/// *A Paper Prince* ///

George Munster

/// *A Paper Prince* ///

Viking

Viking
Penguin Books Australia Ltd,
487 Maroondah Highway, P.O. Box 257
Ringwood, Victoria, 3134, Australia
Penguin Books Ltd,
Harmondsworth, Middlesex, England
Penguin Books,
40 West 23rd Street, New York, N.Y. 10010, U.S.A.
Penguin Books Canada Ltd,
2801 John Street, Markham, Ontario, Canada
Penguin Books (N.Z.) Ltd,
182–190 Wairau Road, Auckland 10, New Zealand

First published in 1985 by Viking

Copyright © George Munster, 1985

Typeset in Baskerville & Italia expanded 10% by Dudley E. King, Melbourne

Made and printed in Australia by
Dominion Press–Hedges & Bell

Munster, George.
Paper Prince.

Bibliography.
Includes index.
ISBN 0 670 80503 3.

1. Murdoch, Rupert, 1931– . 2. Journalists –
Biography. I. Title.
070'.92'4

Acknowledgements

In locating unpublished and archival material for this book, I was assisted by the following: Mr M. Piggott, Australian War Memorial (Canberra); Mr M. Collins Persse, Archives, Geelong Church of England Grammar School (Corio); Mr C. Taylor and Ms S. McCausland, Australian Archive (Canberra); and the manuscript librarians at the British Library (London), the La Trobe Library (Melbourne) and the National Library of Australia (Canberra).

Mr J. B. Ahern of the Herald and Weekly Times Ltd, Mr A. Moore of Advertiser Newspapers Ltd, Ms H. J. Kennedy of the Birmingham Post and Mail Ltd and Professor H. Booms of the Bundesarchiv (Koblenz) have kindly answered written questions on historical points; they are not responsible for the contexts in which I have used the information supplied by them.

I am grateful for the patient and courteous help received from the librarians of the Herald and Weekly Times Ltd (Melbourne), John Fairfax and Sons Ltd (Sydney) and Mirror Newspapers Ltd (Sydney); of the ABC Sound Archives (Sydney), the Australian Broadcasting Tribunal (Sydney), the US Information Agency (Canberra and Sydney): and the Newspaper Advertising Bureau (New York); the State Library of NSW (Sydney), the National Library (Canberra), the Westminster Library (London) and the City Library of New York (Manhattan Branch).

Jackie Yowell of Penguin Books Australia Ltd has patiently commented on successive drafts of this book and her suggestions have greatly improved the final version.

G. Munster
Sydney, August 1984

My greatest debt is to my colleagues in the media – editors, executives, printers, reporters and their spouses – and to my friends in the political world. They will individually recognize their contributions to my text. In gratitude for their patience with me, I dedicate this book to them.

Publishers' note
Sadly, George Munster died very soon after completing this book. That his family, friends and colleagues have spared no effort to help at the final stages before publication is an indication of their deep regard for him and his work. The publishers would like to thank Marie de Lepervanche, Anna Munster, Richard Hall, Rose Creswell and, for his specific helpful suggestions, Tom Fitzgerald.

Contents

To comprehend fully the nature of a people,
one must be a prince, and to comprehend fully
the nature of princes one must be an ordinary
citizen.

Niccolò Machiavelli

Chapter One

/// *Paper Chains* ///

The late 1960s were years of high confidence in Australia and, odd as it may seem with hindsight, Rupert Murdoch was then a representative Australian. If economic growth and nationalism were becoming the creed of the three major political parties, he expounded them as fiercely as anyone; if acceptance and subsequent rejection of the military engagement in Vietnam were characteristic experiences, his newspapers participated in them. When ties with Britian in defence and foreign policy weakened, he approved. He supported the initial awareness of the rights of the continent's Aboriginal inhabitants. Anyone who enhanced his property within the rules of the game was then applauded; he was just as representative in playing a tough business game and winning much of the time. His critics overwhelmingly belonged to his parents' generation. He then went abroad. He had been appreciated in his own country, though without becoming a byword. He was confident that he could enlarge on his expansive performance on another, bigger stage.

He stepped into a media world for which he quickly became an event. The quality papers and the public broadcasters did not deem fire and flood worth regular notice and did not wait for wars or elections to happen. They set about producing news by eliciting statements that provoked counter-statements that led to further comments. Murdoch was doubly welcome to them: he furnished an occasion to look into the media mirror and he was willing to oblige with the first, provocative link in the chains of words. As comment followed comment, each link repeated the name 'Rupert Murdoch'; a star was born. It did not seem to matter where the star came from as long as he shone bright.

It is his earlier path that provides the clues to his momentum and to the

1

directions he might take. He began as an intruder into the comfortably staked-out world of Australian newspaper publishing, which sometimes resisted his expansion and sometimes invited him into the club. He tried to take advantage of both attitudes, more often than not with success. He learnt to keep his eyes on the vulnerable positions of others more than on his own weaknesses; and his course became unpredictable as he oscillated between business co-operation and competition. He learnt to manoeuvre in the undefined area between politics and commerce – a practice in which his father had already excelled.

For many Australian entrepreneurs in the post-war world, the way to survival was to find a discreet path between government assistance and market opportunity. This Australian way of doing business – as well as his occasional attempts to break out of it – is central to an understanding of Murdoch. The criteria that separated tariff protection, subsidy or exclusive licensing in the public interest from crude political patronage were seldom spelt out. In newspaper publishing, this manner of operation entails complications: newspapers cover political events, offer commentary, ride, resist and occasionally initiate political tides. At least half the time they do so in broad daylight. Having spent his first fifteen years as a publisher in Australia, Murdoch has a keen awareness of these complications and insists that he has never used his newspapers to acquire commercial advantages; he has nevertheless entered other areas of business and the onus of proof fell on him to show how he managed to keep his roles separate.

In the mid-1970s Murdoch fell from grace among his Australian allies and admirers. At a high point of the fury against him, a Labor senator rose in the Australian Parliament and brought his sequence of rhetorical questions to this climax: 'Is this country to continue to be run with governments being made and broken, and men being made and broken, by snide, slick innuendoes of a lying, perjuring pimp – Rupert Murdoch?'[1] In Britain, the anger directed at him was expressed more sedately, or more piercingly, in satirical tags; in the United States, the resentment was still to come. In 1976 his fellow Australians failed to understand that Murdoch's international success had made him more thick-skinned about attitudes in his home country, and bewilderment was part of the fury.

That politicians have become loud reverberators of the Murdoch name is not surprising. Politicians live by fragile reputations; they believe that words can propel their careers forward or destroy them. They see newspapers not as chronicles of events just past or forums for comment on the future, but as invaders of their circumscribed field. On his visits to their locker rooms, Murdoch does not discourage these beliefs. On the contrary, he fosters the impression that he is able to deliver a kick beyond the professionals' reach.

Murdoch has become an event to be noticed not only in the media, but by those who manage them. Though its contents are standard popular fare with an occasional excursion into the outrageous, the slender London *Sun* produces balance sheets that are commercially without parallel. In the late 1970s and early 1980s, it made a profit of around one pound sterling for each hundred copies sold, before any income from advertising; four million copies were sold on six days of the week. This one newspaper was the single largest source of Murdoch's publishing profits and the pillar of his capacity to borrow money and thus start or take over other papers. He seldom discusses this source of his strength, preferring to be marvelled at to being puzzled out.

A chain of media properties, such as he has built up, has a structure different from the chains of words he was so good at setting off. Just as steel-works or motor plants enlarge their operations in order to cut unit costs, so newspapers are added to each other to achieve economies of scale. But they economise in ways peculiar to themselves. To push up the circulation of a single daily newspaper is often a slow process, particularly in the saturated markets of the post-war era; and Murdoch himself has not been able to repeat the London *Sun*'s upward spurt. A quicker way of getting more output through one plant is to publish two newspapers where only one has hitherto been printed: a morning is joined to an evening paper, a Sunday to a weekday, or the other way round. The alternative is to develop an inter-city chain, common in the United States since the 1920s, though less economical: the savings lie in shared bureaus, columns and comics, and the bulk purchase of newsprint. Murdoch spreads himself in both directions.

His chain grows also for less visible reasons. Where he can, he couples loss-making operations, started by himself or bought from others, with profit-making ventures. For tax purposes in each of his countries of operation, the profits can be set off against the losses. When a loss-making operation becomes profitable, he may buy or start another that will lose. The chain has a dynamism of its own; the taxpayers in three countries supply the fuel.

His connections with the public sector are often more direct. Starting with television in Australia, he moved into airlines, gambling, mineral and oil exploration. In these ventures he is a concessionaire of positions allocated and protected by authority and subject to limited competition; in some of them, he is a buyer from and seller to governments, a recipient of their guarantees and even a borrower from public agencies. Operating on the interface of business and the state – and publishing newspapers that read sermons to politicians from great heights and publish exposés about them from low recesses – he has not always avoided complications arising from that dual location.

He has been jealously protective of his own privacy and disgruntled by the publication even of his work relationships. These are exaggerated fears, for there is so little to him apart from his political and business activities. At a first meeting, he does not fit the contentious stereotypes that precede him. Wanting to make friends, he bubbles with eagerness, plunges into gossip, bestows fragments of information about his latest doings, shows no urge to pull rank. This was above all the younger Murdoch and, for those like myself who met him early, that impression is difficult to put aside. Today, Murdoch expects to be sized up, listens carefully, and is seeking bearings rather than offering them. This later Murdoch has perplexed many of those who have worked for him in senior positions. He casts them for parts whose outlines are left vague: circulation-lifter for a sick paper, political contact man, resident liberal or conservative, financial wizard or guru on satellites, or a mixture of these roles. If they guess the limits set for them, they prosper; if they step over them, as journalists are apt to do more than anyone else, or if they fall too far short, their relations with him deteriorate in a sharply personal way. The once-outgoing Murdoch is racked with ambivalence, becomes restive, decides on a dismissal and lets others handle the details. In the newspaper world, tales of sackings abound; they usually have a touch of black humour. The stories of dismissals at Murdoch's papers are never funny.

His difficulties with journalists have an obvious source: he is one of them himself and continues to compete. Most of his talents in the journalistic line have been put to use in his business dealings. In the earlier years he liked to be seen jumping on planes, putting his foot in doors and scooping news-papers as ace reporters scoop news. Like theirs, his coups were well prepared. He laid down channels for the flow of information through bankers, brokers and even journalists, very much in the way that reporters develop sources, and just at the right moment he would turn up in person to provide the dramatic touch that made the wires hum with his name. His reputation as an eager shopper spread. He no longer needed to keep his toothbrush by the bedside, for the offers came in and he could finely calculate the moment when he would express an interest.

The one journalist to whom he continues to relate is Sir Keith Murdoch, his father. 'A good father and son relationship is one of the best experiences in life', he wrote in a note to one of his editors.[2] While Sir Keith was alive, his son sported opinions opposed to his father's, though preparing to emulate him in the craft. On Sir Keith's death Rupert learnt that there had been more fame than fortune to the paternal name, but carrying out the father's wishes to the letter, he assumed the small newspaper inheritance. He far surpassed Sir Keith, not by virtue of the tangible property left to him, but because he followed the path of that pioneer through the politico-economic thickets. If Rupert Murdoch's footwork is sometimes too hard to follow, his father's provides a helpful introduction.

While I was preparing this book, Rupert Murdoch went through a phase of shedding his fierce mien and becoming a sedate citizen who attended to public obligations. A year and a half earlier, after he turned fifty, he had been running faster than ever. Was he recuperating and consolidating in 1982? On looking closer, I found out that News Corporation was under financial constraints and its chief executive faced a pause. Was this man, hitherto his own master, becoming the creature of his creation?

The question led me to look more closely at the financial context of his expansion as well as his stalling. When profits flowed strongly again in 1983, his expansionist activities resumed. In writing his story, I found it impossible to separate the man from the money, and so followed them side by side. Rupert Murdoch turned out to be a person without a hidden self; he is what he does; his actions resolve themselves into a pattern of half a dozen manoeuvres in which he has become highly skilled. Taken one by one, these manoeuvres are already known in the commercial world; the one difference, when Rupert Murdoch performs them, is his relentless energy.

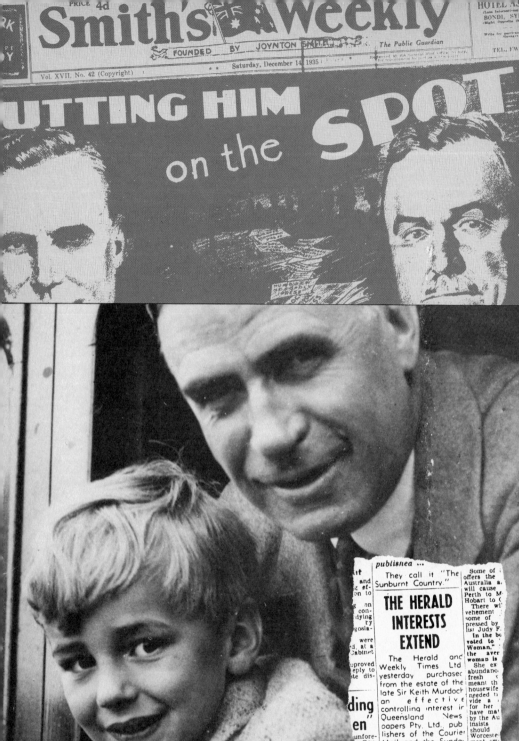

PRICE 4d

Smith's Weekly

FOUNDED BY JOYNTON SMITH   The Public Guardian

Vol. XVII, No. 42 (Copyright)   Saturday, December 14, 1935

UTTING HIM on the SPOT

published ...

They call it "The Sunburnt Country."

THE HERALD INTERESTS EXTEND

The Herald and Weekly Times Ltd yesterday purchased from the estate of the late Sir Keith Murdoch an effective controlling interest in Queensland News papers Pty. Ltd. publishers of the Courier Mail and the Sunday Mail, Brisbane

The big Melbourne company publishes the Herald the Sun Pictorial the Sporting Globe Woman's Day and a number of smaller publications in Victoria

In South Australia the Herald and Weekly Times holds a major interest in Advertiser Newspapers Adelaide, publishers of the Advertiser and the Sunday Advertiser Two members of the Herald board sit as directors of Advertiser Newspapers Ltd.

News Ltd. publishers of The News and The Mail

His series of newspaper amalgamations prove his belief that he prefers the public should never have two daily newspapers if he could manage to make them one.

In Brisbane the Murdoch policy of what is good for the public is shown by the merger of the "Courier" and the "Mail." It is the same in Adelaide with the "Advertiser" and the "Register." In every field of publicity, from the single cable service which now supplies Australia's daily newspapers, to broadcast

torian Government's attitude ing of the Police Commissioner of Victoria.

Not being a politician-juggler, Sir Thomas Blamey requires a much briefer biography than Murdoch. Aged 51 [two years younger than Murdoch], Sir Thomas Blamey re-

And the same as the Police Commissioner's. sane public of Victoria is for the most part disgusted with the blood-curdling "woof woofs" of the newspaper pack.

ing Murdoch is steadily applying a strangle-hold. In brief, he aims to establish newspaper Government, with Murdoch in the role of dictator. His engines of destruction are now directed upon the smash-

Chapter Two

/// *Southcliffe and Son* ///

At the beginning of June 1952 Sir Keith and Lady Murdoch spent a holiday in a friend's house at Surfers Paradise. The coast south of Brisbane had not then been covered with towering apartment buildings, and they could expect that their 2000-kilometre journey out of the Melbourne winter into more clement northerly climes would be rewarded by tranquillity. Sir Keith soon felt better than at any time in the preceding four years: his second prostate operation had succeeded. He had a congenial occupation: to study closely the *Courier-Mail* and the *Sunday Mail*, two newspapers published in Brisbane by Queensland Newspapers Pty Ltd, a company he personally controlled and owned in part. To his satisfaction, the papers' sales were 'splendid', though the advertising content seemed not quite so strong to his practised eye.[1]

As he recuperated, Sir Keith's concern with Queensland Newspapers became more pressing. A share issue had been announced and, to maintain his equity, he had to find the required cash before 20 June. Accordingly he sent his secretary in Melbourne detailed instructions: she was to ask his accountant to put through five separate transactions and to arrange for all the signatures needed. The complications were necessary, for Sir Keith was drawing on funds inside his various companies; at that moment he was not overblest with cash. He had borrowed heavily from banks, life insurance offices and private lenders in pursuit of a project on which he kept his own counsel. It was essential to the success of that project that he should take up the shares and keep control of Queensland Newspapers.

The project was the creation of a newspaper chain separate from the Herald and Weekly Times Ltd over which he still presided as chairman. The chain would compete with the papers of the Herald and Weekly Times in

Melbourne and Adelaide, and would pass to his son Rupert. In 1948, four years earlier when the son was still a legal minor, and the centre of the family estate lay in Brisbane, Sir Keith had committed to writing the intention of creating a newspaper dynasty. It was incorporated in his last will and testament and cast in language somewhat high-flown even for such a document:

WHEREAS I desire that Queensland Newspapers Pty Ltd of Queen Street Brisbane and another Australian Newspaper Company approved by my trustees should continue to express my ideals of newspaper and broadcasting activities in the service of others and that these ideals should be pursued with deep interest AND WHEREAS I desire that my said son Keith Rupert Murdoch should have the great opportunity of spending a useful altruistic and full life in newspaper and broadcasting activities and of ultimately occupying a position of high responsibility in that field with the support of my trustees if they consider him worthy of that support, NOW I HEREBY BEQUEATH . . . [2]

As Sir Keith's business activities unfolded and came to include control of News Ltd in Adelaide, three codicils were added to the will. In the original document the son had been left a substantial parcel of shares in Queensland Newspapers; he finally became heir to a major part of Cruden Investments a family company that held both the Brisbane and Adelaide stock. And sensing perhaps that cash might be a difficulty after his death, Sir Keith cancelled two bequests of a thousand pounds each to private schools in Victoria.

In good health and with the immediate hurdles crossed, Sir Keith returned to Melbourne and began negotiations with Jack Patience, a Sydney lawyer who represented the London Daily Mirror group headed by Cecil King. King's group had acquired the Melbourne *Argus*, a morning paper competing with the Herald and Weekly Times' *Sun-News Pictorial*, and though the *Argus* had been modernised since London bought it in 1949, it did not become a commercial success. Sir Keith's proposition was that if the *Argus* were joined with the publications he personally controlled in Brisbane and Adelaide, and if he brought his skill to the new venture, success for all three papers would be assured. Conveying the proposal to King, Patience advised its rejection, for Sir Keith was to get about two thirds of the controlling shares, leaving the London group with only a third and depriving it of a decisive voice in the future of its investments. King concurred with Patience.

After this rebuff, Sir Keith continued to drive himself hard. He had been afflicted with a heart ailment on and off for eighteen years and he was sixty-seven. He was taking risks. In the first week of October 1952 he faced the possibility of a palace coup against himself. On a visit to Canberra, Colin

Bednall, the managing editor of the *Courier-Mail* , had been taken aside by Arthur Calwell, the Deputy Leader of the Labor Party then in Opposition. Behind closed doors and in a conspiratorial manner, Calwell confided that he knew Bednall and J. F. Williams, the managing editor of the Herald and Weekly Times papers, were planning to get rid of Sir Keith. Expecting the papers to be less harsh to Labor under these two men, Calwell indicated his support. Bednall flew to Melbourne and saw Sir Keith: this was the first he apparently heard of such a move. He assured Sir Keith he had nothing to do with it, and, if anything, he wanted to leave journalism. Sir Keith suggested that Bednall should spend the weekend at Cruden farm, the Murdoch country residence, but having a previous engagement, Bednall declined the invitation.[3]

On 3 October, Sir Keith presided over a board meeting of the Herald and Weekly Times; the next day, a Saturday, he was back in his Melbourne office and in the afternoon he drove the forty-odd kilometres out to Cruden Farm. There, during the night, he died in his sleep.

The funeral was a Melbourne occasion. The cortege wound slowly from the Toorak Presbyterian Church to the Springvale Crematorium. The ten pallbearers who shouldered the coffin represented the federal and state governments; the Herald and Weekly Times, corporately through the vice-chairman and managing editor, and the *Herald* through its editor; Advertiser Newspapers of Adelaide through its chairman; the *Age* of Melbourne through its editor; the *Argus* through its general manager; and the stock exchange, industry and the journalists' and printers' unions through prominent officers. Lady Murdoch was the chief mourner. She was attended by her three daughters, two of her husband's brothers and two of his nephews. But Sir Keith's designated heir-in-chief had been unable to get back in time from Great Britain, where he was enrolled as a student at Oxford. He was thus spared the exchange of courtesies with men who would later stand in the way of the ambitions his father held for him.

The obituaries started a legend. Sir Keith's career was presented in stereotype: by dint of hard work and talent, a lowly reporter became the head of the largest media group in the country. He had transplanted modern popular journalism to Australia. The legend omitted some essentials. Sir Keith owed his rise to an intimacy with politicians; and once he was on top another generation of politicians was in debt to him.

II

Keith Arthur Murdoch began his career as a district correspondent for the Melbourne *Age*. Keith's father, the Reverend Patrick Murdoch, had charge of the Presbyterian church serving the well-to-do Melbourne suburbs of Camberwell and Burwood. David Syme, the proprietor of the *Age*, the biggest and most famous paper in the new Commonwealth, was one of his congregation and an occasional golfing partner. Keith had topped his class at Camberwell Grammar School in 1903 and his father wanted him to go on to the University of Melbourne, but the young man's sights were set on becoming a reporter and earning an immediate income. The distance from the manse to the newspaper office was easy to negotiate. An approach to David Syme produced an assignment to cover the suburb of Malvern, at a rate of a penny-ha'penny for each printed line.

Keith covered the district court and the local council for five years and, living at home, saved £500. He wanted to go to Britain, study at the London School of Economics, have a severe stammer seen to, and break into Fleet Street. Leaving Melbourne in 1908 and returning in 1910, he failed on all counts. He had attended lectures given by L. T. Hobhouse, the Professor of Sociology and former leader-writer on the *Manchester Guardian* but had not sat for examinations; he had done the round of speech therapists, ending with a Mrs Caldwell in Edinburgh who diagnosed a 'mental stammer'; and he could not get full-time employment as a journalist because of his speech impediment. After a year's study and doorknocking, he wrote to his father asking him to sound out the *Age* about renewed employment. Having read the burial service over David Syme, Patrick Murdoch talked to the new editorial head, Geoffrey Syme, and a position was offered. In March 1910 Keith Murdoch started in a promising job at his former paper. A fast short-hand-writer, he was asked to report on the two federal Houses of Parliament, which were sitting in Melbourne.

The Australian Labor Party, providing five governments in the first fifteen years of Federation, was in its heyday. The most durable of the ministries, stretching from 25 April 1910 to 24 June 1913, began shortly after Keith Murdoch climbed the Parliamentary steps. Its Prime Minister was Andrew Fisher and its Attorney-General, William Morris Hughes. Both had good reason to befriend the reporter from the *Age*, the country's leading adovcate of tariff protection for industry and thus read by Labor supporters in preference to the rival *Argus*, which preached free trade.

But at the *Age* journalism was a lifetime career and advancement slow for a young man. When another paper offered him a better position, Keith Murdoch seized the opportunity. Some months after Murdoch had returned to Melbourne, Hugh Denison had started the Sydney evening *Sun* and, at the end of three successful years, Denison decided to buy the news service of the London *Times*, a source that would give his paper international coverage and authority with Sydney readers. Denison arranged to share the service with the Melbourne evening *Herald*, sent his Melbourne correspondent Herbert Campbell Jones to London to pick items from the *Times* and supplement them, and offered Campbell Jones' Melbourne job to Murdoch who promptly moved into an office in the *Herald* building. The *Sun*, too, was protectionist in policy, and Murdoch now came even closer to Labor Attorney-General Hughes, who represented the Sydney waterside where the *Sun* had a wide readership.[4]

The Labor connection led to an even better offer. John Christopher Watson, the first of the Labor prime ministers and a printer by trade, had taken charge of Labour Publications Ltd, got financial backing from large unions and was planning a daily to put his party's point of view. Watson offered Murdoch £A700 a year as news editor and second in charge of the daily, which was to start in the second half of 1914. Murdoch accepted, but kept the offer to himself and remained at the *Sun* for the time being, a fortunate precaution, for when war broke out in August 1914, Labour Publications shelved its plans.

The *Sun* had begun with a nominal circulation of 20,000 and now reached 60,000. The war made it: with the *Times'* news and Campbell Jones' additions on the front page, it rose to 140,000 a day, only 10,000 less than the *Sydney Morning Herald*, that city's leading, seventy-year-old paper. By mid-1915 Denison needed more staff, recalled Campbell Jones from London and brought Murdoch to Sydney to offer him the job at Printing House Square, the *Times* building in London. Hesitating, Murdoch wrote to Andrew Fisher. Murdoch had already tried to get to the Middle East as Australia's Official War Correspondent, but had run second in the ballot conducted by the Australian Journalists Association whose winner filled the position. Would it be appropriate, Murdoch asked Fisher, to enlist in the Australian Imperial Force, most of which was posted on the eastern shores of the Mediterranean? Fisher, who had become uneasy about the sparse reports he was receiving about the country's forces abroad and under British commanders, wrote back asking Murdoch to break his journey to London in Egypt, to visit hospitals and make enquiries about the shaky postal service, on behalf of the Government. Fisher provided an open letter of introduction, and Senator George Pearce, the Minister for Defence, addressed a personal letter to

Lieutenant-General Sir Ian Hamilton, the Allied Commander-in-Chief at the Dardanelles, asking him to permit Murdoch to visit the combat zone. Were the hospital and postal tasks a smokescreen? No records of conversations between Fisher, Pearce and Murdoch have survived, but when the unofficial envoy furnished news on the military situation it was more than welcome. It also furnished the springboard for Murdoch's leap into the upper echelons of British politics.

Reaching Cairo in the middle of August and completing his routine enquiries, Murdoch made his way via Alexandria to the island of Imbros, Hamilton's headquarters. With Hamilton's permission he then continued to two spots on the Gallipoli Peninsula: Anzac Cove, a strip precariously held by Australian and New Zealand forces, and Suvla Bay, about four kilometres to the north. According to his evidence sworn eighteen months later, he discussed the situation with eight Australian generals, a number of officers and other ranks. Back at Imbros he talked at length to Ellis Ashmead-Bartlett, a highly experienced, flamboyant war correspondent who represented the Newspaper Proprietors Association in London. Ashmead-Bartlett criticised the previous month's operations at Suvla Bay and considered the whole Dardanelles campaign a strategic blunder. After listening to Murdoch's alarm at the state of the troops and the grim prospect for the coming winter, Ashmead-Bartlett saw an opportunity to intervene. Here was Murdoch, feeling that the truth should be known 'at home'; here was Ashmead-Bartlett unable to get it past the military censors. Murdoch thought his own views would not carry sufficient weight: something over Ashmead-Bartlett's signature was needed. Accordingly, Ashmead-Bartlett wrote a letter to H. H. Asquith, the British Prime Minister, and Murdoch would take it to London. Words were not minced, least of all on the subject of Sir Ian Hamilton.[5]

Carrying the letter, Murdoch said farewell on 8 September. In Cairo he told Colonel Selheim, an Australian officer, that he had a message for the British Prime Minister; at his next port, Marseilles, British Army officers took it, as well as his report on Australian postal arrangements. Deprived of this document, he began work on a long letter to Andrew Fisher. He wrote all the way on the train and boat journey to London, where the information he had was eagerly sought. Alfred Harmsworth, Lord Northcliffe, was straining to take a hand in the future of the Dardanelles campaign. Early in September, he had called Campbell Jones to his office and asked him whether something could be done about 'those poor fellows on Gallipoli'. He wondered whether Campbell Jones could talk to the Australian High Commissioner who would give his Prime Minister the whole truth. 'It so happened,'

Campbell Jones wrote later, 'that I was able to tell him that an Australian journalist named Murdoch was at the moment on his way to England, after visiting Gallipoli'.[6]

Northcliffe could not be ignored. He had shown that he could make and unmake ministers and ministries when he disagreed with their policies or doubted their efficiency. He took credit for keeping the War Office from R. B. Haldane in August 1914; and in May 1915, his two dailies, the *Times* and the *Daily Mail*, exposed a shortage of munitions on the Western front and provoked the crisis that forced the Liberal Asquith to form a coalition government with the Unionists, as the Tories were called at the time. In pursuit of his policies and his dislikes, Northcliffe was willing to sacrifice some of his papers' sales, and this made him all the more formidable. Fiercely anti-German, he continued to doubt whether Asquith was running the war with sufficient determination. He was now willing to take issue with the Government over Gallipoli, and was heeded by politicians who were inclined to agree or wanted his future support.

Northcliffe was out of town, but Campbell Jones took Murdoch at once to lunch with Geoffrey Robinson (later changed to Dawson), the editor of the *Times*. The following morning, Robinson and Murdoch had breakfast with Sir Edward Carson, the Unionist minister presiding over the Dardanelles Committee that monitored the campaign. From Carson Murdoch passed through a succession of Cabinet members including Sir Edward Grey, the Foreign Secretary and Alfred Bonar Law, the Colonial Secretary and leader of the Unionists. Dictating his letter at Australia House, Murdoch dated it 23 September, and Lloyd George, having asked for a copy, had it printed as a Cabinet document. But not everyone who saw it was favourably impressed. Winston Churchill, one of the campaign's instigators, called it 'lurid'; and Maurice Hankey, another early supporter of the strategy, described Murdoch as 'a horrible scab' in his diary.[7]

Contrary to the date on the letter, it was revised while these meetings took place. As Murdoch wrote in it: 'On the high political question of whether good is to be served by keeping the armies at Gallipoli, I can say little, for I am uninformed. Cabinet ministers here have impressed me with the fact that a failure in the Dardanelles would have most serious results in India.'[8] The letter reiterated much of what Ashmead-Bartlett had tried to convey to Asquith – that the campaign was a fiasco, particularly since August, that prospects were grim, staff work poor and a new commander-in-chief was needed. It ran to nearly 6000 words. Murdoch spiced Ashmead-Bartlett's assessment with a peculiarly Australian flavour. Not only were the Australian troops at Anzac Cove superior to the ill-trained British at Suvla Bay, but the high-placed villains were exclusively British: 'The conceit and self-com-plalacency of the red feather men are equalled only by their incapacity. Along the line of communication, and especially at Mudros, are countless high officers and conceited young cubs who are plainly only playing at war.'[9]

Though regarded as Keith Murdoch's greatest achievement while he lived, the letter was not published until fifteen years after his death. This was fortunate for Murdoch, for he was plainly wrong in a number of details. He alleged that Hamilton seldom visited the Gallipoli Peninsula; Hamilton was able to show that he averaged three visits a week. Murdoch alleged that staff appointments had been made on the basis of personal favouritism; at the secret hearings of the Dardanelles Commission, he was confronted with the existence of a formal appointments structure and could not say how it had been abused.[10] In framing the letter, he had played on the hostility of Fisher – a Scots shipwright who had migrated to Australia – to the British officer class, yet before long Murdoch himself moved among its highest ranks. A request made in the Australian House of Representatives for the tabling of the letter in 1920 was turned down, and Murdoch may well have felt relieved.

By contrast, his published despatches to the Sydney *Sun* conveyed only the most delicate of hints that anything was amiss at Gallipoli. In two descriptive pieces he mailed back from the Middle East, he praised the courage of Australian soldiers at the front, with only a sombre sentence or two in passing.[11] When Ashmead-Bartlett came to London some five weeks after Murdoch, he gave an interview expressing a variety of misgivings which appeared in the *Sun*.[12] Murdoch's own involvement with British politicians was hinted at in a column called 'Diary of a war', which Campbell Jones had started. 'I have been privileged these days to get far behind the scenes – to meet and talk frankly with the men in London whose decisions mean life and death to thousands,' Murdoch wrote in the column, shortly after his arrival. 'Four Cabinet ministers I have seen during the last few days have asked me anxiously what Australia would think of this or that projected move.'[13]

By the time this 'Diary' note appeared, the *Sun* had already come out editorially against a continuation of the Gallipoli campaign. But Murdoch could not resist kicking an antagonist when he was down. When Winston Churchill left Cabinet (in which he had been reduced from First Lord of the Admiralty to the Duchy of Lancaster in May 1915), Murdoch's 'Diary' judged, on the basis of what was called a 'frank talk': 'He had defects which made his war administration impossible. He is heady and is prepared to gamble with the fate of an empire.'[14] Under the restraints of an erratic wartime censorship, some discretion in Murdoch's despatches was understandable. But a deeper pattern in his reporting was becoming established: solid information for a small group of powerful men; crumbs, often stale, for the general newspaper reader. Was this pattern the basis for journalistic achievement, or the first step on another career ladder?

III

Fisher, Keith Murdoch's political patron, resigned from Parliament late in October 1915 and prepared for a journey to Great Britain to act as Australian High Commissioner. Hughes took his place as Prime Minister and, over the next three years, Murdoch became Hughes' confidential and largely unpaid agent, carrying out delicate assignments side by side with his job as a newspaper correspondent.[15]

On becoming Prime Minister, Hughes took up the 'Japanese Question' – the future of the German possessions in the Pacific now occupied by Japan. He feared that postwar Japanese possession would constitute an extension of that country's dominion in the South Pacific and having fished for an invitation, set out to present his fears to the British Government, leaving Australia late in January 1916 and returning early in July. On matters of state, and even for introductions to press proprietors, Hughes initially sought the help of his fellow Welshman, Lloyd George, the Minister for Munitions. But Murdoch knew how to make himself useful, first through his despatches and then through his London connections. He attended the first Anzac Memorial Service with Hughes' party at Westminster Abbey, and followed it to Scotland. Hughes made speeches all over Britain which met with official approval and Murdoch was asked to find a publisher for a collection of them which he did. Two short biographies of Hughes also appeared, and Murdoch was given credit for getting them written and published.

During Hughes' visit, universal conscription for military service was introduced in Britain; as an echo, demands for a similar measure built up in Australia. But in Australia two groups were strongly opposed: the union movement feared that military conscription would lead to civil conscription into the labour force; and the Irish and their descendants (up to a quarter of the Australian population), resented the British failure to honour the promise of Home Rule and felt stirred by the Dublin Easter rising and its severe repression. Hughes asked Murdoch to help him blunt opposition from the left by getting support for Australian conscription from other countries, and

Murdoch secured statements from British and French socialists. The Irish question needed defter handling and, at Hughes' request, Murdoch persuaded Lloyd George and Bonar Law to announce that martial law in Ireland had been lifted at the suggestion of the Australian Prime Minister.

To avoid legal complexities and to sidestep disagreements within his Party, Hughes decided to call a referendum on conscription rather than introduce legislation. The soldiers who had volunteered and were now abroad would of course cast ballots and Hughes had reports that they might strongly object to fighting shoulder to shoulder with conscripts. Hughes' Australian supporters in London were willing to bear the cost of printing a pamphlet addressed to the troops and Murdoch was put in charge of its distribution. On the eve of the poll, the Parliamentary Labor Party began to crack, and when this referendum was defeated, Labor was irreversibly split in two.

Before the year 1916 was over, a lonely Hughes was forming a coalition with his Party's former enemies. Needing a confidant more than ever, Hughes wrote about his situation to Murdoch at some length.[16] In the New Year, Hughes cabled him for advice on whether to attend the Imperial Defence Conference called in London later in 1917, and Murdoch replied with a long assessment.[17] In March Hughes sent Murdoch to Lloyd George, Prime Minister in Britain since December 1916, asking for a conference of Irish nationalists and Dominion representatives to deal with Home Rule. Hughes' concern was domestic: he was governing without a Senate majority, would soon have to call an election, and wanted some of the Irish votes. Though Lloyd George did not oblige, Hughes won the election.

Conscription again became an issue before the end of 1917. Australian troops were fighting in France, losses were heavy, replenishments were called for, but monthly voluntary enlistments were falling off. Pushed by his colleagues in the new Nationalist Party, Hughes announced a second referendum for 20 December 1917. A majority of soldiers had favoured conscription in 1916, and the votes of Australian soldiers abroad were just as important on this occasion. Keith Murdoch had made the political transition from Labor with Hughes without a questioning word. He now anticipated instructions by attending a meeting of Australian businessmen in London to support conscription with money and publicity. But Campbell Jones, Murdoch's journalistic superior in Sydney, heard of the involvement, and instructed him not to participate, and Murdoch informed Hughes of his withdrawal. Defeated on conscription a second time, Hughes was even more in need of friends, and hearing from Murdoch's aunt in Melbourne that her nephew was engaged to Bonar Law's younger daughter, Isabel, he sent congratulations in mock-Scots, adding that he had been awfully upset over the referendum, its aftermath and the venomous attacks from such quarters as Murdoch's friend Campbell Jones.

And now Hughes set Murdoch his most delicate task. A trickle of reports had reached him, hinting at the adverse position on the Western front, where 100,000 Australians were fighting. Hughes had undertaken to attend a meeting of the Imperial War Cabinet in London and had set a departure date for late April; what should his course of action be now? In a way, it was Fisher and the Dardanelles all over again; Hughes was unaware that the Germans had embarked on an all-out offensive and that, in the first drive, they had separated the British and French forces; but he had learnt to be uneasy. Using the Secretary to the Australian High Commission in London as an intermediary, Hughes cabled Murdoch on 31 March 1918:

Most secret. Want your advice and assistance badly.
One. Colonial Office telegrams re present battle meagre and hopelessly belated, contain nothing that has not already appeared in Press previously. I want to know full facts and prospects. Send me full telegram immediately and arrange either that Colonial Office send facts once or twice daily or if they will not or do not then do so yourself. All messages should be sent in Cypher A and addressed to Steward ...

Hughes then drew attention to his forthcoming visit, asked for Murdoch's opinion on peace prospects, referred to his passage through the United States on the way to Britain and ended: 'Kindest regards to Lloyd George and you'.[18]

Lloyd George and 'you' were quick to help. Murdoch had returned from France on the Sunday the cable reached him and the first reply was optimistic in tone: the immediate danger was believed to be over. But the next day Murdoch spoke to his contacts including Lloyd George and foreshadowed the worst: 'There is no doubt possibility of decisive defeat is haunting high quarters ... Another immense attack is regarded as certain'.[19] Good and bad news followed in further cables. If the Germans were fought to a standstill, Murdoch finally reported, peace offers coming from Berlin would be discussed and probably accepted by the Allies.[20]

Having sketched the immediate situation, Murdoch advised Hughes that the Colonial Office was quite hopeless: he would keep Hughes personally posted through the Australian High Commission who could remunerate him 'for the drain upon my pocket'.[21] Murdoch kept up his cables till the end of April; some of them were forwarded to Hughes on his journey via the United States.

While sending these grave appraisals to Hughes, Murdoch also filed for the Sydney *Sun*. The tone of these despatches was more comforting; they dealt with specific situations on the battlefield. Sometimes a despatch directly contradicted the sombre picture he transmitted to Hughes. Eventually the published despatches came into line with the secret cables: 'It is sheer folly to imagine that the Allies will easily, or even certainly, hold the German onslaught. A grave crisis must be met before the enemy design is frustrated.'[22] But the possibility of a compromise peace with Germany was withheld from the *Sun*'s readers.

Hughes came to London, stayed into the peace and attended the Versailles conference. His party included his private secretary Percy Deane and his press officer Lloyd Dumas, whom Murdoch later appointed as editor of the Adelaide *Advertiser* and who, as chairman of Advertiser Newspapers was a pallbearer at the funeral. Given their physical proximity at that time, little survives on paper about Murdoch's continuing relation with Hughes. Frederick Eggleston, a studious young lawyer who joined the Australian negotiating side at Versailles, noted that the people whom Hughes consulted were completely ignorant of European politics: he included Murdoch among them. George Ernest Morrison, the Australian-born political adviser to the President of China and a former *Times* correspondent in Peking, found his compatriot better informed. Struck at first by Murdoch's boastfulness, he soon noted his adroit movements between Northcliffe, Lloyd George and Hughes and the Japanese delegation, all of whom were at loggerheads with each other, and began to have lunch with him.[23]

IV

On 1 July 1921 Northcliffe gave a lunch for Keith Murdoch, the designated editor of the Melbourne *Herald*, in the dining room of Printing House Square and presented him with a set of golf clubs. The party posed for a photograph: the guest of honour was in the front row, flanked by Northcliffe, the editors of the *Daily Mail* and the *Times*, and William Morris Hughes, on yet another visit. A copy of the picture hung in Murdoch's successive offices for the rest of his life.

In his first three years, Murdoch had cultivated 'the Chief', as Northcliffe liked to be called, for his political knowledge and connections. He played golf with the older man, wrote back to Australia about the friendship, yet knew enough about Northcliffe's ferocious moods not to seek a position on his papers. In 1918 the contract with Denison's wire service ran out, and was renewed for a second three-year period. When James Edward Davidson, the general manager of the Melbourne *Herald*, resigned that year, Murdoch's duties widened. Theodore Fink, the chairman, turned to Murdoch for advice on developments in newspaper production and Murdoch in turn sought Northcliffe's help. In 1920 Murdoch covered the Prince of Wales' visit to Australia for the wire service, as well as for the *Times*, and was looked over by Fink in Melbourne. The two men joined the same ship back to Britain, Fink to attend an Empire Press Conference, Murdoch to get back to his London desk. In the course of their shipboard conversations, Fink held out the possibility of the *Herald*'s editorship and encouraged Murdoch to study production in London. Back in Australia, Fink bought a new site for a building to house the post-war *Herald*, put in orders for modern equipment and cabled an offer to Murdoch for the editorship at £2000 for the first twelve months and £A2500 thereafter. Denison matched the offer with the editorship of the Sydney *Sun*, foreshadowing a rivalry between himself and Fink. It appears that Murdoch felt he would have a freer hand in Melbourne and he accepted the position on the *Herald*. He had kept up the friendship with Northcliffe by outrageous flattery and now sought advice on how to improve the Melbourne paper, submitting past issues on which he got extensive comments, followed by hints on office politics.[24] Murdoch had learnt not to model himself too closely on Northcliffe's transparently megalomaniac personality: he concealed his own ambition for some decades, preferred the silken touch and was always unhappy when his manoeuvres, rather than their results, became visible.

As Alfred Harmsworth, Northcliffe had adapted popular journalism to British conditions, while drawing on the production methods, presentation, and price reductions developed in France and the United States. A successful magazine publisher, he had bought the ailing London *Evening News* in 1894 and made it profitable; in 1896 he started the *Daily Mail*, whose sales in 1900, during the Boer War, fell just short of a million copies per issue. The *Daily Mail* was priced at a halfpenny, at a time when the previously 'popular' *Daily Telegraph* cost a penny and the *Times* threepence. The low price was half the reason for the paper's success. Its equipment, based on French and American designs, saved 30 percent of current British printing costs; but the cut in selling price was a gamble on the steadily falling cost of newsprint based on woodpulp, a process developed in the United States. (The Civil War of the 1860s had driven cotton-rag-based paper up to $US440 a ton; by 1899, a ton of wood-based paper was sold for $US42. The new base made newspapers available to ever larger numbers of buyers: the circulations of American dailies rose from 2.6 million to 15 million between 1870 and 1900.) If large runs of the *Daily Mail* were sold, the cost of reporting and typesetting could be spread across them, resulting in a paper that compared well with its higher-priced rivals.[25]

But, for such a mass readership, the content would have to be different as well. Harmsworth directed some of his appeal to a diffuse curiosity, which he had learnt to recognise while running weeklies like *Answers to Correspondents*. But his inspiration came mainly from the United States, whose east coast he observantly toured in 1894, just before buying the London *Evening News*.

The best-known of the popular newspapers studied by Harmsworth was the New York *World*, which Joseph Pulitzer had purchased in 1883. Pulitzer was the greatest of the innovators in popular journalism. He regularly used pictures – originally woodcuts – on the front page, breaking the column rules; he provided sports coverage for men and tailored material to meet women's interests; and he took the 'stunt' – Henry M. Stanley's search for Dr Livingstone – further by sending a woman reporter round the world in seventy-two days, beating Jules Verne's imaginary eighty. These innovations were integral to his purpose of communicating with a new readership. 'I want to talk to the nation, not to a select committee,' he declared. This nation included a large number of New Yorkers who, like himself, had immigrated from Europe and made New York the radical city that came close to electing Henry George as Mayor in the early days of Pulitzer's proprietorship. Though distancing himself from this semi-socialist, Pulitzer defended trade unions, exposed financial frauds and berated the idle rich.

Harmsworth took up Pulitzer's popular appeal, but emptied it of its content. The audience he pursued was typically white collar, fearful of challenges to itself at home and to Britain's position abroad. While Pulitzer had represented a New York district as a Democrat in Washington, Harmsworth unsuccessfully offered himself as a Conservative candidate; while Pulitzer resigned from Congress to get on with his newspaper, Harmsworth followed his commercial success by entering the House of Lords as Northcliffe, engaging in political alliances both inside and outside Parliament. The popular newspaper as it was known in New York was not transplanted to Britain; rather Northcliffe created a mass-circulation organ that told its readers what to think.[26]

Though feared and hated for the inconstancy of his political alliances, Northcliffe tried to inform himself on international affairs and picked foreign correspondents for this purpose. The ambitions of imperial Germany worried him and his fear divided the senior men at the *Times*; the outbreak of the war in 1914 showed him to be right. He hoped the might of

Tsarist Russia could balance Germany; the *Times* published twenty-eight 'Russian Supplements' between 1911 and 1917. But in this case, his confidence turned out to have been misplaced. Northcliffe's mind degenerated in the years before his death. After the war, he saw a Jewish hand both in German aggression (a few Jews were highly placed in German industry), and in the Bolshevik revolution. At one point, the *Times* gave some countenance to the *Protocols of the Elders of Zion*, an anti-semitic forgery concocted before the war by the Tsarist political police.[27] His later beliefs in vast conspiracies were entirely in line with his personalised treatment of political issues throughout his publishing career. 'Never attack an institution! Attack the fellow at the head of it', he told Valentine Williams, one of his favourite journalists.[28] This maxim narrowed the scope of discussion in the British press and allowed the institutions that shape even the individuals at their head to disappear from critical sight.

In the second half of 1921, helped by Northcliffe's comments, Keith Murdoch began to turn the *Herald* into a Northcliffe-style paper. The war had lifted its circulation to a healthy 105,000; Murdoch showed he could do even better than this by seizing on the Colin Ross case, a back-alley shooting. He was soon able to inform Northcliffe that during Ross's trial sales reached 230,000, and that by March 1922 they averaged 144,000.[29] As an evening paper, the *Herald* was able to cover court proceedings on the day they were held, thus beating the next morning's papers to the news. He tidied up the *Herald*'s amateurish lay-out and broadened its appeal by engaging the widely read poet C. J. Dennis to contribute verse and cajoling the singer Nellie Melba, who not so long before bestrode the international stage, from her retirement into writing.

There was little time to lose, for Hugh Denison was preparing to move into Melbourne. To keep the potential intruder preoccupied, Murdoch started negotiations with some of the stockholders of the Sydney *Evening News*, a competitor of Denison's *Sun*, proposing to buy them out. The negotiations went smoothly enough for Murdoch to cable Northcliffe, offering him a stake, and Northcliffe agreed to invest £A5000 provided that Murdoch had control, explaining that control by one man was essential in the newspaper business.[30] The scheme failed when the directors of the *Evening News* issued shares to Sydney retailers anxious to keep the paper's advertising rates low.

Denison's initial attack on the *Herald* was sidelong. In September 1922 he started a Melbourne morning paper called the *Sun-News Pictorial*, modelled on the London *Daily Sketch* and filled with pictures and light-hearted stories to attract young readers bored by the solemn *Argus* and *Age*. Though this morning paper could initially take only a modest place, it would reduce the cost of producing the *Evening Sun*, which Denison launched in April 1923 as a rival to the *Herald*, the only evening paper in Melbourne. But Denison's *Evening Sun* could not match the *Herald*: after two years, it averaged 103,000 sales while the *Herald* stood at 175,000. Denison closed it down and sold the *Sun-News Pictorial* to the Herald and Weekly Times for £175,000. This purchase turned out to be Keith Murdoch's most enduring contribution to that company's prosperity. In 1934 the morning paper surpassed the sales of its evening companion and, with reversals in only one or two years, led the Melbourne field ever after.[31]

In 1925 Keith Murdoch travelled to Japan, the United States and Britain. The concept of the newspaper chain, pioneered by Frank Munsey, was beginning to attract attention. Geographically Australia was much more similar to the United States than to Britain, and the possibility of a chain down under is likely to have struck the astute Murdoch. His business acumen had already been noted by his directors, who made him managing editor in 1926, and even more impressed by what followed, raised him to managing director in 1929. What followed was the establishment of the 'Murdoch press' across the continent, with Sydney alone as the major gap.

Through its chairman, Theodore Fink, and its deputy chairman, W. L. Baillieu, the Herald and Weekly Times Ltd was linked to the influential and wealthy Anglo-Australian group of mining companies known popularly as 'Collins House', after the corporate seat. At Collins House, W. S. Robinson, a one-time finance editor of the *Age* and a wartime adviser to Hughes, played the part of grey eminence: Murdoch had known him well since London. In 1926 Baillieu and Robinson heard in London that the *West Australian*, the leading daily in Perth, was for sale, and they cabled Murdoch to secure an option. The syndicate which bought the newspaper property for £A592,000 consisted of the Board of the Herald and Weekly Times jointly and of Fink, Baillieu and Robinson severally. A new company was formed, which issued shares to locals to smooth ruffled feelings about interstate control. The connection between Melbourne and Perth lasted into the mid-1930s and was renewed much later.

The next move was into Adelaide, where the circulation of the morning *Register* had declined to 14,000. Murdoch bought control for his company and despatched Sydney Deamer, one of his brightest journalists, to push up the circulation, with the object of frightening Sir Langdon Bonython, the octogenarian proprietor-editor of the prosperous morning *Advertiser*, into selling out. An offer of a million pounds did the trick. Once again, a new public company, Advertiser Newspapers, was floated, and, of the million shares, the Herald and Weekly Times took 133,600, Baillieu 120,336, Fink 40,000 and Murdoch 40,000. The *Register* closed in 1931.

Adelaide's evening paper, the *News*, had been started in 1923 by J. E. Davidson, the former general manager of the Herald and Weekly Times, and was now controlled by him through News Ltd. Fortuitously, Davidson died in 1930; Murdoch at once began negotiations with his heirs and the Herald and Weekly Times bought their stock. News Ltd and Advertiser Newspapers Ltd remained separate, each having outside stockholders and each operating at separate premises.

Brisbane had two morning papers, the *Daily Mail* and the *Courier*. The *Daily Mail* was controlled by John Wren, a Melbourne sporting entrepreneur and the *Courier* by the absentee heirs of its founders. Murdoch had an eye on both papers, personally bought control of the *Courier*, arranged a merger, and the joint *Courier-Mail* had its first issue in August 1933. With 40 percent of the stock, Murdoch held the right to nominate the company's directors as long as a stipulated minimum dividend was maintained. Wren got an in-formal concession, assured coverage for his local sporting promotions. The terms, so favourable to Murdoch, emerged from the reputations of the two men. Wren had started his business career late in the nineteenth century with an illegal betting establishment; a Catholic, his name was made an ugly byword by Protestant anti-gambling campaigners for decades thereafter. He had moved out of illegal gambling, had interests in the liquor trade, in hotels, boxing and mining; he was a millionaire, a friend of the Archbishop of Melbourne, and he financed members of the Labor Party. So much the worse; he epitomised the influence of 'bad' money and backroom dealings. Murdoch stood for 'clean' Protestant money, and though he had much less of it than Wren, he was able to dictate the terms on which their joint company would be run: all business communications between himself and Wren would be in writing. He had come a long way since he joined the *Age*: he had a chain and he could make it rattle.

V

MURDOCH – At Avonhurst Private Hospital, Queens road, Melbourne, at midnight on 11th March, to the wife of Keith Murdoch – a son.

The nameless son of the Murdochs had his first publicity, this paid advertisement, on the front page of the Melbourne *Age* of 14 March 1931. He was christened Keith Rupert, after his father and his maternal grandfather, but became known as 'Rupert' so as not to be confused with the father.

In a phrase of the time, Keith Murdoch had been an eligible bachelor when, at the age of thirty-seven, he took up residence in an elegant apartment block used by the country gentry on their visits to Melbourne, and when he bought a house in the fashionable suburb of South Yarra. Tall, with hazel eyes and a straight, broad nose, he was meticulous in his dress and choosy about the places where he allowed himself to be seen. He preferred theatres and art exhibitions to sporting venues and was an acquisition for society hostesses. But he was not an easy catch, for he was attached to a lady who suffered from intermittent but serious bouts of illness, an attachment that was finally broken off.

His engagement to Elisabeth Greene was announced early in 1928; he was forty-two, she nineteen. Rupert Greene, Elisabeth's father, had lived for a generation in Toorak, a suburb of the well-to-do and was an office-bearer of the Victoria Racing Club. It was said that Keith had seen Elisabeth's picture in *Table Talk*, a gossipy weekly published by the Herald and Weekly Times and asked a common acquaintance for an introduction. The Reverend Patrick Murdoch married the couple on 6 June 1928. A select circle of guests was asked to the reception given by the Greenes: in addition to relatives on the two sides, they included Nellie Melba and Sir Harry Chauvel, one of the Australian generals on Gallipoli. Keith had recently bought a country property near Frankston, some forty kilometres from Melbourne, and named it Cruden Farm, after the village of origin of his Scots forebears. The couple started their honeymoon there and went on to Sydney and Brisbane. Busier than ever, Keith was back on the job in July, to resume negotiations for the purchase of the *Register*. He took a bundle of envelopes addressed to Elisabeth on his travels and wrote letters to her en route. A first child, a daughter, was born in 1929 and named Helen after Keith's maiden aunt. After Rupert's birth in 1931, two more daughters followed: Anne in 1935 and Janet in 1939.

As early as 1929 the world depression began to affect Australia through

falling prices for exports. The non-Labor government led by Stanley
Melbourne Bruce sought to meet the situation by cutting heavily into
the unions' powers; Hughes, now one of the ministers, disagreed with
the extreme measures proposed and brought down Bruce's Cabinet. For
Murdoch, this was the time to break with Hughes: he issued a memorandum
to his staff, warning them about Hughes' 'vindictiveness, jealousy and self-
interest'.[32] The next three years were a time in which many old loyalties
were forgotten, factions were formed and parties were split. Keith Murdoch
emerged as a political kingmaker behind the scenes.

After an election, James Scullin, leading a Labor government, replaced
Bruce. He faced deepening problems at once. For some decades, Australian
governments, state and federal, had financed public works and railway
constructions with loans from Britain, paying interest out of tax and re-
borrowing when principal sums fell due. The depression, producing lower
tax receipts, put the squeeze on Scullin. He issued undertakings to Britain
that all commitments would be met, and to do so, cut public salaries and
reduced spending, thus deepening unemployment even further.

His policies were to split Labor. In 1930, E. G. Theodore, Scullin's Treasurer who had stepped out of Cabinet to clear his name from allegations
relating to his earlier years in Queensland politics, began to champion
expansive, quasi-Keynesian policies. Leaving for London to conduct further
negotiations, Scullin appointed Joseph ('Joe') Lyons as Acting Treasurer to
fend off opposition to cutbacks within the Party.

A supporter of financial orthodoxy and regular payments to Britain,
Murdoch quickly found his way to Lyons. Lyons' wife Enid later recalled the
beginning of the friendship:

> In January [1931] the Prime Minister returned to Australia.
>
> Shortly before his arrival, Joe and I were in Melbourne. We lunched one day with
> Sir [sic] Keith Murdoch who said to Joe in greeting: 'Well, Mr Lyons, you will not be
> Acting Treasurer much longer. You will be Treasurer'. Joe said he doubted it; he
> doubted even if he could wish to be. 'Oh, but you will be. Scullin couldn't do
> anything else after what you've done in his absence, and after the way he supported
> you from London. Don't you think so, Mrs Lyons?' he asked, turning to me. 'Surely
> not!' [Lyons] replied. 'What makes you think that?' [Murdoch said]. After the Prime
> Minister's messages from London, it would be just deserting his own policy!'[33]

It was an astute way of arousing Lyons' ambition, of smoothing over any
scruples Lyons had about disloyalty and of playing on his vanity. Scullin duly
reappointed Theodore as Treasurer, and Lyons, joined by a colleague,
resigned from Cabinet at the end of January 1931. Lyons had already talked

to a small group in Melbourne on the non-Labor side, who suggested a new alliance of Lyons supporters in the Labor Party and members of the existing Opposition. Murdoch swung behind this scheme to split Labor and his newspapers began to portray Lyons as 'Honest Joe'. In March, Lyons announced from the backbench that he was willing to head a composite Cabinet drawn from several parties and moved a motion of 'no confidence' in Scullin's Government, which failed.

Murdoch now used his influence with non-Labor politicians to move Lyons into the Opposition leadership in the federal House of Representatives. In April he wrote to the incumbent Opposition leader J. G. Latham, that he should step down in Lyons' favour, and Latham did. As the year went on, Murdoch's association with the new non-Labor leader became a byword in the *Herald* building and beyond. When Lyons would arrive in the overnight train from the national capital, a reporter would be waiting in Melbourne to ask him to lunch at Murdoch's elegant dining room, run by a Swiss chef. The visits continued after Lyons became Prime Minister of a non-Labor government late in 1931 and nobody was surprised when the Honours List of June 1933 included a knighthood for the newspaperman. Sir Keith backed Lyons in the 1934 election, and when Lyons' side was returned, offered detailed advice on the formation of the new Cabinet. He also supported a more personal reward for Lyons. In August 1935, W. R. Rolph, the proprietor of the *Examiner*, a Tasmanian newspaper, wrote to Sir Keith informing him that he was starting a fund so that Mr and Mrs Lyons could complete the education of their large family, and Sir Keith agreed to contribute.[34]

The friendship was strained by a minor item of government policy that happened to affect Murdoch's financial interests. The smaller commercial radio stations had become uneasy about the substantial number of transmitter licences held by Amalgamated Wireless of Australasia Ltd, an equipment and appliance manufacturer then half-owned by the government. In response, the Postmaster-General, proposed to issue a regulation curtailing the number of transmitter licences held by one interest: the upper limits would be five for all Australia, three in any one state, two in all capital cities combined, and one in each metropolis. According to a list of station ownerships later tabled in Parliament, 'the Melbourne *Herald* and its associated publications' were connected with eleven stations round the country, but this list included four licences in Western Australia, a state from which the Herald and Weekly Times was withdrawing.[35]

Murdoch took the whole attempt at regulation extremely ill. After a discussion with Lyons, he wrote him a personal letter. He began by saying that he was presuming on their past relations and went on to complain of

Cabinet hostility to himself. He conceded that the proposed regulation might affect three metropolitan stations in which he had a small interest, and argued that there was no point in cramping AWA. In a five-page hand-written reply, Lyons assured Sir Keith that he hoped to be in Melbourne for a chat before long and that no word hostile to Sir Keith had ever been uttered in Cabinet. On the contrary, all ministers realised only too well what the Government and the Party owed to the papers of Sir Keith's group.[36]

The newspaper world itself was affected by the depression. The *Herald* and the *Sun-News Pictorial* found that advertising rather than circulation fell off and Murdoch obtained cuts in wages and salaries from his staff in 1932 to offset the declining revenues. A greater threat was the decision of the *Argus* to launch an evening paper, in pursuit of more revenue and economies in production. The first issue of the *Star* appeared in October 1933; the next month Sir Keith had the first of his heart attacks, which led to his prolonged absence from the affairs of the Herald and Weekly Times. The early battle against the *Star* was fought by Sydney Deamer, who had become editor of the *Herald* after his return from Adelaide. Under Deamer, and in contrast to the *Sun-News Pictorial*, the *Herald* set out in pursuit of what is now called a 'quality readership'. Its financial page was the best in the country; its London correspondent furnished items such as an interview with T. S. Eliot or an account of a surrealist art exhibition. Its reviews extended from the visual to the performing arts. On some pages, it was more reminiscent of the *Manchester Guardian* than the *Daily Mail*.

Murdoch did not have a substantial equity in the Herald and Weekly Times. In his absence, Theodore Fink, the chairman, tried to cut down the managing director's powers, but Murdoch returned for a board meeting in May 1934 and it reaffirmed his authority. Deamer, who had found Fink more congenial than Murdoch, was sent on a long overseas trip, which he broke to become editor of the Sydney *Daily Telegraph* under a new, rising proprietor, Frank Packer. The *Star* never managed to reach a circulation above 60,000 and was closed in April 1936.

VI

Northcliffe might have recognised more of himself in Sir Keith Murdoch's convoluted politicking than in his paper, the *Herald*. Though seen by the Labor Party as its bitter enemy, Sir Keith contacted D. L. McNamara, the

Secretary of the Victorian Labor Party early in 1935, offering help in the
coming state elections. He suggested that McNamara should submit articles
stating the Labor point of view, at first once a week and, as the poll came
closer, more often. The *Herald* would pay for them at its usual rates.[37] At the
poll the non-Labor parties won with a narrow majority, but the Country
Party leader Albert Dunstan promptly ditched his previous Nationalist allies
and, with Labor support in Parliament though without Labor representation
in Cabinet, became the new Premier. This realignment of parties was engin-
eered with the help of John Wren, Sir Keith's Brisbane partner. Wren
sought, and much later obtained, a licence to conduct trotting races on
Friday nights. The Herald and Weekly Times was not a beneficiary of this
licence, but Dunstan was willing to help on another occasion, the removal of
Sir Thomas Blamey from the position of Commissioner of Police.

Blamey had become head of the Victoria Police in 1925 and his appointment was made permanent in 1931. He had come to the job from the position of Australia's second-ranking soldier and, though often high-handed, he
was incorruptible. Some of his officers were not. In the 1930s leads to crime
stories were hotly pursued by newspaper reporters, who sometimes offered
a variety of gifts to detectives providing the leads. Blamey tried to stop these
practices by ruling that information would be released only at formal news
conferences, and personally presided over some of them. The newspapers
saw Blamey's ruling as a threat to the freedom of the press and continued on
their way. When Blamey retaliated by discriminating against individual
reporters, he was deemed intolerable by all the Melbourne newspaper
organisations.

On 14 December 1935 *Smith's Weekly*, a Sydney-based, nationally distributed publication lifted the curtain on the confrontation. In headlines
draped around pictures of Blamey and Murdoch, it announced: 'Putting him
on the spot/MAN HUNT?/Murdoch Heads Pack Against General Blamey'. The
ensuing article explained:

Sir Keith Murdoch has the Northcliffe complex in journalism. Close students of
Empire and Australian affairs appreciate just how much Murdoch owes to the late
Lord Northcliffe, who took him under his wing and whose influence won for
Murdoch a place in the Press dictatorship which earned for him the appropriate
name Lord Southcliffe ... His proximity to national developments through Lyons
whetted his thirst for power, and each week shows him more eager for political
dictatorship.[38]

Murdoch was not drawn by what seems to have been a leak from Blamey.
He went on a trip overseas, taking his wife and two children. The *Herald*'s

opportunity came with the night of Friday 22 May 1936, when Superintendent John Brophy, the head of the Criminal Investigation Branch, was shot in a car that had stopped in an inner-city park: with Brophy in the car were two women and a hotel waiter. Brophy, four bullets in his body, was taken to hospital and operated on that night. The next morning, a bulletin was issued with Blamey's authority saying that Brophy had accidentally discharged his revolver and grazed his hand. By Saturday afternoon the *Herald* knew the true medical situation and published it on its front page. One cover-up followed the next; each was authorised by Blamey and each was shown in turn to be short of the truth. The evasions led to demands for a Royal Commission which the Premier, Albert Dunstan, granted without hesitation. In the witness box, Blamey offered a version of events which the Commission rejected. When he received the Commission's adverse report, Dunstan demanded and got Blamey's resignation. The *Herald* and its reporters had been represented at the hearings by senior counsel; with Blamey's obstinate assistance, the paper won its biggest campaign.

As the storm was breaking over Blamey, Sir Keith attended a levee at Buckingham Palace. He toured Spain and was at the Olympic Games in Berlin when the Spanish Civil War broke out. His papers began to report Spain prominently and with sympathy for the Republican Government. On his return to Melbourne in October Sir Keith gave an interview to the *Herald* in which he summed up his impressions of Germany. He stressed the build-up for a war in the air, described the sizeable Air Ministry in Berlin and named Marshal Goering as the most dangerous man in that country. But Murdoch also gave weight to the appeasers' views he had heard in Britain – that Germany had been denied raw materials and should perhaps be given back some of her former colonies. He concluded by saying that the British navy was no longer Australia's 'immediate protector'.[39] His impressions of Europe remained vivid and put him at odds with Lyons, who paid a friendly visit to Mussolini in 1937. That year Sir Keith confided to associates that R. G. Casey, the Treasurer, might be a suitable replacement for Lyons, and, considering Lyons' wife an out-and-out pacifist, regarded her with even more suspicion than her husband.[40] She returned the dislike and later alleged that he had tried to undermine her husband by addressing a dinner party with the words: 'I put him there ... and I'll put him out.'[41] Northcliffe had come to life again.

Murdoch was reluctant to confront the isolationist and pacifist sentiments that flourished both on the non-Labor and Labor sides of politics. After the Munich conference, in which Britain bowed to German demands, he campaigned for a form of compulsory military training without gaining much support. Murdoch was convinced of the proximity of war, but he could not persuade others and he bowed to local political developments the following year. R.G. Menzies, a supporter of appeasement even after the British had abandoned this policy, succeeded Lyons on his death, and Sir Keith endorsed the succession.

A year later Menzies decided to use what he took to be Sir Keith's skills. At the outbreak of the war, Menzies had set up a Ministry of Information with the dual purpose of publicising Australia abroad, particularly in the United States, and of creating a domestic awareness of the conflict in Europe. The results at home were less than encouraging and in March 1940 Menzies added the Information portfolio to his prime-ministerial responsibilities. He approached Sir Keith, and they agreed that Sir Keith would become Director-General of Information, reporting directly to the Prime Minister and War Cabinet. The appointment was full-time but carried no salary. Menzies secured approval from his colleagues, Sir Keith consulted the heads of the major newspapers and a public announcement was made on 8 June. He took up his position at the end of that month and disaster at once overtook him.[42]

His first move as Director-General was to requisition prime time on all radio stations, national and commercial. On six nights of the week a departmentally prepared news bulletin would be transmitted over all stations, and on Sunday night a half-hour programme mixing light music and a peptalk would go out with the same uniformity. Their tedium quickly led to complaints, but with government control over radio – directly with the national stations, through the licensing process with the commercial ones – the station executives initially kept their heads down. The newspapers reacted at once to attempts to use their columns. They had accepted voluntary censorship since the beginning of the war, though they complained about specific incidents. Wanting to reduce friction, Sir Keith proposed a remedy: if a newspaper printed a statement deemed false, the government had the right of reply at the same length and in a similar place, without payment. A regulation to that effect was gazetted on 17 July 1940.

The next day, all newspapers except those previously controlled by Sir Keith, strongly disapproved and began campaigns against the regulation. The objection was most strongly put by John Curtin, the Opposition Leader and a former journalist: Sir Keith wanted to be editor-in-chief of every newspaper in the country. Menzies saw the danger of a rebarbative press, agreed to review the regulation and replaced it with a weaker one that was never invoked. In an attempt to bring the press proprietors over to his side by appointing one of them, Menzies had overlooked the animosities latent in that world. By November Sir Keith was in a mood to quit: Menzies had not given him the power he needed. His return to the Herald and Weekly Times was announced in November.

Menzies' conduct of the war increasingly disturbed some of his supporters. His resignation as Prime Minister was followed by the withdrawal of parliamentary support for the Coalition by two independents and, in October 1941, John Curtin became Prime Minister at the head of a Labor Cabinet. Two months later Japan attacked at Pearl Harbor and drove down the Malayan Peninsula. While Sir Keith was in Britain as a guest of its Government during December 1941, Ralph Simmonds, the editor of the *Herald*, asked Curtin for an article, a kind of Christmas message to his readers. Echoing some of the urgent cables Curtin sent Churchill in North America while he was conferring with Roosevelt, the article contained a striking sentence: 'Without any inhibitions of any kind, I make it quite clear that Australia looks to America, free of any pangs as to our traditional links or kinship with the United Kingdom.'[43] This statement was in line with the military realities; American liaison officers were already in Australia, preparing a supply base for the Pacific War. But cabled round the world, Curtin's statement infuriated Churchill and put Sir Keith in an awkward position. He promptly wrote to the *Times*, taking a midway position by criticising Churchill for trying to run the war with a single hand. He advocated that representatives of the Dominions should sit in the British War Cabinet and ignored Curtin's call to the United States. The *Times* placed his letter close to an editorial that referred to it and to Curtin's statement and implied that Curtin had spoken out because he had not been asked into the inner circle.[44]

Over the eight years of Labor rule from 1941 to 1949 Sir Keith's influence was greatly diminished. In 1942 H.V. Evatt, the Minister for External Affairs, put out a feeler about a public appointment for Sir Keith, possibly as a special envoy to Latin America, which was rejected. In some quarters, exaggerated suspicion about Sir Keith was rife. The fact that Berlin shortwave radio picked up items from his papers was the subject of a bureaucratic memorandum; MacArthur, the American Commander-in-Chief in the South-west Pacific, in private conversation with Shedden, the Australian Permanent Secretary for Defence, described Murdoch as 'an Australian Quisling'.[45] Sir Keith did not seek to make relations easier. Expecting an election, he began a series of signed articles in February 1943, assailing the Labor Government and, in Northcliffe fashion, Curtin, at all points. An early instalment repeated a remark attributed to an anti-conscription Labor politician that Curtin had opposed conscription in 1916 because he personally did not want to serve. The purported canvasser of this smear had meanwhile denied making it, and

Sir Keith had to withdraw and apologise the next day, conceding that Curtin had not been eligible for overseas service at the time.[46] Curtin won the election with a large majority, and after another bout of illness, Murdoch sought to regain some influence by putting out personal feelers to Shedden, who stayed in guarded touch with Murdoch over the next few years.

The Opposition had broken into several small fragments, which Menzies now tried to pull together. In the second half of 1944, W. S. Robinson of Collins House organised a dinner to discuss the future of what was to become the Liberal Party. Sir Keith attended, in the company of R. A. G. Henderson of John Fairfax, the publishers of the *Sydney Morning Herald*, Frank Packer of the now successful Sydney *Daily Telegraph* and Eric Kennedy, who had succeeded Denison at the Sydney *Sun*. For Menzies, the support of these proprietors was a matter of the head, not the heart. To his confidant, Lionel Lindsay, he wrote in vituperative terms about Henderson and Packer during the 1940s. He took some trouble with Sir Keith, and the 'Murdoch press' supported him in his 1949 victory, without being able to exercise the lien it once held over Lyons.[47]

VII

James Darling, who became headmaster of the Geelong Church of England Grammar School at Corio, Victoria, in 1930, saw a better future for his stagnating school in the hiring of well-chosen staff. The school had been patronised by the sons of Victorian landed families, with a sprinkling of clergymen's sons. Darling had a vision of a less rigid Australian Eton. The landed families would continue to send their sons; he also wanted those of Melbourne's upper class and in fact, anyone willing to pay for a good education. He sought teachers whose intellectual capacities and academic records impressed him and accepted the fact that they would have ideas of their own. After a decade or more, he had a leavening of such men: K. C. Masterman, the British classics master, who went on to take a chair at the Australian National University; Charles Manning Clark, the son of an Australian clergyman who had been to Oxford, who became the country's best-known historian; Ludwig Hirschfeld, the art master who came from Germany where he had been associated with the Bauhaus movement.

Sir Keith had sent his son to Adwalton, a private primary school in Melbourne and, in 1942, when Rupert was eleven, he enrolled him at

Geelong Grammar, knowing of Darling's reputation. Sir Keith soon made a point of looking over the teachers.

Masterman, Clark and Hirschfeld were the teachers Rupert Murdoch found most congenial. Heading away from his father and in search of an identity, he sought their support. The boy's attachment to Masterman went through the teacher's wife Margaret, to whom he would take his English compositions for help in the construction of sentences. She was an early object of the charm Rupert Murdoch displays towards older women. When the Mastermans were about to take a year's leave, he showed up at their quarters declaring that since Mrs Masterman had been so helpful, he was ready to do the dirtiest of jobs, and proceeded to clean up the bathroom and toilet. Manning Clark, a Christian socialist, aroused the boy's interest in history, but left Geelong in 1944, before taking him very far. But teacher and pupil continued to follow each other's development; more than three decades later, Clark was a steady contributor to the book pages of Rupert Murdoch's *Australian* and Murdoch bought Sidney Nolan's picture *The Bush Poet Henry Lawson (Alias Manning Clark)*. Hirschfeld had encouraged this appreciation of painting, an area where the boy did not clash with his father, who had been a collector since his stay in London during the first world war and had become Chairman of the National Gallery of Victoria. But Hirschfeld looked beyond the framed canvas and the free-standing sculpture, in accordance with the Bauhaus conception of art. He was one of the movers in the school's drama productions, for which he built the sets. In 1946 his major effort was *The Tempest*, in which Rupert Murdoch took the part of Iris in the fourth act.

Having turned sixteen in the next year, Rupert Murdoch began to fill positions in school activities and societies and to make his voice heard. He became co-editor of the *Corio Courier*, the school's news sheet, and spoke at the evenings of 'The Areopagus', a newly founded society that arranged formal debates on the lines of those held by university unions. At The Areopagus' first meeting, the motion debated was 'that this House views with concern the growing predominance of scientific ideas'; the school magazine, the *Corian*, tersely reported that Mr Murdoch had found fault with the Proposer, who in turn found fault with him for misrepresentation. Reporting the society's second debate, on the subject of socialism, the *Corian* noted that Mr Murdoch had amazed his audience with a knowledge of business statistics. The follow-ing year, The Areopagus took up topics that were at issue in the country's political arena. At a debate on the nationalisation of banking, Rupert Murdoch spoke in support, but the *Corian*'s reporter found him short on arguments, accusing his adversaries of having rifled his files. Rupert enjoyed being provocative. In the second debate of the year, when the future of 'public' (i.e., private) schools was under discussion, he was recorded as speaking in his inimitable, racy style: he did not see why birth into a rich family should enable some to enjoy an education they did not deserve. He was now regularly taking the more radical side in debates. Opposing the abolition of trade unions, he jibed at the reporting of the press, argued that one of the reasons of the existence of trade unions was the existence of employers' combinations, and over an uproar, declared that he was 'not a Commo'.[48]

For the major event in its year, The Areopagus invited Harold Holt, R. G. Menzies' lieutenant in Victoria, and Brian Fitzpatrick, an economic historian, to put the cases for free enterprise and socialism. Rupert Murdoch's partisanship was predictable: he called for more controls and said that the previous Menzies Government had been a failure. At the final evening of the year, the American way of life was under debate; Murdoch accused Americans of racial intolerance, deplored their political system and found that the country had fallen into the hands of the capitalists.[49]

If there was any single source for this radical strain, his name was Stephen Murray-Smith. The son of an army officer who had done well between the wars selling horses to the Indian cavalry, and a pupil of Geelong Grammar in the 1930s, Murray-Smith was back from war service, and with one academic year to his credit, obtained a position somewhere below the level of assistant master. He and Rupert Murdoch rapidly became friends and they discussed politics with considerable openness. As they walked around the oval on one occasion, Murray-Smith told his young friend that he and some of his associates regarded Sir Keith as a symbol of what was wrong with Australia – a symbol, of course, without being personal. Rupert Murdoch talked to his parents at some length about this new friend and Murray-Smith was asked to the Toorak home. Sir Keith was all diplomacy; deft with the radical young men on his papers who had opposed Hitler and Franco in the 1930s, he hinted to Murray-Smith at the opportunities in journalism. No offer was made, and according to plan, Murray-Smith went to the University of Melbourne and to a deeper political involvement. Perhaps Sir Keith picked up Murray-Smith's trail through other contacts. The friendship between the two young men did not continue; and when Murray-Smith was expelled from the Communist Party in the second half of the 1950s, his former friend was not receptive to a resumption of relations.

In 1947 Rupert Murdoch matriculated with second-class honours in English Expression but, as he was not yet seventeen, went back to Geelong Grammar for another year. Under less pressure to study, he founded his first journal, *If Revived*, as a successor to the Literary Society's *If*, which had expired in 1934. *If Revived* wanted to give all an opportunity 'to air their

opinions, so long as they are well expressed'. It cast its net wide: the first
issue led off with a contribution on 'Educational Immunisation' by Richard
Searby, one of the best students in the year, though usually on the opposite
side to Rupert Murdoch in the debates of The Areopagus. Daniel Thomas,
later an art critic and gallery director, discussed Gertrude Stein; unsigned
articles defended William Dobell, a painter under attack by traditionalists,
and criticised the racist 'White Australia' policy. The second issue of the
journal presented the cases for and against socialism; Murdoch explained
the Bauhaus as a centre of experimentation, and Richard Searby outlined
the achievements of one Tom Judd, a writer of plays and short stories not
heard of since. The two issues were attractively produced, and unlike Sir
Keith's papers, contained advertisements from the Fairfax, Packer and
Argus groups. At the end of the year Rupert Murdoch won the 'N. B. de
Lancey Forth Prize for Tree Knowledge'.

Under the benevolent eyes of Sir Keith, Rupert Murdoch then became a
cadet reporter on the *Herald*. He was assigned to police and court work,
accompanying a former pupil of Geelong Grammar on the rounds. His first
story in a big newspaper was a report on a court hearing. There were no
by-lines then for lowly reporters, let alone cadets, and, in any case, crimes
had to be fairly dreadful to make even part of the *Herald*'s front page. Before
going up to Oxford in that year, he served another stint as a cub reporter on
the *Birmingham Gazette*.

At Worcester College, where he took up residence in October 1950, he
occupied the De Quincey room, one of the biggest in the college. His political
sympathies were not considered heterodox; he soon joined the Oxford
Labour Club, and befriended Patrick Hutber, later a financial journalist in
London, but his manner was on the abrasive side and he was excluded from
contesting the treasurer's post on the ground that he had broken the rule
against canvassing. His more conservative contemporaries criticised him for
the blend of comfort exhibited in the De Quincey room and his advocacy of
socialism, and when another Australian nominated him for a cricket eleven,
he was blackballed.

Some of the dons thought the young Australian slow in coming up to
Oxford standards, but Asa Briggs and Harry Pitt, two History Fellows of
Worcester, thought he was basically bright and encouraged him. At the end
of the first year he reciprocated by inviting them to join him and George
Masterman, a student from Sydney, on an overland motor trip to the Middle
East, and they accepted.

Sir Keith, who had come to London for a meeting of the Reuters Board of
Trustees in July 1951, caught up with the travellers in Belgrade. The elder

Murdoch's health had not been the best throughout the 1940s, and after an operation and a prolonged absence from work in 1948, he had retired as managing director of the Herald and Weekly Times and stayed on only as chairman. The medical warnings following that illness had led him to re-arrange his affairs, and by 1951 he had clear control of News Ltd in Adelaide. He was going to considerable lengths to get closer to his son and to edge him into the succession he had been setting up. In 1950 he and Elisabeth had gone to Britain to see Rupert settle in. Back in Australia, Sir Keith started to send him information about the family's rural properties and the prosperity they enjoyed as a result of the Korean war boom. The meeting in Belgrade turned out to be their last.

On the way over to London, Sir Keith had snatched a meeting with President Truman. He came away sympathetic to the Truman Administration's plight, then under accusations of treachery by Congressional committees. In Belgrade doors also opened wide for him: the Tito regime was anxious to show Anglo-Saxon visitors that it had really broken with Stalin and a visit to President Tito's residence at Brioni was arranged. Sir Keith went on to Athens by air and reported on the efficacy of American aid to Greece. Sir Keith had been at his journalistic best; Rupert and his friends went on to Turkey by car.

Sir Keith remained uncertain whether he had wooed Rupert into the dynastic project. The following year Hugh Cudlipp of the London *Daily Mirror* group was in Melbourne to inspect the *Argus*. Sir Keith took the visitor to the Melbourne War Memorial on a hillock south of the River Yarra and confided: 'I'm worried about my son Rupert. He's at Oxford and developing the most alarming left-wing views.'[50]

The concern was exaggerated. Rupert Murdoch was back in Melbourne the weekend after his father's funeral, visited Brisbane, and realising the complications besetting the estate, returned to Oxford for another year, to graduate with a third in history.

The gross assets of Sir Keith's estate stood at £A600,000 but its current debts amounted to £A190,000 and death duties were still to be assessed. The estate included only a handful of stock units in the Herald and Weekly Times. In March 1953 Sir Keith's art collection fetched £A35,000 at auction. Halfway through that year, Rupert Murdoch took a job at the *Daily Express*, where Ted Pickering was managing editor. The *Daily Express* was still the place to get to know about newspapers, and Rupert Murdoch was determined to learn what he could before running his own.

Mr. J. W. Shand, QC, announced at [th]e Stuart Royal Commission today he [w]as withdrawing from proceedings.

He read from a prepared statement in which he said: [W]e consider that our continued association with this [co]mmission will in no way help Stuart and we think that the [pa]st few days have established that this commission is [un]able properly to consider the problems before it, and we [th]erefore withdraw".

Two minutes later Mr. Shand rose and walked out [of] the room followed by Miss Helen Devaney and Mr. Villeneuve Smith.

[The commiss]ion has adjourned until it can obtain

FORECAST (metropolitan): A shower or two.

THE NE[WS]

No. 11,236'   Phone LA 1271   48
ADELAIDE: FRIDAY, AUGU[ST]
Registered in Australia for transmission for po[st]

Chairman under fire

LAWYERS CRIT[ICISE] WRONG

Mr. J. W. Sha[nd] C. Villeneuve Sm[ith] Devaney, stated

appeals from the disagree- ments, the three state- ments were signed on the seventeenth (Monday).

Referring to the fact that Stuart was now un- represented, Mr. Blaze[y] said: "It does seem to me that justice could not be done to someone who seems to be momentarily overlooked without ade- quate representation for him...

Miss Helen Devaney

Mr Villeneuve Smith

They walked out, too.

[Mr.] SHAND, QC, and Miss Helen Devaney, [leaving Court]

Courtroom crowd in the scene congregated in the foyer and outside the door for about half an hour discussing possible next moves.

It looked most likely that there would be a long adjournment.

Whoever accepts — or is assigned the brief of rep- resenting Stuart before the commission resumes would have to study three lengthy volumes of transcript.

Factor[y]
66-78 O'C[...]

Chapter Three

/// *Under the Grid* ///

The centre of the city of Adelaide was built, from the days of its foundation, on a square grid bounded by four straight lines. Along North Terrace, the top boundary of the square, an array of public buildings starts with the Railway Station, takes in Parliament House and ends with the Institute of Technology. This face of authority is broken only by the rare monument in a pompous, representational style. The air terminals, hotels and offices opposite, such as those of the evening *News*, seem overpowered. To the novelist Murray Bail, growing up in this city after the second world war was a lesson in geometry. Before he ultimately left South Australia, Rupert Murdoch too was painfully taught how to get his angles right.

Nan and Rohan Rivett, who preceded him, thought Adelaide something of a country town when they arrived in 1951. They had spent three years in London and from there Sir Keith had brought the thirty-four-year-old Rivett to be editor-in-chief at the *News*, to revive it, and to become the mentor of the paper's heir. For those days, Rivett was an unusual person to take charge of an Australian evening paper. He had studied history at Melbourne and Oxford and had gone as a broadcaster to Singapore at the beginning of the war with Japan. Caught in the fall of the base, he spent three years as a prisoner in Japanese hands; life in the jungle honed down his edges and gave him a facility for communicating with a broad spectrum of people. On his release, he chronicled the sufferings of his fellow-prisoners in *Behind Bamboo*, a book that sold 100,000 copies. He had a sense of mission, common to many returned men: he wanted to build a better country. With a straight look in the eye and a firm grasp of the hand, he would strike you as your long-lost older brother.

39

When Sir Keith picked young men for advancement, his choice often fell on those whose fathers he knew. Sir Keith had long known Sir David Rivett, the head of the Council for Scientific and Industrial Research, a body that, among other things, found a way of making newsprint from eucalypts. Sir David had been an uncommonly independent head of the Council; he was married to a daughter of Alfred Deakin, the outstanding Prime Minister in post-Federation days; and he was a trustee of the National Gallery of Victoria over which Sir Keith presided. Rohan Rivett combined radicalism and a solid background in a way that might be palatable to Sir Keith's son.

Rivett's first two years at the *News* were far from easy. The circulation of the paper was stagnant and its profits were down. The estate left by Sir Keith took time to unravel: one of the estate's executors was H. D. Giddy, who succeeded Sir Keith as chairman of the Herald and Weekly Times, the major stockholder in the *Advertiser*, with which the *News* was now competing. When Rupert Murdoch returned from Britain in the second half of 1953, he briskly cut that tangle and – to the astonishment of Adelaide where questions of who owned what were not discussed in public – wanted everyone to know that he was his own man. On 10 November 1953, the *News* published its declaration of independence on its front page: 'The Herald Interests Extend', the headline said. The first paragraph explained: 'The Herald and Weekly Times Ltd yesterday purchased from the estate of the late Sir Keith Murdoch an effective controlling interest in Queensland Newspapers Pty Ltd, publishers of the *Courier-Mail* and *Sunday Mail*, Brisbane.' The report then appealed to local patriotism: two directors of the Herald and Weekly Times were also directors of Advertiser Newspapers; on the other hand, the publishers of the *News* had no connection with the Melbourne company and all its directors resided in Adelaide.

The Herald and Weekly Times bought the Brisbane paper on the hunch that it would soon be able to acquire that city's other paper, the evening *Telegraph*, which it did in 1956. Rupert Murdoch needed money to meet the estate's debts: keeping the Adelaide paper was also a good choice, for the growth of the city and its surroundings was part of the South Australian Government's policy. He accepted with relish the David and Goliath situation bequeathed to him: a small newspaper owned by the Murdoch family competing with Advertiser Newspapers, an outlier of the large corporation Sir Keith had built but not owned, the Herald and Weekly Times.

Before returning to Australia, Rupert Murdoch had gone to see Cecil King, to repeat Sir Keith's offer of combining the Adelaide and Brisbane papers with the *Argus*, and, like his father, he had been turned down. The lines were now clearly drawn. Even before the sale of the Brisbane paper went through,

Sir Lloyd Dumas, the chairman of Advertiser Newspapers, had launched the *Sunday Advertiser* as a competitor to the *Mail*, the weekend companion of the *News*: the first number appeared on 24 October 1953. The daily *Advertiser*'s sales of 167,000 were well ahead of those of the *News*, with around 102,000, but the *Mail*'s sales were around 170,000. Sir Lloyd hoped to carry his paper's daily readership into the weekend. But the *Mail* was well established, and its editor, Ron Boland, appointed by Sir Keith at about the same time as Rohan Rivett, was an old hand at popular journalism. The battle ended with Dumas' virtual surrender, in December 1955, when the *Sunday Advertiser* was selling around 108,000 copies.[1] The two weekend papers merged, each group took a half interest in the company publishing a continuing Sunday paper and the profitable printing contract went to News Ltd.

Their hands free, Rivett and Murdoch formed a team that intended to put Adelaide on its toes. They were excluded from the main wire services, so they engaged special writers as the occasion arose. When James Cameron from the London *News Chronicle*, where Rupert Murdoch had briefly worked, came to Australia to cover the British atomic tests, he doubled for the *News*; when Queen Elizabeth II arrived for her first tour, the *News* had its own correspondent; Walter Murdoch, Rupert's great-uncle, sent a weekly reflective column from Perth; later Walter Lippman's syndicated column became a regular feature. The circulation of the paper went up to 115,000, the profits quadrupled, and the Commonwealth Bank, which had lent the company money to buy newsprint at a critical moment, had acquired a promising customer.

Murdoch and Rivett worked well together as long as each went his own way. Murdoch was fourteen years younger, full-faced and, despite the dark three-piece suits which he wore as a concession to business etiquette, looked so boyish that Adelaide's wits called him 'Rupert the Chick'. But he was full of energy, seeming always to burst out of his clothes; at the paper, he would leave his coat in his office and roll up his sleeves, a mannerism he retained into his older, slimmer days. He left the journalists to Rivett, except to inform himself about politics. His territory was finance, advertising, distribution, the unions, new plant. The years in Adelaide gave him a thorough foundation in the newspaper business.

He established himself in the inner city, eating out much of the time and forming a lifelong restaurant habit. At Maxim's he would run into Clyde Cameron, an influential figure in South Australia's union and political Labor movement, a member of the federal Parliament and an acid raconteur. Cameron, who had called a local branch of the Fabian Society into being, asked Murdoch to deliver an address and Murdoch chose international financial conditions as his topic. On weekends starting with Friday nights, he would go to the races and, with his stockbroker friend Hubert Harvey, he bought a trotter. He liked going to Broken Hill in New South Wales where the company owned a small daily paper, because across the border of South Australia, poker machines were legal, and he liked pulling them to see what came up. His fondness for gambling deluded his competitors into the belief that the young man could not be taken seriously, and he did not mind their delusion.

He was shy and gauche with young women, but he could be persistent. Through a common friend he met Pat Booker, who had come to Adelaide to break off another relationship. Born in Sydney and raised in Melbourne, she had some of the sophistication of those brighter cities. He could not dance, but she saw other attractions in him. They married in a Presbyterian church on 1 March 1956, an event recorded in the *Advertiser* but not the *News*. He could never be brought to learn dancing, and persuaded his wife to come to the races instead, where he now began to win; there weren't many places to go out to in Adelaide on a weekend. After he bought a Sunday paper in Perth, he often flew west for the weekend. Newspapers were beginning to be his big kick.

Rivett was wholly absorbed in being a newspaper editor. The Rivetts had bought a house in the hills and would, after six days at the office, entertain staff there on the seventh, as well as visitors from interstate and abroad. He began on Mondays by switching on the radio to catch the early news, and with an electric razor in his right hand, would click the fingers of his left when an item caught his imagination, to lead the front page or to be the topic of the day's editorial. The radio would be playing again in the car and continue as he picked up a staff member at an appointed street corner, and then on, all the way to North Terrace. He wanted to build the *News* into an educative paper, like the London *News Chronicle*, and he made a special point of training the contributors to the Friday book column. 'I want you to tell my readers', he instructed a university teacher about to review the one-volume abridgement of Toynbee's *Study of History*, 'whether this man is Jesus Christ or not'. Once a year, he would go abroad, usually to Asia. Like Rupert Murdoch, he looked beyond the South Australian borders; good relations with countries to the north were an article of faith with him.

The two men were at one in their ambivalence towards Tom Playford, the state Premier. Playford was for Growth: left to the play of the market, Adelaide would remain a transit point for wheat and wool. Starting during the war and continuing after, Playford industrialised the city and built satellite towns around it. To lure investors to South Australia, he developed the State

Housing Trust until it was building a third of the new dwellings and accom-
modating a growing industrial and service work force. Every new settler was
a potential newspaper reader: the *News* could not be against Playford.

But it was equally difficult to be *for* Playford. He had become Premier in
1938 and had gradually extended a political grid over the whole of the state,
which kept him in power. His enemies called it the 'Playmander'. By 1954
the electoral boundaries were so arranged that one rural vote counted for
three urban votes, and the rural votes largely went to Playford's Party, the
Liberal Country League. The immigrants to Adelaide who bought the *News*
did not count for much. Playford was a firm Baptist: drink was not sold after
six o'clock on a weekday; Sunday was a day of recuperation for industrial
workers and of strict observance for Playford's fellow Protestants. Besides,
when a government is so well entrenched, a newspaper has little prospect of
throwing any weight it has into the balance at election times.

The alternative to Playford as Premier was a long way down the road, but a
man who saw himself in that role made it his business to befriend Murdoch
and Rivett. Donald Allan Dunstan was the son of a trading company manager
in Fiji, where he had spent his youth. From Fiji he went to the exclusive St
Peter's College in Adelaide, took a law degree at the University of Adelaide
and returned to a law practice in Fiji. An itch for politics, acquired as a student,
brought him back to South Australia and in 1953 he won a marginal seat for
Labor. Speaking with a distinctively English accent, married to a woman who
taught French and German at the University, and fond of light wines, he was
an unlikely starter between a teetotal Premier and a beery leader of the
Opposition. But he was tenacious. He formed a circle of supporters who met
at his home, and he persuaded Murdoch and Rivett to drop in and hear the
discussions. They reciprocated by giving him a weekly column to put the
Labor point of view on current issues, balanced by a contribution from the
Government side.

Murdoch, Rivett and Dunstan spoke the same language; they had been to
Protestant private schools, had taken part in student politics and were out of
place in established Adelaide. Nevertheless Murdoch and Rivett did not
fathom Dunstan. When the Labor Party split and its former right wing
became the basis for the Democratic Labor Party with state branches round
Australia, Dunstan was called to the *News* office. Was he prepared to join the
new political organisation? If he was, Murdoch and Rivett could offer him a
great deal of publicity. Dunstan readily figured out that Democratic Labor
would remain a minority group in South Australia, without much influence;
in its strongest state, Victoria, the new party counted on the benevolence of
the Catholic hierarchy; in South Australia, the Archbishop looked at it

askance. In other respects, too, Democratic Labor was not Dunstan's cup of tea: it brought to politics a puritanical intolerance historically absent from Australian Catholicism. Dunstan bluntly turned down the offer.[2]

In April 1957 Murdoch and Rivett had their first major row. Murdoch ordered a large new printing press, capable of producing a 72-page paper. Uninterested in production, Rivett went on his annual trip and sent back a dispatch from India for the first issue to be printed on the new machine. On his return he found that Murdoch had shifted sport from the last to an inside page. How could Murdoch shift *his* sport, without telling him in advance? Murdoch insisted that the back page had to be sold to advertisers to pay for the larger paper. Rivett continued to fume: *he* was the editor. But sport stayed on an inside page: Rupert Murdoch had the last word. Rivett was no longer the infallible mentor, appointed by Sir Keith.

II

Prosperity fed ambition. Retaining a substantial proportion of the profits made by News Ltd Murdoch bought publishing ventures interstate: *New Idea*, a weekly addressed to women and published by Southdown Press in Melbourne and the *Sunday Times*, published by Western Press in Perth, had been acquired in 1956. In 1957 he took a minority interest in the Adelaide radio station 5DN. But the glittering prize ahead was a television licence newly allocated by the federal Government.

In Sydney and Melbourne, three channels had begun transmission. Two in each city were operated commercially, the third was run by the Australian Broadcasting Commission. The major newspaper groups of those cities had stakes in the licensee companies. In Sydney, John Fairfax was the largest stockholder in Channel 7 and the Packer group controlled Channel 9; in Melbourne, the Herald and Weekly Times controlled Channel 7 and David Syme & Co. were a minority partner in Channel 9, controlled by Electronic Industries, an appliance maker. These four commercial channels grouped themselves into two incipient networks: Fairfax joined with the Herald and Weekly Times, Packer with Electronic Industries. According to the Government's plans, Adelaide and Brisbane were each in line for a licence. But as Adelaide had little more than a quarter of Sydney's population it was likely that only one commercial licence would become available there, and, for that matter, in Brisbane. The available advertising money, it was thought, could only support one channel in each city. So much the better for Murdoch. A sole licence would mean not only handsome profits, but could give him an edge over the *Advertiser* in a variety of ways.

The pursuit of a television licence became his major preoccupation. Eager to learn, he toured the world twice, looking at stations and seeking out future programme suppliers. An incidental benefit was the idea of a weekly programme guide based on the American *TV Guide*, which became *TV Week* and commercially the most successful publication he started in Australia. In September 1957 the Postmaster-General announced that applications for licences in Brisbane and Adelaide would be sought, leaving the question of the number of channels in each city open. This question was also left un-determined when an official call for applications went out from the Australian Broadcasting Control Board (ABCB), before whom the applicants were to appear the following year. Murdoch's pursuit of a channel was no secret. He talked to John Williams of the Herald and Weekly Times, to Sir Arthur Warner of Electronic Industries, and to Jim Oswin, the general man-ager of the Fairfax station in Sydney. A potential member of one of the networks, Murdoch was received politely. As the talks proceeded, more concrete offers were put to him: Advertiser Newspapers floated the idea of a joint application, but Murdoch turned it down. Towards the end of 1957 Rupert Henderson, the managing director of John Fairfax, proposed a Fairfax minority in Murdoch's applicant company. Murdoch explained that he needed no money. His ears were wide open, but he made no commit-ment. He wanted as much of the action as he could get for himself.

He learnt rather late that he had been treated as a country cousin. As far back as 23 April 1957 a meeting had been held at John Fairfax's offices in Sydney, attended by the senior people behind the existing licensees and by a radio group interested in a television licence in Brisbane. The meeting considered the implications of further licences for the existing networks. If the Government issued two licences in Brisbane, and, by implication, in Adelaide, then each existing network would have adequate outlets; but if only one commercial channel were set up, then an agreement would have to be made to safeguard outlets for the two networks. John Williams and Sir Arthur Warner undertook to set out the consensus in a memorandum, and a second meeting was held early in May. Over the months, the majority of this group assumed that two licences would be issued in each of the cities, and as the hearings neared, everyone wished everyone else good luck. Rupert Henderson, however, had doubts whether two licences would or should be issued, and as a result of his differences with Frank Packer on this matter, the documents covering these negotiations later became known to the ABCB and the public.[3]

When the hearings opened the country's three major media groups and the two smaller ones, News Ltd and Truth and Sportsman Ltd, had lined up behind six applicants. For Brisbane, the local affiliate of the Herald and Weekly Times sponsored one candidate, the Packer group another; in the third applicant, the Fairfax group and Truth and Sportsman Ltd were substantial shareholders. In Adelaide the Herald and Weekly Times affiliate and the Packer group were similarly represented; the third applicant was Southern Television Corporation, with a 60 per cent stake from News Ltd.

Rupert Murdoch flew to Brisbane for the opening of the hearings on 28 April, and that afternoon asked for leave to make a short statement. He told the ABCB that he feared an allocation of two licences in the Brisbane area might be taken as a precedent for Adelaide, and asked it to regard as irrelevant such questions as the availability of capital or the connections of the licensee with outside networks. Cross-examined the next day, he presented himself as an unabashed advocate of monopoly. Would the possession of a monopoly in commercial television be an extremely valuable asset, he was asked. Yes, Murdoch replied, he had a monopoly evening paper, from the public's point of view an infinitely better paper than the two competing ones in Sydney, and better because there was no competition.[4] On the way back to Adelaide, he was interviewed on Melbourne television: did he want a monopoly? This time he parried by saying that his intention in going to Brisbane had been to see that the monopoly of the Melbourne Herald was not extended further.[5]

At the subsequent hearings for the Adelaide area, he put forward a more elaborate financial argument. If his company operated the sole commercial licence, its total losses over three years would be £A139,060; by the third year, it would operate at a profit. On the other hand, if two commercial licences were operated competitively, his company would lose more than half a million pounds in the first three years. Nonetheless he was prepared to operate under even these conditions, and News Ltd would find the additional capital needed.

The ABCB was impressed with the arguments for single commercial licences and, somewhat shaken by what it had learnt about networking arrangements, released the documents covering the discussions between existing licensees in a special appendix to the Report it sent to the Government. But having been given no guidelines as to the number of licences, it recommended that fresh applications be called for, with clear instructions that only one licence would be issued in each city, that the applicants should have no links of ownership with existing licensees and that they would undertake not to join networks.

In an election year, the ABCB's recommendations were not of sufficient weight to sway a Government that looked over its shoulder at electoral support from the major media groups. Murdoch's company alone would have passed the ABCB's tests. The ABCB completed its report in July; the Government played for time and, when it tabled the Report in Parliament in September, it called for a new set of recommendations on the basis that two licensees be chosen in each Adelaide and Brisbane. The new recommendations of the ABCB were announced on 13 October 1958, after Parliament had been prorogued for the elections. In Adelaide, Southern Television Corporation was to control Channel 9, and the company sponsored by Advertiser Newspapers, Channel 7. The *News* greeted this development with an item on page five, reporting the Leader of the Opposition, Arthur Calwell, as describing the ABCB as a 'poor, spineless, useless instrumentality' and urging its abolition. Undaunted by the budget he had put before the ABCB, Rupert Murdoch left for another long overseas trip a fortnight later, to see television stations and programme producers.

Rivett had long been critical of the Menzies Government's actions abroad, but in the election campaign now afoot the *News* expressed an open disenchantment with other aspects of federal government policy. It greeted the opening campaign speech of the Opposition Leader with the comment that the stimulus promised by him was in accord with the views held by a number of economists. It reacted to Menzies' policy speech by acknowledging his past record but regretting his refusal to consider the Opposition's economic proposals. On the day before the poll it summed up its attitude by sitting on the fence: thousands of people, an editorial said, were unhappy about the Government, but they had equally real fears about the only visible alternative. The major newspapers of the country all supported the incumbent Government. There was little chance that the Labor Opposition might succeed, and the *News* had gone as far as it could in opposing a certain winner.

III

For Rupert Murdoch mid-1959 was full of promise; Channel 9 would open shortly, ahead of its rival. For Rohan Rivett it was a year of newly won fame beyond the borders of South Australia, and of infamy in some Adelaide quarters. He would become involved in a law case that would divide the city.

The involvement began at a lunch hurriedly arranged on 24 July by Frank Borland, the Warden of the University Union, to introduce Father Thomas Dixon MSC. Dixon had become a central figure in the appeal brought by Rupert Max Stuart, who was waiting to be hanged for the alleged rape and murder, late in 1958, of a nine-year-old girl at Ceduna, 800 kilometres west of Adelaide. Stuart was an Aranda from central Australia, employed by a travelling sideshow visiting Ceduna. Dixon had spent some time among Stuart's people as a missionary and knew their language. Stuart's English was poor, and Dixon had gone to the Adelaide jail at the suggestion of a junior chaplain. He was the first to converse with the Aboriginal prisoner in Pidgin and Aranda since the arrest.

The charges found true by a jury and upheld by a three-member bench of the Supreme Court of South Australia were so ugly that neither the *News* nor the *Advertiser* gave the Stuart case much space. When Rivett came to the lunch he knew something about recent developments in it and about Borland's fear of a miscarriage of justice, but he seemed averse to a closer involvement. Borland explained how Dixon came to doubt Stuart's guilt: he had learnt that a confession supposedly dictated by Stuart to police was a crucial part of the prosecution's case and had come to wonder how Stuart, with his poor command of English, could have dictated it. He had taken the document to Ted Strehlow, a university linguist, who had grown up among Aranda and spoke the language like a native. Strehlow then talked to Stuart, wrote an opinion saying that the confession could not have been dictated, and with that new evidence, Stuart's lawyers appealed to the High Court of Australia. The High Court did not overturn the verdict but was impressed with Strehlow's opinion. From this highest Australian court, another appeal was now being made to the Privy Council in London.

Dixon thought he could turn up added new evidence, perhaps even an alibi for Stuart. The owner of the travelling sideshow and Stuart's fellow workers had never been seen by the defence counsel. Nobody knew their whereabouts. Earlier in the week Dixon had therefore made a statement to a reporter from the *Sydney Morning Herald* who had come to Adelaide, expressing a belief in Stuart's innocence and issuing a call for the sideshow people. After a television interview Dixon got a result: an executive from the Brisbane *Courier-Mail* phoned to say that the sideshow was in north Queensland. Interpreting this message as an invitation, Dixon obtained permission to leave Adelaide from the superiors of his Order, and packed his bags. But then he learnt that he had misunderstood: his travelling costs would not be met and, being under a vow of poverty, he could not set off on his own account.

Dixon did not realise that his statements had changed the perspective of the media. Before, newspaper reports on the appeal would have begun: 'The convicted murderer ...'; now they could start: 'An Adelaide priest ...'. But Rivett needed reassurance: he came to the lunch suspecting that Dixon was an opponent of capital punishment who was using Stuart as an example, and he now interrogated the priest about his attitude. Dixon explained the Church's teaching, as it then was: if the State decreed hanging as a penalty, the Church had to abide by the decree. Rivett at once changed tack. The *News* would pick up the tab for Dixon's trip, in the company of its police rounds-man. Any new evidence would first be presented to the Privy Council and the *News* would then have first, exclusive release.[6]

Dixon found the sideshow proprietor and his wife and obtained statutory declarations amounting to an alibi. The following Tuesday, the Privy Council refused leave to appeal, but commented that any new evidence should be reviewed by the South Australian Executive Council, that is, the Governor and a group of government ministers. The next day the *News* opened its campaign with the headline, 'PRIEST: STUART HAS PERFECT ALIBI/Murder case bombshell', published the statutory declarations, and demanded a postponement of the hanging. That afternoon the South Australian Premier, Playford, assured the state Parliament that the Executive Council would look at the evidence. The next day the *News* pushed its campaign with statements of concern from the clergy; the state Leader of the Opposition moved for an investigation; and the Premier announced that the hanging was postponed and a Royal Commission of three judges would be appointed. It was a quick, clean victory for the *News*; it even seemed as if Playford might admit the possibility of a miscarriage of justice in his otherwise blameless state.

He didn't. That evening, with Parliament risen, Playford announced the terms of reference and the members of the Royal Commission. The terms contained no clear indication that the purported confession should be reviewed. Of the three Commission members, two had already sat over Stuart: Sir Mellis Napier, the Chief Justice of South Australia, who was to head the Commission, had presided in the Supreme Court appeal, and Mr Justice Reid had been the trial judge in the first instance. There is a legal presumption against judges reviewing their own cases, and the Commission's terms and membership made Stuart's lawyers hesitate about participating in the hearings. The next day the *News* asked for much wider terms of reference in a front page editorial; next to this editorial it carried a cartoon suggesting that Playford had picked the wrong Commissioners. Adelaide readers had not seen such strong stuff for a long time.

Before the *News* began its campaign, the small band of anti-racists, legal reformers and penal abolitionists around Father Dixon had put out 15,000 copies of a pamphlet opposing the hanging. Now another 10,000 copies were printed; high-school students handed them out at street corners; families who never talked about politics discussed the Stuart case. Playford recognised that Adelaide was aroused, but his actions only succeeded in shifting the centre of concern. They fanned the suspicion that he was above all determined not to have a verdict of his courts overturned. The Stuart case, in which half a dozen police officers were under scrutiny over a confession, became 'the Stuart affair', in which the Premier's judgement was under attack. The grid was beginning to buckle.

Rupert Murdoch now became personally involved. He wanted to look over Father Dixon before the paper went in deeper, and the modest priest was taken to a dinner without being given the chance to discuss the case. Murdoch was happy: Rivett continued the campaign, printing a letter from Strehlow to the state Attorney-General which rejected the authenticity of the confession, and himself went to Queensland to obtain two more statutory declarations in support of an alibi. Interstate and overseas publications, including the London *Times*, kept abreast of events; the London *News Chronicle* had a piece by James Cameron, who called Rivett 'the Zola of South Australia', and Rivett reprinted it. Playford made another concession: he told Parliament he had been assured that the Commissioners would look at the circumstances of the confession.

The hearings of the Commission began on 10 August and, with long adjournments, spread over ten weeks. Jack Shand, QC, one of Australia's best criminal lawyers, came from Sydney to represent Stuart. The apprehensions of Stuart's supporters were strengthened when the Commission told Shand early in the proceedings that it was *his* task to shake their confidence in the verdict, and not *their* task to review the case. The differences between the Commission and Shand grew sharper and, on the fourth full day, Napier interrupted Shand's cross-examination of a retired policeman, saying that though he had not the slightest intention of stopping Shand, he had heard enough. Shand asked for an adjournment and the next morning read a statement saying that never in his career had he been stopped in cross-examination and now he was withdrawing.

For South Australians prepared to question their Chief Justice, Shand's withdrawal was a point of low confidence in the system. It was also the day of the *News'* toughest headlines, whose reverberations would echo till the middle of 1960. Unshaken by Shand, the Commission continued to hear witnesses, letting it be known that it wanted Stuart to be one of them. In his solicitor's view, Stuart could not undergo this ordeal without representation and, with the *News* prepared to foot the bill, local senior counsel was chosen. Before intervening, this second representative withdrew, and a third senior counsel, this time paid out of public funds, arrived from Victoria. Stuart's death sentence had by then been commuted to life and he appeared on the stand. That morning Rupert Murdoch was in the court precincts, glad to be assured by Father Dixon that all would go well. Having heard the final pleadings in October, the Commission adjourned and its report was tabled in December. The heat of confrontation between the *News* and the Premier was lost in the searing summer, but Playford had not forgotten Rivett or Murdoch.

IV

Step by step, it became more likely that a case against the *News* would follow the Stuart Commission. Sir Mellis Napier had shown a distaste for the paper quite early in the proceedings: 'In the very nature of things, we do sometimes read the newspapers,' he remarked, 'and it would be easier for us if we were allowed to go about our business without being told what witnesses are going to say before they are called.' Taken by itself, this pronouncement could have applied to a number of publications that had followed Father Dixon's footsteps, or had occasionally anticipated him in north Queensland before the Royal Commission was appointed. But only the *News* had called editorially for an inquiry, and Napier alluded to this in a further remark that made the target evident: 'It has not been helpful to us that we should be told where truth and justice lie without being able to discover that for ourselves.'[7]

On the day the *News* had reported Shand's withdrawal, it put out two successive posters. The earlier one said 'SHAND QUITS: "YOU WON'T GIVE STUART FAIR GO"'. The later one said 'COMMISSION BREAKS UP/SHAND BLASTS NAPIER'. Throughout the successive editions of the paper, over reports that became fuller in each, the headlines remained constant: 'Mr Shand QC indicts Sir Mellis Napier /THESE COMMISSIONERS CANNOT DO THE JOB'. Rivett had been in close touch with Murdoch all that day and Murdoch knew of the first poster when it was sent out. Murdoch himself drafted the second poster and suggested the line 'These Commissioners cannot do the job'. As editor, Rivett subsequently accepted the legal responsibility for both the posters and the headlines.

The Commission broke up for ten days after Shand's withdrawal and, when it reassembled, counsel assisting it rose to say that attempts had been made to confuse the public mind over Shand's withdrawal; Napier had made it clear that he would stay and listen as long as it suited Shand, who had walked out on a flimsy pretext, and Shand's remarks had been made the pretext for an attack on the Commissioners by a section of the press. Napier endorsed these observations of counsel assisting the Commission.

Shand's departure stirred the Leader of the Opposition into attempting a censure motion, which was stopped at the procedural stage. When another motion was substituted, Playford referred to the press accusations that a confession had been forced out of an innocent man, saying that this was something no Member of Parliament could accept. He then displayed one of the *News* posters and read out the headlines on Shand's departure. The words 'These Commissioners cannot do the job', he said, were the gravest libel ever made against a judge in the state, and at an appropriate time, the Government would consider action.

It was a clear warning. The *News* replied with an editorial, headed 'Let's Get the Record Straight'. It conceded that Shand had not said the words between quotation marks in its heading, and expressed regret for publishing them. It went on to say that the poster saying '... Shand blasts Napier' should have run 'Shand attacks Commission'. This editorial was drafted by Rupert Murdoch. But the *News* had still not heard the end. Counsel representing the Crown before the Royal Commission commented that 'attempted trial by newspaper was a dangerous and malignant thing'.[8]

On 19 January 1960 the Crown laid charges against Rivett and News Ltd over the reports on Shand's departure. They were grave, criminal charges. In the two posters and the headlines, the two defendants were alleged to have severally published a seditious libel, a defamatory libel knowing it to be false, and a defamatory libel, making nine charges against each defendant, who were ordered to appear before a magistrate on 25 January.

The prosecution here argued that, by saying the judges would not give someone a 'fair go', the defendants had committed a 'terrific' libel against the judges. They had said that the Commission broke up, when it was merely adjourned so that Stuart could seek other representation. Shand had not 'blasted' the Chief Justice: to allege that he did was proof of malice. Further exercises in such textual criticism were undertaken. As its first witness, the prosecution called the chief of staff of the *News*, who refused to answer a long series of questions and was committed into custody. A second witness, Murdoch's personal assistant Ken May, was on the point of being committed but, advised by counsel, freely answered questions about the paper's organisation. When the paper's news editor was called on the fourth day, the prosecutor waved an official pardon before him, to undercut a refusal to answer questions on the ground of self-incrimination. On the fifth day, Rupert Murdoch declined to answer a long string of questions.

The defendants called no witnesses and reserved their case for the trial before a judge and jury, which opened on 7 March. Rivett was now represented by a legal team distinct from that of News Ltd and, in some particulars, his line of defence differed from the company's. The prosecution again presented *News* staff as witnesses, who were now cross-examined and gave evidence favourable to their employer and editor. For instance, it was said that newspapers often use quotation marks to summarise a matter, rather than reproduce the exact words, and that the word 'blast' was a journalistic synonym for 'criticise'. But two directors of News Ltd gave testimony that did not help their editor: one admitted that he told Rivett he disagreed with the way Shand's departure was reported, another that he was disturbed by the crude wording of a poster. After eight days the judge instructed the jury that the defendants had not been seditious, but that the jury had to decide whether defamation had taken place.

Before the trial closed Rivett made an unsworn statement from the dock. He recalled his career, then his meeting with Dixon, saying he had formed no opinion on Stuart's guilt on that occasion but decided that the question should be further examined. He still believed that Shand had caused the Commission to break up until further representation was found and that Shand's remarks had been aimed at Napier. With Murdoch's consent, Rivett then disclosed the considerable part played by his publisher in the contested publications. Summing up, Rivett's counsel suggested that the prosecution was politically inspired, was immoderately conducted and stemmed from the Government's pique.

The jurors found that the defendants had not committed defamation knowing it to be false, but disagreed among themselves about whether one poster, which said 'Shand quits ... ', was defamatory. Thus one charge out of the nine remained hanging over each defendant, and it was up to the Government's law officers to initiate another trial or to withdraw. The matter was dropped early in June through a formal plea of *nolle prosequi*. Two days later, the *News* ran an editorial under the title 'An Aftermath'. It said the paper had never suggested that any members of the Royal Commission were unfit to adjudicate the issues before them; it believed that when the number of available judges was limited, as it was in South Australia at that time, exceptions had to be made to the rule against their sitting in appeal against themselves. This was a retreat well beyond Rivett's statement from the dock, let alone from the cartoon originally published; it was also a retraction of the paper's previous suggestion that a judge from outside the state should conduct the inquiry into the conviction of Stuart. Rivett's intimates are certain that he did not write this editorial.

Murdoch and Rivett had seen a good deal of each other when the sedition and defamation charges were first brought, with Rivett sometimes beginning the day with a call to the Murdochs' place. On the night before the repentant editorial appeared, Murdoch was in Sydney, busy in the wings of another media event. The parting of their ways was only weeks away.

V

Murdoch had been wholly serious when he threw out his casual remark to the ABCB about wanting to limit the monopoly of the Herald and Weekly Times. The Stuart affair did not divert him from his purpose. A few days after Stuart took the witness stand before the Commissioners, Sir Stanley Murray, the chairman of News Ltd, wrote a letter to the board of Advertiser Newspapers proposing a merger. He foreshadowed that News Ltd would make an offer to exchange three News stock units for four Advertiser units, plus a cash payment of 40s; alternatively, it was ready to pay 62s 6d for each Advertiser unit. To ensure the independence of the morning paper, News Ltd was prepared to set up an editorial trust similar to those of the London *Times* or *Observer*, made up of such figures as the Chief Justice, or the Chancellor or Vice-Chancellor of the University. This was a remarkable rider, for the Chief Justice and University Chancellor were one person: Sir Mellis Napier.

In market terms the offer was generous: Advertiser stock had been quoted at 36s a few days earlier. But it was not a merger in the normal sense. The stock to be issued carried voting rights only for special occasions, and control of both papers would be in the hands of the biggest holders of News ordinary stock, Rupert Murdoch's family. The bid had been well prepared. It was worth £A14 million in shares and cash, or £A12.6 million in cash alone, at a time when the issued capital of News Ltd was £A560,500 and its shareholders' funds stood in the books at less than £A1.8 million. To cover the disparity, Murdoch had gone to A. N. Armstrong, the head of the Commonwealth Bank's trading division in Sydney, and obtained his backing.

A merger would have made good commercial sense. Sir Keith Murdoch might have approved the production of two papers in one plant and their distribution through one system. In other respects it was unrealistic. The Herald and Weekly Times held over 36 percent of the Advertiser stock, and simultaneously the Adelaide group was the biggest single holder in the Melbourne group. Control of Advertiser Newspapers thus implied a Murdoch foot in the Melbourne door.

Sir Lloyd Dumas, the *Advertiser*'s chairman, took the foreshadowed bid coolly. Three days later the readers of his paper were able to scan his reply on the tenth page. He said that he had consulted a number of the company's shareholders, accounting for more than 50 percent of the stock, and they had said they would not accept the offer if it were made. Sir Lloyd added tartly: 'We believe that our shareholders – and the South Australian community generally – have a real pride in the *Advertiser* and would never agree to its being modelled on the *News*.'[9] This remark was apt to have been read with appreciation at the Adelaide Club, where Sir Lloyd and the three Royal Commissioners were fellow members.

Was Murdoch's bid sheer bravado? He did not proceed with a formal offer, but the fact that he could muster substantial financial backing and was on the march did not escape notice interstate. In the financial world this drew as much attention as anything Rivett had done for Stuart. At the manoeuvres that Australia's media groups performed on the borders of each others' territories, Murdoch would henceforth be counted in.

But in Adelaide he had failed. He had not coordinated his political and commercial moves; they ran in opposite directions. He had not been given the sole commercial television licence, failed to absorb his morning competitor, and finally backed off in a showdown with the Premier. The place was too tight, too small for him. Once he slipped from under the grid, he rationed his visits and never lived there again.

KNIGHT'S SONS IN CITY

Mr. Clyde Packer and Mr. Kerry Packer, directors of Consolidated Press and sons of Sir Frank Packer, managing director of Consolidated Press,

RAW

WEATHER

FLOOD CHAOS

Sydney will have no relief today from the heavy rain, says the Weather Bureau. Seven inches since Wednesday have caused flood chaos. The wettest November on record has brought landslides, road floods, traffic pile-ups, and cancellation of sports meetings—See PAGE FOUR.

ror
PICTORIAL

DWAY MELODY 1961!

Calwell took his Commonwealth car along to Broadway.

MR. MENZIES JILTED

The wedding breakfast was austere and the guests were confined to the family. The Prime Minister, Mr. R. G. Menzies, was at Wagga

Chapter Four

/// *Mirror Images* ///

Sydney's newspaper proprietors were a peculiar lot. Roughly of one generation, they had brawled with each other while they were young and learnt to accept one another as they grew older. The fight over the *Sun* was the last big ring event; it brought the number of groups down from four to three. The contestants were John Fairfax and Sons and Frank Packer's Consolidated Press, and Fairfax won. They had started the *Sunday Herald* after the war, now merged it with the *Sunday Sun* and moved the plant for printing the morning and evening papers from the centre of the business district to the fringe of the inner city. John Fairfax and Sons were run by Warwick Fairfax (born 1901), the chairman and a fourth-generation descendant of the founder, and in his absence by Rupert Henderson (born 1896), the driving managing director. Frank Packer (born 1905) had created Consolidated Press and published the *Daily Telegraph* and *Sunday Telegraph*, but made most of his money from the *Australian Women's Weekly*, and was not hurt badly by losing. The third, much smaller group, Truth and Sportsman Ltd, was controlled by Ezra Norton (born 1897) and published the *Daily Mirror* and *Sunday Mirror*. And then there were two: in 1958 Fairfax financed the purchase of Norton's holdings in Truth and Sportsman by O'Connell Pty Ltd, until then an entity on the shelf of a legal firm.

Sydney's newspaper controllers were acutely conscious of the expansiveness of the Herald and Weekly Times, which had been accentuated after Sir Keith Murdoch's death. On learning that his friend Ezra Norton was serious about getting out of business, Rupert Henderson was determined to thwart any sale to the Melbourne group and, in the event, anticipated a sale to Frank Packer as well. John Fairfax guaranteed a loan of £A885,150 to

57

O'Connell which bought Norton's controlling stock and separately paid him £A500,000 for an undertaking not to start another daily in Sydney. An amalgamation of the *Sun* and the *Daily Mirror* would have been simpler. But the reduction of evening papers to one might have encouraged the Melbourne group, Packer or someone else to start a replacement. In the event, the tortuous arrangement by which O'Connell Pty Ltd competed with John Fairfax allowed Rupert Murdoch to thrust himself into Sydney.[1]

Murdoch's eyes had already lit on the city's western and northern outskirts where Cumberland Newspapers Ltd, a much smaller company, distributed around 400,000 suburban papers once or twice a week. Cumberland Newspapers had been started by Earl White, a former Fairfax reporter, was owned by his family, and after thirty years was reputed to be making a profit of around £A70,000 a year. White, too, had been thinking of retirement and had put out feelers in several directions. When Murdoch heard of these approaches, he chose John Glass, a Sydney businessman, to act for him. White extracted £A1 million from Glass, a good deal more than anyone else had offered. A few days after signing the deal, he realised why so large a multiple of profits had been paid: the buyer was disclosed as Rupert Murdoch, who wanted a foothold in Sydney.[2]

Having taken Norton's papers under his wing, Rupert Henderson had the company renamed Mirror Newspapers and sent executives and one of his best evening journalists to its headquarters at Kippax Street. He thought of refloating the company with John Fairfax and Sons as a substantial but minority stockholder. But the performance of the papers was discouraging. The *Daily Mirror* trailed the *Sun* by 12,000; the *Sunday Mirror*, a recent Norton venture, had fallen from 491,000 to 383,000; and the balance sheet for the first twelve months showed losses. Henderson had other urgent moves on his plate. Television was looking better every month. He wanted to buy out his partners in Channel 7 and to acquire a large studio for local productions, but the joint cost would be around £A2.5 million. Rupert Murdoch had already sounded him out about taking Mirror Newspapers off his hands; why not shed the burden to him? There was opposition from within the company, but the deal was concluded on 21 May 1960. The price was £A1,928,342 with £A600,000 down and the rest in instalments over six years – enough to keep young Murdoch busy for years to come. There was a capital profit for John Fairfax and Sons and the sweetener of further television assets: Mirror Newspapers had a stake in one of the Brisbane licensees and Murdoch agreed to sell the stock to John Fairfax at a later date.[3]

Murdoch's purchase of Cumberland Newspapers had alerted Henderson and Frank Packer to their interests in suburban newspapers, and to the possibility that Murdoch could use that company as a base to launch a major attack on the Sydney market. They therefore combined their suburban papers into a single operation, put Clyde Packer, the eldest of the Packer sons, in charge, and decided to use downtime at Mirror Newspapers to publish additional papers. After the sale of Mirror Newspapers to Murdoch, this downtime was no longer available. Clyde Packer knew of an alternative: Anglican Press, the printery of the weekly *Anglican*, had equipment suitable for small runs and was close to John Fairfax's building on Broadway, where the type-setting could be done. He was friendly with Francis James, who had established Anglican Press, and thus knew that, undercapitalised, the venture was in the hands of a receiver-manager who had called for tenders. He went to James and told him he proposed to deal with the receiver.

He misjudged James who was determined to keep control of the printery. James' eccentricity was well known. The son of an Anglican clergyman, he had attended a flying academy in his teens, been a pilot with the RAF over Germany and, shot down, had escaped from a Stalag on the third attempt. After the war, he had gone up to Oxford, was sent down and, back in Australia, had gone into commercial fishing and then worked as education correspondent for the *Sydney Morning Herald*, using the back of his vintage Rolls Royce, which he parked outside the building, as his office. His tenacity was underestimated; fending off Clyde Packer was child's play to him. He contacted Rupert Murdoch to apprise him of the advantages of keeping the Anglican Press out of Packer's hands. Clyde Packer meanwhile thought he had closed a deal with the receiver.

On the night of 7 June James was dining at Chris' Restaurant in Killara, about twenty kilometres from the Anglican Press, when he was called to the phone. The receiver-manager, who was calling from a public booth, told James that he had been ejected; half a dozen men, led by Clyde Packer and his younger brother Kerry, were in possession of the printery and the locks were being changed. James contacted his lawyers, who confirmed that, in the short run, possession was nine-tenths of the law. The answer was re-occupation. James went home and changed from his customary striped trousers into a track suit.

Learning about these developments, Murdoch sent photographers to the site of the impending battle. At eleven o'clock that night they had their first picture: Clyde Packer stood in the doorway, holding the printery manager by the scruff of the neck and about to fling him into the street. But this journalistic coverage was only a frill; Murdoch had also contacted Frank Browne, the *Sunday Mirror*'s sports columnist, who knew where to find good men and strong at all hours. A rendezvous on the steps of the Sydney Town

Hall was fixed for 12.15 a.m. At 1.00 a.m. the assault began: Browne led one detachment, which battered at the front door with mallets; James, who knew that the toilet window at the back was unprotected, smashed it, slid through and was followed by the other detachment into the printing room for hand-to-hand combat. At 2.30 a.m. a battered Kerry Packer led out his weary brother Clyde, followed by four others. In possession, James opened all doors and gathered his supporters for prayers.

Murdoch had remained at a distance. Joined by friends, he devoured the supper that his wife Pat had prepared and settled down to the next day's headlines. They ran: 'KNIGHT'S SONS IN CITY BRAWL', a reference to Sir Frank Packer's recent elevation, not to Rupert Murdoch's descent. The photographers' vigil supplied graphic support. As the matter moved to the court the next day, successive issues put the *Mirror*'s readers in touch with the more esoteric aspects of the dispute. James remained in control, and Murdoch supported the Anglican Press for a time, sinking about £A65,000 into a holding operation. The days of newspaper brawls had returned.

A year later, Fairfax, Packer and Murdoch were happy to come to an agreement to carve up the market for suburban papers. The Fairfax-Packer venture exchanged its publications in the western and northern parts of the Sydney metropolitan area for some of Murdoch's in the south, and Cumberland Newspapers was given the printing contracts for the lot.[4]

II

At Kippax Street Murdoch faced both the physical and the invisible, but influential, past. Southeast of Central Railway Station, the Truth and Sportsman building had been erected on the fringes of an area where Sydney's adolescent 'larrikins' had fought each other, but light industry and old residences now surrounded it. Ezra Norton had a first-floor office with a separate staircase leading from the entrance at the corner of Kippax and Holt Streets until he had the building reconstructed and left for the inner city, never to return. The O'Connell team found a more spacious, modern building with a newsprint store on the fourth floor. The newsprint was moved to a suburban warehouse; the fourth floor was partitioned into offices and an executive dining room. Murdoch moved into this area, had the partitions knocked down, constructed a big office and hung it, and the corridor, with some of the Australian paintings which, in emulation of Sir Keith, he collected.

Even after extensions of the building further up on Holt Street, the executive suite remained on the fourth-floor level. It provided offices for John Glass and for Douglas Brass, whom Murdoch brought from the *News* office in London, first with an undefined job, followed by an appointment as editorial director. When Glass died, Mervyn Rich, who had worked with Glass in the cinema business, moved in as the group's discreet, efficient finance director, finding the funds for expansion and never questioning the contents of the papers. The executive area became known as 'Mahogany Row', less for its intrinsic luxury and more for the contrast with the reporters' accommodation on the same floor. Though News Ltd continued to be registered in Adelaide, this was for long the effective centre of a far-flung operation. It never grew to be big; the essential facts were kept in Rupert Murdoch's head and in Merv Rich's files, and it was Murdoch who made the decisions without calling for tedious preliminary feasibility studies.

The invisible past was harder to erase. John Norton, Ezra's father, had based his prosperity on the weekly *Truth*, which appeared in Sydney on Sundays and on diverse days and in different versions, in Melbourne, Brisbane, Adelaide and Tasmania. Under John Norton, it owed something to Henry Labouchere's British paper of the same name, a little more to the London *News of the World* and the American Police Gazette, and most to Australian alcohol, which John Norton consumed in large quantities. He would print anything that startled, including the gruesome evidence in the divorce case brought by his wife. Some were horrified by *Truth*, others paid for the information it contained. From time to time, John's son Ezra set about 'cleaning up' the *Truth*s, but when they lost circulation, he returned to the formula. The smug advertisers of the 1950s did the job he could not bring himself to do: they withdrew support from a paper that did not penetrate the 'home'. In 1958 Ezra Norton substituted a more wholesome, though still brash, *Sunday Mirror* for it. Its circulation did not hold and under O'Connell, the *Sunday Mirror* ended up 200,000 behind the *Sunday Telegraph* and 250,000 behind the *Sun-Herald*. The advertisers again stayed away, this time because of the low circulation.

The *Daily Mirror*, an evening tabloid pitted against the broadsheet *Sun* run by Hugh Denison's successors, had been Ezra Norton's baby. He started it in the second world war, overtook his rival and kept in the lead until the *Sun* was bought by John Fairfax and was turned into another tabloid. When Murdoch bought in, the *Sun* was about 10,000 ahead.

For the *Daily Mirror*, Murdoch's strategy was simple; to get readers back by traditional means. Accordingly he chose Ian Smith (born 1909), an old Norton hand, as editor. Smith had edited the *Daily Mirror* in 1950, then brought out the Melbourne version of *Truth* and, having fallen out with Ezra Norton, was working in the office of the New South Wales Premier, where Murdoch found him. Smith had a reputation for boosting circulations and was quickly back in form. In July 1960 a boy called Graham Thorne was kidnapped, and with demands for ransom, their refusal and the boy's murder, the *Mirror* had much to go with for three months. When news of this crime was not forthcoming, *Mirror* reporters scoured the courts and followed police investigators to produce headlines such as 'DAWN RAIDERS FIND DOGS GAGGED', 'BODY IN SAND; DROWNED, BURIED SON, POLICE SAY', or on a poor day, just 'GAMBLER SHOT DEAD'. Murdoch would arrive at five in the morning to help in their formulation. Smith got the sales up and held senior positions at Mirror Newspapers until his retirement in 1973.

The *Sunday Mirror*, Murdoch decided, would trade up; it would go for more sophisticated, if not quite as many, readers. As editor he chose Cyril Pearl, a satirist and social historian who had earlier edited the *Sunday Telegraph* with great éclat. Murdoch had seen a pictorial history by Pearl on a plane trip and had sought him out for ideas for television programmes. Pearl happened to be planning a short documentary about Gallipoli, Murdoch helped to finance it and, through this association, he brought Pearl to the *Sunday Mirror*. There was some irony in the fact that Pearl was famous for a book called *Wild Men of Sydney* which featured John Norton, and which Ezra Norton had tried to suppress.

From Sydney Murdoch saw his past in Adelaide and his former mentor, Rohan Rivett, with different eyes; Rivett, emerging from the strains of the long prosecution, helped with the rift. On the day the *Mirror* front-paged the disappearance of Graham Thorne, the *News* pulled out all the stops for the death of Aneurin Bevan, the British Labour politician. Rivett had once visited the Welsh mining valleys during an Oxford holiday, had seen the depressed conditions and had thereafter admired Bevan. He now wrote a front-page editorial saying that this rebel would be greeted by his peers in heaven, and gave over two feature pages to Bevan's career. It was hardly a topic to hold Adelaide's readers. Rivett had taken the 'Aftermath' editorial in his stride; but his commentary on Bevan read like a coded message: it told his supporters that he was not giving up. Murdoch would not take it and sent a letter south, which Rivett found on his desk the next morning: he was to leave that day. He called together the staff, thanked them one by one for their contributions to the *News* over the years and said farewell. A framed copy of the Bevan front page hung in his study in later years.

In Sydney, the experiment with a sophisticated *Sunday Mirror* did not last. Pearl's staff was small, some of it inherited from a different style of paper, and he had to use contributors to give it a finer edge. Murdoch rarely intervened and was barely involved. He would show up on Saturday afternoons, having been to the races with Frank Browne. He dealt out occasional praise for Pearl's jibes at other newspapers and showed puzzlement at the satirical round-up of the week's events which Pearl had started. From time to time he would reiterate the suggestion that photographs of young women in bathing costumes might brighten the pages, only to be met with an unflinching stare through Pearl's thick glasses. A bit of tit was all right, he finally explained, but one had to be careful with crutch.[5] As the Saturday night wore on, Pat Murdoch would arrive, bringing with her baby Prudence, whom she bottle-fed. It was her hint to Rupert to go home.

He had bought Mirror Newspapers at the top of a boom; in November 1960 the federal Government drastically tightened the economic reins, and advertising for real estate and for the motor trade collapsed. In the year to 30 June 1961, the loss at Mirror Newspapers ran to £A97,901. The *Sunday Mirror* continued to lose circulation, while unable to get upmarket advertising. Pearl left, and an old Norton hand took over. Murdoch's first, tentative reach into quality journalism was at an end.

So was another great expectation. On 10 November 1960 the *Mirror* had printed an interview with the Postmaster-General, who said that Sydney might get a third commercial television licence and that he would consider the matter within six months. The following week a credit squeeze was announced and further television licences for Sydney and Melbourne did not get on the Cabinet agenda till 1962.

III

The mini-budget of November 1960, the first blow by a post-war government at a boom, caught Murdoch flat-footed. He could not understand the implications of the measures introduced; the rest of the press was highly critical. The measures included a rise in the sales tax on motor cars from 30 to 40 percent; the cancellation of the tax deductibility paid on corporate debentures and notes, including those of finance houses, which increased the cost of borrowing to the clients of these houses by 60 percent; and an instruction to banks to restrict lending. The News group did not have a single writer who could interpret the implications of these measures for employment, let alone mount a defence of them against the majority opinion. The *Daily Mirror* reacted with an editorial designed simply to be different. Headed 'Advance Australia Still', it said that this was no time to panic, because the country's people were made of the right stuff. The *Mirror* continued its assurances till Christmas, when it left readers with the cheering observation that Australia had overcome its troubles in the past and would do so again.

Murdoch was not only at sea in economics; he was drifting from one political side to another. Late in July he had disowned Rivett and his own past with an editorial supporting the White Australia policy, one of Rivett's pet targets, printing it both in the *News* and the *Daily Mirror*.[6] Six weeks later he went to Havana, where he sympathetically listened to the views of the regime, and reported back to Australia that Fidel Castro maintained that he was not a Communist and that Raul Roa, the Foreign Minister, had assured him that Cuba would never be anyone's satellite. Having seen Soviet ships in Havana harbour, Murdoch felt it was time the United States reversed their policy towards Cuba, or else that country and other Latin American nations would look to the Kremlin. The future of 200 million people was at stake.[7]

As the 1961 elections approached, Murdoch showed himself less concerned with what the Coalition Government was doing and more preoccupied with what the Fairfax papers, his competitors, were saying. Under Norton, the *Daily Mirror* had leaned to Labor and its readers voted for that Party on class lines. The *Sydney Morning Herald* had never liked Menzies and enjoyed playing an adversary role within the non-Labor spectrum; it was now highly critical of the Government's economic policy, but everybody thought it would stop short of support for Labor at election time. But in mid-October 1961, Arthur Calwell, now the Leader of the Opposition, was invited to see Rupert Henderson who told him that John Fairfax would support Labor and that Maxwell Newton of the *Financial Review* would help with drafting an alternative economic policy.

Murdoch learnt that Calwell might pay further visits to John Fairfax. He arranged to position a photographer in a room facing the front entrance of the Fairfax building off Broadway and the vigil brought results. On 19 November the front page of the *Sunday Mirror* carried a picture of a large, black official limousine with three unrecognisable figures standing beside it, against the background of the Fairfax entrance. The telescopic lens did not have sufficient definition, but Murdoch's words supplied it. The caption above the picture ran: 'Broadway Melody 1961/(SM Herald backs Calwell)'.

The story was separately headed 'Mr Menzies Jilted', and began: 'Wedding Notice. Calwell-Henderson. On 17 November, at Broadway, Sydney, the Hon. Arthur Augustus, 65, leader of the Federal Labor Party, to Rupert Albert Geary ('Rags'), 67, managing director of John Fairfax and Sons, proprietors of the Sydney Morning Herald —' It was the best-informed political report in the pages of the Murdoch papers that year.

After Menzies' campaign speech, the *Mirror* deplored 'Menzies' brand of self-satisfaction' and spoke of Calwell's policies as a 'welcome change', but it backed Menzies in the final week of the campaign, saying that Calwell did not 'match up' and was not its 'image of a Prime Minister of Australia'. In later years Murdoch repeatedly said in public that he regretted not backing Labor in 1961. Whatever the reasons for this failure, the campaign bored him.

By polling day he was in the United States. Zell Rabin, his New York correspondent who had arranged the previous year's trip to Havana, pulled another rabbit out of his hat, an interview with President Kennedy. Between 5.00 and 5.30 p.m. on 1 December (Washington time) Murdoch and Rabin were at the Oval Office for an off-the-record talk. Murdoch at once filed a story and had a picture of Kennedy, Rabin and himself transmitted to Sydney. Pierre Salinger, the President's press secretary, heard of the dispatch and arranged for a cable saying 'Kill Kennedy interview and picture', signed 'Rupert Murdoch', to go through State Department channels. To make doubly sure that nothing got out, Salinger also arranged for Dean Rusk to sign a cable to the US embassy in Canberra that said, in part, 'The President directs the Ambassador contact the Prime Minister if necessary to stop publication'. A duty officer in the embassy who contacted the *Mirror* was told that a picture, but no story, had been received.[8] The *Sunday Mirror* reproduced the picture of the three men in the Oval Office. Murdoch would later tell friends that Kennedy was a boring man.

Menzies came out of the elections with a majority of one in the House of Representatives. He instantly reversed the restrictive economic policies and commercial television licences were back on the agenda.

The existing licensees had done extremely well before the recession. The benchmark for the value of a licence was a payment of £A3.6 million for Sir Arthur Warner's majority holding in Melbourne's Channel 9 by Packer's Television Corporation, at a rate of six pounds for each one pound share. This premium carried a component of goodwill built up over four years' operation, but the major part was simply the value of the licence issued by the Government, which enabled the licensee to extract an economic rent over and above the current return on capital. The recession did not drastically alter this position. Newspapers, carrying small advertisements for jobs and property, had suffered; television channels carried on with consumer-goods advertising.

For all Murdoch's gloomy forecasts before the Australian Broadcasting Control Board, Southern Television Corporation had rapidly moved into a profit position. After the first incomplete year, when it made a small loss, it showed profit levels of above 40 percent on paid capital in the second and third years. The rising profits of television were based on the ability of the channels to raise their advertising charges; and, believing that these charges would fall if more channels competed, advertising agencies vigorously advocated the issue of further licences.

Murdoch set out in pursuit of a Sydney licence with adroit energy and a keen sense of the objections that might be raised against his getting a second channel. In the company he formed for the purpose, the holding of News Ltd was put in the names of two Sydney subsidiaries, to meet the requirement of a 'local interest', and was kept down to 27.9 percent. For his partners he selected representatives of a wide range of interest groups: they included Elder Smith Goldsbrough Mort, the country's largest pastoral firm, two churches and two trade unions. He included American Broadcasting Paramount Pictures, who promised priority in the supply of films in the event that the new station faced a freeze from American suppliers whose product had been signed up by competing stations. He carefully selected his lawyers, adding to them, as a junior, Richard Searby, his acquaintance from Geelong Grammar.

The opening of the licence hearings in Melbourne resembled a law convention. The luminaries of the Sydney and Melbourne bars were all there: they included John Kerr, a future Governor-General. The Sydney licence was sought by no less than nine applicants. The best-connected was United Telecasters Sydney Ltd, which grouped four stockholders all of whom did business with state and federal governments, operated under public licences in various fields and were known for good corporate behaviour: the Colonial Sugar Refining Company (CSR), a major Australian company which handled Australia's sugar sales abroad; the Bank of New South Wales, with a banking licence; and Amalgamated Wireless of Australasia (AWA) and Email Ltd, previously partners in television with John Fairfax and Sons. As they presented their cases, it was evident that most of the applicants, including Murdoch's company, had studied previous hearings and reports and were thoroughly acquainted with the ABCB's preferences. They promised more locally made programmes, more hours of children's television, more education and more religion. The quest for respectibility was accentuated after senior counsel assisting the ABCB suggested in his opening remarks that, in addition to a consideration of the submissions, attention might have to be paid to the applicants' 'intangible quality of character'.

The applications were taken in the alphabetical order of the corporate names and Murdoch, as a witness for Channel Ten Sydney Ltd, was heard first. To anticipate the argument that there were already too many news-papers in the television business, his lawyers put in evidence an article by a member of the US Federal Communications Commission which said that newspaper-owned stations generally performed better and were less likely to sell out. Murdoch personally gave evidence for three days. He stressed that as a newspaper man he knew how to procure news services and organ-ise news-gathering staff. He insisted that a television station had no politics while the character of a newspaper came largely from what he called 'its political policy'. Asked by an opposing counsel why he had lodged an appli-cation, he rejected the idea that he wanted substantial profits and explained: 'I want to strengthen my newspapers with it'. Was it the basis of his applica-tion that he should have a licence because the other two Sydney newspaper proprietors controlled licences? 'Yes, that is one reason why I should get it, yes.'[9] His rivals predictably made play of some of the *Daily Mirror*'s more sensational headlines; they drew attention to a satirical article on Channel 7 and Murdoch's refusal to publish a reply proffered by the Channel, and they accused the *Sunday Mirror* of trying to influence the ABCB by an article it had run. Murdoch firmly denied the suggestion that he had bought newspapers in Sydney in order to be in line for the television licence. Summing up, his counsel said that of all the candidates, Murdoch was best equipped to stand up to Sydney's tough television controllers, whom he had already fought in the newspaper field.[10]

The ABCB completed its report in February 1963 and the Government took six weeks to make a decision. Murdoch sent Douglas Brass, who knew Menzies, to take soundings in Canberra, but a guarded conversation with the Prime Minister gave him little encouragement. By chance, Cyril Pearl, now back to writing history, talked to Menzies in the same weeks. Diverging from history, Menzies scornfully commented on Murdoch's attendance at the races in the company of Frank Browne, whom he described as 'unscru-pulous' (Browne had been jailed for contempt of parliament some years earlier). Despite these private hints, the company sponsored by Murdoch remained the odds-on favourite in the betting books made at the Sydney Journalists Club.

The ABCB had recommended that the Sydney licence should go to United Telecasters, which was not connected with any newspaper; the Government agreed and announced the allocation on 5 April. The Melbourne licence went to a subsidiary of Ansett Transport Industries, which operated one of the two interstate airlines. The hold of newspapers on television was broken; Murdoch's chief argument had worked against him. The *Daily Mirror* publicly congratulated the Sydney winner, but Murdoch did not abandon his wish to get a slice of the market and now took a roundabout route, which led through Wollongong, the provincial steel-mill centre a hundred kilometres south of Sydney.

A year earlier, Channel WIN-4, owned by Television Wollongong Transmissions Ltd, had started to broadcast from a high tower in the coalmining area. It was capable of sending a signal into the southern part of Sydney, and this was part of the reason for its immediate troubles. The North American distributors of television films had been told by their established buyers in Sydney that they must choose between selling to them and selling to WIN-4. Channel NBN-6, which operated at Newcastle, 240 kilometres to the north of Sydney, was in similar difficulties. Both stations took their complaints to the Government and intricate negotiations, and litigation, followed. Meanwhile WIN-4 was running out of money.

Murdoch had watched these manoeuvres while he waited for a Sydney licence of his own. Having failed, he was free to do a deal with Wollongong, who issued 320,000 of their shares to News Ltd for £A160,000. He then embarked on a stratagem not unlike the one he had used when he bought the suburban newspapers on the outskirts of Sydney three years earlier. He flew to New York, saw Donald Coyle, the president of the international wing of the American Broadcasting Company and bought the rights to 2500 hours of television programmes for a million pounds. They included the top-rating 'Ben Casey' and 'Phil Silvers' shows and a small-screen version of 'From Here to Eternity'. Back in Australia he opened fire by telling the *TV Times*: 'We have no intention of confining it [WIN-4] to a country audience. There are two million Sydney viewers within WIN's range and we intend to go after them'.[11] He conceded that they would have to adjust their antennae to receive the signal.

Whether enough people would go to the trouble of making these adjustments was never put to the test. But Murdoch's signal quickly penetrated to Sir Frank Packer's boardroom and Television Corporation offered News Ltd just under a million stock units at 45s 6d each (one shilling above the ruling market), and two seats on the Board. Murdoch accepted at once, acquiring a quarter of Television Corporation. He then joined with Packer and some others to buy 40 per cent of the Newcastle licensee. To strengthen the ties with Consolidated Press, Southern Television Corporation issued 150,000 shares to Consolidated Press and News Ltd sold some of its Wollongong stock to Consolidated Press.

At the end of these intricate moves Murdoch was part of the club that had dealt behind his back in 1957. The subscription fee was between £A2.5 million and £A3.5 million, depending on how the programmes contracted for in New York were counted. What had become of the assurance by Murdoch's counsel that he alone could stand up to the tough controllers of Sydney's newspapers and television channels? Had they bought him off?

IV

Menzies survived the 1961 election with a majority of one in the House of Representatives. At best he could pick the opportune moment for another poll; at worst a sudden death on his side of the House would force the timing on him. Throughout 1962 public opinion surveys favoured Labor, and as the likely Prime Minister, Arthur Calwell seemed almost as important as Menzies. Half stump orator and half wheeler-dealer, Calwell found it difficult to handle his new role. For example, he was unflinching in his support for a continued Netherlands presence in the western part of New Guinea, an issue on which the Government was internally divided: was this because of his personal preference for Dutch Whites over Indonesian Browns, his expecta-tion that electors would share his preference, or part of his alliance with John Fairfax who also supported the Dutch? Even his colleagues did not find it easy to assess the sources of his stand.

Sometimes Calwell simply fell between two stools. The Government had been negotiating for nearly two years to lease a north-western area of Australia to the US Navy who would use it to erect a control station for nuclear-armed submarines. For most of the negotiating period Calwell knew nothing, or did not care to find out, and when the matter became public, he hastily constructed a moderate position, in contrast to the outright rejection of the proposed lease by his Party's left wing. But even that moderate posi-tion was not good enough for John Fairfax, and the *Sydney Morning Herald*, pleased with the economic recovery under Menzies, took the opportunity of expressing a broad disenchantment with Calwell.

Continuing to be more preoccupied with this competitor than with policy, Murdoch noted this development in the *Daily Mirror*: 'A DIVORCE HAS BEEN ARRANGED/Granny's Marriage on the Rocks/BROADWAY MELODY/NOW

SOUNDS FLAT'. In explanation of this piece of humour, he reproduced part of the *Sunday Mirror*'s report of the 1961 Calwell-Henderson meeting.[12]

The decision on the television licences for Sydney and Melbourne had not been announced when Murdoch publicised the Fairfax-Calwell divorce. When it was, both he and Calwell glimpsed the possibility of another alliance. Calwell launched a 'no-confidence' motion condemning the Government for its choice of licensees and, in speaking to it, attacked John Fairfax for trafficking in licences, meaning their purchase of the AWA and Email holdings early in 1962.[13] Before long, Calwell was a regular guest at lunches in the executive suite at Kippax Street, where Murdoch heaped praise on him and introduced him to senior journalists.

Among the journalists, the rising star was Zell Rabin, appointed to edit the *Sunday Mirror* in 1962 and the *Daily Mirror* in August 1963. Rabin was just a year younger than Murdoch, saw the world as the source of headlines and respected little beyond journalism. His mixture of cynicism and enthusiasm was a break with the sometimes solemn, and always older, men whom Murdoch had employed as editors so far.

From a much less privileged background, Rabin had travelled upwards and outwards as fast as Murdoch. From school in Sydney he had gone to university in Brisbane to take a degree in physical education, and there spent much of his undergraduate time on the student newspaper, specialising in attacks on the *Courier-Mail*. Once he had his degree, he called on the editor of that paper to ask for a job, and there his journalistic career began. Sent to New York by John Fairfax and passing thence to Mirror Newspapers, Rabin had been touched by the early stirrings of rebellion in the United States and, when he returned to Australia, he was unwilling to respect even the conventional wisdom of the *Daily Mirror*. In the three months before he took over, the *Mirror* had lived off cables reporting the Keeler-Profumo scandal from Britain. Rabin began to dig up stories closer to home, whether it was a boy who wanted to be adopted, or what the consequences of the Government's anti-trust laws would be. To the distress of some of his reporters, he broke with the paper's standing partisanship for the police by running a campaign over the bashing of a bank manager's son at a police station. The *Mirror* began to find new readers, but in 1964 it was still 8,000 behind the *Sun*. Rabin had only two more years with the paper; he died of cancer in 1966.

But he was able to share Rupert Murdoch's high hopes late in 1963. Encouraged by the deepening divisions in the Labor Party, Menzies took his future in both hands in October and announced an election for 30 November. Murdoch's commitment had been made. The *Mirror* began to report some of Calwell's banal pronouncements as page-three news. When Calwell made his policy speech, it commented 'Off to a good start'; Menzies' speech, which followed, 'failed to inspire'. In the week preceding the poll, it went public with its recommendation 'Time for a change' and, supporting one cliché with another, it explained that Arthur Calwell was 'as good an Australian as Sir Robert Menzies'. Murdoch counted on short memories: few would wonder why his estimates of Calwell or of Menzies had changed in the past two years. But he was sincere enough about wanting Calwell this time to make a substantial contribution to Labor's campaign funds.

Two days before the ballot, Calwell was in Sydney for a final rally in the electorate of a close friend, Les Haylen. Murdoch reserved a table in a Chinese restaurant in King Street and brought Rabin; Calwell was accompanied by some of his staff. In expectation of a victory, Calwell's tongue loosened. He had already made his choice of the next Governor-General – a great Australian, who had shared a Nobel prize in Medicine, Sir Macfarlane Burnet. Though that appointment could not be made for some time, Murdoch and Rabin were boyishly agog at the prospect of more confidences from the next Prime Minister. The next morning's front-page headline ran 'TOP POLL/TIPS LABOR'. The survey was not named, but it had recorded a swing wanted by Murdoch and he did not mind promoting it to a position of authority.

Menzies captured a comfortable majority in the House of Representatives, Calwell remained Leader of the Opposition for another three years and Murdoch went off to Hong Kong on business. Mirror Newspapers was now showing black figures on the bottom line, but a discerning student would see that they were inflated by the absence of interest charges on the substantial loan funds provided by Adelaide. The operation in Kippax Street was marginally profitable and the political influence of the Sydney papers was negligible. Rupert Murdoch needed something more weighty, nearer to the heart of politics.

Strain in Cabinet

Liberal-CP row flares over Senate

Major hostility which has broken out between the Liberal Party and the Country Party is unsettling the harmony of Federal Cabinet.

Throughout Australia both party organisations are on edge as the situation develops.

It is now highlighted by the release of an acrimonious pamphlet by the President of the Western Australian Liberal Party accusing his coalition party of secret dealing with Labor.

Cabinet is feeling the strain as tension generated outside spreads to Canberra.

Contributing to it is the emergence since 1960 of significant differences in approach to national problems between the Country Party Leader, Mr. McEwen, and senior Liberal Ministers.

Mr McEwen's melancholy and the feeling of

GOOD DAY

Trapped skiers rescued after three-day vigil

Ten student hikers who were rescued yesterday after being snowbound for three days on Mt. Franklin, 40 miles from Canberra, read Tolstoy and Shakespeare during their long wait.

The students said last night they had organised their diet for a week stay and were ready to live on jelly beans.

The students went to Mt Franklin for a day's skiing last Saturday but heavy snow blocked the roads and buried their own cars.

They arrived back in Canberra at 10.15 last night.

The students are Hugh Seymour, 21, of 22nd Barton Swan, 18, of Forrest, John Granger, 20, of Deakin, Keith Hutchinson, Andrew Hope, 20, of Eric Kiemer, Ann-Louise Frieuwer, Karen Taylor, Deirdre Knox, and Helen Moore of Bruce Hall, Australian National University.

They were all rescued when the students came on good health a fleet of weapons had gone grades over, four wheel drive vehicles and a RAAF helicopter in a Tuesday effort to locate them.

JELLY BEANS

Anton Granger said that when the students realised on Saturday they might not be able to get out he

FBI finds second headless body

From GUY RAIS

NEW YORK, TUES.

A second body believed to be another victim in the mysterious disappearance of civil rights workers in Mississippi, was found in the same backwater near Tallulah, La., yesterday.

Mafia attack alleged

A 40-year-old Ital-

This body, like the other, has the upper half missing, and is similarly composed.

But, unlike the other, the feet were not together.

FBI men plan to dredge nets today to recover the top half of the bodies and, possibly, the body of the missing man.

The three missing

FRIENDS

Vigor truth in information that dullness will be I and day by day in our columns. To be ever conscious of Australia will welcome this new approach to nations' journalism. This morning, we believe we shall take thousands of friends who on the flitting queen and women of

HE WHO RIDES ON THE BACK OF A SOCIALIST TIGER MAY NEVER DISMOUNT

The above shows the lengths to which the Country Party will go to maintain parliamentary representation. This can't be a once-for-all deal. What must they now do to retain the favor of the A.L.P.?

The Country Party claims that it fights Socialism. Is this how it does it?

More jet links

BY OUR AVIATION CORRESPONDENT

Jet services to link Canberra with Launceston Townsville and Darwin are under consideration by TAA and Ansett-ANA.

Boeing 727 jets would be employed. And the jet services would be in operation by the end of next year.

Both ANA and TAA expect to have Boeing 727 jets operating in Australia

Thinking clearly is that have been smuggled into some restraint is needed. Britain the same way, police said.
United Press International

ONE FLICK

CHICAGO, TUESDAY.

An "electronic" cigarette lighter which uses no electronic ignition principle to eliminate flints, friction wheels and other moving parts was shown yesterday.

Suicide law

Chapter Five

/// *Wizards of The Oz* ///

'This is a new kind of newspaper,' Rupert Murdoch wrote in the advertisements publicising the *Australian*. It was. The first national daily in the
country, it stirred high hopes in its early editors and staff. Murdoch was not
tied to shibboleths; he wanted to put out a paper better than the rest, and
journalists took risks to follow him. There were mishaps, even before the
first number, but over the first seven years, the *Australian* established an
identity, and a place in the affection of its readers. Though fading into a
shadow of its earlier self thereafter, it continued to exist because Murdoch
founded it, was willing to lose more than $A30 million on it over twenty
years and considers it a personal monument. He is right: his loves, hates and
manoeuvres are spelt out there as nowhere else.

On the night of 14 July 1964, the weary, enthusiastic staff were sipping
beer from cans and watching the first issue come off the hastily purchased
second-hand rotary press in Canberra. Eric Walsh, a Canberra reporter for
the *Daily Mirror*, dropped by to compare babies: his wife Meg had just given
birth to a daughter in the Community Hospital and he had come to see how
Rupert Murdoch's latest 'baby' looked. He picked up a copy and, conscious
of the date, spotted the mistake: the running line said '14 July' instead of '15
July', the correct date of the first issue. Shown the error, Murdoch waved his
arms and issued the classic command to stop the press.

In his Sydney years Murdoch had gone through the slog of competing for
daily sales, as he had done in Adelaide. With his coup in television, his thirst
for bolder moves returned: Canberra seemed ripe for attack. The federal
capital's growth rate was the fastest in Australia: at the end of the war the
population was 15,000, in 1960 it was 60,000 and, according to its planners,

it would number 250,000 before the end of the century. The government employed 60 percent of the workforce, with the highest average income in the country. Newspaper-reading was the second-most popular indoor sport: the *Canberra Times* averaged 14,000 sales in the census year 1961.

It had been the sole daily in Canberra since 1928, the year after the Federal Parliament was moved there and had remained a family business, with all the attendant drawbacks. Arthur Thomas Shakespeare, the head of the family, was sixty-six at the beginning of 1964; he continued to write many of the editorials, even sending them in from his vacations, and his son-in-law looked after the business side. The foreign and parliamentary reports were supplied by wire services and, though a professional editor was hired in 1962, the staff remained tiny. The advertising support was so rich that potential competitors had begun to sniff round. In 1961 and 1962 Canberra was alive with rumours of new arrivals from the big coastal cities, but the one starter was of local birth. One of Shakespeare's printers, Ken Cowley, teamed up with Jim Pead, a real-estate man, to put out the *Territorian*, a free paper that quickly showed up the weaknesses in the *Canberra Times'* local coverage.[1]

At the beginning of 1964 Murdoch quietly bought the Cowley-Pead business and, at his behest, Pead acquired a piece of real estate in the same street as the *Canberra Times*. The purchase could not be kept secret. At the opening of Parliament late in February, Shakespeare found himself face to face with Murdoch and asked him what he proposed to do with the land. 'Run you out of business,' Murdoch answered without hesitation.[2] He was following the same stratagem his father used when he bought the Adelaide *Register* to persuade the Bonython family to sell the *Advertiser* to the Herald and Weekly Times.

Shortly after Murdoch's first Canberra moves, Maxwell Newton, the managing editor of the *Australian Financial Review*, phoned him: was Murdoch interested in starting a financial weekly? No, Murdoch told him, but he had other plans and would be in touch. He saw Newton could be a windfall for the Canberra-based daily he had in mind and rang around among his journalistic acquaintances without delay to check Newton's history.

At thirty-four, Newton was the boy wonder in the Fairfax building, yet he was not quite at home there. He had come from the west, where he had climbed the educational ladder for bright boys – Perth Modern School and the University of Western Australia, then a first in economics under Joan Robinson at Cambridge. He had been working in the research office of the Bank of New South Wales when Rupert Henderson spotted him and sent him as a political correspondent to Canberra. He had come back to Sydney as managing editor of the *Financial Review*, which had in three years expanded from once a week to twice and, at his urging, to five times a week. In conversation with his journalists, his energy used to bubble over: Bob (Menzies) said this yesterday, Jack (McEwen) was doing the other today, the paper would set out the right course tomorrow. But by the time he contacted Murdoch, Newton felt at the end of a run. Since its appearance five times a week, the circulation and profits of the *Financial Review* had slumped and Newton feared being associated with possible failure. Moreover, he was unhappy with the management's embrace of the Menzies Government just before the 1963 election, and a variety of differences were developing between himself and his employers.

Murdoch had no difficulty in persuading Newton to come to Kippax Street as editor-designate of the planned new daily. Newton's returning high spirits were welcome; firm plans had been laid and more journalists were about to be engaged. Led by Walter Kommer, who was in charge of the *Financial Review*'s Melbourne bureau and was offered the deputy editorship, a group of Newton's former colleagues agreed to join the venture which Newton nicknamed 'The Oz'.

A series of mishaps, which was to culminate in the wrong date on the first issue, now started. Arthur Shakespeare had not taken Murdoch's jocular remark at Parliament House lightly. The *Canberra Times* was threatened and Murdoch was only the last in the line of potential attackers. Shakespeare had already laid down a line of defence; in April 1963 he had secretly signed an agreement with John Fairfax and Sons, selling them one eighth of the shares in his operating company for £A60,000 and giving them an option to buy the rest in 1967. If a competitor appeared in Canberra earlier, the option could be exercised before that date. Learning of Murdoch's preparations, John Fairfax did not delay and paid Shakespeare £A600,000 for the remaining seven eighths.[3] On 1 May the readers of the *Canberra Times* learnt that the paper had a new proprietor and a new editor, John Pringle. A Scot who learnt the trade in the upper reaches of Fleet Street, Pringle had been editor of the *Sydney Morning Herald* for three years in the 1950s and then spent five years as deputy editor of the London *Observer*. He was given a generous budget and for the first time the *Canberra Times* had a news editor, a features editor, a political correspondent, an economics writer and a chief sub-editor. Within a month it had been overhauled and though its staff numbers turned out to be much smaller than those of the *Australian*, it had an established readership, was first off the mark with a new format and had a versatile and experienced journalist in the editorial chair.

Unaware of Shakespeare's fall-back defence, Murdoch had followed his taunt to the Canberra proprietor with a proposal to buy him out. Now he knew why he had been refused. The presence of John Fairfax in Canberra led to a change of plans. A second daily, no longer aiming to force Shakespeare into a quick sale, might involve a battle of indefinite length. He shifted the emphasis to a daily that would be sold in the major coastal markets, with a separate Canberra edition supported by local advertising. But siting a national paper in Canberra was costly. To begin with, journalists taken there had to be provided with accommodation, and since little was available for rental, property had to be bought. More awkwardly, the two major markets for a national paper were Sydney and Melbourne, where News Ltd had printeries. Murdoch decided that Canberra would make the mattes, midnight planes would fly them to those capitals, and there they would go on the printing presses. Murdoch was in the business of finding solutions, a favourite phrase; it was as simple as that.

Next, he had to find a solution to a problem of his own making. Newton was once more in a cocksure mood, talking at length about the details of Cabinet moves, the direction of economic policy, the failure of other journalists to appreciate what was going on – but what did he know about the mechanics of putting out a paper? The design was under control; Guy Morrison had begun to work on it before Newton's arrival. But would all those matters Newton conversed about be of equal interest to his readers? The circulation of the *Financial Review* was under 20,000: it was bought by a select group. Murdoch began to say that the *Australian* would need 'tinsel' and, as if by magic, it came in the mail from Britain. Saying he had been an editor of the *Daily Express*, a man called Solly Chandler offered his services. He wanted to migrate to Australia where his daughter lived. Murdoch flew him out and offered him sole charge of a page in the new daily.

Murdoch could not direct this demanding operation from Sydney, where he was living. He had to hold together Newton, Chandler and Ken Cowley, who was put in charge of the printing; he had to oversee purchasing, advertising and delivery; his involvement was open-ended. Pat and Prudence, his wife and daughter, remained in Sydney. He took an apartment in the vicinity of National Circuit, where he snatched a few hours of sleep.

II

The print run of the first issue of the *Australian* was 250,000 copies; free copies were delivered to Canberra homes for four weeks. The publicity led readers to expect a better paper: it promised a cornucopia of foreign news, 'facts and trends' reviewed by experts, commentary on literature and the arts; it made much of Maxwell Newton. But it was a hotch-potch and the editorial in the first issue was right when it confessed: 'We are growing up. But we have manifestly not achieved maturity'.

Facts and trends were difficult to disentangle in the leading story: 'Strain in Cabinet/Liberal-CP row flares over Senate'. At some undisclosed time (actually the previous year) the Coalition partners had disagreed over the importation of tanker ships. A little more recently Reg Withers, the president of the West Australian Liberal Party, published a pamphlet criticising the Country Party for riding a 'socialist tiger'. What kind of row was flaring over the Senate remained unsaid. The manner of exposition was that of a weekly correspondent; the absence of a sequel was the paper's own comment on this blistering revelation.

The third page startled expectant readers. Called the 'Peter Brennan Page', it was Solly Chandler's work. It proclaimed itself 'a column that goes round the world's lighter side'. He reproduced five assorted photographs, reported that the Queensland police had 'viewed' a performance of *Who's Afraid of Virginia Woolf* and wondered whether the play would be banned in that state. 'For Those Who Trust the Stars', on Murdoch's insistence, appeared below Chandler's sputnik. When the *Australian* opened its pages to readers' letters the following week, its astrology column was the subject of the largest number of complaints. Running from pages five to seven, overseas reports drawn from the *Guardian*, the *Washington Post* and Agence France Presse partly redeemed the pledges of the publicity; notwithstanding the paper's name, Australian news had been segregated into the second, inconspicuous page.

A distinctive character emerged only on the neatly designed pages ten and eleven. Bruce Petty, who was to develop into the country's subtlest cartoonist, drew Senator Barry Goldwater as the Statue of Liberty holding up a book called *Brinkmanship*. Brian Johns, the political correspondent, sniffed out intermarriage and nepotism in the Department of External Affairs. There were features on William Dobell, whose paintings were about to be shown in a large retrospective exhibition, and on education; a first review opened the series of 'Books of the Day'. It was a discriminating blend of staff work and outside contributions, unusual in the Australian press at that time. The paper then collapsed into a humdrum version of what a newspaper was supposed to be: six pages, including stockmarket quotations, were bundled together as 'The Australian Business Review', a memorial to Newton's first intention; two pages were reserved 'for women'; a miscellany of television programmes, puzzles and sporting news rounded off the issue. The aim was variety: Chez Rupert offered rare steak for Commonwealth Club members and pink icecream for corner-store customers.

On Saturday, when dailies sell best in Australia, the new paper recovered from two dull intervening issues. Newton had engaged Bob Brissenden, a Canberra academic, as literary editor and Brissenden brought together a wide range of well-known writers. The intellectual spectrum ranged from the political right to left of centre, the geographic distribution covered Tasmania, South Australia and Canberra. Max Harris, one of the contributors on that Saturday, was still writing for the *Australian* in 1984. Through the rough times ahead, the Saturday edition would be widely read and would pull up the average sales.

Because the project behind the *Australian* was taken seriously, its performance was closely scrutinised. At the end of the second week, Ken Inglis, the Stuart Commission watcher who had preceded his subject to Canberra, published a long analysis. He saw a disparity between the paper's spacious, agreeable appearance and the indifferent language in which it was written. He noted inappropriate sub-headings and grammatical errors ('a year-round phenomena') and rightly inferred that the sub-editors had learnt their trade at another kind of paper. He objected to the astrology column and traced 'Peter Brennan' to 'William Hickey' of the *Daily Express*. He agreed with John Pringle that the *Canberra Times* would hold its readers in the national capital, but thought that the Canberra circulations of the *Age* and the *Sydney Morning Herald* would drop off.[4]

With the bulk of its staff in Canberra, the *Australian* had advantages in news-gathering that it did not exploit to the full. The federal capital buzzes with items of national politics and bureaucratic infighting and resounds with echoes of international events. As soon as Newton had his staff together, he assigned public-service rounds. Unaccustomed to scrutiny, the bureaucracy took alarm. Sir Frederick Wheeler, the chairman of the Public Service Board and titular head of the bureaucracy, summoned Brian Johns to inquire into the paper's intentions. Newton, uncertain whether the bureaucrats were more use as copy than as sources, did not insist on the paper's right to ask questions. The treatment of the Department of External Affairs in the first issue named no names and was fully understood only in Canberra. For leads, the public-service rounds were more rewarding. Kenneth Randall, the diplomatic correspondent, reported on 21 July that Paul Hasluck, the Minister for External Affairs, had committed Australia to a hard line in Southeast Asia at his first visit to Washington. It was a far-reaching development: the despatch of combat troops to Vietnam the following year arose out of this undertaking.

The *Australian* failed to use this clue in interpreting the cables that soon came into its office. In late July/early August 1964, the first acknowledged shots between American and North Vietnamese armed forces were exchanged in the Gulf of Tonkin. The importance of these events was plain, though their wider meaning emerged only years later when Congress inquired to what extent the clashes had been stage-managed by the Americans. In handling them, the *Australian* compared badly with its competitors. The official Washington version was reported by the *Sydney Morning Herald* in its lead story on 3 August; not a word reached readers of the *Australian*. The next day the *Australian* noted that a US destroyer had been shelled and that the United States planned to retaliate; both items appeared on the second page. On the third day all Australian papers lacked solid news: two short paragraphs on the *Australian*'s front page said that six US warships had left Hong Kong on a secret mission; the *Sydney Morning Herald* did not do much better. On the fifth day the *Australian* woke up: American bombers had raided North Vietnam and the front page and much space inside covered the raids. It next ran with the ball in all directions: a front page announced that the United States were already 'over the brink' and one of the *Australian*'s journalists flew out to Saigon. Unhappily, the South-east Asian correspondent of the *Canberra Times*, resident in Kuala Lumpur, got to Vietnam more quickly and started to file a day earlier than the *Australian*'s envoy. The lasting upshot of the Gulf of Tonkin incidents – the Congressional resolution giving President Johnson the power to conduct hostilities without further reference to the legislature – was buried on an inside page.

Newton and Murdoch decided what was important news and neither was conversant with Asian politics. They had not engaged a foreign affairs specialist who might tell them. But the failure in coverage did not stem merely from the absence of a specialist; at the top disorganisation prevailed. Murdoch, the ubiquitous shirt-sleeved presence, was an evening-paper man, hungry for events translatable into headlines; Newton was a weekly commentator turned editor of a daily. They had spent months preparing a mix that didn't blend. After the early excitement the disadvantages of the Canberra location weighed more heavily. There were nights when the charter planes could not take off at the fog-bound airport, the printing in

Sydney or Melbourne accordingly ran late and readers saw their papers around eleven in the morning. They voted with their pennies: in the second half of July, sales averaged 74,782; in November, when copies were no longer given away in Canberra, sales were down to 51,834.

Seeing failure ahead, Newton began to emphasise his differences from Murdoch. He seized on a report saying that a small group of dissidents within the Sydney Anglican Synod objected to the use of public funds to support private schools and wrote an editorial headed 'State Aid and the Privileged'. 'The argument for giving a helping hand to underprivileged Catholics is surely weak enough,' he enlarged, 'and can really only be justified on the basis of saving Catholic children from the consequences of their parents' religious convictions.'[5] Canberra's population included about 30 percent Catholics; the visible result was a flood of protest from offended readers. The less visible and just as predictable outcome was a rift between Newton and Murdoch, whose concern was the sales figures of the *Australian*. In private, Newton was pessimistic about the future of the paper and suggested to one or two confidants on the staff that they would be wise to look for alternative berths.

Having chosen mid-winter as his starting time, Murdoch faced the silly, newless, summer season before the paper had established itself. He now sent feature writers round the country, an initiative that could have been taken earlier, and filled much of the space with serialisations of books. Some were appropriate to Canberra, such as C.P. Snow's *Corridors of Power*; others, like the memoirs of 'Mad Mike' Hoare, a British mercenary in Africa, may have been grabbed for their low price. In February the world was more generous with news opportunities: President Sukarno moved in the direction of Peking and the paper's diplomatic correspondent went to Djakarta; President Johnson sent waves of bombers over North Vietnam and, thanks to the *Guardian*'s Victor Zorza, readers learnt of a strain on Moscow-Peking relations. The mood inside the *Australian* was expressed in some lines of the anonymous 'Canberra Blues' published in the Folksong column on 13 February 1965:

> Let's sing a song of Canberra, the nation's capital,
> It's a pretty city, but it's got no heart at all,
>> You got those bad Canberra blues,
>> Get on the booze,
>> You get those awful Canberra blues.

Newton certainly had them. Some days he could not be found on the premises; then he sent Murdoch a letter setting out the conditions under which he would continue as editor. Murdoch declined to accept them.

Newton left on 8 March and that afternoon the staff were told of his departure. They read his version in the *Canberra Times* the next morning: 'Perhaps
I was wrong, but the experience of editing the *Australian* under complete
direction in recent times has, in my view, made it impossible to achieve the
essential principles, aims, and standards of quality which fired the enthusiasm and dedication of a large team of men and women, including
myself.'[6]

Walter Kommer took his place. Two weeks later Murdoch called Kommer
and two senior journalists to his office and told them that the Board of News
Ltd had decided to close the paper. Visiting Sydney, Murdoch called one
night into a restaurant to catch a friend and, unusually distraught, confided
that he might have to sell the *Australian* to someone like Roy Thomson, who
was on the lookout for new properties.

Selling to Thomson would have been an admission of failure with a bitter
twist. The shrewd Canadian proprietor had gone to Britain, bought more
newspapers and, moving into television on the ground floor, had made a
fortune from a commercial licence. He had tried to spend some of his spare
cash in New Zealand by buying the Wellington *Dominion* early in 1964.
Murdoch then took time off from the preparations for the *Australian* to buy
25 percent of the stock of Wellington Publishing Co Ltd on the open market,
while Thomson and two New Zealand publishers went through the motions
of formal bids for all the issued capital. Murdoch came to an agreement with
the Board of the *Dominion*'s publishers; his three rivals were stale-mated and
withdrew. It was Murdoch's first appearance as an open bidder in a foreign
arena; it cost him a little over £A500,000; and News Corporation now had a
stake of about 21 percent in the *Dominion*.

The temptation to close or sell the *Australian* passed. Newton might have
been delighted if it had followed so close on his own departure. At the end of
March 1965 he spoke to a sizeable audience at St Mark's Library, Canberra,
and attacked Australian newspapers at large for being 'shopping guides': the
Canberra Times and to a lesser extent the *Australian* and the *Financial Review*
were possible exceptions. The *Australian* was more of an exception than
Newton cared to say: its advertising content was smaller than that of most
dailies. Later in the year Nationwide News Pty Ltd, the operating company,
filed a balance sheet showing that £A634,952 had been tied up in assets,
another £A682,288 had been spent on 'net costs of operation' up to 24
December 1964, and another £A122,292 had been lost in the remaining part
of the financial year. This was the first and last profit-and-loss statement to
spell out the position of the *Australian*; thereafter, intra-group arrangements
obscured the results.

III

Rupert Murdoch's direct contact with Adrian Deamer began with a phone call, followed by a lunch. Deamer had swum into his ken by accident; he was not looking for another editor. Deamer was then working for the *Sun-News-Pictorial*, the largest and technically the best daily in the country and Murdoch had a sneaking admiration for that kind of paper. While on holidays in Sydney, Deamer was invited by a common friend to talk to Douglas Brass, who suggested a further meeting to Murdoch. Deamer had last seen Sir Keith's son by the tennis courts of Cruden Farm where his father had taken him, and later heard about him from an angry Rohan Rivett. His thirty-five-year-old host at the Melbourne lunch turned out to be utterly persuasive and offered him a job as assistant editor of the *Australian*. Deamer was acting editor of the *Sun-News Pictorial*, but he was bored with the routine and, being on the outspoken side, he was unlikely to go much further in the Herald and Weekly Times hierarchy. He discussed the move to Canberra with his wife and handed in his resignation the next morning. He duly became the *Australian*'s most widely admired editor; in 1970, three years after he took effective control, its sales had nearly trebled.

What struck him when he went to Canberra in February 1966 was the pervasive muddle. The overwhelming impression of the day's paper, which he marked up on the plane, was its poor presentation; at the airport no transport awaited him. At Mort Street, an eager Rupert Murdoch wanted any comment Deamer could offer, but when the journalists were called in for introductions, it turned out that Walter Kommer alone had been told of Deamer's coming. Murdoch then took the day's paper apart, a procedure so novel that the journalists guessed the source of the critique and Deamer spent much of the following week drinking with his colleagues to smooth ruffled feathers. An air of insecurity hung over the place and journalists were hard to keep, harder to replace.

Murdoch alone was making progress. He had chosen a system of facsimile transmission used in Britain, which would transmit the pages of the *Australian* to their Sydney and Melbourne printeries, and was awaiting permission to use the coaxial cables laid down for use by the television stations, though the Canberra-Melbourne link would not open until late 1966. He was settling into Canberra. He had begun to look for a property in the surroundings, something like Sir Keith's Cruden Farm and, with the help of Jack McEwen, the Deputy Prime Minister, he found 'Cavan', halfway between Yass and Canberra. The old, one-storey stone house and several thousand surrounding hectares cost him $A196,000 of his own money. He laid down an airstrip, bought a plane and hired a pilot. For a time, Cavan became so much a part of him that he toyed with the idea of becoming the local member of parliament.

But for which party? After Menzies' narrow victory in 1961 Murdoch told Ken Humphreys, a close business associate at the time, that McEwen was the only alternative Prime Minister. McEwen did not publicise this ambition for the good reason that the Country Party which he led relied on rural votes, could not be the major partner in the coalition with the Liberals, and that he himself could be Prime Minister only in some short period of crisis. He had no illusions about politics, and was even bitter, but he welcomed the attentions of the young newspaper proprietor, who told him a good deal of what was happening within the Government, and even invited Murdoch to the model farm at Shepparton, to which he periodically withdrew. Murdoch spoke with admiration of this man of great strength, drawing his journalists' attention to McEwen's craggy profile as proof. One of his favourite anecdotes was how McEwen had smuggled him out of his parliamentary suite when Menzies' imminent arrival was announced. They shared a belief in economic growth and saw protection for primary and secondary industry as the means for getting it. But in Murdoch's papers, with their dominantly urban readership, the Country Party was not favoured and, after he dropped Calwell and with Menzies gone into retirement, the *Australian* announced on election day 1966: 'No alternative to the Holt Government'.

Meanwhile, Murdoch had changed his mind about Canberra, and in October 1966 he told the annual meeting of News Ltd that the management and production of the *Australian* would move to Sydney, while a strong editorial staff would stay in Canberra. The move became the subject of long deliberations: how many would go, how many remain behind? He insisted that the *Australian*'s journalists had to be kept away from those of the *Daily Mirror*, lest they were contaminated. He proposed a separate office in the eastern suburbs of Sydney, from which relays of couriers would take copy to Kippax Street, and then dropped the idea. Despite all the complications, the move was announced in March 1967. It seemed like a victory for the *Canberra Times*.

The gloom was broken by a sudden prospect of buying Sir Frank Packer's publications. About to turn sixty and troubled by his eyesight, Sir Frank let it be known that he was considering a sale of Australian Consolidated Press, the operating company for his newspapers and magazines. Murdoch offered $A22 million (all sums looked bigger from 1966 onwards when one Australian pound changed into two Australian dollars). Rupert Henderson, having retired as managing director of John Fairfax, offered $A24 million in his own name, but made the offer subject to a close audit of the books: Henderson in fact dummied until John Fairfax could make a decision, which it did shortly after. John Fairfax and Murdoch then began to parley over a joint purchase. Murdoch went to London, and Henderson, followed by his successor Angus McLachlan, continued to talk to him there. The terms of a joint purchase were close to agreement when Murdoch heard from Sydney that Television Corporation, of which he was a director, had called a sudden board meeting.[7]

Packer, it turned out, had been getting impeccable valuations for Australian Consolidated Press from his competitors in order to rearrange his own affairs. When the board of Television Corporation met, its directors were asked to approve the acquisition of Australian Consolidated Press in exchange for an issue of 6.1 million stock units to Consolidated which was firmly controlled by the Packer family. This proposal put a value of $A21.35 million on Australian Consolidated Press, slightly below Murdoch's bid and more so below Henderson's, but it assured Television Corporation of a continued link with the print media. Sir Frank and three other directors who sat on both Television Corporation and Consolidated Press abstained from voting and the transaction was agreed to by six votes to one.

The reshuffle was most unwelcome to Murdoch. He could not buy Packer's papers; the proportion of News Ltd's holding in Television Corporation was sharply diminished and any future prospect of controlling it had disappeared. Before the reshuffle Packer had held 35 percent and Murdoch 25 percent. They had an agreement that if Packer, through Consolidated Press, bought more than 42 percent, he would have to offer a pro rata proportion to Murdoch. Sir Frank now offered 1.2 million units of the issue to News Ltd; the result would leave Murdoch with 25 percent still, while Packer controlled 62 percent, and Murdoch rejected the offer. According to the agreement, Consolidated Press had the right of first refusal if News Ltd wanted to sell, and Murdoch now offered the block of shares to Packer. The prevailing market price, however, was rather lower than in 1963: Murdoch had then paid $A4.5 million and he now got $A3.3 million. He partly retrieved the situation later in the year, when News Ltd bought all the outstanding stock in Southern Television Corporation, including Packer's, and got control of $A2 million in cash inside the television company. Murdoch's concern then became where to put his cash: the Australian media world had become too small for him.[8]

While looking for overseas opportunities, he concentrated on tidying up. The *Australian*'s move to Sydney improved its circulation, but a prolonged national strike by journalists once more imperilled it. When the journalists went out, the executives stayed in, but they were soon transferred to the

Daily Mirror and, for a week, the *Australian* did not appear. As a negotiating tactic, Murdoch hinted that it might not be published again. When everyone was back at work, he threw a party for the stay-ins at Blues Point Tower where his second wife and he had established themselves. He had first met Anna Torv when she interviewed him for the staff journal of Mirror Newspapers and they had met again at a party. She had gone to Canberra as one of the *Australian*'s door-to-door promotion teams and stayed to work as a reporter, and a friendship developed. Pat Murdoch sought a divorce, and in April 1967 Anna and Rupert began a marriage which brought them three children. There was bitterness between Pat and Rupert for a time, but a decade and a half later Rupert came to Pat's aid when her second marriage broke up and Pat, Anna, he and some old friends from Adelaide had a reunion dinner in Madrid.

At the end of 1967 Kommer and Deamer came to an arrangement about the running of the *Australian*. Kommer's interest lay on the commercial side, Deamer's on the journalistic. They proposed to separate their functions: Kommer would be called the managing editor, Deamer the editor. Murdoch agreed to their proposal and, seizing on Kommer's business bent, soon sent him to Western Australia, where the News group had acquired mineral exploration leases.

IV

Harold Holt, who succeeded Menzies as Prime Minister, drowned off a Victorian beach on the weekend before Christmas 1967. In the confusion that followed, Rupert Murdoch had his first chance of federal king-making.

Having been Deputy Prime Minister, Murdoch's friend John McEwen was sworn in as Prime Minister three days after Holt's disappearance. This was to be a temporary arrangement, for the long-term Prime Minister would have to be the leader of the majority partner in the Coalition, the parliamentary Liberal Party. The Liberals fixed 9 January 1968 as the date for making their choice. William McMahon, the Deputy Leader under Holt, was a strong candidate. As soon as the date was fixed, a push on behalf of Senator John Gorton, as an alternative to McMahon, began within the Party. McEwen then dropped hints that he might be unwilling to serve in a Cabinet headed by McMahon. He and McMahon had long been at loggerheads over matters such as tariff levels and wool marketing, but the threat not to serve under a leader chosen by the majority partner in the Coalition had to be backed by more serious reasons. If it were carried through, it could split the Coalition.

Early in January, reports crept into the media saying that McEwen was concerned about McMahon's 'associations'. Murdoch then came to his friend's aid. On 6 January, the *Australian* carried the front-page banner: 'Why McEwen vetoes McMahon/Foreign Agent/is the man/between the leaders'. The article below it went on to speak of McMahon's association 'with an agent of foreign interests who had sought to undermine Australia's tariff policy' and identified this agent as 'Mr Maxwell Newton, a former managing editor of this paper'. It said that Newton received money from foreign interests, for which he held a general watching brief over all matters concerning Japanese imports into Australia'. Murdoch had obtained the information from McEwen, whom he had met at the Hotel Kurrajong in Canberra.

On the morning of the leadership ballot, the *Australian* made its allega-tions more specific by printing extracts from a contract between Newton and the Japanese Export Trade Organisation (JETRO), which included a watching brief on tariff development.

After leaving Murdoch, Newton had started a series of newsletters. McEwen and the high tariff policies endorsed by his Department of Trade were constant targets of Newton's polemics. His advocacy frequently ran in parallel with the internal advocacy of the Treasury where one of Newton's close friends from Perth Modern and the University of Western Australia, John Stone, was a rising star. When McMahon became Treasurer in Holt's first Cabinet, he became a frequent critic of high tariff policies in Cabinet. Newton went on to add a lobbying business to his newsletters and attracted clients who were in conflict with the Country Party on other issues.

The watching brief for the Japanese trade organisation was a very small part of Newton's business. There was no suggestion that he had received information in his task from Treasury. McMahon was accused of guilt by association and was defeated by Gorton in the leadership ballot. The dis-closure of the combination of journalism and lobbying may have been to Newton's disadvantage. For Murdoch, the interlude meant a growing friend-ship with Gorton. The question of how Murdoch had obtained the extracts from the contract between Newton and JETRO remained in the dark for the next seven years.

In 1975 a former officer of the Australian Security Intelligence Organisa-tion (ASIO) told the Royal Commission into the Intelligence Services in camera that after Holt's death an ASIO officer stationed in Sydney had come to Melbourne with information so sensitive that he would convey it only to the Director-General, Sir Charles Spry, who then passed it on to the Prime Minister, McEwen. The information, the officer gathered, was similar to that thereafter disclosed in the press about Newton and JETRO; he did not know how his Sydney colleagues had acquired it in the first place.[9] The Royal Commission noted in a classified part of one of its subsequent reports that ASIO had also broken into McMahon's Sydney home in 1967, but found nothing there to interest it.

Gorton and Murdoch went on to form a warm association, in the course of which Gorton kept Murdoch abreast of political developments. An intense nationalist, Gorton implemented measures that McEwen had only talked about.

Late in 1968 Murdoch bought shares in the London-based News of the World Ltd and put forward a proposal to transfer some of his Australian assets to London, as a result of which Murdoch would get control of the British company, though it would retain a majority of British shareholders. There was no precedent for knowing how this transaction would look to a nationalist government that was uneasy about overseas corporations taking control of key Australian assets. Murdoch feared for a time that McMahon, as Treasurer, might put obstacles in his way, but Gorton sent reassuring signals and Murdoch was grateful. Having helped to elevate Gorton, Murdoch came to regard him as a 'great Australian'. McEwen would not be Prime Minister again, Gorton supplanted him in Murdoch's affections, and McMahon had to wait for his next chance until after McEwen's retirement.

V

As an editor Adrian Deamer was patience itself. The paper was an end, not a means; its public face, not its influence behind the scenes, was his first concern. He fought shy of friendships with individual politicians. Though he met many, he left the job of reporting their actions and judging their characters to his writers.

To put the paper into shape took time, but the result was striking. Five years after its first careless rapture, it had taken on a thoroughly professional look. On 15 July 1969 the *Australian*'s front page led with a report on the moon race between the United States and the Soviet Union; the second story examined the effects of the labour market on the making of the next budget;

a third report dealt with the beginning of a shooting war in Northern Ireland. The second, third and fourth pages carried Australian news; the sixth, seventh and eighth overseas cables; the ninth, pictures of the moon's surface. On the editorial and feature pages, ten and eleven, four journalists looked forward into the next five years.

Over a fortnight, the difference from the paper of 1964 was even more striking. Columnists and critics appeared on regular days, some once a week, some once a fortnight; readers would know when and where to look for film and theatre, music and art. On weekends the paper summed up the past seven days and presented a magazine. In these matters Deamer simply applied well-tried precepts: some of the best, and also some of the dullest, papers in the English language are well organised. He managed to channel the early enthusiasm, and added to it. The *Australian*'s self-conscious solemnity was balanced by satire: his greatest find was Mungo MacCallum who wrote a column 'The Morning After' on the informal side of parlia-mentary life in the Saturday summing-up. By the early months of 1969 sales passed the 120,000 mark.

Deamer approached politics in a humane spirit. He was less concerned with who was winning, more impressed by who was suffering. The pre-occupation came through most strongly in the feature pages. In 1968 the cartoonist Bruce Petty went to the Middle East and sent back drawings of Palestinian refugees; in May 1969 Deamer bought a series of articles on North Vietnam by Oriana Fallaci. Back in 1965 the *Australian* had opposed Australia's participation in the Vietnam war in an editorial written by Dou-glas Brass on the occasion of the announcement that a first Australian battal-ion would be sent north. After this intervention widened and when Vietnam policy became a hot domestic issue, Murdoch's judgements followed the line of his federal political allies. Gorton continued the 'forward defence' policy laid down by his predecessors; in an editorial on 30 October 1969, the day of the federal poll, the *Australian* was behind him, saying that 'thoughful voters' would support the Prime Minister, because of his approach to the 'over-riding problem' of defence.

Within a few weeks, however, the *Australian* changed its stance and demanded drastic action on Vietnam. Brass had exploded over the My Lai incident and on 4 December wrote a signed article for the *Australian*, in which he saw the shooting of unarmed villagers as symptomatic of the war's futility. The next day a front-page editorial demanded the withdrawal of Australia's troops. The *Australian* thus became the first daily to speak for half the country against the military presence in Vietnam.

Murdoch's extended stay in London, where he had bought the daily *Sun* to go with the Sunday *News of the World* and had a dream run with the daily, gave the *Australian* a good deal of autonomy. When he was back in Sydney, he was out of touch, unpredictable in his opinions, put too much store on snippets of information which he sometimes kept to himself and sometimes passed on. All this made a consistent public line in his papers somewhat difficult. Deamer later complained: 'He is an absentee landlord visiting Australia for short periods three or four times a year and making snap decisions while he is here'.[10] His absences did have their bright side.

On occasion the snap decisions turned out to be wrong. When Murdoch returned to Australia on the last weekend of July 1970, he announced plans for instant expansion to his executives. There would be a *Sunday Australian*, edited by Bruce Rothwell, Melbourne-born and recently a deputy editor of the London *Daily Mail*; there would be a *Finance Week*, a joint effort with the London *Financial Times*. Brass, who had turned sixty, would retire as editorial director of the group; a little later, he persuaded Tom Fitzgerald, the financial editor of the *Sydney Morning Herald* and founder of the fortnightly *Nation*, to replace Brass. Ken May, whom he had brought from Adelaide in the first half of 1969, would remain in overall command at Kippax Street. Flushed with his success in Britain, Murdoch thought he knew the next moves appropriate to Australia: feasibility studies for new papers were not needed. *Finance Week* lasted six months, the *Sunday Australian* eighteen, and Fitzgerald left in 1972.

When Murdoch departed some weeks later, Ken May took him to the airport and there received last-minute instructions for changes in the *Australian*; the satirical columns by Ray Taylor and Phillip Adams, whom Deamer had brought to the paper, were to stop; Mungo MacCallum would be moved from Canberra to Sydney, thus ceasing his watch on parliamentary hangovers; Bruce Petty's cartoons were not to touch on the Arab-Israeli conflict. May transmitted the instructions to Deamer, to whom Murdoch had not breathed a word. Deamer resisted: if MacCallum went, so would he. He was in a strong position: in March, aided by a stockmarket boom, the *Australian*'s sales passed 143,000 and Ken May respected this tangible achievement. A compromise was worked out. Taylor was dropped, Adams stayed; MacCallum lingered in Canberra and found another paper that gave him scope; Petty continued to draw, though not about the Middle East.

In February 1971 Murdoch was back for the launching of the *Sunday Australian*, to which he brought his mother from Melbourne. Though the new paper counted on carrying with it the *Australian*'s weekly readers, it pitched its appeal markedly lower. Its main market would be in New South Wales; on the Sabbath, Melbourne newsagencies were closed and distribution through other channels was sporadic. It therefore leaned towards the popular Sydney Sundays, including perennials like a children's section.

In other respects, the paper's form and content were inappropriate. It did not have the clean, spacious look of the daily and strove for the busy look of a British broadsheet. The main news items were kept short. There seemed to be some difficulty with filling the early pages: the first issue included such items as a report that the average age of Australian brides had fallen to 23.84 years. This was in the style of the *Daily Mail* of 1896.

The *Sunday Australian*'s biggest disadvantage was that Rothwell was out of touch with much that had happened in Australia since he had left it. The longest feature article in the first issue – its prize exhibit for weekend reading – was an instalment of James Cameron's impressions of Australia, and two more instalments followed in subsequent issues. Visiting celebrities had once been pursued by Australian airport reporters for their most passing comments; in 1971 Australian readers could not care less about the reactions of a veteran British journalist. The best indication of the *Sunday Australian*'s direction was its treatment of Germaine Greer's *Female Eunuch* which was just appearing as a paperback in Australian shops: the short review was written by a puzzled male.

For Rupert Murdoch the occasion was marred by the treatment meted out to him by *Four Corners*, a television current affairs programme of the Australian Broadcasting Commission. He had thrown open Kippax Street and submitted to an interview; he must have hoped for free and even favourable publicity for the *Sunday Australian*. Instead, segments of the interview were cut into a critical report called 'What Makes Rupert Run', which took in some of the less complimentary things being said about his British papers. It was the beginning of a grudge he bore against the Australian Broadcasting Commission. As it was, he was amidst a dispute over his fitness to control London Weekend Television and he went back to London to sort it out. The *Sunday Australian* would never involve him as the *Australian* had done.

Though out of sympathy with satire, he had divined the demands for change, the widespread feelings of dissatisfaction in Australia. When a row broke out between John Gorton and Malcolm Fraser, the Minister for Defence, a few days after Murdoch's departure, he rang from London asking for details and offered the comment that Gorton was no longer the right Prime Minister. Independently Deamer had a call from Fraser who wanted to put his case; but a decision had already been made and the next editorial said 'Gorton must go'. From the falling out between Gorton and Fraser, McMahon emerged as Prime Minister, Fraser temporarily moved to the backbench, and Murdoch swung to the Opposition.

In his way, McMahon recognised the new mood. He set in train the withdrawal of Australian forces from Vietnam, in line with Nixon's policy of Vietnamisation and to defuse popular protest. But he had altogether the wrong personality for expressing the developing quest for an Australian identity. Gorton was tall, had a face scarred in the second world war, went in for underwater fishing and spoke with the deliberate drawl of the farmer he had been for a time. McMahon was small, balding, urban, and occasionally lisped, yet he presented himself as a tough squash player and the virile husband of a younger, glamorous woman. He could not convey a consistent impression and the cartoonists, including Bruce Petty on the *Australian*, had a field day.

His policies swung from one side to the other. He raised old-age pensions, appearing as the welfare Prime Minister, and then ran into rising unemployment. He was the economically rational ex-Treasurer one day and the next he fell back on racism. In April 1971 the South African Springbok Rugby League team, internationally ostracised, announced an Australian tour. Opponents of apartheid began a campaign and called on the Government not to grant visas to the team, but McMahon persisted. The *Australian* ran an analysis of sport under apartheid by an expatriate South African teaching at an Australian university and then dropped the issue. As the tour came nearer, the anti-Springbok campaigners gained the support of the union movement, which threatened to boycott the team's transport around the continent. McMahon announced that Air Force planes would carry the footballers if airport workers enforced a boycott. Late in June a confrontation between the unions and the armed forces seemed imminent. On the day of the Springboks' scheduled arrival, the *Australian* carried a front-page editorial headed 'Cynical misuse of the Prime Minister's Power' and forecast that the Government's support for the tour would polarise the country. The forecast was right; on the issue of the unions versus the armed forces, people would take sides more readily than on apartheid, and Queensland declared a state of emergency.

Murdoch came for another visit in July. Calling Deamer to his office, he thumbed through a pile of *Australians*, stopped at the Springbok front page and commented : 'This is the worst thing that has happened to the *Australian* since the State Aid editorial.' It was an ominous reference to his rift with Newton.

For some days Murdoch was in and out of Deamer's office; his refrain was that the satire in the paper was not funny, it was merely negative. He then left for Cavan and, still restless, rang Tom Fitzgerald from there to complain that the *Australian* had become unbalanced. Fitzgerald defended the paper with examples and Murdoch observed that Fitzgerald must have read it more closely. He seemed satisfied for the moment, but his discontent persisted. On the morning of 22 July he was back in Kippax Street and saw, first John Menadue, the general manager of News Ltd, and then Fitzgerald, the editorial director, to say that Deamer had to go. He took ten hours to carry through his decision. At eight that night, he told Deamer he wasn't bringing out the paper he, Murdoch, wanted; perhaps Deamer would like another job in the group. Deamer replied that he would be editor of the *Australian* or nothing, and went home.

Murdoch was duly prepared; earlier in the day he had instructed his Melbourne office to get Owen Thomson back to Sydney by that night. Thomson had been chief sub-editor at the time of Deamer's arrival in Canberra and later made his name as a feature writer with a series on the wool industry. His ambition was undisguised: he had asked both Rothwell and Deamer for the job of assistant editor of their papers, and though he did not succeed his requests made an impression on Murdoch, who met him at the airport that night and told him he was acting editor of the *Australian*. Recounting the meeting, Thomson dwelt on the reply: 'What's that "acting" bit, Rupert?'

At the end of the week, the *Australian* announced Rothwell as editor-in-chief of the two *Australians* and Thomson as acting and deputy editor of the daily. Murdoch then turned to a more difficult task: changing the Canberra guard.

elegraph

SYDNEY, WEDNESDAY, FEBRUARY 25, 1976   Price 12c

aughty Benny
n the money

SECRE
ARAB
MONEY

THE AUSTRALIAN

Backers struggle to delay showdown

WHITLAM FIGHTS
FOR HIS LIFE

Caucus rebuff in call
for Federal report

THE MAN WHO CAME TO BREAKFAST

Taped speech
Reuben Scarf
party opened
door to Arab

THE AUSTRALIAN

Whitlam on the verge of resigning from politics

HAWKE FLIES HOME
FOR CRISIS TALKS

Talks at breakfast
with Arab visitors
lasted 90 minutes

'Funds do have to be accepted
from all sorts of sources'

PAY UP
PAY UP
AND
THEY'LL
PLAY
THE
GAME

TOKYO

pics
y page 22

ps: City 26 Liverpool 27.

Chapter Six

/// *Friends Like These* ///

'How do we get rid of this Government at the next elections?' Rupert Murdoch did not expect an answer from his executives at the table; he was declaring an allegiance to his guests, Gough and Margaret Whitlam. He had asked them to the Hungry Horse at Paddington, a couple of miles from the centre of Sydney, where he was a habitue and the management met his wish for a private room at short notice. It happened to be 28 July 1971, and Whitlam had begun the dinner by alluding to the departure of Adrian Deamer from the *Australian* the week before. Murdoch responded with a giggle and quickly moved to a discussion of the long slit down the side of Sonia McMahon's dress, on which his newspapers kept him thoroughly informed. It was not the kind of exposure Margaret was likely to subject herself to, Whitlam assured the company. For most of the evening, the conversation had run shallow, and as an attempt to come closer, the occasion was a failure. Murdoch's late rhetorical question tried to pull it together: he liked results. He had looked over McMahon on two visits to Canberra, and he had continued to dislike him. He would henceforth support the only alternative on offer and he wanted to be sure that Whitlam would become a personal friend.

For his part, Whitlam was prepared to believe that Murdoch was something of a 'financial genius'. Though businessmen did not figure prominently in Whitlam's pantheon, Murdoch's quick work in acquiring the biggest Sunday paper in Britain and then coupling it to a daily with a soaring circulation was an achievement not to be discounted. The international stage appealed to Whitlam; he had no less an opinion of his own performance on it. He had just been to Peking; McMahon had promptly condemned him as a

95

stooge of the Communists, and then Henry Kissinger followed on Whitlam's heels. A telex advising Kissinger's presence in China came through to the Tokyo Foreign Correspondents Club while Whitlam was talking to news-paper people there, on his way back. It foreshadowed a later visit by Nixon. 'Kissinger has won the next election for me', Whitlam announced ecstati-cally; he was already Prime Minister in his thoughts. At the Hungry Horse and for the next sixteen months he was cautious about giving undertakings to people who might hold him to them in future, and this caution added to his air of reserve.

The acquaintance between Murdoch and Whitlam had begun at a Can-berra restaurant in February 1967. Cyril Wyndham, the Federal Secretary of the Labor Party, decided that, as the newly chosen Leader of the Opposition, Whitlam should meet people that counted. Despite his support for the Coali-tion Government, Murdoch continued to have links with senior Labor poli-ticians. He discreetly supported his old friend Don Dunstan, who had become Attorney-General in the South Australian Labor Cabinet, and when Dunstan became Premier a few months later, the *News* and Channel 9 were in the box seat for early news releases. But the first meeting did nothing to diminish Murdoch's attachment to McEwen, and for the time being, he wrote off Whitlam as 'vain'.

The Whitlams were house guests at Cavan on 1 September 1970; the property had become Murdoch's reception centre on his visits back to New South Wales. The *Australian*'s editorial before the 1969 election, though sup-porting the Coalition, contained a friendly reference to the Labor leader. Gorton lost half his parliamentary majority at this election, and when Murdoch's papers changed their support for the Vietnam war, they came closer to Labor, and in Britain Murdoch was supporting Harold Wilson. On this occasion Whitlam was cordial, though formal. Generous about Murdoch's papers, he singled out Mungo MacCallum's Saturday columns, unaware that Murdoch was irritated by them. What Murdoch looked for was inside information on politics, not an outsider's ideas on journalists: it was a lesson Whitlam found difficult to learn. Nor was Rupert Murdoch like Sir Keith, who had been humble on the way up, and had retained the skill of playing men without leaning on them. Rupert Murdoch would flatter only fools; with others, he conducted relations on a plane of equality. He ignored the possibility that he might be deemed an interloper in their affairs or that they might hold reservations about the press.

Despite the commitment at the Hungry Horse, Murdoch's papers gave little sign of campaigning for Labor. On dismissing Deamer, Murdoch had impulsively decreed that a copy of the *Australian* should lie on every front

lawn at Pymble, a Sydney suburb whose sedate executive and professional residents were less likely to change their reading habits than their
dentists. His proposed method was to make the *Australian* a businessmen's
paper, but apart from its coverage of mining, the paper never succeeded
in that aim. Murdoch's one clear intervention on federal politics was to
commission three articles for the *Sunday Australian* from John Gorton,
who continued in McMahon's Cabinet as Minister for Defence.[1] In the
first article, Gorton complained of the leakiness of ministers over whom
he had previously presided, and was at once forced to resign. The interlude did not benefit Gorton, who never held office again; it embarrassed
McMahon; and it signalled that Murdoch was wary of the incumbent Government.

When News Ltd bought the titles of the *Daily* and *Sunday Telegraph* in
mid-1972, the assumption that Murdoch was making another move to
unseat the Government was accordingly widespread. It was also false.
Murdoch paid Sir Frank Packer's asking price of $A15 million, a figure effec-
tively much higher than the $A22 million he offered in 1967, when the
transaction would have included the profitable *Women's Weekly*, all the plant
and a grab-bag of real estate. The Packer family shrewdly recognised that
the pursuit of a strategic position, the seizure of a unique chance, had
become Murdoch's business way of life. Clyde and Kerry Packer took him to
a boxing bout on the night of 31 May and, parked in the car outside the
Town House Hotel where Murdoch had booked in, they broached the possibility of Father selling the two papers. By Friday, Father was in a mood to
conclude and on Saturday, lawyers, accountants and executives were drawing up the contract at Sir Frank's offices in Castlereagh Street. It was
Murdoch who was in a hurry; he had booked a flight to London the following Wednesday and wanted to be at hand for the announcement and first
moves. To take advantage of lower stamp duty, the formal signatories chartered a plane to Canberra on the Sunday, and after their return a goodwill
gathering was held at Sir Frank's office.[2]

Sir Frank's papers had supported McMahon's rise during the 1960s and
McMahon had come to look on the Packer family as close friends. Knowing
McMahon's faith in the power of the media to sway elections, Kerry Packer
suggested to Father that the Prime Minister should be informed of the sale.
Sounding shaken over the phone, McMahon expressed a wish to see Sir
Frank and issued an invitation to his Sydney residence that night. Pleading
frailty, Sir Frank persuaded the Prime Minister to come up the short distance
at Bellevue Hill, where they both lived. After the gathering broke up,
Murdoch phoned Whitlam with his side of the news.

In the half year that followed, the *Telegraph*s were the least politically committed of Murdoch's papers. Murdoch wanted to retain their existing readership. The key to commercial success was the printing of the old and the new, the morning and the evening papers, under one roof, so Murdoch bought some of Packer's plant, in addition to the deal for the titles, and engaged a few of his printers. For the previous twelve months, the Kippax Street operation had been in the red, with the *Sunday Australian* as the biggest loss-maker; the weekend after the purchases, it was unceremoniously buried inside the *Sunday Telegraph*, while the *Sunday Mirror* continued to be published. Rothwell, still editor-in-chief, devoted his energies to editorials and features in the daily *Australian*.

In the next financial year, Kippax Street flourished. But the most tangible gain came from an afterthought. No longer in major dailies, Packer sold his shares in Australian Newsprint Mills to the Herald and Weekly Times, putting the Melbourne group ahead of John Fairfax as the largest single stockholder. Merv Rich, who as finance director had the job of putting together the funds for Murdoch's instant deal, guessed that John Fairfax might now want the 1.25 million stock units held by News Ltd in the paper mill; as a junior partner, Murdoch had never been happy holding the stock. The sale produced a capital profit and cash, but the long-term result was even better. News Ltd's contract with the mill, running to 1976, stipulated that prices per tonne would not be raised by more than two dollars each year. Between 1972 and 1976, international price levels for newsprint nearly doubled and newspapers raised their retail prices sharply. The prices at which Australian Newsprint Mills sold were based on the lowest available import price, and because the Australian dollar firmed over those four years, local prices rose a little less sharply than international levels. At the beginning of 1974, the Australian mill raised its price to contract customers by $A10 a tonne and at the beginning of 1975, by another $A62. News Ltd, however, successfully insisted on getting deliveries at the 1973 price level, plus a mere $A2 annual increase, and saved millions of dollars. On expiry of the contract, Murdoch reduced his dependence on Australian supplies and shifted the bulk of his purchase to Finland. Through his increasing British needs, with his daily paper there moving towards a four million circulation, he had become a huge, favoured customer of the Finnish mills.

II

Though Murdoch met Whitlam only twice in the second half of 1972, he was convinced that he was sitting at the incoming Prime Minister's elbow. Even after they had publicly fallen out in 1975, he told a television interviewer: 'I was close to him [Whitlam] at the time, or certainly very friendly to him'.[3] Murdoch's belief was fostered by Whitlam's associates, who were aware of Murdoch's wish to be part of the action and thought his support useful, while having to deal with Whitlam's preference for keeping his distance.

Standing a head above most Australians in his socks, Whitlam was seldom close to anyone. Under his ready, barbed wit, he had retained his boyhood shyness. From his early days, he had to communicate with a deaf mother and his speech continued to be punctuated with long pauses. Even more than Murdoch, he sought to live up to an image of his father, a federal Solicitor-General with a high sense of propriety. But in the Labor Party, deals had to be done, alliances formed, money raised. He left those mundane tasks to others and put in an appearance once the bargains were concluded. He was confident that he had the press in hand. He relaxed at Parliament House among a small circle of staffers and journalists, whose hopes for the future of the country he had raised just by being Whitlam. Even when their editors opposed Labor, these journalists reported him sympathetically. But by the second half of 1972, Whitlam's inner circle no longer included any Murdoch journalists.

Keeping Murdoch happy became a job for Mick Young and Eric Walsh. Young had succeeded Cyril Wyndham as Federal Secretary of the Labor Party: Walsh, after moving from the *Daily Mirror* to John Fairfax, began to work for the Labor campaign in the second half of 1972. The two operated from a serviced apartment at the Park Regis in inner Sydney, put at their disposal by Dick Crebbin, the head of the Marrickville food group. Their most delicate task was to orchestrate replies to Liberal suggestions that Catholic authorities should worry about the future of government financial assistance to their schools. They succeeded in dividing the Sydney Catholic hierarchy; their skill was acknowledged by the *Financial Review*, who dubbed them 'Whitlam's Irish mafia'. Compared to that operation, keeping an eager Rupert Murdoch on side was child's play.

As early as 10 October, McMahon announced an election for 2 December. In the manner of the pre-tabloid London *Daily Mail,* Rothwell initiated a series of profiles of political figures, led by one on Whitlam. The most striking, though unintended, revelation was the gap between Murdoch's actions and his journalists' awareness of them. Dennis Minogue wrote in his piece on Whitlam: 'It has been suggested that Sir Peter [Abeles], attracted by Labor's proposals on transport, has become the party's largest individual donor, though this seems unlikely in the light of the $25,000 Metals Workers [union] donation'.[4] Abeles, the chief executive of Thomas Nationwide Transport and some eight years later Murdoch's business partner, tended to spread his financial donations between several parties; Murdoch himself was contributing nearly $A75,000 to the Labor Party's advertising outlay, as he subsequently disclosed.[5]

Since he had taken his family and himself to London in 1969, Murdoch had chosen October/November as the time for intensive attention to Australia. He would tour his establishments, deliver a report to the annual general meeting of News Ltd and, on the first Tuesday, go to the Melbourne Cup, the horse race that was a public holiday in Victoria. In 1972 he was also to follow Deamer as that year's Arthur Norman Smith memorial lecturer on journalism at the University of Melbourne, where he painted a skilful self-portrait of the benign press baron who welcomes criticism even when it is not wholly responsible.[6] But he could not wait until Melbourne Cup Day to burst into political action. An advertisement in the *Australian* set him off. It consisted of a montage of newspaper headings that dramatised the theme of 'leadership by crisis' and was signed by one Patrick Sayers on behalf of 'Business Executives for a Change of Government'. Sayers was a youngish Sydney importer, who used to inject a touch of spoof into the campaign against the Vietnam war and had been resurrected as a signatory by Young and Walsh. Murdoch had been saying ever since his return that Whitlam lacked credibility in the business community, and seeing the advertisement, thought it a step in the right direction. He rang Park Regis at once to draw Young's and Walsh's attention to it and was unabashed when told that Sayers had been resurrected by them. He asked for more insertions in that style and offered to meet the cost of their appearance in newspapers he did not own.

He remained apprehensive about Whitlam's standing with business. In an intricate to-and-fro between Kippax Street, Park Regis and Whitlam, a further proposal emerged: Whitlam would announce that he proposed to appoint Dr H. C. Coombs as his personal economic adviser on taking office. Coombs had been the Governor of the Reserve Bank under Labor and Coalition governments, and since his retirement from that post, had devoted himself to the welfare of Aborigines and the administration of the performing arts. Nevertheless Coombs turned out to be interested, sounded out Sir Frederick Wheeler, the permanent head of the Treasury, to see if he objected, and then accepted. The proposal to appoint Coombs was announced on the evening of 12 November and appeared as the main news item in the following morning's *Australian*. It may not have swung the business community's votes, but Rupert Murdoch felt he had made a significant contribution.

Young decided on a further effort to cement the alliance after Murdoch's attendance at the Cup race and contacted Murdoch's secretary with a proposal for a cruise on Sydney Harbour the coming Sunday, so that Whitlam and Murdoch could talk at length. The arrangements were taken out of Young's hands by Jim Macpherson, Murdoch's all-purpose executive, who found a boat, arranged for the wine and picked up the tab. On Sunday morning Whitlam was still reluctant. 'Do I have to come?' he queried Young over the phone. But under strict instructions, he turned up at the designated Darling Harbour jetty, bringing his wife Margaret, Young and Walsh aboard. With Murdoch were Macpherson and John Menadue, once Whitlam's private secretary and now an executive at News Ltd. A two-man crew started the engine, the boat chugged under the Sydney Harbour Bridge and threw anchor for lunch at a cove to the northeast. 'Rupert felt close to royalty at last,' a Whitlam associate joked later. He may have overlooked the fact that Murdoch, unlike some of his parents' generation, had little use for royalty unless it had more than ceremonial power, and that Murdoch might hope for more than reflected glory from his association with Whitlam.

In its editorial on Whitlam's policy speech two days later, the *Australian* described Labor's promises as 'exciting'; they constituted 'a radical alternative to the Australia which exists today'. By contrast the editorial on McMahon's campaign opening portrayed the Prime Minister as bidding for the support of those who were 'satisfied with the way their society is going'. The theme of subsequent editorials supporting Labor was simply *change*, without an examination of its direction, a reflection of Murdoch's personal inability to sit still. Nor could he stick to expressing himself in his newspapers. Dragging John Menadue from his tasks, he took him one morning to the Park Regis apartment, which he had come to regard as the best-placed observation post for watching the campaign. Young and Walsh were both on the phone and broke off briefly to usher in the callers. At that hour the apartment had not been serviced yet and empty beer cans from the previous night lined the skirting boards. Murdoch expressed the hope that Labor would run the country better than the apartment.

Murdoch knew that the readers of the *Australian* were too thin on the ground to make a difference to the outcome in any one seat, even if he persuaded all of them to share the paper's views. The *Daily Mirror* had a bigger and more concentrated audience, but at the time it was engaged in a circulation battle in which it was a mere 5000 ahead of the evening *Sun*. The *Daily Mirror* did not buy into the election battle until nine days before the poll. Murdoch himself then wrote an unsigned column for the second page under the heading 'Mirror Election Viewpoint', and to make it lively, introduced his fellow media proprietors into the first instalment, dubbing the Packers' Channel 9, which continued to be friendly to McMahon, 'the dirtiest sideshow in town'.[7]

McMahon gave up hope of making any impression on Murdoch, though before it was all over he sent Malcolm Fraser, his Minister for Education, on a ritual call to Kippax Street. Fraser was received with courtesy, allowed to go through the motions of explaining government policy and was escorted out. Accompanied by Menadue, Murdoch flew to Melbourne on 30 November for a dinner with Whitlam, after the Opposition Leader's final rally at St Kilda. An electoral win seemed in the bag. The next morning, the Australian National Opinion Poll, then part-owned by News Ltd, was to forecast an assured Labor win. Whitlam was once more accompanied by Young; Murdoch, with Menadue at his side, considered himself as part of the family. The talk went on well into the night. Murdoch later recalled the occasion under cross-examination by an advocate for the Australian Journalists Association in a hearing on television licences (see Chapter 11). According to this evidence, an expansive Whitlam had discussed diplomatic appointments he would make, including the Australian High Commissioner in London, who would be ex-Senator John Armstrong. Young and Menadue had criticised this choice and Murdoch interjected, in what he called a light-hearted and silly way, that it would not be a bad job for himself. Whitlam's recollection carried a different emphasis: as part of his quarrel with Murdoch in 1975, he confirmed to a journalist that an intermediary for Murdoch had made an approach for the High Commission, offering that Murdoch would place his assets in trust for the duration of the appointment. Murdoch then issued a denial through his secretary. Memories are apt to fail: Murdoch's testimony was in error on a minor point in placing the dinner on the night before the poll instead of two nights before.[8]

Whitlam did the *Australian* one favour after being elected though before taking office. The paper had prepared a series on the immediate actions of Labor ministers and the first instalment dealt with Whitlam's intentions. McMahon had conceded defeat on the Saturday night; on Sunday morning, a journalist on routine duty took the galley proofs to Whitlam's Cabramatta home, where Whitlam read them and made corrections. The article appeared on Monday morning.

Had Murdoch contributed to putting Whitlam into office? Apart from causing friction between McMahon and the still popular John Gorton, his papers had done little to damage the Coalition over the previous years. Political scientists tend to think that, by the time campaigns start, news-papers can make little difference to the outcome: this opinion is commonly backed with finer data than are available for the 1972 campaign. On the raw data that do exist, it is hard to argue that Murdoch's support carried much weight. His papers were in the numerical majority in New South Wales, where the swing to Labor was 3.8 percent. In Victoria, where the anti-Labor publications of the Herald and Weekly Times dominated circulations, the swing to Labor was 5.5 percent.

Both these swings were bigger than the national average of 2.5 percent. Moreover, the New South Wales swing in 1972 was much smaller than the 7.7 swing to Labor in 1969, when Murdoch's and all other metropolitan papers had supported the Coalition. Operating in an area of uncertainty, campaigners do not take the hard-headed view of the press that these figures would suggest. Few follow Milner's view of Northcliffe: 'I believe he is only a scarecrow, but still the fact remains that most public men are in terror of him'.[9]

Whitlam, who was something of a Milnerite, was subsequently criticised within his Party for failing to keep Murdoch on side. He continued to see Murdoch at the insistence of his advisers. Whitlam was in London at Easter 1973, but was greatly preoccupied with his first prime-ministerial visit; Walsh, who had become a press secretary, and Young, who happened to be in London for a conference of socialist parties, accepted Murdoch's invita-tion to his office in Bouverie Street. Over the weekend Whitlam went to Murdoch's country house in Essex. Fifteen months later Whitlam was in New York to address the General Assembly of the United Nations. Murdoch was also there, having moved to New York where he was running a weekly paper. Having promised to dine with David Frost, Whitlam had a quick breakfast with Murdoch, who sought to admonish the Prime Minister about the state of the Australian economy, a subject on which Whitlam had already heard too much for his liking at home. In November 1974 Whitlam at last had Murdoch to a dinner at his official residence, the Lodge.

For all his casual treatment of Murdoch, Whitlam did attribute some importance to the press; on taking office, he let loose an unprecedented number of press officers on Parliament House. He wanted his Government's deeds reported at length; he just didn't think that the men who owned the media mattered very much in determining elections. Later in life, he believed that Murdoch had backed him in 1972, as he backed Malcolm Fraser in 1975, in order to take credit for the victory.

III

Some years before Labor took office, Murdoch had moved into a high-risk area – minerals for the world market. The involvement led to a clash with the Labor Cabinet.

The bauxite deposit at Mount Saddleback sounded too good to be true; its natural advantages could make raw material production the cheapest any-where in the world. It was relatively close to existing ports, thus cutting construction costs for transport; it was handy to coal deposits, which could be useful as an energy source for reducing the bauxite to nearly pure alum-inium hydroxide that could be shipped at a lower net cost to overseas smelt-ers. Murdoch formed Alwest Pty Ltd as a vehicle for the project and entered a partnership with Broken Hill Proprietary Company. In 1970 the two ven-turers reached an agreement with the West Australian Government, but the following year the world market for bauxite and its derivatives turned down and work on the project was postponed. Prices went up again after the Caribbean bauxite producers formed a cartel in 1973 and Reynolds Metals, the only United States smelter not mining in Australia, joined the venturers. Reynolds Metals was prepared to invest $A300 million at Mount Saddle-back, thus becoming the majority partner. The rise of oil prices after the October war in the Middle East made the use of the low-cost coal deposits, and therefore the project as a whole, even more attractive.

Extending its predecessor's policies in favour of Australian ownership, and anxious to stem the flooding of the money markets by incoming funds, the Government stood in the way of the consortium's plans. The obstacles were well publicised. The first was the 'variable deposit requirement', under which investors introducing major sums from abroad had to deposit a pro-portion with the Reserve Bank at zero interest. The proportion varied from time to time: early in 1974 it stood at 33.3 percent, so that to spend $A300 million at Mount Saddleback, Reynolds Metals had to marshal $A450 million. The second hurdle was a requirement of 51 percent Australian ownership before export permits for minerals were granted.

Nevertheless the consortium made a submission to Cabinet early in 1974. The moment was propitious: a Labor Government sought re-election in Western Australia and wanted to present the project to the electors. But a powerful section of federal Cabinet saw the submission as a test of its adherence to its announced policies. Frank Crean, the Treasurer, opposed the waiver of the variable deposit requirement asked for in the submission; Rex Connor, the Minister for Minerals and Energy, would not yield on

Australian majority ownership. They were supported by Tom Uren, the Minister for Urban Development and Moss Cass, the Minister for the Environment, both of whom circulated papers on the risks to the Perth water supply and the hardwood stands in the vicinity of the mine. Whitlam had no way of countering this combination. The submission was rejected by a full Cabinet on 18 March 1974.

On 10 April Whitlam announced the dissolution of both Houses and an election for May. He lacked control of the Senate, half of which had been elected in 1970 and half in 1967. The *Australian*, then as before the best indicator of Murdoch's attitude, was edited by James Hall, who had succeeded Owen Thomson. Hall, formerly the paper's literary editor, was not greatly perturbed when told by Ken May that the News group's election line was straight down the centre. Rothwell had gone back to Britain, Murdoch was tied down in New York with his new weekly, the *National Star*, and Hall liked to have plenty of elbow room. Was Murdoch perturbed with Whitlam's economic policies, as he had become at Harold Wilson's? Or was he taking other matters into consideration? These questions were not asked, let alone answered, at Kippax Street.

Returned with a reduced majority in the House of Representatives and with increased numbers short of a majority in the Senate, Whitlam addressed himself to the mounting rate of inflation. The advice from Treasury was to slam the economy with higher taxes and severe limits on credit, but the advice was mistimed. A squeeze on the money supply had begun late in 1973 and was working its way through the system. While advisers argued with advisers, companies engaged in land and building speculation collapsed. This was the part of the business community closest to Labor in 1972; the honeymoon was now followed by divorce proceedings. Against this background, Cabinet faced an insoluble dilemma. The rate of inflation alarmed banks and insurance companies, and Treasury and the Reserve Bank spoke for them; on the other hand, unemployment, recommended as the temporary remedy for inflation, would lead to retaliation from the unions and drive away the low-income earners who were one of Labor's electoral bases. On top of everything, the international boom collapsed, and with it the mining industry, which had stimulated growth.

Once Whitlam had settled on a compromise budget, he cast around for new machinery to deal with the conflicting advice pressed on him. The arbitrators would be housed in the Prime Minister's department, and to lead them, he lured John Menadue back to Canberra as permanent head of the department. One of Menadue's early tasks was to bypass Connor, who had become a bogey to the mining industry, and thus put a few projects back on the agenda. Alwest was one of them. The consortium agreed to an Australian majority, another submission went to Cabinet and, on the night of 30 January 1975, Whitlam announced the Government's approval, subject to an environmental report. The announcement had an element of window-dressing. In an unsigned comment, the *Australian* said two days later: 'There is no certainty that the Alwest alumina project will get off the ground, though the Federal Government has given it dilatory approval. The Alwest consortium will have to overcome a drastic shortage of investment funds and a scarcity of markets against strong international competition before the project becomes a certainty.'[10] This was a roundabout way of saying that Reynolds Metals was getting cold feet. In June the project crossed the environmental hurdle, but Reynolds Metals still hesitated. The News group ultimately sold its share in the venture in 1979.

For Murdoch, Alwest was too complex a matter over which to take public issue with Labor. But even before his hopes for the project came to an end, he stumbled across a piece of information that put him well ahead in understanding the political developments of the coming twelve months. It concerned a matter that seemed abstruse at the time – the power of the Senate to withhold or postpone Supply, that is, to stop the Bills providing legislative authority for the Government's annual expenditure. Murdoch's source on the possible use of Supply was impeccable: Sir John Kerr, the Governor-General.

On a weekend in mid-November 1974 Murdoch was at Cavan, surrounded by journalists and executives. He was now something of the hometown astronaut, who had soared in Britain and landed in America, whose handling of the levers and whose stamina you had to admire and whom you watched out of the corner of your eye. Even his mother had come up from Melbourne to look. On Sunday afternoon Murdoch announced that the Governor-General would call in. The guests took the announcement in their stride; it was a case of one neighbour calling on another. Sir John had been known as a gregarious man even while he was a barrister and this sociable streak had become more pronounced after he had become a widower in 1974, when he started to drop in for drinks at the least likely gatherings. He took Cavan in an easy stride; how did news stories come into being, he asked some of the editors. He was a little disingenuous, for he had had a fruitful association with the media in his barrister days and had used them to launch his pet projects on the public.[11]

Having settled down to drinks with a small group that included Rupert Murdoch and the veteran Canberra commentator Ian Fitchett, Sir John embarked on a survey of the Whitlam Government's coming problems.

They included the difficulty of getting legislation through the Senate and the possibility that Supply might be withheld by it. Fitchett thought this suggestion somewhat odd: for one thing, the annual Appropriation Bills, which authorise the Government's expenditure, had passed through the Senate just three days earlier; for another, Fitchett had legal training, including an associateship with a High Court judge, and knew that though the Senate's power to withhold Supply was written into the Constitution, it had never been exercised. Murdoch sat still and took it all in. Kerr had been thoroughly briefed when he had examined Murdoch in the television licence hearings in 1962 and, who knows, lawyers like him got hold of information from all sorts of quarters.

An elaborate, closely guarded scenario for dislodging the Labor Government had been drawn up a year earlier by Senator Reg Withers, when the Opposition still had a clear Senate majority. In a letter to Snedden, then Leader of the Opposition, Withers drew attention to the Supply power, but suggested that instead of rejecting the Appropriation Bills, the Coalition should defer approval until the Government agreed to a general election, or, if it refused to do so, until the Governor-General stepped in to resolve the deadlock between the two Houses. Snedden rejected the scenario. One obstacle he saw was a convention that dissolutions were granted only on the advice of the incumbent Prime Minister; it was a convention closely modelled on the relation between the British House of Commons and House of Lords.[12]

In November 1974 the Coalition lacked the numbers in the Senate to stop Supply. But in the next ten months two Senate seats held by Labor became vacant and, in breach of another convention, they were filled by men prepared to vote with the Opposition. Over this period, Sir John Kerr elaborated his thoughts on the role a Governor-General might play in a crisis, and Murdoch would be in a position to follow his thinking.

IV

The Murdoch papers were the last to become hostile to the Whitlam Government, but when they did, they were the most strident. Murdoch had never had much time for the adversary role, in which a newspaper ranges from the patient examination of issues to the exposure of malfeasance; when the *Australian* had shouldered some of those tasks in the Coalition years, he put an end to it. During the second half of the Labor Government, his competitors had a feast while he was indecisive. He entered the fray when divisions were becoming bitter and suspicion abounded, and he himself became a large target for some of that anger and suspicion.

The *Australian* was in the middle of a crisis of its own when the bricks began to fly outside. In mid-June 1975 James Hall was replaced by Leslie Hollings, his assistant editor, and shortly afterwards Bruce Rothwell came back from London to be placed over Hollings, with a British news editor arriving in his wake. Murdoch had previously told Hall to develop a philosophy and a distinct line in the *Australian*, without indicating what they should be. When circulation slipped, Hall offered to resign but was asked to stay; some weeks later, Ken May told him that Murdoch no longer wanted him as editor. Under Hall, working for the *Australian* was agreeable; some of the journalists saw Rothwell's arrival, and the changes he made, as a move in a Fleet Street direction and, late in August, the House Committee of the Australian Journalists Association (AJA) met the visiting Murdoch to ask for greater staff participation, a polite way of indicating dissatisfaction. Murdoch sounded conciliatory, but once he had left, tensions sharpened. Robert Duffield, one of the editorial writers and a member of the House Committee, clashed with Rothwell and was moved to another slot; in his place, John Hallows, a resident conservative columnist in earlier years, was engaged to write editorials on a fee basis. The editorials were strongly anti-Whitlam; news stories on federal politics carried the by-lines of Canberra-based correspondents less regularly and, rewritten in Sydney, were published as being 'by our political staff'. Such shifts are painful to journalists who have supported an earlier commitment; they resolve the situation by moving into areas less concerned with making political judgements or by taking jobs with other organisations. At the *Australian* in the last quarter of 1975, there was no time for readjustment; the country was headed for a showdown.

In the first half of the year, the Opposition would have handsomely won an election. Confused over the drift of the economy, the Whitlam Government had embarked on a secret search for loan funds from Arab sources through a dubious broker, Tirath Khemlani, whom it authorised to raise four billion and then two billion dollars. Khemlani failed, and when the details trickled out the Government harvested suspicion and ridicule. A budget on orthodox lines restored it to some standing, but the 'Loans Affair' was not over. The Melbourne *Herald* found Khemlani and with him, proof that Rex Connor, the Minister for Minerals and Energy, had continued negotiations after authority had been withdrawn from him. Connor, who had lied about this matter to Whitlam and to Parliament, was dismissed.

Malcolm Fraser, who had displaced Snedden as Opposition Leader, early in the year, activated Withers' 1973 scenario by announcing the deferral of Supply on 15 October.

The next day the *Australian* headed its editorial: 'No more petty tricks – let the people decide'. It stood by Fraser's action and asked Whitlam to call an election (16 October). Two days later, its main front-page story announced: 'Governor-General will act soon, says Fraser'. A second, single-column story forecast that Sir John and Lady Kerr (Sir John had remarried since his visit to Cavan) would be among the first victims of a refusal of Supply and might have to pay the staff at Government House out of their own pockets (18 October). Sir John had become a close reader of newspapers. The *Australian*'s reports led him to phone Whitlam the next day, to profess his embarrassment at an attempt to intimidate him. He took the opportunity to ask whether he should consult the Chief Justice, Sir Garfield Barwick, as to his course of action on Supply. Whitlam advised against recourse to the Chief Justice, raising among other objections the possibility of a related action in the court over which Sir Garfield presided.[13]

Over the next eight days Fraser reiterated his demands, with the transparent intention of creating an atmosphere of crisis. Despite their repetitiveness, the *Australian* gave Fraser's pronouncements front-page exposure: 'Fraser says Kerr must sack Whitlam' (20 October); 'Fraser accuses PM and says he must go' (24 October); 'Whitlam acts like a dictator – Fraser' (27 October). Its editorials were addressed to a more exclusive destination. The first in a series of three – 'Stalemate and Sir John' – condemned a Government plan to pay public servants in the absence of a parliamentary vote and expressed sympathy for the Governor-General: 'Let us hope that the situation will never reach the stage where Sir John will have to intervene because of clearly unconstitutional actions' (22 October). The next effort was prompted by a comment from Sir Robert Menzies upholding the propriety of the Coalition's course and ended with an opinion on Sir John's separate meetings with Whitlam and Fraser on one day: 'The Governor-General has authority to use his own methods of consultation, at his discretion – and he has made a useful start in doing so' (23 October). The last in the series was headed: 'Decision rests with Kerr'; it enlarged on the sources from which Sir John should seek advice: 'These range from the Attorney-General to eminent authorities of his own choosing, the Chief Justice, for instance, or eminent counsel' (24 October). That Sir John had actually wanted to seek the Chief Justice's advice and that Whitlam had withheld his agreement the previous weekend was known by very few; in due course, the Governor-General went against Whitlam's wishes.

If Sir John was capable of being embarrassed by a newspaper, he also knew how to use it to his advantage. In the second week of the Supply crisis, two of the *Australian*'s feature writers compiled a profile, which was published as 'The Man in the Middle', a title striking a note Sir John wanted to be heard. One of the writers, Graham Williams, talked to David Smith, the official Secretary at Government House; the other, John Lapsley, pursued the footprints left by Sir John in Sydney. The draft article included an allusion to his fondness for drink, but this was deleted (25 October). Sir John confirmed this view of himself when he addressed the Returned Servicemen's League two days later: the *Australian*'s headline summary was: 'I can't take sides: Sir John Kerr' (28 October).

That day, a letter drafted by the AJA House Committee and signed by seventy-six members was sent to Murdoch. It expressed concern about the *Australian*'s becoming a laughing stock among influential people with whom the journalists were coming into contact and, without objecting to the paper's policies, it found the way they were carried through in the editorial and news columns to be 'blind, biased, tunnel-visioned, ad hoc, logically confused and relentless'. The signatories said that they found it difficult to be loyal to the traditions of journalism if they accepted 'the deliberate or careless slanting of headlines, seemingly blatant imbalance in news presentation, political censorship'. Murdoch had not answered the letter when Kerr dismissed Whitlam on 11 November. The day after that event three AJA office-bearers sent Murdoch a second letter, announcing their intention to distribute a bulletin setting out their members' grievances, offering to publicise his reply and asking for a meeting. Murdoch instantly wrote back, saying the proposed bulletin made dialogue impossible: 'If you insist on providing ammunition for our competitors and enemies who are intent on destroying all our livelihoods, then go ahead.'[14] The following Monday, the AJA held an unofficial meeting at the Journalists Club and put out a six-point communique, and that night two office-bearers appeared on 'This Day Tonight', a television programme transmitted by the Australian Broadcasting Commission.

Kerr's dismissal of Whitlam was greeted with indignation by Labor supporters and was criticised more temperately by some of Labor's opponents, including newspapers, who saw a breach of convention such as Sir John's as a bad precedent. The *Australian* did not address this issue: it simply declared the economy to be 'the real debate' (14 November). Murdoch's papers were thrown unquestioningly behind Fraser. The first three weeks of press coverage were surveyed by a group at La Trobe University. They divided the space given to the election in four daily newspapers circulating in Melbourne into three categories, which they labelled 'non-by-lined news', 'by-lined news' and 'combined editorial and news comment articles'. In the *Australian* non-by-lined news ran to 15,865 column centimetres; of this total, 21.37 percent were favourable to Labor, 45.2 percent favourable to the Coalition, and 33.4 percent neutral. By-lined news ran to 4255 column centimetres; 26.4 percent were favourable to Labor, 13 percent favourable to the Coalition and 51.14 percent were neutral. Editorial and news comment ran to 5085 column centimetres: none was favourable to Labor, 56.3 percent were favourable to the Coalition and 43.7 percent were neutral.[15] When Murdoch denied 'bias', as he did, he may merely have meant that the *Australian* was not totally regimented.[16] Fraser was delighted with the paper and invited Leslie Hollings to become his speechwriter, thinking that the editor wrote the editorials. Hollings declined the offer.

The bitterness that had arisen between Whitlam and Murdoch came into the open shortly before polling day. The *Australian* took up the allegations of another commentator that Connor had sought additional loans with Whitlam's consent (4 December) and Whitlam sued for defamation. The next day, the leading item on the *Australian*'s front page presented the latest monthly unemployment figures as growing; but this was using raw data; if it had used seasonally adjusted figures, as it had done before, and as other newspapers were doing, it would have reported a fall in unemployment (5 December). The resurrection of the Loans Affair brought sharp attacks on Murdoch from several Labor figures. Addressing the Queensland Press Club in Brisbane, Whitlam said that the hostility of the Murdoch press stemmed from his Government's refusal to approve the Alwest project; Murdoch retorted that Whitlam's allegation was 'highly irresponsible and entirely false'.

Whitlam's remarks had immediate resonance. In Perth, wharf labourers refused to handle newsprint consigned to the *Sunday Times*. Murdoch flew to Western Australia and from there went on television across the continent to deny partiality in his papers and to contradict the suggestion that the *Australian*'s treatment of the unemployment figures stemmed from his instructions. Despite his assurances printers at Kippax Street struck that weekend and went back only on condition that their point of view be given space in the papers.

On Monday 9 December journalists on the *Australian* held yet another meeting and this time decided to stay out until Wednesday on ethical grounds. The next day a Deputy President of the Arbitration Commission ruled that a breach of the professional code of ethics was a valid issue in the dispute and asked Murdoch to meet the journalists' representatives, whom he had hitherto refused to see. The meeting between Murdoch, two of his senior executives and eight AJA representatives broke into personal recriminations, but having made their point, the journalists returned to work that night. The episode was invoked against Murdoch on subsequent occasions by journalists whose papers Murdoch tried to buy. Yet Murdoch continued to believe that as the proprietor he was right: if journalists wanted to determine the editorials, he said to one of them at an early stage of the dispute, they could set up their own newspapers. As for Whitlam, who was defeated on 13 December, Murdoch soon had the opportunity of teaching him another lesson.

V

Henry John Fischer was known in the Sydney of the 1960s as a figure of the extreme right. He started a fortnightly called *Australian International News Review*, whose contributors ranged from Vietnam hawks belonging to the Coalition, such as Malcolm Fraser, to pre-war sympathisers with European fascist regimes. In its early issues the fortnightly apologised for the maligned regimes of South Africa and Rhodesia; it later discovered merit in some of the Arabian sheikhdoms. The common factor among the regimes the paper defended was their racist policies. After the fortnightly's short life came to an end, Fischer spent some time in the United States and returned with an increased interest in Arab matters. He sought to make contact with a variety of immigrant Arab groups, but was rebuffed. Then, suddenly, he had a job with a non-profit foundation set up by Reuben Scarf, a wealthy Christian Lebanese.

At the Scarf Foundation, Fischer seemed a changed man. He signed the Foundation's cheques, some of which were donations to Arab causes, and began to be accepted by Arabs and Arab sympathisers, including Bill Hartley, a former Secretary of the Victorian Labor Party and still a significant figure on the left. The Scarf Foundation supported two rural developments in Iraq and Fischer repeatedly visited that country, making a variety of business contacts. Perhaps other contacts as well: Richard Hall, a commentator on the intelligence world, later wrote that Fischer acted as an envoy for the Australian Secret Intelligence Service.[17] Neither Australia nor the United States then had embassies in Baghdad.

On 17 February 1976 Fischer contacted Murdoch, who was on the Continent, insisting that he had something important to convey and that he would tell only Murdoch in person. On 20 February he was in Murdoch's

London office telling a tale that Murdoch later described as incredible. For his revelations he received no payment, despite his journalistic background, but Murdoch provided a bodyguard for him. The incredible tale had a hard core of truth.

When the Labor Party's campaign committee met five days after Whitlam's dismissal, the question of funds for advertising was a major part of the discussion. Hartley took David Combe, the Federal Secretary, aside and suggested the possibility of Arab help: Reuben Scarf might be an intermediary in an approach. Like many businessmen, Scarf was disenchanted with Labor and, in his place, Fischer went to Baghdad as a first stop. Though he stressed that Australia's even-handed policy in the Middle East was in jeopardy and that the CIA was involved in Whitlam's dismissal, the Iraqis regarded him with suspicion. They therefore despatched two of their men to Australia, who travelled via Tokyo where they picked up visas. On their arrival at Sydney airport early in December, they were met by a protocol officer of the Department of Foreign Affairs, the editor of an Arab-language newspaper and Henry Fischer. It is a reasonable presumption that from then on they were under surveillance by Australian security organisations: Arabs with political ties are associated with terrorism in the counter-espionage mind and have to be watched.

Whitlam met the two Iraqis at Fischer's flat on the morning of 10 December. He outlined recent Australian events and expounded Labor foreign policy. The question of funds was left to Combe, who expected at least $250,000. The envoys left for Hong Kong the same day, accompanied by Fischer, whose bona fides had been established by the morning's meeting. The Labor Party spent heavily on advertising; no money reached Combe. In the New Year, the Party's bankers wanted to know when the overdraft customarily extended at election time would be reduced and at a meeting with senior Party officials, Combe and Whitlam made a clean breast of where they had expected funds to come from. The arrangement with the Iraqis, and the fact that Whitlam had been involved, concerned them greatly. The customary Labor way of turning wishes into events is to float them as coming developments to the media. After the electoral defeat, some Labor politicians wanted Whitlam to retire and thought that releasing information about the Iraqi breakfast was an opportunity for hastening the process. A selection from the admissions made by Combe and Whitlam promptly reached Laurie Oakes, the chief political writer for the *Sun-News Pictorial*.

After Fischer rounded out his tale of the Whitlam-Iraqi meeting, Murdoch took the story personally in hand and started to phone round the world to confirm separate aspects. On 24 February, when he knew that the Packer-owned *Bulletin* was past that week's deadline, he rang the weekly's political writer Alan Reid in Canberra and learnt that Oakes was about to file a story covering part of the events. Not wishing to fall behind, Murdoch cabled a first instalment to Sydney, where it appeared in the next morning's *Daily Telegraph* and *Australian* as coming from 'a special correspondent'. Some of the details were shaky, the headlines were changed in two successive editions of the *Australian*, but the core – that Whitlam had met two Iraqi envoys and that money had been promised – was right. The next day, 'a special correspondent' continued the exposé in the first edition of the *Australian*, but 'our political staff' filled in details in the second edition. The headline in both instances was 'Whitlam fights for his life'.

The disclosures would have been more damaging to Whitlam within the Labor Party if they had appeared elsewhere and if it had not been Murdoch in person who wrote the articles. There were resolutions round the country in branches and trade unions asking Whitlam to continue as Leader of the Parliamentary Party. The solicitors of the volatile Fischer issued a statement saying that writs would be issued against eight newspapers in New South Wales, which included some of Murdoch's. Murdoch came back with an interview given to one of his journalists in New York, whom he told that all stories on the subject by papers in his group were 'completely substantiated'. Did he seek the downfall of the Labor Party and the public disgrace of Whitlam? 'Nothing could be further from the truth,' Murdoch responded. 'We have always worked for the maintenance of two strong democratic alternative parties'.[18]

Whitlam remained Opposition Leader till the end of 1977. During the electoral campaign of 1975 and its aftermath, he brought a sheaf of legal actions against Murdoch's papers. Late in November 1977 the two dinner partners of 1970-72 spent an hour in a Melbourne motel room, during which an out-of-court settlement of Whitlam's actions and a handsome figure were mentioned. Their legal advisers did the rest. As an enemy Murdoch benefited Whitlam more greatly than as a friend.

DIANA DORS EXCLUSIVE: TH

CK PAST OF TV SEX

He made me feel
16 again, we were
perfect together

NEWS OF THE WORL

No. 7,3

BRITAIN'S BIGGEST SELLING SUNDAY NEWSPAPER

FARM GIRL FL

ved Tony Curtis

QUIZZED

Chapter Seven

/// *The Invader* ///

Sir William Carr greeted his breakfast guest with genuine enthusiasm. 'Thank God, you've come!' he said to the youngish Australian as he ushered him into the apartment. He had been through two anxious months and the last seven days had been particularly disturbing. But two nights before, his nephew Clive Carr and his son William had dined with Rupert Murdoch in the company of Harry Sporborg of Hambros, the banking advisers of the News of the World Organisation (NOTW), and a plan for averting the Carrs' loss of control over the company had taken firm shape. All that remained that Wednesday was for Sir William to size up the Australian and give the final approval. Murdoch went along with Sir William's jovial manner though his own plans would soon diverge from Sir William's hopes of staying in command. On later occasions, he would recount the naive welcome with wry amusement.

Murdoch received the first signal of a takeover threat to NOTW at Kippax Street on the morning of 17 October 1968; six days later he was at Sir William's Cliveden Place apartment in London. A telex had reached Sydney when the London clocks had not yet struck midnight; an announcement had been foreshadowed in the *Evening News*, and after the London market closed, Robert Maxwell, a Labour MP released his letter to Carr and explained his plans over the BBC. Some ten weeks later, Murdoch, not Maxwell, was in control of the *News of the World*, Britain's largest Sunday paper and, with a circulation of over six million, the biggest in the English language.

Murdoch added all his ingenuity to the expertise of his British banking advisers, Morgan Grenfell, to counter the bid by Maxwell's Pergamon Press.

117

Maxwell proposed to offer three Pergamon stock units for four ordinary NOTWs, plus redeemable stock in Pergamon. Since NOTW stock came in voting and non-voting ordinaries, he offered more loan stock for voting than for non-voting ordinaries. The finance writers in the morning papers put the value of the bid for voting ordinaries at 37s 6d, for the non-voting ordinaries at 36s, and computed its total value at over £stg26 million.[1] Though News Ltd had spare funds as a result of the sale of its holdings in Television Corporation and the acquisition of Southern Television Corporation, they were not within reach of mounting a cash bid against Maxwell. To offer stock in News Ltd in exchange for NOTW was even more difficult; Murdoch did not want to lose control of the Australian company and there were other legal obstacles back in Australia. Something different was needed, to which the Carr family's consent was essential.

Maxwell meanwhile dwelt on the strength of his position. He revealed that he held pledges from the family of Professor Derek Jackson, a cousin of Sir William Carr, for over 25 percent of the NOTW voting ordinaries. Moreover, as finance commentators pointed out, NOTW's profits, and hence the market prices of its stock, had been on a downward path, while Pergamon Press had shown steady growth since it was listed in 1964 and the market price of its stock had risen from 25s in 1966 to the current 45s.

Commentators like such comparisons, but Sir William resisted the offer. Even before Maxwell confirmed his intentions, Hambros plugged into the fray, bought substantial parcels and pushed up prices beyond Maxwell's bids: the morning after Maxwell revealed his plan, the voting stock was traded at 44s 6d. Carr then called a board meeting, which advised stockholders to do nothing until they received a circular. These were standard defensive moves. But unless a helper could be found, Hambros could only hope to force up Maxwell's price, not keep him away from NOTW.

Murdoch had been actively looking for a way of getting into British newspapers for at least a year and had engaged Morgan Grenfell as his scouts. On receiving the first news of Maxwell's intentions, he contacted Lord (Max) Catto, the head of the banking firm, and simultaneously instructed Frank O'Neill, the head of the News bureau in London, to transmit information about the *News of the World*: it was not a paper on Murdoch's shopping list until then. A flood of balance-sheet data superseded the colourful fare that was normally telexed to the *Sunday Mirror* at that time of the week. Not enough: Murdoch was on the international phone to anyone and everyone who could tell him something about the paper and its owners. Visitors came into his office while he was making the calls. He was oblivious; he seemed possessed.

He was ready to leave instantly, but Max Catto, having sounded out Hambros, saw no need to hurry. Murdoch stuck to his intention of attending the Caulfield Cup, Australia's second most important race meeting of the year, and took a plane to Melbourne on Friday night. In London the clocks were still striking noon when Maxwell's brokers, who had also gone into the market, pulled out. Hearing whispers of a further bid, Catto tried to contact Murdoch with advice not to delay his arrival in Britain. But Murdoch was out of contact; Catto caught Norman Young, the chairman of News Ltd, in Adelaide and Young then found his elusive chief executive. The next morning Murdoch collected his ticket and passport at Sydney airport and met Catto at Heathrow early Sunday. They drove to Catto's place in Hertfordshire to discuss the position. That night Murdoch checked into the Savoy, his usual *pied-à-terre*.

Maxwell and the media were busy responding to an editorial composed by Stafford Somerfield, the editor of the *News of the World*, on the 'little local difficulty' at his paper. Somerfield said that he would not be able to work with Maxwell, who was a socialist MP, and he doubted whether the paper's independence could be preserved under such an owner. Alluding to Maxwell's Czech origins, he contrasted him with a paper that was 'as British as roast beef and Yorkshire pudding'. Facing Maxwell on television, Somerfield replayed these themes. His xenophobia, though going down ill with the cosmopolitan City, provided wide publicity for Carr's attempt to resist.

By then, Maxwell had made certain that London's major press proprietors would not bid against Pergamon. Roy Thomson, who owned the *Sunday Times*, at once declared that he was not interested. Max Aitken, who owned the *Daily* and *Sunday Express*, and IPC, who published two popular Sunday papers and the *Daily Mirror*, were both liable to be called before the Monopolies Commission if they made a bid. The one possible counter-bidder on Fleet Street was Associated Newspapers, whose *Daily Mail* had no Sunday stable-mate. Over the weekend Maxwell talked to Lord Rothermere, the chairman, and got an assurance that Associated Newspapers would not intervene. Rupert Murdoch's arrival went unnoticed.

The market, however, was going against Maxwell. Myers, a firm of stockbrokers associated with NOTW, had joined Hambros in buying. After the weekend, Maxwell had to raise his price: he foreshadowed an offer that would put the voting stock units at 50s each and the overall value at £stg34 million.

Murdoch could match Maxwell's new bid even less than the first. But the plan he was working out with Catto was still applicable. Some of the Australian assets of News Ltd would be transferred to NOTW; in exchange,

NOTW would issue new stock to News Ltd. If the Carr side of the factional-
ised family, as owners of about 30 percent of the voting stock agreed, Sir
William and Rupert Murdoch would be in unchallengeable, joint control.
When Murdoch called on him, Sir William saw no danger: his own position
as chairman was covered by a seven-year written contract. Murdoch asked
that he himself should become joint managing director with Clive Carr: Sir
William was delighted to agree.

The lack of ready money had haunted Sir William ever since Derek Jackson
brought up the question of selling. Jackson had never sought close involvement
with the paper; he had pursued a scientific career and then moved to France
where he lived with his sixth wife. When Sir William visited Paris in summer
1968, Jackson talked of opening the trust that bound the various members of
the family; in short, he wanted to sell his own million shares and the rest for
which he spoke. Carr did not know where to find the cash for several million
shares and, as he soon learnt, there were worse complications on the horizon.
Jackson would want more than the going 28s per unit; and if more than 28s
were paid, the City Takeover Panel would consider the purchase of Jackson's
stock as a springboard to control and would require an offer to all stockholders.
Somerfield heard of these difficulties in September; Sir William, he recalled,
looked ghastly as he enumerated them over drinks.[2]

Determined to sell, Jackson wrote to Sir William saying he was putting the
matter into N. M. Rothschild's hands. On behalf of the Carrs, Hambros
offered 28s, a price later described by Jackson as ridiculous. Rothschilds
went to Robert Fleming, a merchant bank close to Pergamon Press and
Maxwell's mid-October bid was the upshot.

The negotiations between the Carrs and Murdoch began to leak out. On
the night of 23 October, the date of the breakfast, Hambros confirmed that
they themselves had talked to Murdoch and on Thursday morning business
commentators forecast a share exchange that would forestall Maxwell. That
afternoon Murdoch held a press conference, flanked by Catto and a
hurriedly hired public relations man. He told his audience that he proposed
to acquire 40 percent of NOTW, buying 9 percent on the market and getting
the rest in exchange for Australian assets. (Morgan Grenfell were buying 3.5
percent on behalf of News Ltd and Hambros were promised that their
excess holdings would be taken over.) The finance writers in the audience,
already unhappy about Hambros' attempts to block Maxwell, believed that
as a result of Murdoch's proposal, minority shareholders would be left with
stock that would fall well below the present market value. Was Murdoch
willing to match Maxwell's offer? He did not have enough money for that,
he replied. Outside the business pages, however, he was welcome, though

with little discernment. The *Times* called him 'the quiet Australian' and the *Economist* reported that he had inherited 'his father's considerable empire just half a dozen years ago'.[3] He had already seen Vere Harmsworth, Lord Rothermere's son, and he now called on Roy Thomson at the *Times* and on Hugh Cudlipp at the *Daily Mirror*. At the end of the week, Hambros announced that a minimum of two months were needed to work out the details of the exchange.

II

The issue that would assure joint control of NOTW had to be passed by an extraordinary general meeting. Sir William Carr could speak for over 30 percent of the needed votes; with the stock bought by Murdoch and Hambros, the allies were confident of a smooth passage. The immediate hurdle to cross was the City Takeover Panel, which could rule against the proposal. But it could not enforce its rulings and the lack of power made it unpredictable. The Government suspected that the Panel too often gave bidders the benefit of the doubt in order to avoid a confrontation, and was toying with a form of more stringent control over City conduct. The Bank of England, standing between the Panel and the Government, kept a close eye on City events: it acted as landlord to the Panel, whose Secretary was an employee of the Bank. In the contest for NOTW, the Panel was more than unpredictable; it successively jumped several ways.

Shortly after his arrival in London, Murdoch went to see the Panel's chairman, Sir Humphrey Mynors, who told him: 'You have the green light'. After the rights of minority shareholders were raised by the press, Murdoch saw Mynors again, who suggested that News Ltd should speed up the decision on what Australian assets would be transferred to NOTW and allowed him to tell the media that in the Panel's view the takeover code had not been breached. Murdoch took the hint, and a plane back to Australia that very night.

Maxwell's side counter-lobbied. The day after Murdoch's intentions became public, Rothschilds called on the Panel and Robert Fleming, for Maxwell, wrote asking that stock bought after the contest opened should be precluded from voting at the extraordinary general meeting. The week after, Hill Samuel, who also acted for Pergamon, joined Robert Fleming in a submission that two months' delay for the production of details was excessive.

Sir Leslie O'Brien, the Governor of the Bank of England, then took a hand, with warnings to City groups that the Panel might have to be reorganised under a full-time chairman, a hint that Mynors was being too soft. Two days after Murdoch's departure, O'Brien conferred with Tony Crosland, the Cabinet minister overseeing financial affairs. At the end of the week, twelve days after Murdoch arrived in London, the City Panel met in plenary session and announced late in the evening that Hambros, Morgan Grenfell and Hill Samuel had agreed not to vote with their newly bought stock on the issue to News Ltd. It was a victory for Maxwell. The Carr-Murdoch camp had counted on 51 percent of the votes; of the stock now eligible to vote, it held only 38 percent, Maxwell held 32 percent and 30 percent were with uncommitted parties.

The NOTW board struck back with a circular asking stockholders for written pledges of support over twelve months and for signatures assigning a right of first refusal to purchase to Hambros, who offered a nominal sum for the signatures. Pergamon countered with a complaint to the Panel that this offer cut across the vote freeze and NOTW countered saying that the circular was drafted before the freeze. The Panel was silent and on 12 November, two NOTW directors and a Hambros man flew to Australia to inspect the assets on offer from News Ltd.

Unaccountably, Maxwell wavered. He had still not made his formal offer and now let it be known that he would not make one till the Panel ruled again on what shares could be voted. The Press understood him to be avoiding the costs of an underwriting agreement unless he had a reasonable chance of success. His formal offer came late in November. The market value of Pergamon stock had declined; he now offered additional loan stock and his offer put 51s on NOTW voting ordinaries. Pergamon stock had ceased to be supported heavily in the market and the Maxwell camp embarked on a less costly, more gimmicky move. Hill Samuel commissioned a Gallup poll that asked respondents for their opinions of takeovers, giving the NOTW bid as an example. Maxwell sent a broker to Australia to find out more about News Ltd; and when Murdoch's papers there began to discuss the selling methods of International Learning Systems, a Pergamon affiliate, Maxwell issued writs for defamation.

Murdoch was back in London early in December 1968, beaming confidence and facing the cameras with Anna and a baby. A formal agreement between News Ltd and NOTW had been signed in Canberra. Sir William Carr wrote to his stockholders finally setting out the terms: NOTW proposed to issue 5.1 million voting ordinaries, amounting to 35 percent of the expanded voting stock, or 26 percent of all the ordinary stock. With the stock already held by it and its friends, News Ltd would then hold 40 percent of the votes; in return, it would inject assets earning £stg1.1 million a year before tax, a figure it would guarantee. Murdoch would be managing direc-tor with full executive powers at a fee of £stg20,000 a year – the conditions had changed further in Murdoch's favour – and the meeting to authorise the deal would be held on 2 January. Carr added encouraging news: profits would be up by 62 percent next year, NOTW had realised a nice sum on the sale of investments and the Treasury had approved the payment of a higher dividend. In an aside about Pergamon, he said that the price of its stock had been supported by the purchase of 579,000 shares on the part of its asso-ciates.

Maxwell had asked for acceptances of his formal offer by 24 December and now extended the closing date. No longer in a strong position, his camp sought the intervention of authority. The trustees for the Jackson family took out writs, seeking injunctions against the directors of NOTW, News Ltd and Hambros to prevent the agreement from going ahead and asking an award of damages against some of the defendants for breach of fiduciary trust and/or conspiracy.

Maxwell sought another injunction, restraining the trustees of the NOTW pension fund from voting 600,000 stock units under their control; his request was refused on New Year's Day. Hill Samuel and Robert Fleming came in with a circular noting that NOTW voting ordinaries had fallen to 39s 6d or 10s below the Pergamon bid. It was whistling against the wind, for with the help of pledges the Carr camp once again had a sizeable proportion of the votes.

The Connaught Rooms had been rented for the large audience expected at the extraordinary general meeting on 2 January 1969: 500 turned up. When Sir William Carr walked to the platform and took his seat, the audience gave him a two-minute ovation, no great surprise since half of those in the hall were NOTW staff who had been issued with voting stock. Carr's speech, written by Somerfield and one of the executive directors, traced the contest to Jackson's wish to sell, charged Pergamon Press with ignorance of newspapers, and declared Australia to be a fast-growing country. Murdoch spoke from the hall for three minutes, ending with an · expression of pleasure at Sir William's staying on as Chairman. Maxwell rose to ask questions, was given three minutes to speak and stressed the money value of his offer. Sir William deprecated mere money from the chair, and called for a show of hands: 299 were for the issue, 20 against. The ensuing ballot gave the board 4,536,822 votes, with 3,246,937 against it.

That night Murdoch gave a party at his apartment on the Embankment, where he had just moved. Max Aitken of the *Daily Express*, which had supported Carr and Murdoch, was one of the guests. Carr, feeling unwell, briefly paid his respects. His doctors suspected cancer and he went into hospital the next day. From the continent, Derek Jackson commented later in the week: 'I regard the News of the World Board as raving mad'.[4] But he soon sold 1.4 million voting ordinaries to News Ltd at 40s each and the rest of the Jackson family holdings were placed by Hambros. With Jackson's parcel, some old and some new purchases and the issue, Murdoch controlled 49 percent of the voting stock and no longer needed Sir William.

III

Two years later Rupert Murdoch explained his methods on an Australian television programme: 'We tended to take sick newspapers, ones that were not worth much, that people thought were about to fold up. And by energy and drive, and getting people around us that were good, we managed in most cases to turn the corner, and this is how we've built a fairly large company.'[5] He could not have been thinking of the *News of the World*. If the paper was sick, it got worse under his control. He used the cage to great effect, but the beast had its own life cycle, and when Murdoch fed it pep pills, it was he who got bitten.

The *News of the World* was still spoken of as a British institution, a little jocularly. With his talk of Yorkshire pudding, Stafford Somerfield had tried to capitalise on this sentiment. Not long before, one British adult in two, man or woman, had read the paper on Sunday. However its editors or owners cast their votes, it was deeply Tory, respecting order and authority. Its sauce was licensed: it was poured on acceptable targets, unless its rivals had to be scooped. It demonstrated, Sunday after Sunday, how pride goes before a fall and how pederasty will end in the courts. The props of order were upheld by proof that justice was at work; the ressentiment of its readers was given acceptable targets. But, like other British institutions, the *News of the World* was in slow decline.

The decline can be quantified. Its circulation had reached a high point just after the second world war and sustained that level for nine years. When a Royal Commission on the Press surveyed the Sunday domain in July 1947 – a low month for British newspapers – the sales stood at 7.9 million copies, or 26.9 percent of all Sunday paper sales. Its closest rivals were the *People* with a circulation of 4.67 million and the *Sunday Pictorial* with 4.0 million. The dailies then lagged far behind the Sundays, as they had done in the nineteenth century. The *Daily Express*, with 3.8 million, barely led the *Daily Mirror* with 3.7 million.[6]

What was it that readers found in the *News of the World* to make them so keen to buy it? In 1949 Mass-Observation published a study in which the *News of the World*, as Britain's largest paper, figured prominently. Some 26 percent of its readers said they liked its 'news', a proportion higher than that of the readers of any other Sunday paper, including the quality *Sunday Times* and *Observer*. Was this possible? To see what they understood by 'news', Mass-Observation asked the same readers which government was in power in Yugoslavia; the score of *News of the World* readers giving correct answers was the lowest among all the readerships. Mass-Observation concluded that readers of the *News of the World* confused news with gossip; two-fifths of them were willing to admit that they liked scandal.[7]

The uncertainties expressed in these answers were eloquent testimony to the packaging. The editorial pages, read by few, were adorned with articles by clerics of several creeds and by members of parliament from three parties. In the more widely read court reports, who could say what was news and what scandal?

The *News of the World* began to decline when commercial television was introduced in 1955. In the first half of 1954 its sales still averaged around 8.1 million; for the corresponding first half of 1956, they were 7.5 million, sliding to 6.5 million in 1960 and 6.1 million in 1961. The paper then absorbed the *Empire News*, gaining 660,000 and, by dint of other efforts, was selling 6.2 million at the start of 1968. Its rivals did not suffer in the same way. In 1954 the *Sunday Pictorial* stood at 5.45 million, in 1960 at 5.3 million and in 1968, its renamed and refurbished successor, the *Sunday Mirror*, at 5.1 million. The figures for the *People* (later *Sunday People*) at those same times were 5.2, 5.275 and 5.5 million. Thus, commercial television could not be blamed for the decline of the *News of the World*.[8] A more pertinent development was the growing popularity of the posh Sunday papers. Between 1956 and 1968 the sales of the *Sunday Times* rose from 618,000 to 1.46 million, and those of the *Observer* from 601,000 to 900,000. The *News of the World* used to have readers in the middle classes, but the posh Sundays understood the changes among those strata better. They were now more apt to be scandalised by spymasters than scoutmasters, by greed more than by sex. The investigations in these papers were fuller; they spent more money on them.

Even if the NOTW board had understood these changes, they could not reverse them: they could not repeal the Education Act of 1944. Appointed in 1960, Stafford Somerfield had a free hand to update sex; he opened his cheque book to actresses and 'vice queens'. His most provocative exploit was the serialisation of Christine Keeler's reminiscences in 1963. Keeler had allocated her time to both John Profumo, the Secretary of State for War, and Evgeniy Ivanov, a Soviet Assistant Naval Attaché. The press and the Opposition pursued this association as a matter dangerous to national security and after Profumo falsely denied a liaison with Keeler in Parlia-ment, it acquired political relevance. On these presumptions, the *News of the World* opened its pages to a highly paid prostitute. The chequebook turned out to be a temporary expedient. Though money was still being made, costs were creeping up and early in 1968 the cover price rose from six to seven pence. The holding company had partly diversified out of publish-ing, with bids that sometimes failed, and these admissions of decline prompted Derek Jackson into getting out.

Murdoch first tackled management problems. Sir William Carr had boasted that good relations with the printing unions were among his main assets and suggested that Murdoch should continue in his way. For their part, the union officials liked Carr. The dominant union at Bouverie Street, NOTW's offices, was the Society of Graphical and Allied Trades (SOGAT) and, before going to hospital, Carr asked Bill Keys, its senior man, to head a delegation that would meet the new managing director.

The encounter took place on a Saturday night; new arrangements were to be made. Murdoch swept in with a retinue, sat down and astonished the delegates by opening up with the words: 'I'm now going to fucking tell you ...' and laying down the law about the British union movement for three minutes. Keys replied: 'If you want to take over this newspaper, wash your mouth and come back to us'. Murdoch stormed out, returned ten minutes later and asked everyone into his office for drinks. The industrial arrange-ments at NOTW were reviewed, and agreed on; it was the quickest deal negotiated by London printing unions in a long time. Their officials realised that Murdoch's opening tone was uncharacteristic and wondered who had put him up to it.

Murdoch then moved on to the higher echelons. The advertising director left. Sir William Carr followed more slowly. The doctors had cleared him of the suspicion of cancer, but had found a large aneurism and after a vacation he went back to hospital for an operation. During the months of Carr's illness Murdoch first obtained his resignation from various subsidiaries and, in June 1969, from the chair. Carr took the title of president. Murdoch became chairman.

Under Carr, the editor of the *News of the World* had had control over its content. Stafford Somerfield, the first Murdoch victim-editor to set down his experiences at length, has recalled how quickly his role changed. Murdoch began by altering the paper's contents bill and by asking to be informed when reporters went abroad. To Somerfield's remonstrations, Murdoch replied that he hadn't come from Australia not to interfere. On a holiday in Spain, Somerfield learnt that Murdoch was dropping the leader page, and returned just in time on the Saturday night to have it restored for the second edition. There was a suggestion that Somerfield should move from editor to editorial director but, with Murdoch busy in Australia, nothing came of it.[9]

IV

The response to the paper's slow decline was another dose of sex. At the end of August 1969 readers' memories were stirred with a photograph of Christine Keeler that all but showed her nipples; an accompanying report said that she was having a row with a photographer who, having taken pictures of her for a book, was offering them for sale elsewhere. The *News of the World* was, in fact, opening its cheque book again. Three weeks later its front page annnounced: 'World Exclusive/CHRISTINE KEELER/at last the/FULL STORY'. The promise continued:

Next week in the *News of the World* we are going to start printing the FULL STORY OF THE LIFE OF CHRISTINE KEELER.

This is the story the world has been waiting for. A wonderful story. A story which in years to come will be retold in the nation's history books.

Christine Keeler will tell:

The full story behind the tragedy of John Profumo the War Minister who lied to the House of Commons about his secret relationship with her.

A purported extract from the coming revelations said: 'Jack showed me 10 Downing Street and the ministry where he worked. I never met a man like this before.'

Profumo, who had resigned from Parliament in 1963 after admitting he had misled it, was now working at Toynbee Hall, an East End charity presided over by Lord Longford, a Labour peer. Longford at once issued a statement protesting against the forthcoming publication; so did others, regarding it as an intrusion into Profumo's privacy. In reply, the *News of the World* agreed that

Profumo should be forgiven, but that the part he had played should not be forgotten. The paper had only the serial rights, a book would be published anyway. The first instalment, however, did not deal with Profumo.

The promise to pioneer historiography was met with wide disfavour. Lord Devlin, who had conducted an inquiry into the security aspects of Profumo's conduct in 1963, now headed the Press Council, a body to whom the public could address complaints. In an address before the proprietors and senior executives of Fleet Street, Devlin, as outgoing chairman, said that when a man's public life ceased, he became entitled to all the protection claimed by a private citizen and that his misfortunes were not to be used for the purpose of making money; no name was mentioned. Murdoch was in the audience. Cardinal Heenan, the Catholic Primate, who had been preparing an article on the permissive society for the *News of the World*, refused to contribute. A former captain of the Welsh Rugby side announced that he would not write for the paper again. Interviewed by David Frost on London Weekend Television, Murdoch pleaded that the series was a precautionary tale for politicians, and when Frost suggested that a book by Wayland Young shortly after the event had already brought all the 'new facts' in the *News of the World* series to light, Murdoch said he had not heard of it. Ian Hamilton commented on the interview in the *Listener*: 'Murdoch had put his case, altered it, contradicted himself, got angry, been revealed as misinformed'. Hamilton felt a little sorry for Frost's victim: 'There is a point at which the legitimately tough grilling of a public figure starts shading into blood sport.'[10]

It turned out that Keeler had little to say about Profumo. Since her memoirs did not appear in book form, it is difficult to say whether the paper had overstated what was to come or had been deflected from a fuller version by criticism. Following Lord Devlin's hint, the Press Council nevertheless took up the cudgels.

Its first step was to announce a meeting for 15 October to consider the Keeler memoirs without waiting for a specific complaint from the public. It relied on a declaration issued in 1966, which said that newspapers should make no payment to persons 'engaged in crime or other notorious misbehaviour' when the public interest did not warrant it. It drew up a complaint that alleged that the publication of 'sordid details' was an exploitation of sex and vice for commercial purposes; that payment was unethical if the public interest did not warrant it; and that dragging up a man's past, under similar circumstances, was also unethical. It invited Somerfield to appear before it and suggested that Murdoch might also wish to appear. Somerfield and the Press Council then exchanged pleasantries. Somerfield said that he had rejected that particular part of the declaration in 1966 as a step in the direction of censorship, still had the same attitude, and found it difficult to see how the Press Council could refer to the contents of the memoirs when only one instalment had appeared. His refusal to appear before the Council was followed by another invitation, followed by a second refusal, a further invitation and a third refusal. The Press Council then deliberated, found the complaint proven and censured the *News of the World*.

Why did both men refuse to appear before a body, to which NOTW continued to belong, when Murdoch had been willing to face a hostile television interviewer? Perhaps because each might have said different things. Somerfield later wrote: 'He [Murdoch] was wrong in his judgment and wrong to interfere in the way I wished to present the story.'[11]

Both had failed to see the questions that might have led them to something worth printing six years after Profumo's resignation from Parliament: how could the triangular situation between the Secretary of State for War, Keeler and the Soviet Assistant Naval Attaché have escaped British security? If it had, this was a matter of public concern worth airing six years later. If it had not, then what? Christine Keeler herself was not likely to provide the answers.

In 1975 Profumo was awarded a CBE 'for charitable services to Toynbee Hall' on the recommendation of Harold Wilson, who had relentlessly pursued Profumo in 1963. Had Wilson, impressed by Profumo's charity, repented of his earlier zeal or had he learnt more? A version of events more likely to influence history books was published in 1982 by Nigel West in his book on MI5, the counter-espionage agency concerned with people like Soviet attachés.[12]

Evgeniy Ivanov had been identified for MI5 as a member of GRU (Soviet military intelligence), by Lieutenant-Colonel Oleg Penkovskiy, a member of that same organisation. Ivanov's father-in-law was chairman of the Soviet Supreme Court and his sister was married to another GRU officer at the Soviet embassy in London; he was therefore considered as a desirable target for 'turning', that is, secretly working for Britain. Put under surveillance, Ivanov was found to be a visitor to a house occupied by Stephen Ward, an osteopath with a high-society clientele, whom he also supplied with women. MI5 enlisted Ward, in an effort to entrap and then blackmail Ivanov. Ward reported back that he and Keeler, a woman resident at his house, had visited 'Cliveden', the home of Viscount Astor, for a weekend; Ivanov and Profumo had also been visitors. MI5 were alarmed by Profumo's presence, believing that he could complicate their plans to entrap Ivanov. Sir Roger Hollis, the Director-General of MI5, therefore passed information on what was afoot to Profumo through the Secretary to the Cabinet. On the day Profumo heard, he wrote to Keeler breaking off the liaison. This was in August 1962.

In December a West Indian, trying to get admission to Ward's house by using a gun, was charged by the police. Keeler became a witness in the case against him, aroused newspaper attention and started negotiations for her life story. When Ivanov heard of these negotiations, he packed his bags and returned to Moscow. In turn Profumo heard of Ivanov's impending departure and called on MI5, where he learnt that Ivanov had not been turned. Thus, far from being a security risk, Profumo was aware of MI5's plans though without participating in their execution. He subsequently suffered as a result of his discretion as much as of his indiscretion.

Telling the police of her liaisons with Profumo and Ivanov, Keeler added that Ward had asked her to find out when atomic weapons would be sent to West Germany. MI5 accordingly considered whether it should prosecute Ward under the Official Secrets Act, but instead inspired a prosecution against him for living off immoral earnings. In retaliation Ward threatened to expose Profumo's affair and contacted the Opposition. Macmillan, the Prime Minister, now had to be told that Profumo had had a liaison, despite his denial, and asked for Profumo's resignation. Ward ended by taking his own life.

MI5 could not be accused of lacking vigilance, but according to West, it does not seem to have been clearly aware of Profumo's brief liaison with Keeler. Its machinations to entrap Ivanov destroyed Profumo politically and Ward physically. This plot did not fit easily into the stereotyped exposes of the News of the World, even if Murdoch and Somerfield had suspected a part of it.

In the half year when Keeler's ill-informed reminiscences were rehashed, the paper's circulation rose by nearly 200,000. Nevertheless, Somerfield was summarily dismissed in February 1970.

V

For all the ingenuity of his plan, Murdoch's victory over Maxwell turned out to be absurdly easy. Maxwell had started with all the advantages, offering highly priced stock and Murdoch had publicly admitted that he did not have enough money to match the offer. There was something odd about the way the Maxwell camp made so little effort to buy NOTW stock on the market: keeping the acquisition price down was not the explanation. The clues to the failure began to appear in the second half of 1969.

In May Maxwell talked about a sale of Pergamon Press to the New York conglomerate Leasco and, the following month, Leasco announced a bid for all Pergamon stock at a total value of £stg25 million. As a start, Leasco bought 38 percent of Pergamon on the market. The sellers included Maxwell's family companies: he was getting out. The bid was withdrawn before the end of August; the explanation offered by Rothchilds, Leasco's advisers, was that questions eroding Leasco's confidence had arisen. Next Pergamon's own banking advisers and stockbrokers resigned.

The City of London Panel then stepped in, and trying to protect stock-holders that had not sold their Pergamon holdings, persuaded Leasco to renew its bid. Leasco agreed, on condition that the new price would be based on a multiple of the average profits for 1968 and 1969 as determined by independent auditors, and not on the 1968 disclosed profits, which Leasco did not accept. Independently the Board of Trade appointed a prominent accountant and a senior lawyer to conduct an inquiry into Pergamon Press. In mid-September Leasco withdrew its revised bid, but being Pergamon's largest stockholder, sought the appointment of a group of directors who had been agreed on by institutional stockholders and itself, as replacements for Maxwell and his associates. At the meeting where the directors were chosen, Maxwell complained that the people now sharpening their knives against him were those who had brought Murdoch from Australia to thwart his bid for NOTW. The vote went against him.

The Board of Trade inspectors filed an astringent first report on Pergamon in mid-1971. They said that Maxwell had shown an unjustified optimism in reporting to shareholders and investors and, on some occasions, had disregarded unpalatable facts. Maxwell tried to prevent their inquiry from continuing by taking out a writ of prohibition and suing the inspectors in person. The court held that the inspectors had erred in denying Maxwell an opportunity to rebut their preliminary findings, but did not grant him an injunction against the publication of further reports. The second interim report in April 1972 alleged a history of overstatement of Pergamon's trading profits; a final report in November 1973 alleged that the real purpose of certain transactions between Pergamon Press and one of Maxwell's family companies was to increase the value of Pergamon's shares in the market. Maxwell replied that Pergamon's main trouble was Leasco.

It took the public three years to learn how weak a reed Maxwell had been. Murdoch had meanwhile enjoyed the reputation of being a giant-killer. Un-abashed, Maxwell started to rebuild his position, and as a result he would come up against Murdoch in other contexts. When they met again, they knew each other.

REACH FOR THE NEW SUN

YOUR SUN will be different on Monday. Very different.

But it will still be YOUR kind of newspaper.

It will be in a new, easier-to-handle tabloid form. Smaller pages, but many more of them. It will have lots of new names. Lots of new, exciting ideas.

But the most important thing to remember is that the new Sun will still be the paper that CARES.

The paper that cares—passionately—about truth, and beauty and justice.

Independent, aware

The paper that cares about people. About the kind of world we live in. And about the kind of world we would like our _____ to live in.

of familiar features—the popular Pace-setters page, for example—will be there.

The new team

The incomparable TEMPLEGATE, Britain's most famous tipster, will be in the team.

So will brilliant DEIRDRE McSHARRY, the writer who dominates the fashion scene.

Witty, incisive JON AKASS will continue to write for the paper. UNITY HALL, ELIZABETH PROSSER, KEITH MASON, _____ ARNOLD and lots of other

In the first week alone Sun readers will be offered:

● A series of long extracts from **The Love Machine,** the world's best-selling novel of 1969.

● Inside-soccer stories by the top names —a million pounds' worth of soccer talent.

● The supreme readers' service—your problems answered by the world-famous John Hilton Bureau.

● Opportunities for women to win new CARS, COLOUR TV SETS, and a "NEW-YOU" session at a famous health farm.

● New and original cartoons.

There will always be something new in the new Sun.

Lively, entertaining

'BLITZ

Chapter Eight

/// *At Sunrise* ///

The printing presses at Bouverie Street lay idle for six nights a week. Could anything else be housed in the cage? When Pergamon Press foreshadowed its bid for NOTW, the *Economist* put the obvious question; 'A Daily Maxwell?'[1] Murdoch, promptly asked whether he would start a daily, parried by saying he didn't know there were any for sale. One soon was.

IPC had a doomed child. In 1961 Cecil King, then IPC's chairman, bought the Odham group which published *People* and a stack of magazines: the *Daily Herald*, of which the Trade Union Congress owned 49 percent, came with the purchase. To get Odhams and buy out the Trade Union Congress, King guaranteed the *Daily Herald* a life of seven years. He relaunched it as the *Sun* in 1964 and extended the *Sun*'s life to January 1970. Limping with a 1.3 million circulation alongside the *Daily Mirror*'s five million, it was an embarrassment; under the common ownership it could not take on the *Mirror*. By 1969 the *Sun* had cost IPC over £stg 12 million in losses and its circulation was dropping below a million copies. Perhaps someone else might do better with it.

The first trier was Robert Maxwell, who approached Hugh Cudlipp in April 1969. In mid-May IPC made a statement through its solicitors saying it expected an approach for the *Sun* from a group of prominent Labor Party members; Maxwell publicly agreed with this statement. His deal with Leasco appeared to be going through; in July the IPC Board announced that it would cease to publish the *Sun* in January. The unions, put on notice, began to talk to Maxwell who set eight weeks for the completion of new contracts. His plans disappointed them: he aimed for a circulation of 500,000, would sell only in major centres and his working capital would be £stg 500,000. To the unions, this meant a drop in *Sun* employees from 1150 to 400 or 500.

133

Late in August Maxwell's deal with Leasco had become shaky and an agreement with the unions was no closer.

Murdoch had watched from the sidelines while Maxwell made the running. The morning after Maxwell pulled out, he was in Cudlipp's office at
Holborn Circus, and on television that night he spoke of a 'straightforward,
honest newspaper' he might publish.

IPC dealt with him on the terms it negotiated with Maxwell; the price
would range between £stg 250,000 and £stg 500,000 according to the
paper's lifespan; the payments were in instalments of £stg 50,000 a year. It
was a basement bargain. By the end of September Murdoch had an editor,
Albert ('Larry') Lamb, who had been in charge of the *Daily Mail's* northern
edition, and SOGAT had given him its blessing. The temporary delay lay
with the National Graphical Association (NGA), whose members held jobs in
the machine rooms of the *Sun* and now asked for similar jobs at Bouverie
Street. In mid-October, the difficulty was ironed out. Murdoch announced
that the first new *Sun*, changed from a broadsheet into a tabloid, would
appear on 17 November 1969.[2]

The Press Council's inquiry and the David Frost interview had not diminished his thirst for personal publicity. Still a broadsheet of a mere dozen
pages, the *Sun* of 15 November carried an appeal to readers to stay with the
new paper, signed by 'Rupert Murdoch, Publisher'. With an eye to the
Labour stalwarts who had been reading the paper, he promised: 'The most
important thing to remember is that the new *Sun* will still be a paper that
CARES. The paper that cares – passionately – about truth and beauty and
justice.' On the Monday, the new tabloid continued under the slogan 'Forward with the People'. Other signposts to its direction were the front-page
leading story, 'HORSE DOPE SENSATION/*Sun* Exclusive', a page-four picture of
Anna Murdoch touching the button that made the presses roll, a page-nine
interview with Harold Wilson, and a serialisation of Jacqueline Susann's
novel *The Love Machine*, which filled several of the remaining pages of a
forty-eight-page issue.

There was a hitch before Anna Murdoch touched the button. A fire broke
out in the stereo room, delaying the making of the plates, and the night
trains that were to take the papers to the provinces had left when the printing began. In London, the man to deal with such emergencies is known as
the 'chief publisher'; but the other 'Publisher' had overlooked appointing
one. Two union officials who had come to oversee the observance of the
agreed rules were on hand, and one of them, Bill Keys of SOGAT, took
charge and rang round for trucks. The deliveries cost a packet, but Murdoch
paid up without blinking an eye.

The early issues were rough. Lamb found it difficult to hire staff away from other papers, the news coverage was scanty, competitors had anticipated some of the planned gimmicks. And was there a policy? Murdoch was stung by criticism that the *Sun* had no principles, and in reply to 'pundits' who said so, he ran a long page-two editorial at the end of the week. He laid it all out: the *Sun* opposed capital punishment, was against apartheid in South Africa and colour discrimination in Britain; opposed the country's entry into the Common Market; wanted to see the Vietnam war ended, hated the hydrogen bomb but backed a nuclear deterrent. Above all, it endorsed the 'permissive society', which was not 'an opinion' but 'a fact': 'Anyone – from the Archbishop of Canterbury to Mick Jagger – is entitled to put forward his own moral code.'

The *Sun* found its way into a world of sartorial propriety by trial and error. On the first Monday, it featured a picture of a woman with a deep cleavage in her dress on the third page; on Tuesday, a woman in a bikini appeared in the same spot; on Wednesday, the seventh page featured 'two views of Hylette', one of which displayed her left breast; on Friday's third page, the bikini top was gone and both breasts were hidden under folded arms; on Saturday, a deep cleavage harmonised with the late autumn. After these fashion guides had run for a month, Tom Baistow wrote in the *New Statesman*: 'Mr Cudlipp sensed correctly that what Mr Murdoch would go for first . . . was Jumbo's soft underbelly – those unreconstructed proles who may have felt the *Mirror* was getting too highbrow.'[3] Baistow had the emphasis right. Murdoch was no Hugh Hefner; he had no interest in playmates; he was personally prudish. The business of Rupert Murdoch was business.

The *Sun*'s political stance called for greater delicacy. It had to keep one eye on the existing pro-Labour readers, another on potential customers buying the Conservative dailies, whose pence were just as good. The *Sun* declared itself politically independent; the interview with Harold Wilson was followed by a column written by Cecil King, who had spectacularly quarrelled with Wilson the year before and had been ejected from IPC as a result. Faced with an overwhelmingly Tory press, Wilson found it all the more important to cultivate the invader. Wilson had not overlooked Murdoch, even at the *News of the World*, and at the end of August had asked him to Chequers, the Prime Minister's country residence, along with Max Aitken of the *Daily Express* and Michael Berry of the *Daily Telegraph*, to hear a five-hour exposition of a plan to confront the unions. Two days later Wilson backed off and, among political insiders, the Chequers evening became notorious proof of Wilson's inconstancy.[4]

There were tangled circumstances counselling a friendship on both Murdoch's and Wilson's side. The Government had the power to refer major newspaper purchases to the Monopolies Commission and an expansive proprietor like Murdoch could not wholly foresee what occasions might arise in future. Wilson had to heed the printing unions, who cast a block of votes at the Annual Conference of the Labour Party and had friends in the House of Commons; when jobs were at stake, the printing unions expected a Labour Prime Minister to lend a sympathetic ear. Hugh Cudlipp had learnt early in 1969 that any amalgamation of the *Sun* and the *Daily Mirror* would not go through because of union opposition. In some of these matters Murdoch could draw on the wisdom of Lord (Arnold) Goodman, the senior partner of Goodman, Derrick and Co, whom he had engaged as solicitors. As a director of Observer Holdings and the Observer Trust, and about to become Chairman of the Newspaper Proprietors Association, Goodman was familiar with the world Murdoch had entered. He moved just as easily in the higher reaches of politics. Though he sat with the Liberals in the Lords, Goodman was trusted by Wilson, who had bestowed the barony on him in 1964 and used Goodman, Derrick and Co for his personal legal work. With all that, Wilson came to lunch at Bouverie Street three or four times between November 1969 and the general election of 1970. Flanked by Larry Lamb, Murdoch could not be more cordial.

Over those months, Wilson became more and more confident of a victory. A series of by-elections pointed to a gradual decline in anti-government feeling, and on 18 May, a general election for exactly a month later was announced. Before Murdoch had owned them, the *News of the World* did not take editorial stands at elections and the *Sun* inevitably supported Labour. Murdoch waited until 17 June, when he devoted two columns of the *Sun*'s front page and half of the second page to explain 'Why it must be Labour':

In the past few weeks the *Sun* has kept its promise to bring you all the election news.

Our coverage has been, as we promised, detailed, analytical and non-partisan.

We also promised that we would tell you, when the time came, which way the *Sun* would vote.

THE TIME HAS COME, AND THE *SUN* WOULD VOTE LABOUR.

The editorial explained that Wilson had a better team, that cared more about ordinary people, social justice, equality of opportunity and the quality of living – things the *Sun* also cared about. It rejected the Conservative appeal to 'law and order', and said that immigration, which Enoch Powell and his followers wanted to restrict further, should not have been made an issue. Neither Party was sufficiently aroused by environmental matters or industrial pollution.

The night after the votes had been cast, the *Sun* believed it was on the winning side. Accepting the piece of folklore that, under the British voluntary system, Labour supporters need an inducement to turn up, it explained on the next morning's front page: 'Hot sunny weather brought a rush to the polls yesterday and made the outlook bright for Harold Wilson'. But the sun above shone down impartially: the Conservative vote exceeded the Labour vote by nearly a million, and another two million voted Liberal. With 330 votes in the House of Commons, Edward Heath led a comfortable Conservative majority against 267 Labour members, six Liberals and six others. The *Sun* was ready to give him advice: 'And now Ted, Take Charge', it counselled on 19 June. 'Well done, Ted Heath. The British love to see an outsider come surging up to pass the favourite.' Who were the baddies? Why, the pollsters who predicted a victory for Wilson: 'The election has been a rebuff to the opinion polls. That's good for democracy anyway.'

The *Sun*'s political flexibility did not harm its sales. Though the *Daily Mirror* was the main rival in the long term buyers were coming over from the *Daily Sketch*, a tabloid stable-mate of the *Daily Mail*, from the *Mail* itself and from the *Daily Express*. At the time Murdoch took over, the *Sun*'s sales were around a million copies; in December 1969 Tom Baistow had reported that the *Sun* was putting its circulation gains at 450,000, of which only 150,000 came from the *Daily Mirror*. Early in March Murdoch told Cecil King that the *Sun*'s circulation was about to reach 1.5 million, of which 300,000 came from the *Mirror* and 80,000 from the *Sketch*.[5] The circulation average for the half year to June showed a more complex picture: the *Express* lost about 125,000, the *Mail* 43,000; the *Sun* exceeded 1.5 million, the *Mirror* was just under 4.7 million.

Associated Newspapers, whose proprietors had welcomed Murdoch to London, felt the *Sun*'s heat most strongly. Harmsworth Newspapers, the group's London operation, was publishing three dailies, the *Mail*, the *Sketch* and the *Evening News* and the once-a-week *Weekend*, and was losing money. The *Sketch* with a circulation of 764,000 at the end of 1970, had been kept going because it shared the *Evening News*' plant, and could thus spread overheads, and because it had been hoped that the *Sun* would close. But the *Sun* was racing ahead, averaging 1.72 million in the second half of 1970, while the *Mail* itself lost another 100,000. In March 1971 Harmsworth Newspapers called in the unions and told them the *Sketch* and the *Mail* would merge in May when the *Mail* would become a tabloid. That half year, the *Sun* passed the two million mark.

A private loss offset the corporate gains. In mid-December 1969 Anna and Rupert Murdoch went for a holiday to Australia, leaving the firm's Rolls Royce with Alick McKay, the Australian-born deputy chairman of NOTW. A man enquired at the Greater London Council after the ownership of the car, tried to obtain the name of the person running it and apparently traced it to the McKays' home by following it. On 29 December McKay came home and found the place in disarray and his wife Muriel missing. Shortly after, he received calls purporting to be from 'M3, the Mafia', followed by ransom notes demanding a million pounds. Muriel McKay was not found, alive or dead, and two brothers, Arthur and Nizam Hosein who originated in Trinidad, were charged on counts of kidnapping, murder and other serious offences. Before the arrests, a distressed McKay had sought the help of the media as well as of the police; during the search, and the accompanying speculation, wide credence was given to a presumption that the kidnappers had wanted to abduct Anna Murdoch, not Muriel McKay, and hence asked for a huge sum. In summing up at the trial, Mr Justice Shaw commented that the person normally using the Rolls was Rupert Murdoch: 'To the outside world a man of great substance, just the sort of man whose pocket is long enough to enable him to pay a substantial ransom if his wife were held hostage'.[6] The abduction of Muriel McKay was the beginning of Anna Murdoch's disenchantment with Great Britain. An incident at the trial that aroused less attention also influenced Rupert Murdoch's convictions.

After the jury found the Hosein brothers guilty on all counts, Arthur Hosein exercised his right to make a speech from the dock. He alleged that injustice had been done: 'The provocation of your Lordship has shown immense partiality. To his Lordship I would say that, from the moment I mentioned Robert Maxwell, I knew you were a Jew.' Maxwell had been introduced in a weird part of Hosein's evidence. Maxwell was not in fact Jewish, but an anti-Nazi Czech who had fled his country and joined the British Army. By referring to Maxwell's original name – 'Jan Hoch' – the *News of the World*'s 'Yorkshire pudding' editorial might have created that impression in Hosein's mind. Mr Justice Shaw, on the other hand, *was* Jewish. 'Not that I am anti-Jewish myself,' Hosein added, in a near-parody of a common saying.[7]

The kidnapping strengthened Murdoch's proclivity for keeping information about his family and his places of residence to a small circle: he now had a justification, the exposure to kidnappers. Hosein's paranoic speech confirmed him in his suspicion of anti-semites; people of that ilk were capable of anything. He became indiscriminately pro-Israel, though not much wiser about anti-semitism.

II

Raised, and still rising, in Australia, Murdoch took it that a direct road led from newspapers to television. In Australia anyone can legally buy a news-paper, but foreigners are kept from the control of television stations by law. In Britain, as in Australia, the place of outsiders in Fleet Street was not chal-lenged: the Astors came from New York, Beaverbrook and Thomson from Canada; they had taken titles and were absorbed. The position in commercial television, initially a licence to print money, was less straightforward. The transmitters were owned by the Independent Television Authority (ITA), which let six-year contracts; the contractors produced programmes and sold advertising time. The ITA was empowered to terminate contracts at any time, a power intended less to be exercised and more to provide influence over programming, personnel, and changes in ownership.

The Act operating in 1969 was vague about who should be debarred from being a contractor. It defined one type of disqualified person as 'an indi-vidual . . . not ordinarily resident in the United Kingdom, the Isle of Man and the Channel Islands, or being a body corporate, is incorporated under the laws of any country outside the United Kingdom, the Isle of Man and the Channel Islands'. Other parts adverted to newspaper ownership of con-tractors and said that, if this kind of connection was not 'in the public inter-est', the ITA could use the power to terminate contracts. The long debates in the Commons and the Lords preceding the passage of the amended Act of 1964 suggest that compromises were reached to leave Thomson, whose ultimate holding company was located in Canada, in control and to allow other Fleet Street investors to keep what they had. It now provided a loo-phole for Murdoch; whatever his personal status, NOTW was clearly resi-dent in the United Kingdom.

The question of Murdoch's right to enter British television was tersely settled by a written reply given on 15 February 1971 by Christopher Chat-away, the Minister for Posts and Telecommunications in the Heath Cabinet. Chataway was asked whether he would seek assurances from the ITA that no change in London Weekend Television's shareholding had taken place which may enable the Authority to take action under Section 11(4) of the Act. Chataway answered 'The ITA tells me that, after careful consideration, it decided not to take action'.[8]

Murdoch was in, seemingly to stay, and he promptly used his well-exercised muscle. Two days later, he obtained the agreement of his fellow directors to the dismissal of Tom Margerison, the managing director of London Weekend Television (LWT).[9]

Since mid-1968, two contractors had been transmitting to the London region. For most of the week Thames Television, whose major shareholder was the electronics company EMI, exercised this privilege. From Friday to Sunday night it was LWT, whose voting shares were more widely dispersed. Thames Television had a number of advantages; LWT's only night for big audiences was Saturday. As a result, LWT's balance sheet for 1969–70 showed a loss.

Before the tell-tale figures appeared on the bottom line, some of LWT's directors had started to talk to Thames Television, to explore a merger or some other form of cooperation. The ITA had deliberately split the region into two by having two contractors and was not likely to give its agreement. In May 1969 Tom Margerison chanced to meet Rupert Murdoch at an award-giving function and, shortly after, suggested to him the possibility of investing in LWT. Margerison's colleagues were beginning to disagree about how to divide up the budget and he was looking for allies. By autumn the split reached the Board level, with disputing executives speaking through outside directors, who consequently disagreed with each other. The squabbling was too much for Arnold Weinstock, one of the outside directors, head of the General Electric Company and holder of 7.5 percent of the voting shares. Weinstock sold his parcel. Murdoch, who bought it, with the approval of the ITA, shopped around for non-voting shares, which constituted the overwhelming bulk of the issued capital and, in succession to Weinstock, became a non-executive director, a position that gave him a quick, first-hand view of LWT.

To be an investor and non-executive director was not good enough for Murdoch. Three weeks after ITA's first approving nod, he told some of his fellow directors that LWT was undercapitalised and that he was willing to inject £stg500,000 in order to overcome this problem. A share issue by LWT could raise this money; his sole condition was that he would attend meetings of LWT's executive committee. A kite was flown through two Sunday papers to test public reaction. The full Board of LWT then made a counter-proposal: it would issue one new share for each existing three, and if present holders did not take up the issue, NOTW would be free to do so.

LWT's history favoured Murdoch. It had not been floated on the stock market; a good deal of the non-voting stock was in the hands of executive directors and senior staff who had bought it with the help of bank loans on which they were paying interest without receiving a compensating dividend. After Aidan Crawley, the chairman, and Tom Margerison assured the ITA that Murdoch would not become an executive director and that no major sackings were planned, the ITA agreed to the issue. NOTW then controlled between 30 and 35 percent of the non-voting stock.

Executive director or not, Murdoch sat on the executive committee where he promptly suggested new programme schedules. When the ITA heard of this its eyebrows were raised. Tom Margerison resisted Murdoch, but after Chataway's nod in Murdoch's direction, Murdoch felt free to dismiss the managing director, and without further ado took off for Sydney to launch the *Sunday Australian*. He left behind a press release saying that he would henceforth chair the executive committee – in other words, choose the programmes. This was the second-last straw for the ITA; the last was a succession of calls from the heads of other programme contractors, such as Lew Grade and Sidney Bernstein, who said that the ITA was becoming a laughing stock. After a two-and-a-half-hour plenary session on 25 February, the ITA issued three demands which LWT was to meet within six weeks: programme plans were to be submitted for approval; a managing director and a programme controller were to be appointed, subject to ITA scrutiny; and the next managing director's name would not be Rupert Murdoch.

Interviewed in Sydney by the Australian correspondent of the *Times*, Murdoch agreed that the ITA had every right to cancel LWT's franchise if it did not live up to its intentions. He disagreed about the need for ITA approval for programmes: 'What do you have to have a managing director for?' He declared that LWT's morale had already improved; it had better leadership. From whom? 'No one has got any doubts that I might be a success.' The troubles at LWT were 'all a bloody storm in a teacup'.[10]

It was vintage South Australian red, too strong for British tables. A few days later, David Frost phoned from London. Frost, a co-founder of LWT, held 5 percent of the voting shares and ran the LWT public affairs programme on which he had bruised Murdoch six months earlier. He had been in the United States during the fracas, when it was rumoured that the axe might be put to his programme. He now had a proposition of common interest to put to Murdoch: LWT needed a new face, an executive chairman with public standing and television experience. His nominee was John Freeman, famous as an interviewer some years earlier, a past editor of the *New Statesman* and a Wilson appointee to the High Commission in New Delhi and the embassy in Washington. Murdoch at once made enquiries, encouraged Frost to make contact with Freeman, and rapidly returned to London for discussions with the proposed appointee. When the choice was publicly confirmed, the diplomatic Freeman said that he had only got to know Murdoch well in the last three days: 'I like him very much. He is a man of enormous flair in the field.'[11]

LWT started to show a profit in 1971-72 and continued to do so, at a rising rate, for most of the 1970s. Half way through, it became part of LWT (Holdings) Ltd, which made purchases in other areas, including Hutchinson, the book publishers. At the end of the decade LWT (Holdings) was not doing quite so well. The book publishing subsidiary was in the red and commercial television had been on strike for eleven weeks. News International, the renamed NOTW, sold out in March 1980, realising £stg4 million, a capital profit on 1970, though the figure was perhaps not quite as high a sum as it might have got a few years earlier. John Freeman remained chairman.

III

The *Sun*'s profits exceeded all expectations; its sales passed three million in 1973. The *News of the World* was not doing so well; that year, its sales fell below six million. Assisted by Larry Lamb, who presided over both papers as editorial director, Murdoch reached for the pep pills. And then was badly mauled again in the ensuing 'Lambton affair'.

Antony Claud Frederick Lambton, the fifty-one-year-old Member for Berwick-upon-Tweed, had a reputation for high living, including, so it transpired, occasional visits to one Norma Levy and her women friends, who provided unorthodox sex as a business enterprise. Lambton had been the eldest son of the Earl of Durham when he first entered the House of Commons and was then known by the courtesy title 'Lord Lambton'; to re-enter the Commons in 1970, he renounced his hereditary peerage, but continued to use the courtesy title, and this made him more of a potential object of press interest than he might otherwise have been. But his true undoing was the acceptance of the junior post of Parliamentary Under-Secretary for Defence (RAF) in the Heath Ministry. He answered questions on the Royal Air Force in lieu of Lord Carrington, the Minister for Defence who sat in the Lords, and this connection with national security was used by some newspapers to justify an invasion of his privacy with bugs and hidden cameras.

The *News of the World* initially handled the results of its scrutiny with a show of decorum. An article on 20 May 1973 said that the activities of political figures involved in vice were being reported to the Home Secretary, who in turn kept the Prime Minister informed. Two days later, Lambton resigned from the front bench for what he called 'personal and health reasons'. The next day *Stern*, a German weekly, alleged that a high-ranking British diplomat was involved in a prostitution scandal. Taking this blow on his chin, Lambton issued a statement conceding that he had 'a casual acquaintance with a call girl'. London police had told him that the woman's husband had taken photographs and sold them to the newspapers. The same day, the *Evening News* alleged that two men had tried to sell compromising pictures of Lambton, that the *News of the World* accepted the pictures without paying for them and that they were handed back after a desision 'at the highest level'; the *News of the World* had then called in the police. The silhouette of Rupert Murdoch was now visible in the background.

The *Times* took the matter further by reporting that two men had called on the *News of the World* to sell pictures and information about Lambton, and then quoted Larry Lamb as saying that the editor of the *News of the World* had rejected the pictures: 'There was nothing new in what they had to tell us. We started the story and had it buttoned up long before they came to the office. We do not buy this sort of thing anyway.'[12]

These reports were fuzzy and they fell short of reporting much of what had transpired. There were only two factual admissions: that the *News of the World* had started enquiries that led it to Lambton's female acquaintance; and that it had refused to pay the woman's husband for his assistance. These two admissions, however, were enough to shift the focus from Lambton to the *News of the World*.

Following Larry Lamb's statement, Edward Heath gave an outline of police actions to the Commons; and Lambton, going on television, charged that if newspapers were prepared to buy such material, they helped blackmailers. On the defensive now, the *News of the World* printed an account of its contacts the following Sunday. It had been in touch with Norma Levy and her husband Colin; 'relevant pictures' had been taken by the paper's own photographer. The contacts had begun when two men called at Bouverie Street with undeveloped film and a cheque in Lambton's handwriting. In a by-lined article, a reporter said the film was put in his custody, hidden and later turned over to the police. The *News of the World* also carried a picture of Norma Levy and two men, all clothed, lying on a bed. An editorial declared: 'This paper is not, never has been, and never will be, involved in blackmail.'[13] On the same day, the *Sunday People* reported that Norma Levy had spoken to its reporters from a hide-out. It printed a photograph of a teddy bear whose bugged nose had been connected to a tape-recorder, and another photograph showing Norma Levy's bedroom.

The *Times* at once seized on the phrase 'relevant pictures'. It again contacted Larry Lamb, to ask him whether his newspaper was in possession of pictures showing Lambton 'in compromising positions'. Lamb repeated that 'we' had pictures which were 'relevant' and had been taken by staff photographers. He was not prepared to say what they showed and could not explain the origin of the 'compromising pictures' to which his paper had referred.[14] The *Daily Express* had even less success when it asked questions of Rupert Murdoch.

A week later, the *News of the World* was a little more candid: 'Of course the *News of the World* took pictures of Lord Lambton in compromising situations. Were we supposed to have accepted the unsupported evidence of "pimps and prostitutes", as the *Daily Express* calls them. But these pictures were never published, nor were they intended for publication.'[15]

The course of events, as it emerged from later admissions of *News of the World* and reports by Lord Diplock and the Press Council, was this. The News of the World had begun a general inquiry into London vice, and received confirmation of Lambton's involvement from what it called an 'unimpeachable source' in March. On 9 April the Home Secretary was informed of police investigations and four days later a reporter tried unsuccessfully to interview Lambton. On 5 May Colin Levy, the husband, and an associate, Peter Goodsell, came to Bouverie Street and on 10 May the paper tried to make sure that the story was beyond challenge. Diplock expanded on these admissions. He reported that Colin Levy and Peter Goodsell had tried to cine-photograph Lambton in bed, but lacking the technical resources and skill, they sought help from the *News of the World*. In the days following their call, staff members of the paper installed a tape recorder and photographic equipment in the flat Lambton visited. On 9 May, Colin Levy recorded a conversation between Norma Levy and Lambton, and the next day a staff photographer took pictures of Norma Levy, another woman and Lambton in bed. Having decided not to buy the story, the *News of the World* handed the tape recording and, according to Diplock the negatives and prints, back to Levy. On this incident, Diplock issued a severe censure:

The action of the *News of the World* resulted in two men with criminal records being supplied with convincing evidence, which they previously lacked, of the involvement not only in sexual irregularities but also in criminal offences in connection with drugs of a junior Minister who had access to SECRET and TOP SECRET information of value to the intelligence services of a foreign power. These potential instruments of blackmail they handed over to Levy and his associates to whom it was therefore open to make what profit they could out of them.[16]

When Diplock's report appeared, the *News of the World* retorted that the pictures were not handed back to Levy, for the good reason that he never parted with them; and it complained that Diplock had no first-hand knowledge of the circumstances under which these issues had arisen and had not tried to learn by asking the paper to appear before him.

The Press Council had meanwhile instituted an inquiry into the coverage given to the Lambton affair by several papers, but waited till Diplock reported on the security aspect. Murdoch now had the chance to put forward what he would have said to Diplock if asked. He conceded that he had no defence to Diplock's charge. He *did* have an excuse: to get a degree of cooperation, the possibility of money had to be held out, but everybody on the paper was under instructions not to make a payment. His answer to the charge of creating a security risk was that police had been kept informed throughout. When working in this seamy area, he saw no alternative to getting photographs of Lambton; the pictures were taken as a matter of proof. In the paper's belief the police were dragging their feet; if events had not overtaken it, the paper would have taxed Lambton with the matter.

Making its findings under a code derived from prevailing Fleet Street practices, the Press Council accepted that the *News of the World* had been in touch with the police throughout, that it genuinely believed that the police were not diligent enough and that it was entitled to publish its allegations. The Press Council argued that if a serious public ill was to be exposed, then methods could be used not justified in a less serious case. The user of these methods employed them at the risk of his own reputation, 'and nothing but success is an acceptable excuse'. The *News of the World* acted indefensibly in leaving material in the hands of Colin Levy and Peter Goodsell and was therefore 'severely censured'.[17]

Lord Diplock's job was to look into security aspects; there was no need for the Press Council to take them up. But the Council failed to answer a number of questions that had been asked quite early in the controversy. The *New Statesman,* for instance, had asked whether a paper was entitled to invade Lambton's privacy just because it kept the police informed; in its opinion, privacy urgently awaited legislative action.[18] And what of Lamb's and Murdoch's endorsement of the permissive society, set out in the first week of the new *Sun?* Consistent with it, they should not object if Lambton's conduct was different from their own; the only question deserving investigation was whether Lambton's conduct endangered national security. The police, said to be dragging their feet, had reported on Lambton to the Home Secretary: had he dismissed the possibility of a threat to security? If not, had he warned

Lambton? The *News of the World* did not pursue these questions; what then was it investigating? Was the paper, the Press Council might have asked, pursuing a seamy story which it felt entitled to publish just because one of the characters was a junior minister and called 'Lord'?

The Press Council's report was not published till March 1974, but the part played by the *News of the World* brought Murdoch much private disapproval. Added to this distress was a road accident, in which a car driven by Anna Murdoch knocked down an elderly woman; a coronial inquiry found that the death was accidental, but even the minimal publicity dismayed her. Sensitive to these events, Arnold Goodman asked Harold and Mary Wilson to have dinner with the Murdochs, whom people were avoiding. Goodman hinted that Wilson should not accept unless he would really turn up. The dinner went off well, but it failed to reconcile the Australian couple to living permanently in London. After Rupert became committed to expanding into North America, Anna made it plain that she preferred New York.

IV

The worst recession since the war surfaced in the western industrial countries during 1974. The OPEC suppliers had trebled oil prices and Britain, importing most of its oil, was badly affected, running into a quadrupled trade deficit. Almost at once, coalminers went on strike to get a share of the rising fuel price and the Heath Government countered by decreeing a three-day working week to meet the threatened energy shortage.

The new political and economic situation confused Murdoch, as the lesser Australian downturn had done in 1961. The confusion was all the deeper because British newspapers had entered into a crisis of their own. Between 1971 and 1973 the popular dailies had gained 36 percent in advertising revenue; in 1974-75 the gain was 8 percent, an effective loss after reckoning inflation. This was part of the recession; the major squeeze came from the rise in newsprint prices. With an index figure of 100 for 1970, newsprint in Britain rose to 188 in 1974 and 231 in 1975. World shortages accounted for some of the rise, the decline of the pound sterling for the rest. When British newspapers spoke of 'stagflation', they were able to draw on the experience of falling demand for advertising and rising costs of raw material.[19] The *Sun* added another half million to its circulation in 1974, but the profits of News International, the renamed NOTW, were less than half of those in 1973.

Economic growth was a constant article of Murdoch's faith. Neither the Conservatives nor the Labour Party now promised it and his papers floundered between them. He showed some initial sympathy for Wilson's plan to control prices and incomes, but union pressure for higher wages, which extended to Fleet Street, made him uneasy. The *News of the World*'s lead stories showed the confusion reigning in Fleet Street. The paper began the year with an attack on Heath for wanting to shut down television stations at 10.30 p.m. as part of his energy conservation measures: 'Today the *News of the World* has this message for Premier Heath', the front page announced on 6 January; it opposed the early closing time.[20] The next Sunday it told Harold Wilson that the Labour Party was too weak to restrain the unions.[21] On 7 February, still in conflict with the coalminers, Heath announced an election for 28 February, initiating the shortest campaign in forty years. Put to the political choice, the *News of the World* retreated to one of its more traditional front pages: 'My Terror/By the Bathtub/Killer's Mistress'. As a concession to politics, Heath, Wilson and the Liberal leader Jeremy Thorpe made statements on page two, and the Chancellor of the Exchequer, Anthony Barber, put the Conservative case on page four. An editorial complained of Heath's secrecy and Wilson's blank cheque to the unions.[22]

The next Sunday it had a biological bombshell: 'Phantom Babies Sensation': an investigation had revealed that women 'could have abortions without being pregnant'. The *Lancet* and other specialist journals did not follow this lead, perhaps because they realised that the *News of the World* had failed to distinguish curettes from terminations.[23] For close students of politics, however, there *was* something in that Sunday's issue. An editorial well inside bore the heading: 'Why we think it is to be Heath': a peril faced Britain, no less than in 1940; sacrifices on a wartime scale were needed. It rejected 'the pragmatic Mr Wilson, who trims his sails to every breeze' and supported Heath, who had the guts and strength to see it through.[24] Earlier in the week, the editorial had been cabled to New York for Murdoch's detailed approval, and Harold Wilson, who happened to get hold of a galley proof, anticipated that the *Sun* would go the same way.

Having tested the tide, Lamb and Murdoch jumped on board the Conservative ship on Wednesday. 'The Devil and the/Deep Blue Sea', said the *Sun* in two banner headlines. As a drawing on the left disclosed, the Devil was Wilson, sitting atop Nationalisation, Unions and Taxation; on the right was Heath, astride an outmoded boat, with a sailor's cap and an ancient telescope. A caption explained: 'In spite of the record, Ted's Tories look the better bet.' Some of the phrases and most of the arguments of the *News of the World* were reiterated in a long editorial.[25]

The winter weather did not deter voters from turning out: 78.2 percent of those eligible went to the ballot boxes, compared to 72 percent in the summer of 1970. In a House of Commons enlarged to 635, Labour won 301 seats, the Conservatives 296 (though more voters supported them than Labour), the Liberals 14 and others 23. To continue in office, the Conservatives needed the support of the Liberals, who refused the terms offered to them, and on 5 March Wilson formed a minority Government. Those who bet on Heath had lost their money.

After several defeats on the floor of the House, Wilson called another election for 10 October. Notwithstanding their flexibility, the *Sun* and the *News of the World* had not backed the winner since Murdoch took over. This time they placed no bets. Two days before the poll, the *Sun* announced down a column of the first page: 'We're /SICK/OF THE/TED AND/HAROLD/ SHOW!/See/Page/Two.' There it explained that neither Heath nor Wilson would do: 'THE ISSUE ON THURSDAY IS QUITE SIMPLY ONE OF SURVIVAL. ALREADY THE VULTURES ARE DARKENING THE SKIES'. It advised readers to vote for the best candidates.[26]

This time Labour attracted a million more votes than the Conservatives; the Liberals lost 650,000 supporters and the votes cast for the remainder were up. Labour now had 319 seats, the Conservatives 276, the Liberals 13 and the others 27. Wilson was there to stay for another four years; the *Sun*'s circulation would continue to go up, that of the *News of the World* down, and the joint profits would be better than ever. Rupert Murdoch himself would spend a great deal of time beyond the vultures' reach.

JANUARY 17, 1977

TIME

Rupert
Murdoch

New York

New York Post

THE INTERNATIONAL NEW
News
January 17, 1977
THE DAILY
Splash
PRESS

STRALIA ... 60c   NEW CALEDONIA ... FR 180
PAPUA NEW GUINEA

Chaper Nine

/// *Give Me Your Poor* ///

He had been exploring the United States for some years. To begin with, he merely followed up opportunities as they arose; but the American scene was too complex to take in at a glance and he set about establishing a bridgehead in a systematic way, making contacts and buying knowledge. His British success paved the way; he could now borrow in sizeable slabs.

The first casual opportunity was *Look*, put on sale by Cowles Communications in 1970. Murdoch sent an executive from Sydney to New York for six weeks, to see if the losses could be turned round. Like other illustrated magazines, *Look* tried to match the audience sizes of national television programmes to attract advertising. It sold subscriptions at half the production cost of the magazine and then tried to sell space at high rates. They turned out to be too high and the advertisers stayed with television. Like everyone else who knocked on the door, Murdoch went away and *Look* closed in October 1971. In the course of looking, he noticed that *Life* had similar problems; its losses were sending down the market price of Time Inc., its owners. If he could get control, which would not be easy, he would shut down *Life* and raise profits. It would be a massive gulp, and before Murdoch could do more than ruminate over the prospect, Time Inc. put an end to *Life* and overnight restored the vitality of its stock.

Getting a start in daily newspapers would be much harder. Though there were over 1700 of them and 250 had circulations over 50,000, there were plenty of buyers and they had pushed up prices. In 1970, Times-Mirror, the owners of the *Los Angeles Times*, had paid twenty-four times the annual pre-tax earnings for *Newsday*, published on Long Island beyond the New York metropolitan limits. The purchase price became a benchmark around which

151

buyers and sellers bargained for profitable papers with prospects of improvement. The buyers, typically, were existing chains who brought better management to their acquisitions and spread the costs of their Washington bureaus, columnists and other services over the members of the chain.

The spectacular closures of the pictorial magazines made that side of the publishing business even more fluid. Between the end of the war and 1970, the number of magazine titles had risen from 6500 to 9500. The majority were highly specialised, by trade, hobby, city or state; some had captured the national market riding on the crest of a wave, with no more than an idea and a line of credit to start with. In this fluid situation, Murdoch could buy a weekly, or start one of his own.

His eyes dwelt longest on the *National Enquirer*, a newsless tabloid equiva- lent of the *News of the World*. It was owned by Generoso Pope jnr, the son of an Italian-language publisher in New Jersey. Gene Pope had taken an engin- eering degree at MIT, worked for the psychological warfare section of the CIA, and bought the *National Enquirer* in 1952. Having pushed its super- market sales, with a fare of crime and celebrity stories, to a million, Pope began to think of higher things. He went through the backnumbers of the *Reader's Digest*, decided that health and nutrition, psychic phenomena and government waste had a wide appeal and moved his headquarters from New Jersey to Lantana, Florida, in 1971. By early 1974, backed by several hundred representatives who stacked the papers at supermarket checkouts, Pope was selling close to four million copies a week, which grossed him around $US50 million a year. In an elaborate fencing match spread over eighteen months, Murdoch tried to persuade Pope to sell the *National Enquirer*. Murdoch's first offer was considered derisory by Pope and Pope's selling figure was thought sky-high by Murdoch, as it was probably intended to be. Murdoch therefore went it alone with a paper directly competing on Pope's ground. The printing would be contracted out; apart from the run- ning losses, the only initial investment would be a large promotion on tele- vision.

The plans for the supermarket weekly were well advanced when a daily newspaper property, the Express Publishing Co. of San Antonio in southern Texas, came on the market. Harte-Hanks Communications, a middle-sized chain chiefly operating in the south, had bought Express Publishing from a local family in the 1960s. It had made few changes to the three papers – the morning *Express* (approximate sales 80,000), the evening *San Antonio News* (approximate sales 63,000) and a joint Sunday paper (approximate sales 135,000). The *News* competed with the Hearst-owned evening *Light*, whose

sales averaged 135,000. Harte-Hanks drew an annual profit of $US1.2 mil-
lion from San Antonio and was willing to part with Express Publishing for
$US18 million, fifteen times the pre-tax earnings, a modest price by Ameri-
can standards, though high when measured by Murdoch's borrowing costs.
But if the earnings were to be tax-free, if the losses of the weekly Murdoch
was planning could be set off against the earnings in San Antonio, then the
buy was attractive.

Murdoch came, bid and bought. Anna and he were in the *Express* building
to announce the purchase to the wire services on 25 October 1973. He
redesigned the lay-out of the evening paper and insisted on snappy headlines. It turned out to be his best deal in the United States. By 1976 the
circulation of the *News* was up to 76,000 and though that of the *Express*
declined a little, the joint circulation of the two exceeded that of the *Light*.
San Antonio was exactly the sort of place which fitted his newspaper style;
its citizens liked to be shocked in a gentle way. The *New York Times* summarised local reaction by saying: 'Mr Murdoch has raised circulations as well as
the ire of local civic leaders.'[1] If they had realised the concessions Murdoch
was making to local susceptibilities, they would have been more forgiving.
The *News*, for instance used 'bare' as a verb, as in 'Teacher Sex Try Bared' or
'Bizarre Cult Rituals Bared', and not as an adjective, as his papers did elsewhere; and its revelations were, from a transnational perspective, on the
mild side: 'Armies of Insects Marching on SA', 'Nightcrawlers Drive Town
Nuts' and 'Uncle Tortures Pets With Hot Fork'.[2] The banner 'Killer Bees
Move North' secured a niche in the museum of non-events.

After that first announcement, Anna and Rupert Murdoch saw little of San
Antonio. The *National Star*, named to compete directly with Pope's *National
Enquirer*, went out on 4 February and absorbed much of his energies that year.
He hired Hill and Knowlton to handle his public relations and held a press
conference in New York, to which he brought much of the abrasiveness he
first displayed at Geelong Grammar. America's papers were aimed at the rich
and powerful; not so the *National Star*: 'We are not interested in the publishing
judgements of Madison Avenue or professors of journalism,' he announced.[3]
The first print run was 1.2 million; he expected sales of 800,000. He would
spend five million dollars to promote the weekly on television and 40 percent
of supermarkets would carry it. Larry Lamb, who was with him, pointed out
that Murdoch had pioneered advertising for newspapers in Britain. The first
issue lured buyers with the headline 'Thousands Kneel to Miracle Boy
Michael', a Pope-like report on a faith-healer, and the centre-spread dealt with
killings in Detroit. By August Murdoch had shown the way far enough to
appoint an editor, James Brady.

The plans for selling and promoting the *National Star* had gone wrong. It was not nationally available until April, and then only 30 percent of super-markets carried it. In the second half of the year, television advertising was discontinued. Some years later, Marty Singerman, the circulation manager, admitted: 'The advertising budget at that time was too much for what it [the weekly] was doing.'⁴ Pope had carefully and gradually mapped out the terri-tory; to Murdoch it was unfamiliar and he failed to crash in. In mid-1976 he called off his direct challenge to Pope and redesigned the paper. The word 'National' was dropped from the name; the *Star* was given the subtitle 'The American Women's Weekly'. Contrary to an early announcement that advertising would not be sought, a forty-eight-page issue now carried up to sixteen pages of advertising and, in 1977, promotion on television began again. Available in the majority of supermarkets, it was heading for a circu-lation of three million.

Murdoch knew from the beginning that he had a great deal to learn about the United States. He had earlier done business with television people; he now had to find out what he could buy in the newspaper line, where he could borrow money and who was who. His first and most enduring adviser was Howard Squadron, a senior partner in a mid-Manhattan law firm. When Murdoch's group consulted him about the purchase of *Look*, Squadron had one other celebrity client, Bess Myerson, the vocal Commissioner for Con-sumer Affairs in New York City and, at the time, the only Jewish winner of the Miss America title (1945). Alert and competent, Squadron handled Myerson's divorce from her second husband, obtaining the exclusion of the media from the hearings and the suppression of the cause of action. Such achievements may not commend a lawyer to a media proprietor, but Murdoch saw beyond. Squadron was immersed in Jewish community poli-tics. Before beginning legal practice, he had worked for the American Jewish Congress, was still active in it, and later would become its first non-rabbinical president. These activities meant political contacts at all levels, from City Hall to the White House, Jewish and otherwise. Squadron's political know-how was invaluable.

On money, Murdoch sought advice elsewhere. For a time, he retained Eliot Janeway, an acquaintance of Cecil King. After a career that took in working for Henry Luce and Lyndon B. Johnson, Janeway was running an economic consultancy and writing a syndicated business column. He watched the media market and told Murdoch who was who in the financial world. On the banking side, Murdoch went to Allen and Co. Inc., where Stanley Shuman handled his transactions. Allen and Co. Inc. had been set up as an investment house by Allen and Co., the Wall Street partnership of the legendary Charlie Allen and his brother Herbert. Starting with little, the Allen brothers made it into the top dozen New York dealers and a fortune above $US100 million, with a Philippine goldmine bought for a song just before the Japanese invasion, with an investment in Syntex, the patentee of the active ingredient in the birth-control pill in the 1950s, and with holdings in Columbia Pictures in the 1970s. Allen and Co. Inc. are renowned for a discretion bordering on secrecy, and this has brought them clients such as the late Shah of Iran as well as Rupert Murdoch. The association continues; Allen and Co. Inc. have taken a small position in News Corporation and Stanley Shuman is now on its Board.

Murdoch also cultivated his fellow publishers, who were curious about the man that had had so successful a run in London. From the time he started the *Australian*, he had been in contact with the Washington Post Company, buying the news service it sold in conjunction with the *Los Angeles Times*. When Katharine Graham, its head, came to Australia in March 1973, he put himself out to provide a big welcome. The Summit, a revolving restaurant atop a tall building in Sydney, was taken over for a night and a galaxy of politicians, publishers and business executives invited to dinner. Late that year, he spent a weekend at Glen Welby, Graham's property in Virginia, and there he met Clay Felker, the founder of the magazine *New York*.

Murdoch has a particularly winning way with women older than himself: he used it to the utmost with Dorothy Schiff of the *New York Post*. He first tried to take her to lunch in the early 1970s, calling her office on South Street, but she was out of town, and he lunched with Mortimer Hall, her son, instead. When he was established in the United States a couple of years later, he succeeded in taking her to dinner; she found him 'disarming'.

Without anyone realising it, Murdoch was assembling the cast for his first off-Broadway season; and, contrary to his own plans, it opened in two separate theatres, with two distinct scripts.

II

As she moved into the eighth decade of her life, Dorothy Schiff was more than ever a woman of great resourcefulness. She had shed two psycho-analysts, three surnames, four husbands and five rival dailies. She was the publisher of New York's only evening paper, competing with two very different morning papers. At times, she would seem quite detached from her venture; she stayed in her penthouse on East 69th Street, had editorials read to her over the phone, and occasionally received journalists whom she seated under her crayon Picasso to discuss possible columns. At other times she would descend on South Street to discuss financial details, down to the out-of-town expenses of a reporter, or to take a call from Washington. Though few had met her, the staff all called her 'Dolly'. She got on better with some of the union officials than with her fellow publishers, whose association she had quit. The *Post* had become predictable, but she was not. When the paper began to show a small loss and was likely to continue as a marginal proposition, she found a buyer willing to part with over $US30 million. She then had the good sense not to boast about her shrewdness and to let Rupert Murdoch do the talking.[5]

Looking through the *Post* over the thirty-seven years Dolly Schiff owned it is like reading an immense Jewish novel – with a difference: the heroine has long been out of the ghetto, takes her distance from Zionism and the synagogue, rubs shoulders with the Roosevelts. But in its indignation and in its sentimentality, its advice on human relations and its gossip, those pages have the unmistakable flavour of New York Jewry. And at no time more so than in the 1950s, when the *Post* fought the battles of the liberal Democrats in retreat. Jack Newfield, a radical of the 1960s, looked back to the *Post* of that time as his 'warm, humanitarian Jewish mother ... I learnt to hate Joe McCarthy and revere Eleanor Roosevelt'.[6]

Her inherited wealth gave Dolly Schiff some of her staying power. 'Grandpa' Jacob Schiff was the biggest of the German-Jewish bankers that established themselves in New York in the late nineteenth century. He married a Loeb, took Kuhn Loeb and Co. into railroads, buying into them, lending them money, selling their paper. He died in 1921, leaving a mere $US40 million: the greater part of his fortune had gone into setting up Jewish charities and educational institutions. His son Mortimer married the daughter of another banker and left $US31 million in the depths of the Depression, an inheritance divided between John Schiff, who stayed in the investment house, and Dolly. The other source of Dolly's durability was her readiness to defy the family's traditions. When her mother stopped her from going beyond the first year at Bryn Mawr, she took a correspondence course; an Episcopalian bishop officiated at her first marriage; and while her grandfather and father were Republicans, as a matter of class, she became a New Dealer, was a regular guest at Hyde Park, Franklin D. Roosevelt's weekend place, and at his suggestion bought the *Post* in 1939. The paper had been, and continued to be, one of the few dailies to support the President. Her second husband, George Backer, had headed the newspaper company for the first three years but in 1942 she took over and the following year she married the executive editor, Ted Thackrey. Their disagreements over the 1948 presidential elections were argued out in the *Post*'s columns, and when they split up in 1949, she resumed the name Schiff.

She stamped her personality firmly on the paper in the next decade. After publishing an expose on Joe McCarthy, James Wechsler, the editor, was hauled before McCarthy's Senate sub-Committee and questioned about his youthful involvement with a Communist organisation. Wechsler had volunteered this information to a Congressional investigator, in order to clear a government official falsely accused of belonging to the same group. McCarthy's subpoena smacked of intimidation of the press, and Wechsler's supporters saw the incident that way.[7] Dolly Schiff was not intimidated; she soon hired Eleanor Roosevelt as a columnist and tried to send her to Peking. She also wrote a column, based on interviews: one of her scoops was a meeting with Frank Costello, a leading figure in organised crime, another a conversation with Albert Einstein about Israel.

Despite her exploits, the *Post*'s circulation fell below 300,000, and she then gave it a more popular turn. She moved Wechsler to the editorial pages, put the news-minded Paul Sann in charge, and ran murders on the front page. She stayed in business, and in 1967 the last of her evening rivals, the *World-Journal-Tribune* (a merger of the *World-Telegram*, the *Journal-American* and the *Herald-Tribune*) closed its doors. The *Post*'s circulation then jumped from 400,000 to 700,000. She needed more space for printing and bought the building of the former *Journal-American* in South Street from the Hearst group. In the early 1970s the *Post*'s circulation hovered around 600,000, but fell below that mark in 1974, and after she put the price up to 25 cents to meet costs, the half-yearly average went down to 489,000 in 1976. The city's two morning papers, the *Daily News* (around 1.9 million) and the *New York Times*, were also in decline, but they were getting the bulk of the advertising, at least 80 percent of the lineage and 90 percent of the dollars.

Selling a family business, when you don't have to, is a slow process. Dolly Schiff spent the summer of 1974 with her daughter Sarah Ann Kramarsky on Long Island. The Murdochs had taken a house in East Hampton; she met them three or four times at Clay Felker's place. Murdoch talked about money, power, and about what a poor newspaper the *New York Times* was. His talk was balm to Schiff, and to Felker, whom the *Times* professed to despise for his slickness. Murdoch had ambitions beyond San Antonio and the *National Star*, and in the second half of 1975 he came clean and asked whether the *Post* was for sale. Schiff wasn't ready; the next spring she appointed two of her offspring to company positions. Murdoch was not put off, and after the summer he raised the subject again; they negotiated and on 19 November signed a letter of intent, leaving the exact price to be determined till Murdoch had studied the books. In fact the loss for 1976 was over half a million dollars. Both of them made reassuring statements to the *Post*. Schiff: 'Rupert Murdoch is a man of strong commitment to the spirit of independent, progressive journalism. I am confident he will carry on vigorously in the tradition I value'. Murdoch: 'The *Post* will continue to serve New York and New Yorkers and maintain the present policies and traditions'.[8] Both rang Clay Felker to tell him they had met before he reintroduced them.

The night the letter was signed Murdoch went to the '21', a bistro where political and business people wheel and deal, to celebrate with some of his executives; Anna had gone back to London to furnish a new flat, in the expectation that they would divide their time between the *Post* and yet another paper Rupert was about to buy in Britain. There was every reason for his high spirits. He had prevailed on Dolly Schiff to endorse Jimmy Carter before she sold to him, as his Texan papers had done after he met the Georgian candidate on a plane. The *Star* was approaching profitability, and if the *Post* made a loss for another year or two, it could be offset against the *Star*'s profits.

The next day, there was more talking to do. The *Times* had already billed him as merely a 'brash millionaire'; he would now repair that deprecatory view. He explained that he and his family had been full-time New Yorkers for three years; when he took over, the *Post* would retain its format and its 'political policies', but the writing would be tighter, there would be more photographs, more stories. He would be very competitive and strengthen the circulation. Schiff too was expansive. Her lawyers had prompted her to sell because of the impending changes in the federal tax system that would make it prohibitive to pass the paper on to her children. Rupert Murdoch and she had the same birthday, 11 March, and though she did not believe in astrology, she loved coincidences. On Saturday night Clay Felker gave a dinner for Murdoch at Elaine's restaurant; he brought Gail Sheehy, Shirley MacLaine, Felix Rohatyn, the investment banker, and Pete Hamill, a columnist on the *News*. Everybody talked about how the *Post* could be improved.

A graduate just out of journalism school could see some of the possible improvements. The *Post* carried over thirty columnists a week; it was short on news, taking its national cover from the *Washington Post-Los Angeles Times* service. It had nurtured some of New York's sharpest writers, Pete Hamill included, and let them go elsewhere. It was sometimes inaccurate, even in tracing Rupert Murdoch's business career. Dolly Schiff worked with a tight budget; if Murdoch loosened the purse strings, he might improve the contents and perhaps also the circulation.

At the centre of media attention, Murdoch began to talk of his plans at length. In an interview with John Consoli of *Editor and Publisher*, he explained that even the *Star* often had stories, or angles on them, that the dailies missed; there was plenty the *Post* could do. He would not be putting colour into the paper, because the plant lacked that capacity, but he would not rule out a *Sunday Post*. To Robert Haupt, the Washington correspondent of the *Australian Financial Review*, he described the purchase as a tremendous opportunity; it was 'like having the *Sun* and the *Mirror* in Sydney in one newspaper – and New York is four times as big as Sydney ... it's mind-boggling'. With Alexander Cockburn of the *Village Voice*, controlled by Felker, he opened up. He would improve the authority of the *Post*'s writing on the arts and on finance, the women's section and the television coverage. These were the 'ribs' of the paper, which had to be fixed first. There were too many columns in the bloody paper; he couldn't read one of them, and another, to which Kissinger leaked, sucked up to the Washington establishment. The *Post* writers were too busy with essays about city government and neglected the courts. There was something wrong with the news-gathering: the *Star* had the story of Patty Hearst's release by her kidnappers ten hours before it appeared in the *Post*. A great many stories were around; for instance, Governor Carey had been carrying on at the '21' the other night. Murdoch's advice was 'Just doorstep Carey every night.' Murdoch also had words of wisdom for his rival, the *Daily News*: it should be 'violent and blood-and-guts'.[9]

At Allen and Co. Inc., Stanley Shuman put together the loans for the deal. One third came from an unsecured loan from the European-American Bank and Trust Company, part-owned by Murdoch's London bankers, the Midland Bank; another third came from London, where News International deposited a slightly higher sum against the loan advanced in New York; the last third came from Australia, where cash holdings, the sale of investments and borrowings provided the money. An important aspect of the arrangement was that News International in Britain and News Ltd in Australia should each take a half share and no more. 'In this way', Murdoch explained, 'a central bank in London or in Australia can't order you to pay dividends, since you don't have control stock. It means you can plow back the profits'.[10]

On 30 December 1976, having settled the exact sum to be paid to Dolly Schiff, he took control of the *Post*. The implementation of his ideas for improvement was postponed until he got another acquisition out of the way. The course it took made him appear something less than a warm, humanitarian, Jewish mother.

III

On the second Monday of January 1977 the editors of *Time* and *Newsweek* dropped their reluctance about giving events in the media too much prominence. The cover of *Time* showed King Kong with the face of Rupert Murdoch bestriding the rooftops of Manhattan: 'Extra!!! Aussie Press Lord Terrifies New York'. *Newsweek* mocked up the front page of an imaginary *Daily Splash*, with a picture of Murdoch: 'INSIDE: Aussie Tycoon's Amazing Story! – PRESS LORD TAKES CITY'. Murdoch's face was also due to appear on the front page of Clay Felker's knowing weekly *New York*, as part of a drawing of a killer bee by David Levine. This cover page was not sent to the printer. Murdoch was in control of the magazine before the deadline and edited it in person.

Felker did not quit without a fight. The winner Murdoch made the magazine covers; Felker had produced the dramatic scenes that reporters found irresistible. He was the city's spotter of trends, tastes, writers. He had created a new form of publication, the city magazine. In the media market, the sum of $US26 million ultimately paid by Murdoch for the New York Magazine Company was diminutive. Felker's trying to hang on and losing was the show worth watching, every minute of it.

The friendship had puzzled Felker's friends more than their falling out. Did Felker partly want to be a successful businessman like Murdoch? Did he expect to pick up a trick or two from the determined Australian who talked so freely about using 'OPM' – other people's money? Was he in need of another appreciative listener? Murdoch's cultivation of Felker was easier to understand. He was an outsider on the way into New York, as Felker had been. Felker retained a Balzacian gusto for what was what and who was who, from the boards of insurance corporations to the beds of mafia families. He developed these themes in *New York* and put the best early pieces between hard covers in *The Power Game*, for which he wrote an introduction. He had little patience with the typewriter, but he could talk for hours, taking in information or passing it out. Murdoch paid for such knowledge elsewhere; Felker gave it freely.

At fifty-one Felker still expected the best to happen. Since he had started the magazine, with a title bought from the closing *Herald-Tribune* eight years earlier, a great deal had come right. The son of two working journalists in Webster Grove (Missouri), he had gone to Duke University and then spent quite a time in magazines. He had passed through *Life* and *Esquire* to the *New York* Sunday insert of the *Herald-Tribune* and in its last months that insert had carried Tom Wolfe's excursions into 'oops-wow' journalism, established the persona of 'Adam Smith' on Wall Street for George Goodman, and started the 'Underground Gourmet' column. His severance pay had bought the rights to *New York*, a Wall Street friend raised finance, and the weekly magazine went out in 1968 in a lavish format designed by Milton Glaser. With its success, Felker raised his personal style: he bought a duplex apartment and dined out most nights. The New York Magazine Company itself was flush: it merged with the *Village Voice* in 1974 and, in 1976, on Felker's recommendation, started *New West* as a fortnightly equivalent in California.

The New York Magazine Company's stormy passage from Felker to Murdoch began on the evening of the celebration at Elaine's. On the way out Murdoch confided that he was about to fail in the purchase of the London *Observer*, and Felker, still being the genial host, opened up on difficulties of his own. His directors, who didn't understand publishing, were restive over the likelihood that there would be no profit, and therefore no dividends, at the end of the current year. A fortnightly, *New West*, had been launched in California, its success had pushed early costs beyond the agreed budget and the profits from *New York* would thus be swallowed. Murdoch was all attention. They had lunch eight days later, but Murdoch did not go beyond a casual hint that his commercial eye had turned to an acquisition of the magazine.

For some weeks, Felker's chairman Alan Patricof had already been taking soundings about selling a controlling interest. Patricof was a financier on the fringe of Wall Street, had helped to get initial backing and was now a minor stockholder. Felker himself held around 10 percent, was the chief executive and had an agreement with Carter Burden, the largest stockholder, which provided that Burden had to offer his block of 24 percent to Felker before selling it to anyone else. This agreement was made when Burden, a Vanderbilt heir and a City Councilman, agreed to a merger of the *Village Voice*, in which he had invested, with the New York Magazine Company in 1974. Accordingly Felker believed that he had a decisive voice in who could control the publications.

The day after the lunch between Murdoch and Felker, Stanley Shuman of Allen and Co. Inc. contacted Patricof to find out more about the company.

Murdoch, believing at that moment that Felker held the keys to control, phoned him in California and asked him to come to News America's offices on Third Avenue, the base of Murdoch's North American operations. There Shuman and Murdoch made a first offer on 9 December 1976. The company's stock units were being quoted at two dollars; they would pay five dollars. If Felker wanted *New West*, they would spin it off and let him have a third for a million dollars. Felker sparred and two days later gave a categorical refusal. Still thinking he was in control of the situation, he took the precaution of sounding out Katharine Graham, who promised that the Washington Post Company would help if bidding got under way.

Murdoch had to loosen Felker's lien on Burden's stock and to face the obstacle of New York State laws regulating bids for control over listed stock. According to that law the bidder had to stand in the market for thirty days, while counterbids could be made. The New York Magazine Company had a mere 1.6 million units on issue, and with so little stock around, a prolonged battle over control could send prices sky-high. There was, however, a standard way around the official bidding process, known as the 'creeping tender'. Instead of making an outright offer, the intending buyer could make oral agreements with sellers, until they had promised him enough stock to control the corporation. He would then call in the promises and offer to pay for the outstanding stock at the standard agreed price. Stanley Shuman now used his savvy of this procedure. He picked the largest stockholders on the list and offered to pay for their holdings at whatever rate Carter Burden was willing to part with his 24 percent.

The crucial figure in the moves that followed was Peter Tufo, Burden's lawyer, who had earlier drawn up the agreement between Felker and Burden and knew its provisions from beginning to end. They included an escape clause: if New York Magazine Company failed to make an aggregate profit over four successive quarters, Felker's right to first refusal of Burden's stock would lapse. The next quarter would end at midnight of 31 December 1976. On 17 December Tufo had dinner with Shuman and Murdoch. The right midnight hour had not yet struck; Tufo kept things going for two weeks without clinching a sale.

Still relying on his agreement, Felker went to Missouri to see his aging father. He was back in New York on the Monday morning after Christmas, when Burden came on the line from Idaho. His message was that formal negotiations for a stock sale were afoot: he had been offered seven dollars. Felker's right to have the first option had not lapsed, Burden was adhering to the letter of the agreement, and the next day, he gave the same information to the company's legal advisers. Felker now mobilised support. On 30

December Katharine Graham was in New York with Felix Rohatyn, her investment adviser. Rohatyn spent much of the day trying to speak to Tufo, and late in the afternoon succeeded in conveying to him Felker's offer for Burden's stock, with a back-up from the Washington Post Company who would bid for the rest of the units on issue. Following up, Rohatyn went to Tufo's office the next morning, but the offer was turned down. Katharine Graham then abandoned her bid and, with an announcement to that effect, the battle for *New York* began its media run the next morning.

Murdoch was out of New York on New Year's day. The day before, Shuman, back from a holiday in Florida, hired a chartered plane, put Tufo on board, collected Murdoch upstate and started for Sun Valley, over three thousand kilometres east, where Burden was skiing. Once midnight had struck, Burden was free to accept an offer for $US8.25 a unit, which grossed him around $US 3.4 million. The visitors went back east, Shuman tied up the remaining ends, and a signing party was held at Murdoch's Fifth Avenue apartment on the night of 2 January.

Felker had also moved. With a lawyer of his own, he spent most of New Year's day looking for a federal district court judge who could make out a temporary order restraining Burden from selling. He succeeded in the afternoon and, since it was Saturday, the judge said that a further hearing would take place some time the following week. On Monday, at eight in the morning, the Second Avenue offices of *New York* were packed with the writers on the two papers. Felker, who was closeted with his advisers, could not come and sent a statement that was read on his behalf: 'I intend to fight, and fight as hard as I can.' The writers debated an appropriate course of action. They did not want Murdoch as their boss, agreed to support Felker, and passed a resolution which they sent him: 'We suggest you do not meet with Murdoch.' Calling a news conference, they defined themselves as a 'talent package' that could not be bartered. From then on, television, radio and newspapers covered every move.

A meeting of the Board took place that evening. After the restraining order, Burden's stock was in legal limbo, but Murdoch came prepared. He had proxies for the stock pledged to him and could cast votes accordingly. Felker brought his customary supporters. Alan Patricof, himself an intending seller, presided; he began by removing two directors known to be on Felker's side and a successful motion seated Murdoch and Shuman in their places. After an hour and a half's debate, a waiting delegation of five journalists was called in and Byron Dobell, the managing editor, made a strong pitch on behalf of Felker; the other four agreed with him. In the debate across the table the directors traded phrases like 'fucking liar';

Murdoch stayed calm and called Felker the greatest editor in America. At one o'clock Murdoch emerged with Felker and his friend Milton Glaser and suggested that the three of them should work out something.

The writers also delegated Richard Reeves and Ken Auletta, two of their number, to mobilise opinion that might persuade Murdoch to back off. Auletta talked to Howard Squadron, telling him that if Murdoch persisted, there might be no writers for *New York* and *Village Voice*. 'You won't scare us, kid,' Squadron replied. 'He wants the publications.' The talent package met again on Thursday morning, and was joined by the non-writing staff. The meeting agreed that each person would make an individual choice; those not wanting to work for Murdoch would walk out. By noon the suite of offices was empty.

Felker spent Tuesday and much of Wednesday locked away, until the federal court ordered him to see Murdoch. He continued to be reluctant to do so. He had changed his advisers, engaging a firm specialising in corporate battles, and on Thursday morning he was warned about the no-profit loophole in the agreement with Burden: the Court might not continue the temporary restraining order. Accompanied by Glaser, Felker saw Murdoch at five that afternoon: they told him they simply wanted him to withdraw. Murdoch pleaded that he had just failed in London; he could not lose face a second time. They broke up. At midnight, Felker's new lawyer turned up at the duplex to announce that an acceptable settlement had been offered and advised acceptance of the offer before the next day's hearing. He also reminded Felker of the clause in his employment contract, which debarred him from taking a job at any other magazine in the states of New York, New Jersey, Cincinnati and California, or with a magazine in any other state if 50 percent of the circulation was sent across the state border. Once Murdoch had control of *New York*, Felker was effectively precluded from taking another job and a prolonged legal fight might cost around half a million dollars. On the other hand, Murdoch was offering to scale down the effects of the employment clause, buy Felker's 10 percent of the stock and give him time to repay a debt to the New York Magazine Company.

Murdoch too had a wakeful night. The deadline for sending the coming issue of *New York* to the printer was 6.30 am Friday. Some of the copy had disappeared, none of the staff was at work. Aided by executives from the *Post* and some of the Board of New York Magazine Company, he met the deadline. The next day he appointed James Brady, his choice as the first editor of the *National Star*, as editor of *New York* in Second Avenue.[11]

At five o'clock on Friday afternoon, Howard Squadron announced to the Court that agreement had been reached. Some of the staff went, others stayed. Felker spent a holiday in the Caribbean, with Gail Sheehy, pondering what to do next. He managed to persuade Associated Newspapers, one of Murdoch's London competitors, to take a stake in *Esquire* and became its editor.

Murdoch at once cut costs on *New York*, and left *Village Voice*, with its massive local advertising, largely alone. *New West* continued to make substantial losses and was sold on give-away terms in mid-1980. The buyers had made a success of *Texas Magazine*, an imitator of *New York* in the south. The nuances of good taste were not altogether Murdoch's forte.

NEW YORK POST

FRIDAY, AUGUST 19, 1977 25 CENTS

Vol. 176, No. 232

© 1977 The New York Post Corporation

DAILY PAID
CIRCULATION
2D QUARTER 1977
609,

FINAL
CLOSING MARKE

The Post endorses
Ed Koch for Mayor

Ed Koch can be the able, decisive Mayor New York City so desperately needs.

Koch has demonstrated in this campaign that he is the most likely candidate to tackle the tough problems confronting this troubled city.

He has displayed initiative and intelligence in an independent, aggressive effort to place himself and the issues before the public.

Koch has wisely made the stimulation and creation of jobs his

man has earned him a reputation for consistency and effectiveness

Many of the candidates are say-

issues confronting the city, although we question some of his priorities.

Mario Cuomo has displayed as a mediator and Secretary of State that he is an intelligent, thoughtful and highly moral person who might do much to ease the tensions in the city.

But Cuomo has not shown the toughness we think the job of Mayor demands. His campaign has vacillated, and with it his candi-

SAM
BAIL

NEW YORK POST
FINAL

SAM'S LAWYER WANTS OUT

Son of Sam's amazing letters
HOW I BECAME A MASS KILLER
BY DAVID BERKOWITZ

recommendations on homicide suspects while co
Continued on Pag

EXCL **IS' LIFE STORY**

g hillbilly • Page 19

Chapter Ten
___

/// *Post Mortems* ///

Before moving into Dolly Schiff's offices in South Street, Murdoch talked of one kind of *New York Post*; when he got there, he put out another. In the long interview with Alexander Cockburn, he described it as a Jewish middle-class paper; he wanted to broaden its appeal to get Italian, Irish and 'whoever else' readers.[1] He was neither Jewish, Irish, Italian, nor even middle-class; he was an Australian who had multiplied his millions at the lower end of Fleet Street. He would not delegate the job of reshaping the *Post* to anyone else and he published the kind of paper that was in his journalistic reach.

He pruned the *Post* and grafted onto it branches from the London *Daily Express* and the Sydney *Daily Mirror*. An early graft was on the sixth page, which carried a column in the manner of 'William Hickey' of the *Express*, and was simply called 'Page Six'. A cartoon by Paul Rigby, who was flown in from Sydney, was placed on top of the column. Under Rupert Murdoch as publisher and editor-in-chief, two personal assistants were appointed: Neal Travis from the *Mirror* and Peter Michelmore from the News Ltd bureau in New York. Ted Bolwell, an expatriate Australian on *Time* became titular editor and stayed till the middle of the year. Paul Sann, Schiff's executive editor, went into retirement at the end of January. The building was abuzz about the 'kangaroos'.

When Murdoch had come from Adelaide to Sydney, his favourite word was 'tinsel'. The early Murdoch *Post* was to glitter with the stuff. The paper adopted Farrah Fawcett-Majors, a star in the television show 'Charlie's Angels'. She was glad of any publicity she could get, for her contract was running out. In March, the *Post* devoted twenty-one items to her, but it owed her no debt for the circulation rise that followed. The Newhouse Newspaper Group was about to close down the *Long Island Press*, which sold 150,000 of

167

its run by home delivery in Queens, a borough within the City boundaries. The three metropolitan dailies and the island's *Newsday* all went after the readership about to be abandoned. Murdoch, with the biggest stake in a circulation rise, bought the delivery list, did a deal with the Deliverers' Union and sent out copies to the homes. The *Post*'s sales averaged 615,908 in the half-year to September 1977, up about 127,000 on twelve months earlier: the greater part of the rise stemmed from the list purchase.

Murdoch was still a long way from convincing advertisers that they should take space. The situation was very different from that in Sydney, though not in the 'mind-boggling' way he had enthused about. The two Sydney papers jointly sold more copies than the *Post*, in a city with 40 percent of New York's population, and were packed with advertising from grocery and appliance chains and from department stores. Sydney's retail trade was highly concentrated: three large grocery chains had a presence in most suburban centres; three or four departmental store names could be found at the four points of the compass. In New York the grocery trade was dispersed and the stores used the local free press. The big department stores put their messages in the morning papers to get their messages to Manhattanites or to commuters before they left home. Murdoch could make up for these differences only with a very large circulation. How was he to get it? In June 1977 he told a meeting of the Newspaper Publishers Association: 'What we are looking for is a special chemistry for each and all of our publications . . . the *New York Post* is only beginning to search for it'.[2]

Like an alchemist, he searched for the elixir in the dark. At 9.34 on 13 July 1977, the New York power supply failed; the cut lasted twenty-four hours. Drawing on its experience thirteen years earlier, the *Times* shifted its printing to New Jersey and continued publication; the *News* and *Post* did not appear for a day. On 15 July the *Post* came back with a 'Blackout Special' and headlines in letters bigger than New York had yet seen: '24 HOURS/OF TERROR'; a pull-out section inside the paper was captioned 'A City Ravaged'. The *Post* carried little information that was not already in the two morning papers; the difference lay in the hyperbole. This did not amuse Osborn Elliott, the Deputy Mayor for Economic Development and a former editor-in-chief of *Newsweek*, who instantly despatched a letter: 'So your *New York Post* has now covered New York City's first big crisis since you took over. Are you proud of what your headlines produced?' The *Post* had mentioned several thousand looters and arsonists; in Elliott's view, looting was limited and homicides were below average. The *Post* replied by accusing Elliott of being 'Os the ostrich'. Neither side gave numbers to resolve the argument. The only hard figure available was a rise of 75,000 on the *Post*'s usual Friday sales.[3]

The next chemical experiment was the coverage of a criminal psycho-path who killed, in all, six young people and injured another seven between 29 July 1976 and 31 July 1977. The crimes were committed with a .44 calibre weapon of a brand so common as to make it difficult to identify the weapon and thus trace the killer. In March 1977, when the toll was three dead and four injured, the investigators concluded that the crimes had all been committed by one man, whom they called 'Son of Sam', a tag that drew in the media. In April there were two more dead, with whom the killer left a note signed 'Son of Sam': a chain of messages between murderer and media was coming into being. The killer began to enjoy the attention. In June, Jimmy Breslin, a columnist on the *Daily News*, received a letter purporting to be from this man. After consulting the police, who found the fingerprints imperfect and hoped to draw more prints, Breslin published the letter and asked the writer to turn himself in. His advice was not taken: late that month, the .44 weapon claimed two more victims.

The letter to Breslin contained a passage indicating the killer's game. 'Tell me Jim, what will you have for July 29 . . . You must not forget Donna Lauria [his first victim] and you cannot let the people forget her either. She was a very sweet girl but Sam's a thirsty lad and he won't let me stop killing until he gets his fill of blood.' On 28 July Breslin reprinted part of the letter, and the next day his paper gave a great deal of space to the anniversary of the first killing. The *Post* was just catching up. It had no new information but, undeterred, it led off with the line 'GUNMAN SPARKS SON OF SAM CHASE'. It reported that a police officer had pursued a man who carried a gun and, in the second-last paragraph, told readers that, according to police, the man was definitely not 'Son of Sam'. The killer bees had come from San Antonio to sting New York readers.

'Son of Sam' killed another young woman and injured her escort on the night of 31 July. The next day, the *Post* headlined its report: 'NO ONE IS SAFE FROM SON OF SAM'. It continued to scratch for information, revealing on 4 August: 'MOBSTERS JOIN HUNT/Godfather orders: Get Sam'. It had pur-portedly learnt that Son of Sam was hurting the night trade at bars and discos owned by mafia connections and that Carmine Galante, a mafia chief-tain, sent out word that the criminal had to be found. On 6 August it noted that a plastic bag was under examination and that lovers' lanes were deserted. Two days later, it took off into fiction by serialising Lawrence Sanders' *First Deadly Sin*, explaining to its readers that 'Son of Sam' might have read this novel. The murderous villain of the novel was a publishing executive.

On the night of 10 August, a man called David Berkowitz was arrested, and identified by police as 'Son of Sam'; in the late morning of 11 August the *Post* ran the headline 'CAUGHT!' and sold a million copies. The next day one of the *Post's* photographers was arrested, along with three journalists work-ing for other papers, for breaking into Berkowitz's apartment. Berkowitz, though in the hands of the police, had no rest at the *Post*. On 15 August, the paper produced the best-remembered front page of the year: 'Son of Sam's amazing letters /HOW I BECAME A MASS KILLER/BY DAVID BERKOWITZ/THE MAN POLICE SAY IS SON OF SAM'. Below, and continuing inside the paper, were several letters Berkowitz had written in 1972. They were addressed to a young woman who had kept company with Berkowitz for fifteen months and, on the authority of the *Post's* reporter, had not been 'intimate' with him. Lacking the gift of prophecy, Berkowitz was not then able to reveal how he would become a mass killer; lacking the same gift, the *Post* paid $500 for the letters, not knowing that the *News*, having paid $200, would run them a few hours earlier, with different headlines. Some months later Murdoch told an interviewer from the monthly *More* that the headline 'How I became a mass killer . . .' was 'inaccurate and wrong, and I'm going to take the blame for it'. He had forgotten who wrote it, but he had approved it. He had asked himself whether the man would get a fair trial, and answered the question by saying that the *Post* had done no more than everybody else.[4]

Both the *News* and the *Post* had been criticised for their coverage even before Berkowitz was caught. The *New Yorker* wrote: 'By transforming what should be a quiet police operation into a political issue, the press has forced the Mayor and the Police Commissioner to reduce the day-to-day protection provided by the police around the city, in order to concentrate on the search for the murderer . . . It will make a fair trial of the killer nearly impossible'.[5] Jimmy Breslin replied in his column; for the *Post*, Robert Spitzler, a carry-over from the Schiff days, said: 'If it offends the delicate sensibilities of the Algonquin crowd [the Algonquin Hotel is frequented by *New Yorker* staff], so be it'.[6]

Murdoch was still raw about criticism when he spoke to *More's* inter-viewer: 'For God's sake, let's not get the British system'.[7] He meant the British law of contempt, not the British style of popular journalism. After the blackout, the *Post* had announced that Bolwell, the editor, was leaving. The Berkowitz episode had been dealt with by Rupert Murdoch himself; the Britisher Roger Wood, who once worked with the young Murdoch on the *Daily Express* and had been brought to the *Star*, now became editor. 'It's drama,' Wood explained to an Australian journalist on the *Post*, 'it's drama'.

II

It took Sir Keith Murdoch a decade from making a splash with crime to putting a Prime Minister into office; Rupert Murdoch, after practice else-where, moved on both matters at almost the same time. A new mayor would be chosen in the autumn of 1977, and in New York the Democratic primary, for which two million New Yorkers were on the register, was the decisive event. On 19 August, three weeks before the first run of the contest, Rupert Murdoch made known his decision: 'The *Post* endorses Ed Koch for Mayor', said the front page.

The choice of a mayor initially seemed of some importance to New Yorkers. New York City had been on the edge of bankruptcy in 1975 and was rescued by a series of federal loans that would fall due in 1978. The pre-carious financial position had much to do with fifteen years' mismanage-ment and the incumbent Mayor Abraham Beame effected little change. The next mayor, a Mr Clean, would need to inspire confidence in the renego-tiation of the loans; it would be of advantage if he also promised to be firm with City Hall's registered Democrat employees, whose numbers he might have to cut and whose salaries he might have to freeze. This would at least mean the appearance of a break with the local party bosses, who obtained City Hall jobs for their supporters and were friends of Beame.

The first Mr Clean to offer himself was Mario Cuomo, the non-elected Secretary of State in the New York State Government. Cuomo had the support of nationally influential Democrats such as Averell Harriman and the financial backing of Ed Carey, a brother of the State Governor. The next Mr Clean was Ed Koch, the Representative for Manhattan in Congress. Koch could point to a long liberal commitment: Americans for Democratic Action rated his voting record above 91 percent and the AFL-CIO scored him 91 percent for his pro-union stand. Koch projected flexibility. He told people that though his parents were Polish Jews, he personally got on better with conservatives than with liberals. He had two liabilities: all previous mayors had been men with families and he was a confirmed bachelor; and he had supported legislation to give gays equal employment opportunities on one occasion. As a Jewish candidate, he would have an edge in the Democratic primary, for 40 percent of registered Democrats were Jewish, compared with the 38 percent Irish and Italian that were registered, and the winner in the primary would go on to top the mayoral poll. There were, however, three other Jewish candidates, including Abraham Beame. The Black candi-date was Percy Sutton, but though 20 percent of New Yorkers were Black, few were on the Democratic primary register. The Hispanic candidate was Herman Badillo; he could succeed only if voters did not follow ethnic lines. If issues were pushed into the background, the contest would be between Koch and Cuomo.

Rupert Murdoch made personal inspection tours of the candidates over some weeks. When Cuomo entered the contest the *Post* gave him good coverage; Murdoch later said he became slightly disillusioned with him. He spent a day with Badillo in the South Bronx, was impressed but was talked out of an endorsement by the *Post* staff. According to a retrospective account he gave to *More*, Murdoch found Koch very different from the image at their first meeting, and subsequently saw him as 'very specific'.[8] The *Post*'s attention to its readership played a part in the decision to back Koch; as Murdoch said to a writer for the *New Republic*: 'The traditional primary voter in New York City is the sort of liberal Jewish voter, which is very much the old audience of the *Post*.[9]

That liberalism, however, was dropped by Koch, who turned the primary into an ethnic contest. His strategy surfaced in his choice of two campaign co-chairpersons. One was Bess Myerson, once Howard Squadron's client and now a columnist on the *Daily News*, the other Edward Costikyan, a Tammany Hall figure without affiliation to a major ethnic group. Myerson introduced Koch to David Garth, a specialist in campaign publicity who took Cuomo's platform and rewrote it for Koch, thus eliminating issues. Myerson arranged to be seen with Koch, walking hand in hand with him; rumours of a romance gained currency and Koch's vote for gay opportunities was forgotten. The contest would be fought on ethnic lines; it was liable to emphasise communal division. The Jewish-owned *New York Times* saw this possibility when it made its endorsement on 31 July: 'Mr Cuomo, To End the Tribalism'.

Having announced his choice less than three weeks after the *Times*, Murdoch found the first response encouraging. After the *Post*'s endorsement, funds flowed to Koch. Murdoch took a personal hand in the conduct of the campaign. Koch wanted the support of Mario Biaggi, a conservative Democrat with a following in the Bronx; Biaggi came to Murdoch's office, but walked out still backing Cuomo. Murdoch went much further in his partiality than the other two papers. The *Times* gave extensive coverage to all candidates and invited Cuomo and Koch to a debate in its office in the subsequent run-off. The *News* endorsed Koch, but Breslin and Hamill declared their preference for Cuomo in their columns. The *Post*'s pages were thrown uniformly behind Koch. An analysis of its election news between 19 August and 8 September, the day of the first primary, showed four favourable front-page stories for Koch, one front-page photo, four favourable head-lines on pages two to five and nine items on 'Page Six'. Cuomo was given no favourable mentions on the front page or on pages two to five; he received prominent snide comments such as 'The Blonde Millionairess Whose Big Bucks Back Cuomo'. It became difficult to distinguish editorials from reports. The day before the ballot, the *Post* led its first page with the line: 'KOCH – A MAN WHO WON'T BE PUSHED AROUND'. The presentation left it open whether this was news or comment.[10]

In this first ballot, Koch scored 20 percent, Cuomo 19 percent, a result that called for a run-off primary. Koch was less specific about what he proposed to do in City Hall than Murdoch had found him in private. He favoured the restoration of the death penalty, a power outside the office he sought; he handed President Carter a letter on how the United States should act in the Middle East; and he visited a synagogue on Jewish New Year's day with Bess Myerson, who canvassed for votes after the service. The *Post*'s support culminated in an editorial: 'Vote Today: Vote for Koch'.

Koch won and continued into the main campaign as the Democratic candidate. Cuomo re-entered with the support of the small Liberal Party. By then the *Post*'s journalists had had a gutful. To readers, its style of campaign-ing may have been a novelty; to the journalists it seemed unprofessional. They drew up a petition, expressing what one journalist described as a 'dis-quiet over slanted news coverage'. Murdoch heard of it from a reporter on another newspaper and reacted with anger. He summoned the representa-tive of the Newspaper Guild in the building and told her he had the right to run the paper as he saw fit. She posted a notice on the bulletin board reporting Murdoch as saying that anyone questioning his integrity should seek employment elsewhere.[11]

The gap between Koch's campaign policy and actions grew after he took over at City Hall. He made substantial concessions to municipal unions, granting the Transport Worker's Union an effective 9 percent wage rise. He appointed a Hispanic lawyer as Human Rights Commissioner, but when she sought details on employment in the Mayor's office, he asked for and got her resignation. He showed little concern about communal tensions; when violence between Blacks and Jews erupted at Crown Heights in June 1978, he appointed others to study the situation. His actions fitted with a negative aspect of ethnic politics described by the New York sociologist Stephen Stein-berg: ethnic groups have class reasons for tearing down ethnic barriers in front of them and they have class reasons for raising ethnic barriers behind them.[12] Murdoch might not be very keen on pluralism inside his own papers, but he continued to be entranced with the chameleon who had become

Mayor. Over the next five years the *Post*'s changes of political hue commonly coincided with Koch's.

The excitement of the election did not keep Murdoch from planning new publications to come out of South Street. In October 1977 he told a gather-ing at the Sales Executive Club that it was only a matter of time before he produced a Sunday paper.[13] He was reluctant to set a target date; in the event, it was set for him by circumstances not wholly of his making.

III

The political differences between the three New York dailies did not stand in the way of their evolving a common strategy against the printing unions. In the early 1970s computer technology promised lower labour costs. The major hurdle to its introduction was crossed in 1974, when each of the publishers signed a contract with the New York Typographical Union No. 6, permitting the introduction of 'cold type' – in fact, doing away with metal type altogether.

The printing process used since the invention of the linotype machine in the 1880s fell into two distinct stages. In the first stage journalists, having written their stories on bundles of papers, handed them to typesetters who turn them into lead-antimony slugs on linotype machines: this job is called 'type-setting'. The slugs, together with headlines and stereotyped photo-graphs, were then arranged in 'formes' by compositors; this job is known as 'comping'. The second stage was to make 'mattes' on the basis of the formes, fit the mattes onto rotary presses and print, in the narrow sense of the word. The computer technology does away with the metal slugs and thus dispenses with the compositors; it also changes the work of the typesetters, who now sit in front of computer terminals, not linotype machines. Computer setting eliminates jobs, but it is speedier, cleaner and less burdensome.

In New York both typesetters and compositors belonged to No. 6. To soften the blow of lost jobs, the proprietors guaranteed lifetime employment for No. 6 members; in return, the union agreed not to strike for a ten-year contract period. Though three separate contracts were signed, each con-tained a 'me-too' clause customary in New York printing agreements. This means that if either publishers or printers make concessions in any one place of work, similar rearrangements should be made in the other two work-places. The *Post* was thus in the same boat as the other two dailies with respect to 'No. 6'. This was its first link with the *News* and the *Times*.

Though Murdoch is seldom at ease with his competitors, he was drawn into a closer association with them in the second half of 1977. All three had further contracts with ten more unions (including the Newspaper Guild), with a currency of four years and due to expire on 30 March 1978. Having made headway with technology in 1974, the *Times* and the *News* now looked at the possibility of cutting labour costs in the second stage of the printing process. The 'pressmen', who operate the rotary printing presses were working on a contract basically drafted in 1923. The machines had undergone a good deal of automation since then, but they were manned according to an old formula. A reduction of staff was technically feasible and financially desirable, but it would need the agreement of William Kennedy, the President of the New York Printing Pressmen's Union No. 2, to which the pressmen belonged. To deal with Kennedy, the publishers needed unity; 'me-too' clauses were not enough. The *Times* and the *News* had had unhappy experiences with Dolly Schiff over the decades, and she had left their grouping, the Publishers Association of New York, in 1974. The breach in the fortress wall had to be filled.

On 8 August, Arthur Ochs ('Punch') Sulzberger gave a dinner at the Board Room club. His guests were W. H. ('Text') James and Joseph Barletta, the publisher and general manager of the *News*; Walter Mattson, his own general manager; and Rupert Murdoch and some of the *Post* executives. The diners talked about the contract renewals and agreed that in next year's negotiations they would concentrate on the reduction of the rotary press crews. Murdoch decided he would personally handle everything to do with union negotiations and, in November, the *Post* rejoined the Publishers Association.

The *Post* had less to gain from these reductions than the two other papers, but even a small cut in costs was welcome. Each pressman cost his employer about $US30,000 a year in wages, overtime and benefits. The *Post* employed about 150 pressmen, the *Times* 585, the *News* 720. In their most optimistic moments, the employers hoped to halve their pressmen; the *Post* would then save $US2.25 million a year, the *Times* $US8.75 million, the *News* $US12 million. Before the expiry date of the contracts, each publisher tried to show he was in earnest and willing to face a strike. Murdoch flew in a planeload of non-unionised staff from San Antonio and went through a trial production run with them on a Sunday; the *News*, which had sent some of its executives to a training school in Oklahoma, did dummy runs; the *Times*, less fervent, said that it had Oklahoma graduates on tap, but did not try them out.

If no bargain was struck, Kennedy might pull out not only the pressmen, but members of other printing unions. Ten of the eleven unions belonged to the Allied Printing Trades Council, known as the 'Allied'; only one of the

Allied members, No. 6, had a no-strike contract, which was not up for rene-
gotiation. The eleventh union, the Newspaper and Mail Deliverers, was outside the Allied and separate negotiations would have to be held with it. The
proprietors thought it good tactics to bargain with Kennedy last, and
Murdoch took charge of negotiations with the Newspaper Guild on behalf of
all three. With the clash over the Koch coverage fresh in his mind, he put up
two proposals: the Guild should accept a one-year freeze on salary rises, and
should give the *Post* the one-up right to discharge any employees considered
incompatible with the *Post*'s 'publishing philosophy'. He estimated that the
staff cut would cover about a third of the 460 Guild members, including
clerks, in the *Post* building. The Guild publicly dubbed Murdoch's second
proposal an 'Auschwitz clause'; the other proprietors privately thought that
he was asking too much. Just then, Punch Sulzberger ran into A. H. Raskin,
his recently retired labour correspondent and told him: 'The man is wild.
We'll support him on the things we have in common, but not on the crazy
kind of thing he's after with the Guild'.[14]

The expiry date for the whole set of contracts passed and they were
adhered to while further talks were expected. But Murdoch and the Guild
reached an impasse. When the Guild called a strike, the rest of the Allied
refused to join in and a compromise was reached. Murdoch abandoned the
'Auschwitz clause', the Guild agreed that 120 of its members would be
retired with increased severance pay and eighteen at the bottom of the
seniority list would be laid off. With the rest of the unions, no bargains were
struck; William Kennedy flatly rejected a first offer from the employers. To
speed things up, the employers announced 4 July as a deadline: if Kennedy
and they had not signed by then, they would then post their own rules for
manning and shifts. The summer months are the lowest for sales and advertising; it was then they could best face a short strike. Kennedy sat tight; he
feared that the employers were out to break his union. An unexpected strike
elsewhere then broke over both sides, and as both sides got lost in details,
they could no longer control the situation.

The first strike, called by the Newspaper Guild at the *Daily News*, lasted five
days. The *Daily News* expected its two co-publishers to shut down in support,
but Murdoch was out of touch on an international jet and nobody else could
make the decision. A temporary compromise was reached, and to gain time the
publishers postponed the deadline for the signature of contracts to 8 August.

On 18 July Mattson, Barletta and Murdoch met for dinner at the Christ
Cella restaurant. They proposed a new negotiation position. So far they had
talked to the pressmen about the number of men in attendance at each
press; now they would talk about the numbers in each room: this would be

more advantageous to themselves, though less acceptable to the union. What else was said became a matter of subsequent disagreement. Mattson and Barletta maintained that there had been consensus that the publishers would fall back to press numbers if Kennedy rejected the new formula; Murdoch maintained that no fall back was discussed. For the moment he was more uncompromising than the rest and suspected that the *Times* was ready to sell out. His suspicions were deepened when he heard that a *Times* executive and Kennedy had met. The *Times* maintained that the meeting concerned a detail of computerisation, previously agreed in principle; Murdoch, however, rang Barletta and expressed his outrage.

Just before the deadline expired, the Federal Mediation and Conciliation Service sent one of its negotiators, Kenneth Moffett, from Washington. Despite a day's grace, no compromise was reached; the publishers posted unilateral rules and Kennedy called a strike, supported by all the unions involved. The three papers ceased production on 9 August.

In New York, business seldom misses new opportunities. By the end of August, three new dailies, the *Daily Metro*, the *City News* and the *Daily Press* were on sale. Their combined circulations were about a million, a third of the dailies now on strike. Some of the sales came from the home deliveries they took over. Believing the *Post* to be particularly vulnerable to competition in Queens from *Newsday*, which had not shut down, Murdoch supplied the *Daily Metro* with several hundred thousand dollars, took a lien over it and purchased 150,000 copies of each issue, which he sent to the *Post*'s home subscribers. This arrangement gave rise to allegations that he intended to run the *Daily Metro* as a morning paper after the strike ended. Murdoch denied these suggestions and, in fact, the *Metro* closed when the *Post* reappeared.

This publicly voiced suspicion was groundless; others, privately held, continued to be about. In the 1962-63 strike, Dorothy Schiff had made an early, separate peace with the unions. The *Post* was now financially the weakest of the three papers: in negotiations with the unions, Murdoch put its losses at $US10 million for 1977 and forecast a loss of $US8 million for 1978. The *News* and the *Times* therefore attempted to 'cement him in', as they later put it. He was made president of the Publishers Association and acted as its spokesman in the dispute. In front of the microphones and cameras in the Doral Inn, where talks were intermittently held, he was an articulate performer, erasing the King Kong image pinned to him early in 1977. But the outward unity which Murdoch projected was precarious; and the differences between the three publishers soon overshadowed the dispute between them and the union leaders.

Enter Theodore Kheel, a mediator in most post-war newspaper disputes and a man on the sidelines so far. Kheel was a senior partner in a law firm and had made his name settling industrial disputes in subways and municipal employment as well as in publishing. He used his wits, his wide network of acquaintances and more recently, Automation House, a non-profit organisation studying industrial disputes he had set up. In 1978 the publishers, more militant than usual, kept him out because they thought he leaned too far to the union side. Kheel was not perturbed, broadcast a running commentary on the strike over the television station WCBS and kept up to date. Murdoch had several earlier contacts with Kheel, who had been a legal adviser to the New York Magazine Company in Felker's day and was then on the other side. Nevertheless, he had turned to Kheel after acquiring the *Long Island Press* delivery list for help with the Deliverers' Union, and grateful for Kheel's advice, had donated $15,000 to Automation House. As union negotiations began to take much of his time, Murdoch hired Martin Fischbein from Automation House as a personal assistant; when the presidency of the Publishers Association was offered, Murdoch sought an opinion from Kheel, who suggested acceptance.

Kheel took his entry cue from a public proposal made by Murdoch. Murdoch had announced that the publishers were reverting to unit manning and asking for a reduction from twelve to eight journeymen, an offer promptly rejected by Kennedy who stuck to the maximum of a one-man cut. In this stalemate, Kheel wrote an article for the *Daily Press* saying that Kennedy's blank refusal made it possible for the eight other unions to cross the picket lines and that, accordingly, the Allied was now the arbiter over the continuation of the strike. Five days later, the Allied appointed Kheel as an adviser. On the same day, Kheel had a discussion with Murdoch. Both were polite; Kheel explained that he wanted to establish the facts about pressrooms for his clients; Murdoch was wary of this explanation.

Five days later, on 11 September, Walter Mattson, the executive on the publishers' side with the closest knowledge of printing technology, privately saw Kheel. Murdoch was not told that this meeting would take place, and with Kheel's entry heightening his suspicions of a sell-out, asked Fischbein to find out what Kheel was doing. From a switchboard operator in Kheel's law firm whom he called at her home, Fischbein learnt that Kheel was with Mattson at that very time. Murdoch at once contacted Barletta and suggested that both of them were being double-crossed. Barletta was not convinced, for the good reason – which he didn't tell Murdoch – that he himself had initiated the meeting between Kheel and Mattson. Late that day, Murdoch was officially informed that Mattson talked about pressroom technology. He refused to accept that this had been the sole purpose of their meeting. He had several monkeys on his back, with the faces of the Australian newspaper proprietors whom he fought single-handed in earlier years. The *Times* and *News* executives, who did not see them, exacerbated Murdoch's suspicion, which became a major factor in what followed.

Murdoch focussed his suspicions on Kheel whose influence grew after Moffett, the federal mediator, returned to Washington. Murdoch refused to have Kheel in a central position. When Kheel invited all parties to Automation House, Murdoch would not come, privately describing Kheel as a 'megalomaniac'. His alternative was that everybody should go to Washington, set up there for the duration and talk under Moffett's auspices. A first meeting took place on the last Monday of September, but the meeting was adjourned to Wednesday 27 September at the Federal Plaza in New York.

Murdoch had made up his mind on the morning of that day. He called in the *Post* executives and told them he would have to get out. He then took Howard Squadron, who was handling the legal side, to a lunch with Barletta of the *News*, where Squadron talked at length about Kheel's role. After the meal, the three men headed for the meeting at the Federal Plaza and stopped outside. As Squadron prepared to enter, Murdoch said: 'Go in and throw the bomb'. In the negotiating room, Squadron condemned Kheel at length: he had moved into a vacuum and was becoming the de facto arbitrator. In the *Post*'s view, Kheel's place was outside, or at most as a silent observer inside. The *Post* would withdraw from the negotiations unless Kheel reverted to that role.

Anticipating Squadron, William Kennedy stormed out, and Squadron announced the *Post*'s withdrawal. Murdoch immediately turned a somersault and sought a separate peace with the unions.

IV

The strike was holding up a project to turn round the losses in South Street. When the other New York publishers planned new publications – and both had looked at evening papers in recent years – they went through elaborate exercises in market research, made production studies and consulted advertisers. These preparations did not seem relevant to Murdoch. All he needed was a few more journalists, and he got them with the minimum of noise.

Late in May, Ross Waby, the head of the New York bureau of News Ltd, was sent to Australia with a simple mission. He was to recruit about a dozen journalists and photographers, ostensibly to join the bureau. The requirements: mobility, age between twenty and thirty, readiness to put a foot in the door. Waby offered $US20,000 a year, a sum attractive to Australian reporters less than halfway up the ladder, and return fares guaranteed. The chance of working in New York, otherwise offered only to journalists destined for advancement, was readily seized. Waby was vague about details; but who would want to look into the closed mouth of this gift horse?[15]

Waby was still recruiting when reports of the strike at the *Daily News* reached Australia. The Australian Journalists Association warned its members that they could find themselves breaking a strike, an early false alarm. The recruits took out visas allowing them to work as foreign correspondents in the United States and soon a dozen dribbled into the Third Avenue office. As each arrived, he was given $US300 pocket money and booked into the Lexington Hotel. 'Not a bad pub,' they told each other. They were then directed to find permanent accommodation. Having seen to mundane things, they started on stories for publication in London, Sydney, Adelaide. The relaxed pace did not fit their preconceptions of working for Rupert Murdoch and a variety of rumours circulated. The *Post* continued on strike, nobody went near the picketed building and the rumours died down.

After Squadron threw the bomb at the Federal Plaza, Murdoch lost no time, and within hours was face to face with William Kennedy, negotiating for a return of the pressmen to the *Post*. Kennedy sparred, and Murdoch passed to the Deliverers, whom he offered a weekly rise of $US68, to be spread over three years. This offer broke the existing deadlock over pay rises, and learning that Murdoch was negotiating from a changed position, Kennedy agreed to come to a meeting at Squadron's office at two o'clock on Sunday afternoon. They talked for fourteen hours and, early on Monday morning, a separate peace was declared. Murdoch would adhere to whatever ultimate terms Kennedy agreed on with the other two publishers on manning and job security; as a sweetener, Murdoch promised to hold separate negotiations about machine maintenance and cleaning up, and to go to independent arbitration if no agreement was reached. In two more days, Murdoch settled with the rest of the unions on this 'me-too' basis and, on the morning of 5 October, the *Post* was in production with a run of a million copies and 128 advertisement-packed pages. 'WELCOME BACK!' the front page said.

While the buyers looked, Murdoch took the plans for a *Sunday Post* off the drawing boards and on Saturday night the new paper came off the presses.

'Monopoly is a terrible thing,' Murdoch said shortly after to A. H. Raskin, 'till you have it.'[16] In Australia, his conflicting statements on competition were familiar.

The *Times* and the *News* continued to be locked into negotiations with the unions, while Murdoch was free to proceed with another planned move. Waby told the Australian recruits to report the next morning at seven o'clock in the *Post* building, where they were directed to the back of the reporters' floor, finding themselves shoulder to shoulder with a handful of American reporters and a contingent of subeditors from San Antonio. The group was told that they were working on the *Daily Sun*, with Neal Travis as editor and Steve Dunleavy as news editor, and rounds were assigned. Some days later Murdoch appeared in his ceremonial shirt-sleeves to give battle orders. The paper was directed at low-income earners; long explanations were not required in New York: the stories should be short, sharp and contain plenty of quotes. The first page should carry no more than fifteen paragraphs and the second paragraph should be a quote. There were to be no stories about homosexuals.

Travis produced two dummy issues. Tit-and-bum photos came from London to fill the third page; a gossip column written by a reporter previously on the Melbourne *Age* was placed on page six. The paper would have twenty-four pages and would be sold for ten cents, compared to the *Post*'s twenty-five, and would be on sale at five in the morning. Murdoch did not have to spell out the meaning of the phrase 'low-income earners'; the intended buyers were self-evident. Together with the publishers and journalists, the project for the *Daily Sun* showed how far popular journalism had moved since the days of Joseph Pulitzer: it was to be of White Australians, by White Australians, for the dimes of New York Blacks.

The imminent publication of the paper was announced on 19 October. Murdoch began negotiations with the Deliverers Union, who set stiff terms, estimated to add two million dollars to a tight budget. Other unions had second thoughts. The negotiations could not be concluded, and after four weeks' ghostly existence the *Daily Sun*'s appearance was postponed indefinitely.

Travis announced at once that he was leaving to write a novel. The following year it appeared under the name *Manhattan*, and told the tale of the magazine *Manhattan* which a Canadian magnate tried to take over, to find himself foiled when its editor got backing from a mafia syndicate. The central character was a caricature of Clay Felker; the Canadian magnate stood in for Rupert Murdoch, without closer resemblance. The message was that in a choice between Murdoch and the mafia, every decent editor should

choose Murdoch. Murdoch was not displeased and Travis briefly reappeared early in 1983 as a weekend columnist in the *Australian*. Waby's
recruits stayed on for a time at the *Post* and then dispersed.

The separate peace bought from the unions brought Murdoch immediate
benefits. Through most of August and September with the three dailies off
the streets, *New York* and the *Village Voice* cashed in on advertising, with the
Voice nearly doubling its content. Having reopened, the *Post* ran at a million
sales and the *Sunday Post* nearly reached that figure; with this circulation, the
department stores advertised as they had never done before. Clay Felker
commented to *Business Week:* 'The man is brilliant. He has incredible energy.
He's made fools out of the *Times* and *News* people, taken them for a ride,
outmanoeuvred them at every turn.'[17]

By coming back with the *Post*, Murdoch added urgency to his competitors'
wish to reopen. The rich Christmas season was close; and since mid-term
elections at the state and federal levels were due early in November, politicians, eager to see their names in print, began to urge an end to the strike.
Kheel was stronger than ever. Drawing attention to Murdoch's abandon-
ment of the other two publishers, he put into circulation Robert Browning's
poem 'The Lost Leader': 'Just for a handful of silver he left us . . .' Kennedy
could not be shifted about yielding more than one man from each press, but
he was willing to make concessions about the number of shifts worked, in
return for continued employment for all his members. The employers
agreed to Kennedy's formula and the only reductions in jobs were by attrition. The key issue was thus resolved on the lines of Kennedy's pre-strike
proposal. With a great many strings left untied in the rest of the contracts,
the strike ended and the *News* and the *Times* reappeared on 6 November.

By the end of that month, the *Sunday Post*, unable to compete, was down to
400,000 sales and closed. The effect of the strike on South Street was more
complex. The *Post*'s figures for the six months after the strike showed an
average increase of 19,000 for Monday to Friday and a decline of 29,000 on
Saturdays. A more enduring effect was that by experimenting with two new
publications at a moment of crisis, failing to bring out one and making little
headway with the other, Murdoch closed off two ways that could put the
whole operation into black figures. He did not accept his defeat over the
Daily Sun with equanimity and issued a writ for $US75 million, charging the
Deliverers and the *Daily News* with conspiracy.

But the strike and its aftermath did point up the continuing decline of the
News. In the year ending 30 September 1979, its Monday to Friday sales fell
from about 1.8 million to 1.6 million; its Saturday sales from 1.6 million to
below 1.4 million; and its Sunday sales from 2.6 million to below 2.4 million.

To an outsider free of the passions and preconceptions of the main players, the decline of the *News* would suggest a simple strategy for the *Post*. As the *News* moved into an operating loss and began to look at closure, the *Post* would divide the spoils with the *Times*. The *Times* would acquire the upper layer of the readership, while the *Post* would move into the lower level of the advertising. Though this strategy was logical, it was quite different from that pursued by Rupert Murdoch, who was unable to envisage co-operation with the *Times* – and throughout the dispute had sought to make common cause with the *News*. The *Times* now reciprocated. On the evening that the first post-strike issue was put together, Richard Reeves, writing for Clay Felker's *Esquire*, was in the *Times* building, where Abe Rosenthal, the executive editor, said to him: 'I think that Rupert Murdoch has already failed in New York. He'll be out of town in a couple of years, and I hope to see it happen. He's taken the *Post* from a marginal newspaper to a big loser because he's incapable of putting out a good product.[18]

Rosenthal overlooked the continuing decline of the *Daily News*, a prospect that would keep Murdoch in New York. He overlooked Murdoch's profits elsewhere, and his capacity for developing American profits outside the *Post*. Murdoch would not sit and wait for the *News* to go out of business. He would find plenty to do elsewhere and move at the appropriate moment.

THE AUSTRALIAN

NUMBER 478   WEDNESDAY NOVEMBER 21 1979   20 CENTS

Bid for Herald and Weekly Times

NEWS GROUP'S $126mill OFFER

TV, radio would be nationalised

...SPAPER publisher Mr Rupert Murdoch ... ... the business world yesterday with an

A CONTINUING LOVE AFFAIR WITH NEWSPAPERS

Murdoch moves closer to biggest

Drillers hit onshore ga

VICTORIA'S first on-shore drilling rig struck gas yesterday with an estimated flow rate of 7 million cubic feet a ...

The promising gas find was made just north of Port Campbell in the south-western part of the state by Beach Petroleum in its well North Paaratte 1.

Chief executive of Beach, Mr John Boskins, said the test was very dry there were no signs of oil or condensate for the test period.

While the flow ... encouraging, he stressed that more detailed testing would be done to help determine the commercial significance of the discovery.

Port Campbell is in the Otway Basin, about 290 km from Melbourne.

Mr Boskins said that previous wells drilled in other companies in the area had been seeking much deeper targets and had failed to find any hydrocarbons.

Although still to be proven commercial, the initial flow is comparable with flows from new wells recently tested in the on-shore Surat Basin in Queensland.

Both the chairman of the Victorian Gas and Fuel Corporation, Mr Neil Smith, and the Victorian Minister for Minerals and Energy, Mr Balfour, described the North Paaratte well as encouraging.

Mr Smith said it could be ...

Gas export approved

THE Federal Government yesterday gave approval to N and LPG from the West Shelf project in Western Australia to be exported over a period from 1986.

Permits were issued to joint ventures in the project — California Asiatic Oil, Mobil Oil, Mitsubishi, Woodside Petroleum, Shell Development, Shell Development, Hematite Petroleum, and Petroleum Development.

Mr Jeff Harworth has ...

TE NEWS

... Australian ... ... the 15 months to ... ... Australian Turf Club ... ... broker Wayne Craig ... was disqualified for the ... ... after the steward ... ... adjournment in the ... ... the running of ... ... at Saturday's Ascot ... ... pike and Craig were ... ... sundry Australian ... ... Jockey Club with ... ... with failing to ...

LABOR SALES FOR MINORITY — PAGE 2

OSAKA GRANDS STADIUM — ...

Ansett tipped to head club

MR Bob Ansett, the managing director of the Budget Rent-a-Car group, may replace Mr Lloyd Holyoak as chairman of the Victorian Football League club, North Melbourne.

Mr Holyoak, president of the club for the past three years, announced his resignation yesterday.

FULL STORY — BACK PAGE

Wardley still dogs airline

THE future of Mrs Deborah Wardley almost held more attention at Ansett's annual meeting in Melbourne yesterday than the recent take-over battle for the company.

Shareholders asked only two questions, including one on the future of Mrs Wardley — Australia's first female commercial airline pilot trainee.

FULL STORY — PAGE 13

Rupert really has to go into the wilderness for some time.

"It has been a very long, hard pull for Rupert to get back into this position. Even if he fails I am very happy that he is now able to make this attempt.

"Really, I suppose it was the making of Rupert, having to work so hard at the start.

"If his father had lived it would have been a very different life for Rupert, but as it is he's had the great opportunity to prove himself. I'm happy my his father's dea..."

... interview continually breaking off in sighs and answer phone calls, issue instructions and display an eager elation and energy which bailed an enormously strenuous day — and days before.

Mr Murdoch, born in Melbourne, was at Oxford University completing a Master of Arts degree when his father died. He had, he said, no real plans to expand from The News when he took control of ...

CONTINUED PAGE 4

KING SIZE

You'll stay for the taste.

Great tobaccos smoothed by the white Microlite filter for mild, yet truly satisfying flavour.

Chapter Eleven

/// *An Australian Base* ///

Expand! Expand! Between 1979 and 1981 Murdoch bought and bought again. By June 1981 his group had quadrupled its annual turnover to $A1.2 billion. A cold economic wind was blowing over Britain and the United States, and he rediscovered the advantages of sunny profits from Australia, where the expansion was most spectacular.

The plunge started with a tidbit from Bruce Gordon, an Australian working as a vice-president for Paramount Pictures in New York. Gordon owned under one percent of the stock in United Telecasters Sydney Ltd, the licensees of Channel TEN-10, and kept a close watch on his investment. He knew also that, along with the old Adelaide licence, Murdoch was now in control of TWT Ltd in Wollongong, and through Wollongong, held just under 5 percent of the stock in TEN-10. In April 1979 Gordon made a shrewd guess: one of TEN-10's founding stockholders, Email Ltd, would be willing to sell its 11 percent holding, for it had just bought out a large competitor in appliances, its main business, and would need cash. Gordon thought he would do Murdoch a favour by drawing his attention to the possibility of Email selling and phoned him accordingly.

Murdoch contacted Merv Rich, his finance director, in Sydney. By 14 May Rich had bought Email's parcel. He also secured a second lot from the CSR Co., which took the opportunity to get out of television and divided its holding between Murdoch and the channel's largest stockholder, AWA. After these transactions, News Ltd held 21 percent of United Telecasters Sydney, AWA 26 percent. Reluctant to play second fiddle, Murdoch gave instructions to buy over three million shares in the open market, and News Ltd then had 48.2 percent of TEN-10.[1]

Murdoch had already begun to pick up pieces of Australian property again. In 1978 he purchased a sheep property for $A3.5 million and early in 1979 he had a visit in New York from David Hill, the key economic adviser to the New South Wales Premier, who sounded him out about tendering for a licence to conduct Lotto. He joined up with Vernons of Britain and the local Packer group in a venture that became highly profitable.

The television purchase too made rough commercial sense. Among the Australian media, television was growing fastest. The fifty commercial stations grossed $A475 million in 1979-80, and the six channels in Sydney and Melbourne took more than half of this gross amount. United Telecasters Sydney had made over $A4 million post-tax profit in 1977-78. It had a key position in one of the three networks linking channels in purchasing overseas product and financing local material, the network in which its chief partners were channels owned by Ansett Transport Industries (ATI) in Melbourne and Brisbane, as well as an Adelaide station that competed with Murdoch's Channel 9. This was a complication to be ironed out in due course. The strong Sydney channel would give Murdoch an even stronger voice in a network; he ultimately paid $A36 million for 100 percent and, at nine times post-tax profits, it seemed cheap.

With the purchase of the stock in TEN-10, News Ltd stepped into the lush rainforest of Australian television law. The Broadcasting and Television Act was being administered by the Australian Broadcasting Tribunal (ABT), which superseded the Australian Broadcasting Control Board in 1977. Its predecessor could only make recommendations to the minister responsible while the ABT, cushioning the Government against pressures, renewed licences, approved their transfer and could even revoke them. In 1979 the ABT was still feeling its way about how it should use its powers, but on one point there was no ambiguity. The Act did not allow any one legal 'person' to hold more than 5 percent of the stock in more than two television licences, except for those who had already done so in 1965. Having added Universal Telecasters Sydney to the channels in Adelaide and Wollongong, Murdoch was outside the law. Knowing this, he sold Wollongong to Bruce Gordon's family company Oberon Broadcasters for nearly $A4.3million. Gordon had to approach the ABT for approval, which seemed a mere formality.

This approval was still pending when the ABT opened hearings on the transfer of TEN-10 on 4 July 1979. The hearings were presided over by Bruce Gyngell, the ABT's chairman since 1977. Gyngell was thoroughly familiar with industry conditions and knew the leading personalities, having acted as master of ceremonies at the very first commercial transmission in 1956 and having subsequently been a senior executive in two networks.

After his appointment to the ABT he tried to live down a reputation as an 'industry man', as was being alleged by public interest groups, and talked as freely about the transcendental meditation that he practised as about ratings. But having no legal background he was vulnerable: in the past two years, professional lawyers had come before him to raise intricate points that might facilitate or frustrate deals that ran into eight figures. With him on the ABT in July 1979 sat Keith Moremon, who came from film distribution and had a sharp commercial sense, but he too had no legal background. When Gyngell and Moremon wanted legal advice, they sought it in the federal Department of the Attorney-General, from officers who drafted laws and spent little of their time in the adversary situations of the courts.

From the first hours of the TEN-10 hearings, Gyngell and Moremon sat over proceedings in which the lines of legal battle were firmly drawn. Four outside parties sought leave to appear and to various degrees, all of them opposed the TEN-10 licence passing to Murdoch. Gyngell refused to hear the New South Wales branch of the Australian Journalists Association but granted leave to Senator Gareth Evans to represent the Australian Labor Party. The initial presence of these two bodies recalled the public animosities between them and Murdoch in 1975-76.

Evans, an academic lawyer before going into politics, had put a written submission to the ABT in which he foreshadowed an argument based on an unexplored part of the Act: a company was not eligible to hold a television licence if a person who was 'not a resident of Australia' controlled 15 percent of that company; he proposed to show that Rupert Murdoch was 'not a resident'. Evans now repeated this argument orally, and announced two further contentions. He would show, first, that control of the Sydney channel by News Ltd was not in the public interest, for the group's previous record in the media was such that, if it got control, the independence and objectivity of the channel's news and information services would be adversely affected. Secondly, Evans proposed to argue that 'a wholly unhealthy aggregation' of media ownership in Sydney would be created by the transfer of the licence to News Ltd.[2]

Henric Nicholas, an experienced advocate before the ABT and now appearing for News Ltd, at once took up this tough challenge, contending that the onus of proof of all these points rested with the objectors. He called James Macpherson to give evidence for the group. Having been a general manager of NWS-9 and being now a director of the group, Macpherson was familiar with media operations, but on the stand he was terse and cautious. To some of the more probing questions of the objectors, he answered that he would have to consult the Board's minutes. Would the new owners continue existing station policy and keep the managers, as the previous owners had promised to a recent licence renewal hearing? 'We have no plans to put before the directors of United Telecasters for any change in the management or staffing'. Was it still the object of the group to have a Sydney channel to strengthen its newspapers, as Murdoch had said in 1962? The acquisition was now a 'purely commercial venture'. Was the price paid for the shares bought so far $A17,365,899? 'That's about it.'[3]

Macpherson's evidence was not dramatically compelling. Murdoch read the transcript and returning to Sydney towards the end of the month, decided to make a personal appearance and raise his legal representation to a senior level. He engaged Alec Shand QC (a son of the Jack Shand who had made a short, stormy appearance in the Stuart Royal Commission) and took the witness stand on 26 July. Murdoch deployed his cheek and charm, enunciated policy and, taking advantage of the ABT's loose rules, went on the offensive. He explained that a connection between newspapers and television channels was wholly beneficial; the Australian Broadcasting Commission, which was not linked to a newspaper, had the only TV news service subject to serious criticism. (He did not refer to its coverage of the *Sunday Australian* opening in 1971.) He painted a picture of himself as a beleaguered man, the Orphan Annie among his fellow proprietors: 'My life has been spent fighting them, starting with a very small newspaper, standing up to attempts to push me out of business at the age of twenty-three in Adelaide.'[4] The authorities were against him, too: 'A previous conservative government brought in a special law to protect those monopolies [John Fairfax and the Herald and Weekly Times] and to make certain that outsiders like myself could never get as much.'[5] He was victimised abroad: 'Who in this room can say that I am not a good Australian or a patriotic one. Who else chooses to be battered and bruised ten months of the year in being an Australian when it would be easier not to be one?'[6] Most of the targets of these extempore sallies were not in the room, but sometimes his fluency carried him away, as when he said to Gyngell: 'Are there to be new rules every time you sit?' Gyngell shot back 'I think you are very close to a degree of impertinence'.[7]

Evans used the opportunity given to him by Murdoch's appearance to pursue the question of residence in cross-examination. He produced a copy of *Who's Who in Australia*, which showed two addresses for Rupert Murdoch, Cavan and New York. Murdoch coolly answered: 'It is a Herald and Weekly Times publication.' Evans then showed him the *International Who's Who* with only a New York address. Murdoch: 'I never put that there'. Murdoch then gave details of his annual timetable: this calendar year he would spend three months in Australia, the previous year he had spent two months here, the year before three or four months . . . He held a 'green card' in the United States, which gave him the right to take up citizenship after five years, but he chose to remain Australian. Before letting him go, Evans pressed the question of Murdoch's further intentions: would he be content with the licences in Sydney and Adelaide, or did he intend to take over Channel 0 in Melbourne? 'There is no substance to that rumour, and I do not see why I should give up a profitable station in Adelaide for a loser in Melbourne.'[8]

When the hearings were completed, a man with legal qualifications, appointed as acting member of the ABT, wrote the decision. The decision saw no force in the objection that Murdoch was 'not a resident': the intention of the Act had been to limit ownership by overseas companies. It found that little evidence had been advanced that the common ownership of newspapers and television stations threatened the public interest, and specifically rejected objections to News Ltd, which were based on its newspaper record alone. It conceded that the aggregation of ownership was an important issue, but said that a reference would have to be given by the Minister if the ABT were to examine the problem. The transfer of the licence to News Ltd was accordingly approved.[9]

The decision was silent on a particularly knotty issue. In his evidence Murdoch had agreed that he had bought the shares in United Telecasters Sydney 'unconditionally', meaning that the purchase was not subject to the ABT's subsequent approval. In other words, News Ltd had been the simultaneous owner of more than 5 percent in three channels while waiting for the transfer of the Wollongong licence to be approved. Was this situation in breach, or was it not? By failing to touch on this aspect of Murdoch's purchases, the ABT gave the impression that unconditional acquisitions were in order and thus encouraged their further occurrence. Mark Armstrong, a specialist on broadcasting law, later wrote that the ABT's failure to comment was taken by Murdoch's advisers 'as a signal to storm the citadel'.[10]

II

Sir Reginald Ansett, the chairman of ATI, was a crusty exponent of pioneering enterprise who basked in the warmth of government benevolence. His astute way of reconciling these attitudes brought ATI to the top in Australia's transport industry and established him, in the absorbent phrase of the time, as a great Australian. A steady 60 percent of ATI's revenue came from its airlines, whose profits were assured. Trans-Australia Airlines (TAA), the rival in the interstate traffic, was owned by the government, which was just as anxious for its company to show a reasonable return on capital as Sir Reginald was for ATI to do likewise. The government therefore instituted a 'two airlines policy'; there were no further competitors for the interstate traffic, and when costs went up, a rise in the fares of both operators was apt to follow.

In this enviable position ATI expanded beyond transport. Sir Reginald relied on ATI's sheer size to discourage corporate raiders, allowed his personal holding to slip below 2 percent, and counted on political friends to aid him in an emergency. His confidence was well placed, for his control survived a major test. In 1972 Thomas Nationwide Transport (TNT), based in Sydney under Sir Peter Abeles as chief executive, bought 23.4 percent of ATI's stock. The Victorian Government stepped in and limited TNT's voting rights to 10 percent, whatever its holding. Shut out of control, Abeles accepted a compromise giving TNT three seats on the ATI Board in return for a signed undertaking not to buy more than 23.5 percent.

Sir Reginald took this new position as an incentive to diversify further. He bought into Diners Club and into Biro-Bic, and then took a fatal look at Associated Securities Ltd (ASL), a finance company that had gone too deep into real estate. Believing that ASL could recover when given liquid funds, ATI bought close to half of ASL's stock before the end of 1976 and injected cash through issues of ordinary and preference shares. Abeles did not like what he saw: he considered that much of ASL's land was overvalued, and he reduced TNT's holding to under 14 percent. Early in 1979, Abeles was shown to be right. ASL went into receivership, ATI wrote off $A19 million and its stock units started to fall, reaching a low of $A1.16.

By moving into Channel TEN-10, Murdoch had acquired Sir Reginald as a network partner. He quickly learnt that the Sydney channel got on less than famously with ATI's Melbourne and Brisbane stations, and he concluded that the network operation would be smoother if TEN-10 in Sydney and Channel 0 in Melbourne were under common ownership. The simplest way of bringing this about was to buy ATI holus-bolus, but the market price of its stock was already on the way up and two others were in pursuit of ATI. At the end of June, well before Murdoch had thought about ATI, Abeles announced that TNT was once again buying ATI; just after him, Robert Holmes a'Court, the head of Bell Group Ltd in Perth, chimed in by saying that Bell now held 12.5 percent of ATI. Both these buyers were in the transport business and eyed ATI for that reason. Sir Reginald, taking their buying to heart, forged an alliance with Ampol Petroleum Ltd: Ampol bought 20 percent of ATI's stock, ATI bought 20 percent of Ampol and the two parties entered into an agreement to keep their holdings at that level, not buying more or selling out without the other's permission.

By early September, there were accordingly three major stockholders in ATI and Murdoch had little chance of getting control. He could, however, attempt to get a voice in its future, thus securing Channel 0 in Melbourne from the ultimate victor in the developing contest. Between 14 and 26 September 1979, Abmacroft Ltd, a subsidiary of News International in London, bought just under 5 percent of ATI; and after a dinner conversation between Murdoch and some of their directors, Morgan Grenfell and Hambros, two of News International's merchant banking friends, bought another 4.5 percent between them. The three holdings formed a block, not decisive alone but useful to another, bigger, buyer as an ally.

By the second half of October over 60 percent of ATI was in four pairs of hands. If any one of the four started to bid for the rest a wild auction might follow. Since Murdoch's interest was still limited to getting the Melbourne television channel, he was able to step in as a mediator. A summit meeting of Abeles, Holmes a'Court and himself was set up for Saturday 27 and Sunday 28 October at Cavan, an oddly peaceful place for three hard-driving, competing magnates. They had one relevant thing in common: wholly self-reliant, they could make decisions on the spot without extensive recourse to a board of directors.

Abeles is a biggish, outgoing, apparently affable man. Born in Vienna, educated in Budapest, he had come to Sydney after the war and, by a series of mergers, had become the head of the country's biggest surface freight handler. He remains conscious of being a newcomer to Australia and has acquired defences in depth against his vulnerability, which range from a habit of doing favours for casual acquaintances to putting retired politicians on his boards. According to Abeles, everyone has to be on Sir Peter's side.

Holmes a'Court, physically slight in comparison, is reserved and deliberate in speech. He is distantly related to British aristocracy, was born in Zimbabwe where his father farmed, was educated in South Africa and Perth and went into business after a law degree and legal practice. He made his money through a series of successful stockmarket deals which rested on a flexibility between buying and selling at the right moment. Like other West Australians, he is suspicious of what happens on the east side of the continent: that weekend he took written notes of the talks.

Murdoch played his listener role. The outcome of the negotiations gave him just what he wanted – a firm promise of Melbourne's Channel 0.

Holmes a'Court had gone to Cavan with an open mind as to where his advantage lay. He left as the apparent buyer of the others' ATI stock. He agreed to take the stock held by TNT, by Murdoch and the two British merchant banks for $A2.50 a unit, half in cash and half in twelve months' time; he proposed to make a similar offer to Ampol. But his purchases were subject to a number of conditions: the most important was that ATI would buy the operating assets of Bell Group Ltd, thus funding the cash purchases of the three blocks of stock units from Abeles, Murdoch and Ampol. Once Holmes a'Court was in control of ATI, he would offer Channel 0 in Melbourne to News Ltd and the Brisbane channel to Ampol.

Joined by an Ampol representative, the summiteers met Sir Reginald on Tuesday, who agreed to their proposal in principle: ATI would get an independent valuation of the Bell Group assets. Thinking that the scheme was about to go through and that he would shortly be offered Channel 0, Murdoch told Merv Rich to find a buyer for the Adelaide station NWS-9; an early sale would make the Melbourne acquisition easier. Rich approached the owners of the Newcastle channel NBN-3 and the transaction was completed on 16 November at a price of $A19 million. Hambros supplied the buyers with finance.

By that time, the valuation of the Bell Group assets had been dragging on for nearly three weeks. This delayed Murdoch's access to Channel 0; perhaps a satisfactory figure might never be agreed on. Thinking aloud to Peter Abeles, Murdoch suggested that perhaps News Ltd would try for the Herald and Weekly Times Ltd as a whole.

Having sold the Adelaide television operation, he put everything into high-speed motion for a daring bid. Just before making it, he called together three Queen's Counsel to check through the legalities and, on the evening of Monday 19 November, they cleared the bid. The next morning, telex messages to the stock exchanges announced the intention of News Ltd to acquire 50 percent of the Herald and Weekly Times Ltd at $A4.0 a stock unit. The Melbourne group had 63.25 million units on issue; the bid was thus valued at $A126.5 million.

Once deemed impregnable through its cross-holdings with Advertiser Newspapers and Queensland Press, the Herald and Weekly Times was now vulnerable: the holdings of the Brisbane and Adelaide affiliates in the Melbourne company amounted to less than 15 percent. As a second defence, the Herald and Weekly Times had relied on the fact that it controlled, directly and through its affiliates, four television channels, and that under the Broadcasting and Television Act a new controller of the company would have to dispose of at least half of them. But this did not deter Murdoch: the ABT's decision on TEN-10 encouraged him to think that he could dispose of three of the channels after he had gained control of the Melbourne group.

The essence of what turned into a bitter struggle was speed and money. Once the telexes had gone out to the markets, Murdoch added panache by visiting the Herald building to call on Keith Macpherson, the chairman of the Herald and Weekly Times, to deliver the bid in person. He then visited his second cousin Ranald Macdonald, the managing director of David Syme and Co., to tell him that all existing agreements between Melbourne publishers would remain in force, gave a first interview outside the *Age* building, caught a plane to Sydney, paid his respects to James Fairfax and Kerry Packer and, late in the afternoon, talked to Bruce Gyngell and two of the staff of the ABT.

The next morning the *Australian* carried the front-page headline 'Murdoch moves closer to the biggest conquest', and a second report, 'After a long struggle, the chance to realise a dream', which was flanked by a photo of Rupert Murdoch's mother.[11] In an interview with a Fairfax paper, he explained: 'I think it completes the building of a tremendous Australian base for our world-wide company.'[12]

His confidence was not well based. Before the bid was announced, the stock units he sought had stood at $A2.78; on Tuesday, they rose to $A3.75. Queensland Press then instructed Potter Partners, the country's biggest brokers, to buy against Murdoch; a group of unnamed friends were enlisted as backers, later revealed as John Fairfax. By Thursday morning, buying brought the holdings of Murdoch's opponents to 37 percent, including the stock owned before the bid was launched. Meanwhile, the Herald and Weekly Times formally rejected the offer and approached the Trade Practices Commission, which had a non-specific mandate to prevent market domination. It agreed to investigate the consequences of a successful bid by News Ltd.

On Thursday morning, the unit price reached $A5.52 and the brokers for News Ltd sold about 3.5 million units for a sum of $A19.3 million. Murdoch later explained that he quit for fear of being locked into a minority holding. He had not expected that John Fairfax would rally to the Herald and Weekly Times, nor that the Trade Practices Commission would present a threat.

He made a handsome profit on buying and selling stock, but the dream of succeeding his father as chief executive of the Herald and Weekly Times was at an end.

It was now back to ATI. Holmes a'Court's deal with Sir Reginald Ansett was falling through, and Holmes a'Court, once again ready to move out of a holding, offered Murdoch 11 million ATI stock units, which the Bell Group had bought earlier in the year. The price and the terms of sale would be the same as those he had offered to the summiteers at Cavan. Murdoch accepted over the telephone and the next day News Ltd announced that it would seek another 4 million units in the market. As the brokers plunged in, he rang Bruce Gyngell to tell him he was 'having a go' at ATI.

Sir Reginald Ansett's carefully constructed alliance with Ampol was no longer a defence. If TNT brought its equity up to 23.5 percent and if News Ltd completed its market buying, each of them would have parcels larger than Ampol's. In a last-ditch effort, Sir Reginald wrote to the Attorney-General and to the ABT, saying that the holdings of News Ltd in ATI were in contravention of the Act. Having received no answers, he had to choose between Abeles and Murdoch, and chosing Murdoch, he sold the Ansett family holdings to News Ltd. On 13 December, Sir Reginald named Murdoch chief executive of ATI, staying on as chairman himself.

Murdoch turned around and worked towards a partnership with TNT. He first released Ampol from its undertaking not to sell its ATI shares and News Ltd became the buyer of its parcel. He then set aside TNT's limit, and Abeles announced a formal bid for all the ATI stock. Murdoch replied that News Ltd would not sell, Abeles modified his bid, making it for the outstanding stock alone, and he and Murdoch agreed that after the mopping up, News Ltd and TNT would each own half of ATI. Abeles became joint chief executive of ATI with Murdoch; in the *Australian*'s phrase they were 'co-pilots'.

The half equity in ATI had cost News Ltd between $A90 and $A100 million. For half a television channel in Melbourne, which was Murdoch's original target, this was quite a sum. But having got into ATI, he discovered a way of flying much higher than his father's office in the Herald and Weekly Times building.

III

For nearly two years, the purchase of half the Melbourne television station Channel 10 (as Channel 0 was renamed after a frequency change) hung in the legal balance. Murdoch was caught between the rules of the stockmarket and those of television regulation. The idea underlying the market is that anyone can buy and sell; payment is on the nail; the rules are concerned with assuring equal access to information for buyers and sellers. The allocation of television licences is more like approval for the lease of a dwelling: the owner chooses the lessee, the neighbours can object. In Australia, there is a rider saying that new channel tenants cannot hold more than two leases. The rules of the market and those of licensing are in potential conflict: which set of rules has to be complied with first? After the Sydney decision, Murdoch assumed he could buy out the existing lessee/licensee first and talk to the owners' representatives afterwards. His assumption was wrong.

After buying into ATI, News Ltd knew of course that it held too many 'prescribed' interests and sought to bring itself back within the limit by having ATI sell its Brisbane station. Ampol Petroleum, who had been pro-posed at the Cavan summit, was still a willing buyer. On talking to Martin Cooper, a lawyer with a close knowledge of television regulation who had come into the group with the TEN-10 purchase, Murdoch was reminded of an obvious hitch. ATI continued to own 20 percent of Ampol and, after the Brisbane licence went to it, News Ltd would indirectly hold 10 percent, and thus still be involved in a third 'prescribed' interest exceeding the 5 percent limit. Cooper was told to find solutions. The first step was a reduction of ATI's holding in Ampol to 16 percent, but this was not enough. Ampol then looked for a partner in station. It had already been talking to Broadcasting Station 2SM Pty Ltd in Sydney, who now agreed to take just over a third. Ampol would keep under two thirds and the indirect interest of News Ltd would be under 5 percent, within the legal limit. Between them, Ampol and 2SM paid $A17 million to ATI. A third of this sum was a major outlay for 2SM and Ampol, as the larger partner, agreed to make it an interest-free loan and guarantee a minimum dividend.

With the formal obstacle seemingly overcome, a subsidiary of News Ltd applied to the ABT for approval of the acquisition of its interest in Channel 0/10. The Australian Labor Party again objected and this time was repre-sented by Alistair Nicholson as senior counsel and Stewart Morris as junior. In a written submission, Nicholson said he would argue that breaches of the Act had occurred and that he would bring evidence in support, but that the ABT had erred in the past by putting the onus of proof on objectors. When the hearings began on 1 April 1980, Nicholson explained that he would not produce primary evidence of the breaches but would seek to explore the matter in cross-examination. Presiding, Bruce Gyngell ruled that cross-examination would be limited to thirty minutes, refused to investigate breaches suggested by Nicholson and demanded an apology for the imputa-tion that News Ltd had acted unlawfully.

Nicholson was driving at quite a simple point. By buying into ATI at various times, on the stockmarket or elsewhere, News Ltd had simul-taneously owned at least three prescribed interests and thus breached the Act. Its failure to come to the ABT first should count against News Ltd in this application. Since this question had been raised in passing in the TEN-10 hearings, yet was ignored in the decision, Nicholson's insistence on it as a central issue could not be welcome to the ABT.

Nicholson and Gyngell clashed even on minor issues. The ABT staff had prepared a paper showing that if approval were given, News Ltd would have 'prescribed' interests in three licences; the paper discussed how this breach could be overcome but did not discuss whether breaches had already occurred. When Gyngell was asked about this omission, he announced that the Attorney-General's Department had advised him that there could be no breach until the stock transfer was registered. For Nicholson, what counted was beneficial ownership, not the date of registration; and though the ABT was assisted by senior counsel who intervened in the hearings, Nicholson had little hope that this legal point would be satisfactorily settled at Tribunal level.

Accordingly, he prepared for a walkout and a contest in another forum. The next day he asked Gyngell to confirm their differences one by one and Gyngell obliged. By then they were extensive: Nicholson was not allowed to show by cross-examination that breaches of the limit on the number of News Ltd holdings had occurred; nor to produce secondary evidence of these alleged breaches, such as reports by companies to the stock exchanges; nor to introduce evidence supporting allegations of criminality. On the other hand, Gyngell would not order the production of documents showing how News Ltd had acquired its interest in ATI, which could be primary evidence. In the afternoon, Murdoch appeared as a witness and the clash came to a head. Before thirty minutes of cross-examination had passed, Gyngell asked Nicholson to request an extension of time, but Nicholson insisted on the right to continue cross-examining without specific permission. Rejecting Gyngell's concession, he gathered his papers and walked out with his junior.

He immediately applied to the High Court for an interim order prohibiting the ABT hearing and for a writ of mandamus telling the ABT how to conduct the inquiry. After this formality, a full bench of this highest legal instance in the country heard Nicholson's request for three days. It issued a stiff reprimand to the ABT, told it that breaches of the Act were a fit subject for its inquiries and ordered it to conduct appropriate investigations.[13]

By the time the ABT reopened for hearings, Gyngell had been appointed to another public position and though he had not taken up his new appointment, he stepped down from presiding over the inquiry, and a week later, Moremon was joined by Catharine Weigall, a lawyer newly appointed to the ABT. In line with the High Court's instructions, a plethora of documents was subpoenaed and a parade of witnesses called. Shand, who was appearing for

News Ltd, had to accept that breaches of the Act arising out of stock purchases were relevant, but denied that they occurred and, if they did, they had been condoned and approved by the ABT. The details of the ATI acquisition were laid out, Abeles and Holmes a'Court, as witnesses, recalled the Cavan summit and Murdoch testified for three days. On 6 June all the evidence seemed to be in, the pleas were completed and the ABT adjourned indefinitely, a way of saying it was ready to make a decision.

Early in July, when the ABT began to hear applications for the renewal of the three commercial licences in Brisbane, Stewart Morris, Nicholson's junior, intervened to demand that the ownership of the former ATI channel should be investigated. He argued that if it turned out that News Ltd still had a 'prescribed' interest, then the licence should not be renewed. For people connected with television, this was too dire a prospect. While a transfer was blocked, the asset remained intact; a refusal to renew a licence left no more than the plant, films and contracts. Morris' intervention seemed like an attack on property rights and was tactically unwise. Yet it turned up some astonishing material.

Sidestepping the possibility of a non-renewal, the ABT met Morris' demand for an investigation by reopening the hearing into the Melbourne licence. The centre of the investigation was 'warehousing', a term that had crept into financial usage for a variety of arrangements under which one legal entity held stock on behalf of another entity for the time being, without that other entity becoming the formal owner. Morris was fishing for evidence of some sort of 'warehousing', and when the ABT subpoenaed more documents from Ampol, he got a start. Ted Harris, Ampol's chief executive, had written a memo for his Board saying that while the company would buy 66.5 percent of the Brisbane licensee, the remainder would be held 'under appropriate warehousing arrangements'. Harris was now asked what 'warehousing' meant. There were many constructions of the word, he replied; to him, it meant an opportunity to repurchase the stock, subject to certain terms and conditions.[14] The suggestion behind Morris' attack was that 2SM's holding in the Brisbane channel continued to be under Ampol's control; hence News Ltd's indirect interest still exceeded the legal limit. With that suggestion in the air, the ABT once again adjourned indefinitely.

As a result News Ltd was in danger of being denied Channel 10 in Melbourne. To forestall such a development, it sent the ABT a telex saying that neither it nor ATI had been aware of the arrangement between Ampol and 2SM; if, however, the ABT found that News Ltd held a prescribed interest in Brisbane, the holding in Ampol would be reduced to below 10 percent. And if this proposal were not acceptable, further hearings should take place.

The further hearings began on 15 August. Shand called Martin Cooper to describe his part in negotiations between ATI and Ampol. Cooper testified that he had negotiated only with Ampol's legal officer and had not become aware of any arrangement between Ampol and 2SM till much later. Cross-examined, Cooper was shown two sheets of writing that he agreed were in his hand. They appeared to be drafts for sale agreements between ATI and Ampol and between ATI and 2SM. Next he was shown a piece of orange notepaper, again in his hand, on which the fifth item down the page said enigmatically 'Warehousing'. Cooper said he had no idea of what he meant by that word.[15] The ABT again adjourned indefinitely.

On 26 September approval for the transfer of the Melbourne licence was refused in a public decision. The reasons were released later in a document which argued that a set of breaches of the Act had occurred, partly through unconditional purchases; in other words, Nicholson was right and Gyngell wrong. But the ABT went on to explain that if these breaches were the only considerations for refusing approval, it would exercise its discretion in favour of the News Ltd interests. It advanced two other considerations as the basis for refusing. It could not agree that the possible advantage of having a new management in the channel outweighed the disadvantages of the old management; and it put weight on the effect of network operations, holding that if News Ltd got the Melbourne channel, the Sydney and Melbourne channels would have a combined voting power of five-sevenths against two-sevenths held by Brisbane and Adelaide in the network that would come into being, thus restricting the freedom of choice of the smaller network members.[16]

Before this refusal was handed down, the ABT had been shaken up beyond recognition. Gyngell had been replaced as chairman by David Jones, a Melbourne lawyer; the High Court had imposed deeper responsibilities of investigation; and prescribed interests could be acquired unconditionally only at the buyers' peril. Its authority was stronger than ever, yet it hesitated to use it. No matter what the change in personnel it still carried the corporate responsibility of having approved Murdoch's application for TEN-10 in Sydney, after he made unconditional purchases resulting in more than two prescribed interests. It was now reluctant to regard a second run of such purchases as a sufficient reason for refusal, though the High Court had decided the legal issue and it put the weight of considerations on much weaker grounds.

The length of the proceedings had helped Murdoch in a major way. If the ABT had wanted to order News Ltd to divest itself of its Melbourne interest, it had to issue the order within six months of the acquisition. Time had run out; no order could be made. The future was obscure, but Murdoch was in factual possession of the channel and could strike back.

IV

Murdoch continued to see setbacks as a loss of face; his image as the young man most likely to succeed had been of great help to him in the past. After the failure in the bid for the Herald and Weekly Times, it was unthinkable for him to shed ATI's channel in Melbourne. He was ebullient about growth in Australia, basing his confidence on the mineral resources, but he now nodded vigorously in the direction of the bankers' view of the world. He believed in 'small government', he told the Australian Institute of Directors in April 1980; the Western economies had been 'over-stimulated, over-regulated and overtaxed'.[17] These views had rubbed off onto him in his many-sided efforts to borrow. At the London dinner where the purchase of ATI stock was discussed with Morgan Grenfell and Hambros, the main topic was a Eurocurrency loan for $A60 million, to be led by Hambros. After becoming ATI's co-pilot, he arranged to borrow several times that amount from an American government bank.

His lawyers lost no time in seeking a way out of the impasse created by the ABT. In order that decisions made by administrators could be put to the test, the Whitlam Government had created the Administrative Appeals Tribunal (AAT); bodies such as the ABT were included among the administrators. A latter-day beneficiary of Whitlam's concern for social justice, Murdoch now went to the AAT, seeking an initial 'directional decision', which he obtained. The opening was equally wide for other parties to pass through. Some wished to oppose a reversal of the ABT's decision, such as the Australian Journalists Association, which was granted leave to appear for the first time. Others, such as the Packer group, which had linked channels in Sydney and Melbourne, wanted to put a case defending networks.

Though judges sit on the AAT, it does not work like a court of appeal that restricts itself to questions of law; under its loose procedures anything previously presented can be put again and new material may be introduced. The AAT hearings took three times as long as the ABT's and Murdoch spent nearly seven days on the witness stand.

Mr Justice Morling disposed of the question of past contraventions of the Act by News Ltd almost as soon as the proceedings opened in April 1981. In his opinion, the breaches had the ABT's approval and did not warrant the refusal of a licence. Murdoch thus crossed the biggest hurdle, for the Act had been administered on the assumption that it was the ABT which approved and disapproved of the transfer of prescribed interests. Shand, again acting for the News group, then concentrated on the merits of networks. He found it easy to show that networks were firmly established and more complex in their operations than the ABT had assumed. Morling ultimately decided that common ownership of channels within a network was not against the public interest.

The ace in Shand's deck was Murdoch himself. In a first three-day season from 12 to 14 May, he improved on his buttonholing number before Gyngell in 1979. His most telling lines were items of inside information. He had 'nearly' grown up with Malcolm Fraser, the Prime Minister, whom he remembered at the age of five; he spoke to Sir Peter Abeles once a day on the average, wherever either of them happened to be; his apartments in London and New York were paid for by the company; he interfered with his papers a lot less than he used to; he was the best customer of Telecom, the Australian phone system; he thought politicians were paranoid about the media, but there were admittedly two sides to that. What were his politics? 'You would be surprised.'[18]

He was less good-humoured in his second stint, from 13 to 17 July. Shown a critical article about himself in the *New Statesman*, he observed about his fellow-Australian Bruce Page: 'We refer to the editor, Mr Pol Pot of Fleet Street [sic].' Examined on the interview given to the *Times* about London Weekend Television in February 1971, he replied that the interviewer was not very reliable. On being asked why the chairman and general manager of United Telecasters had left, contrary to what had been foreseen at the ABT hearings on Channel Ten-10, Murdoch requested a discussion in a confidential session, and was granted it. When Mr Justice Morling emerged, he said for the record that the departures related to managerial matters. Was he sensitive about the journalists' strike in 1975? Yes, he was; it was an injustice and did the *Australian* a great deal of damage, as it was intended to do.[19] Morling was impressed; Murdoch was no monster. In his decision he described him as 'a man of drive and experience in the related field of journalism' who would be 'a distinct asset to the licensee'.[20]

The AJA rested its case on a premise Murdoch was prepared to share before the AAT, that news reports should be objective while editorial comment can be free. It focused on the events at his Sydney papers which surrounded the elections of 1975 (described in Chapter 6). Murdoch, his executives and a small number of journalists denied that the papers had failed in objectivity and News Ltd argued that it had restrained journalists who had failed to be objective.

The rules of 'objectivity' in journalism are so vague that, in specific instances, a case can be made to indicate either a breach or an observance of the implicit rules. When quantitative measures are applied, qualitative considerations are overlooked: of two items of equal length, each unfavourable about a contending political party, one can be devastating in its revelation, the other commonplace and without impact. Even before fellow professionals, a case based on lack of objectivity is therefore hard to mount; before a judge, the onus of definitive proof lay with the AJA.

The alternative track to take was to emphasise the autonomy of journalists – their right to follow their best judgement in writing stories. This was a proposition Murdoch found wholly unacceptable at the *New York Post* and it would have provided grounds for substantial disagreement between him and his challengers. This track would have been consistent with the evidence the AJA tried to present; and it could have been supported by the decision on the relevance of the AJA's code of ethics given by a deputy president of the Arbitration Commission in 1975. But it was risky, for Mr Justice Morling might have thought that managerial prerogatives were being challenged.

In the event Morling refused to be impressed by examples of Murdoch's bias put to him; he was also unconcerned at arguments about political and social consequences flowing from media concentration.

Nonetheless, some of the testimony before him raised matters hitherto obscure; the proceedings, it appeared, were only one part of a wider discussion on media control and regulation.

In April 1981, Richard Searby had become chairman of News Ltd, now the main subsidiary of News Corporation, the holding structure for the world-wide operations. Since his days with Rupert Murdoch at Geelong Grammar, Searby had an impressive scholastic and legal career that led to seats on the boards of corporations such as CRA Ltd and Shell Australia. On occasion he acted as a consultant to the Australian Government and as a close personal friend of Malcolm Fraser, he gave a party for the then Prime Minister's fiftieth birthday in May 1980, which Murdoch had attended. Searby had first taken a directorship on News Ltd in 1980 and Murdoch had increasingly sought his advice, even bringing him to London for the purchase of Times Newspapers.

Searby's name came before Morling in a roundabout way. In Murdoch's first stint of evidence, an advocate for a public interest group asked Murdoch whether he, in his capacity of chief executive for big companies, held discussions with governments from time to time, directly or indirectly.

Murdoch answered 'No' twice over and then qualified his reply, saying he meant not regarding television; late in 1980, he had met a number of politicians who had examined him about the structure of air fares to Western Australia.

This probe was followed by questions to the Government in the House of Representatives. The complexities raised by the purchase of licences on the stockmarket led the Government to announce amendments to the Broadcasting and Television Act. Late in May 1981, Bill Hayden, the Leader of the Opposition, asked about the preliminaries to the drafting of the amendments and Ian Sinclair, the minister responsible, replied that consultations with all the parties concerned had been held. Sinclair added that he himself had not spoken to Rupert Murdoch for three months and all discussions had taken place with lawyers. Did Sinclair's reply contradict Murdoch's denial of any discussions, even indirect?

On the morning of 16 July the *Age* headed its front-page story: 'TV chiefs saw bill/PM gave draft to Murdoch, Packer'. The report below cited 'senior public service sources' who alleged that the Prime Minister supplied advance copies of the draft amendments to Kerry Packer's and Rupert Murdoch's organisations. It was believed, according to the *Age*, that Richard Searby conducted negotiations with the Prime Minister and that the News group gave a legal response to the drafts between 12 and 16 May, a time before Cabinet confirmed the amendments.

Murdoch had been in the witness stand the previous afternoon and continued that morning. At eleven, Nicholson took over the cross-examination and asked Murdoch whether he had enquired of his fellow directors about any communication with the Government. Searby had told him, Murdoch replied, that he had been consulted by the Government over the years; in the first two or three months of the current year he had been asked on one or two occasions about the Broadcasting and Television Act. Searby had acted in a private capacity and had told Murdoch nothing about the consultations. Murdoch now understood that the consultations had been private in the truest sense.[21]

The *Age* developed its story the next morning: 'Fraser, Sinclair clash over bill/News man's role under question'. Fraser had released a statement confirming he had discussed a draft amendment with Searby, who had not passed on the substance of the discussion. Sinclair stuck to his parliamentary answer: he had believed that Searby was acting for News Ltd, and in that role had been 'in intensive consultations with a number of ministers'. Searby himself issued a statement through the News organisation:

The evidence Mr Murdoch gave today is entirely correct. I did not convey even the fact that I had these discussions either to him or to anybody in the News group. I do not distinguish in that respect these discussions from any discussion which I have had from time to time with members of the Government.[22]

Apart from this explanation, Searby chose to remain an enigma. He did not volunteer to appear before the AAT and was not summoned before it. The role of a legal consultant to the Government without a brief was unusual, but it is capable of explanation. The Government had decided to keep the amendments out of the hands of its bureaucracy and only parts were shown to a small number of senior advisers. The reason, apparently, was that differences between the Minister for Communications and his Department had been put on paper the previous year and had been revealed before the ABT. The step of formally briefing Searby was bypassed because that process went through the bureaucracy. Fraser simply obtained advice from a trusted friend. The roles Searby attempted to separate were merged by Sinclair.

Morling gave his decision in December 1981. He approved the holding of News Ltd in the Melbourne channel, overturning the ABT's decision. He deplored attacks on Murdoch, saw no harm in a network where two stations were under common ownership and felt television stations might derive advantages from being owned by newspapers. The Government had already enacted amendments allowing buyers to make purchases in advance of ABT approvals, giving them six months to tidy up the situation. Morling's other rulings were more in the nature of personal opinions than legal precedents, but they amounted to a severe discouragement to future outside interveners in television licence inquiries.

The brief glimpse the public had of Richard Searby gave rise to much speculation. Would his presence influence Murdoch to come closer to the Government, and within it, to Malcolm Fraser? Murdoch supplied the answer to a small group at a dinner he attended in Sydney the night before the August 1981 budget. He was seated at one remove from Fraser, and during the meal the conversation turned to the Middle East and the American request for an Australian component in the Suez peace-keeping force over which Cabinet had been hesitating. As they rose at the end of the dinner, Murdoch seized Fraser's upper arm and exclaimed for all to hear: 'Show a bit of muscle, Malcolm, show a bit of muscle!'

He left nobody in doubt about who was calling the tune.

TEXAS MILLIONAIR
BUYS DAILY NEW

TEXAS millionaire Joe L Allbritton letter of intent to buy the New York the newspaper said this afternoon

The agreement is contingent on reaching cord with the unions for concession days, News editor Michael O'Neill told

Allbritton, onetime publisher of the defunct Washington Star entered the picture yester day when he made a dramatic telephone call from Paris

It came after multimillionaire real estate tycoon Donald Trump suddenly pulled out of negotiations with the parent Chicago Tribune to buy the tabloid

A Daily News executive said the purchase to Allbritton would include real estate in Brooklyn and Queens but that the Tribune Co would keep the News main of fice building in Manhattan

JOE ALL...
take over ...
bilities for ...
severance ...
total close...

Medical tests for Reag

WASHINGTON — President Reagan will undergo medical tests today after experiencing a slight distress...

news conference last night, was fine today.

In 1967, while he was governor of California Reagan underwent surgery to remove calcium...

not identify the doctors who would examine Reagan.

The President was to make the brief round trip by helicopter this...

physician Rugg. will examine...

Rugg... morning...

Israel steps out of the Sinai
DRAMATIC SPECIAL COVERAGE ON PAGES 4, 30 & 59

PLAY WIN GO II

NEW YORK POST

FINAL WALL STREET EXTRA

910,000

TEXAS JOE BUYS NEWS

VON BULOW'S LOVER TELLS ALL

Allbritton has 30 days for deal with unions

Chapter Twelve

/// *Up in the Air* ///

Murdoch had to put off two appointments at the White House over the last three months of 1979 for the sake of his Australian buying burst.

A meeting with President Jimmy Carter first came up in a discussion at his upstate house where Gerald Rafshoon and Joel McCleary visited him in June. Murdoch asked them about the President's energy and economic policies, and they jumped in to suggest that the President himself could best answer these questions. Both men would soon be involved in the Campaign to Re-elect Carter. McCleary moved into New York in September and, having newspaper endorsements as a priority, sought to fix the appointment that had been discussed, though the final date, 19 February 1980, was arranged through another channel. By then Murdoch was not only sought after by the White House for the *Post*'s endorsement; as 'co-pilot' in ATI, he had become the Boeing Company's largest potential buyer of aircraft, and Boeing suggested another meeting – with the financiers of its export sales – for the same day. Murdoch managed to arrange exceptional terms for the purchases; and the question of why the two appointments fell so close to each other came to be carefully scrutinised.

The *Post*'s endorsement in the Democratic primary for New York State was important to Carter, for his chief rival there was Senator Edward Kennedy. Kennedy's record of support for Israel was unbroken; Carter's policy was to lean to the moderate Arab states in search of a broad Mid-Eastern settlement. Kennedy was likely to gain overwhelming support in New York, not only from Jews but from many other supporters of Israel. When Joel McCleary arrived, he quickly established contact with Howard Rubinstein, a public relations consultant and active Democrat, who happened also to be retained by Murdoch. McCleary, who considered Rubinstein an excellent judge of trends, talked to him almost daily and, through him, was able to get a reading of how the political landscape looked from the *Post* office. What he heard, and soon what he saw on the front pages, encouraged him. Late in 1979 the *New York Times*, followed by *Reader's Digest*, started to re-examine the Chappaquiddick incident, Kennedy's vulnerable spot. The *Post* took its scrutiny of Kennedy's life much further; it found a woman who talked about an affair with him, and his evenings became its breakfast food. With the chance of a Carter endorsement around the corner, Howard Rubinstein suggested a White House meeting and the date was picked in the Washington campaign office.

The two men talked for an hour and a half. 'It was a terribly long conversation', Murdoch recalled for a Senate committee. 'Apart from general subjects, such as Iran . . . he spoke about New York City, it was a long conversation, which I can't repeat in full.'[1] Carter had done little other than worry about the hostages taken on 4 November, and had not moved from the vicinity of Washington since then. Murdoch foreshadowed an encouraging development: though he would not commit himself on the main contest, he promised endorsement for the New York State primary.[2] Three days later a restrained editorial well inside the paper said: 'The Democratic primaries: the *Post* endorses Carter'. It dismissed Jerry Brown, the Governor of California, and criticised Senator Kennedy. Though it expressed reservations about Carter's commitment to New York City, his past policies on the Middle East and his failure to persuade Congress to make welfare a federal responsibility, it declared him a 'fast learner' on these and other issues.

How had the *Post* arrived at this judgement of the President? Perhaps a part of its readership, which had accepted David Berkowitz's explanation of how he became a mass murderer, did not ask such questions; but another part might wonder why an endorsement was published when the primary was not due until 25 March. When the *Times* endorsed Cuomo late in July 1977, five weeks before the first mayoral primary, the *Post* called this action 'precipitous' (meaning precipitate). Could the editorial be addressed to the readers in New Hampshire, where voting would take place in four days? Or was it meant to be forgotten when the figures went up? On that score, precipitation was sagacious. Though Carter was endorsed by Ed Koch as well as Murdoch, Kennedy took 59 percent of the votes; private surveys suggested that at least three out of four Jewish Democrats supported him.

II

The hosts at the meeting on Vermont Avenue were John Moore, the chairman of the Export-Import Bank (Eximbank) and Charles Houston, the vice-president of its Asia Division. Jack Pierce, Boeing's treasurer, who had arranged the date, brought another Boeing man. Murdoch's party included Donald Kummerfeld, recruited from Governor Carey's staff and now president of News America, and an executive from Thomas Nationwide Transport. Murdoch, in the role of ATI co-pilot, gave a star performance.

A trained lawyer, Moore made no reference at the meeting to Murdoch's next appointment though he had been told it was at the White House. Moore liked to separate his position as chairman of the government-owned Eximbank from his past as a campaigner for Carter, and wisely so, because a lot of fuss was made of that connection later. The Florida-born Moore had worked with the Atlanta law firm Alston, Miller and Gaines from 1956 to 1976; having participated in Carter's gubernatorial campaign, he was put at the head of a commission to examine Georgia's mental health programme after Carter became Governor in 1971. When Carter started running for the presidency in 1976, Moore and his family took off for New Hampshire, where they doorknocked in the primary; and in the transitional period of late 1976 to early 1977, after Carter had been elected to the White House, Moore headed a group investigating financial conflicts among Carter's supporters. A month after the inauguration he took charge of Eximbank, whose functions were upgraded.

Moore would have attracted little attention had he been the only lawyer from Atlanta to gain high public office. But so had Philip Alston, the senior partner in Moore's law firm, whom Carter sent as ambassador to Australia. The two partners stayed in touch; and when Alston was back in Washington, in early 1980, for a visit of the Australian Prime Minister, he had dinner with Moore at the Metropolitan Club. It was a further coincidence that Alston was on the same flight as Murdoch across the Pacific, where they exchanged a few words.

Murdoch, however, did not come to Eximbank to seek favours. He came to dispense them. Ansett Transport Industries would buy planes from Boeing, if the terms were right, and it was up to Eximbank, as the financier, to make the terms sweet. Murdoch explained that under its new controllers ATI no longer felt bound by the 'two airline policy' to which his predecessor had adhered. True, TAA, the other airline owned by the Australian Government, had ordered four A-300 Airbuses from Airbus Indus-

trie, the European consortium; and hitherto ATI had been inclined to go to
the same people as TAA. Murdoch now had five Airbuses on offer and had
to give a decision by 29 February. The last offer for finance from Europe
had been made on 8 February; the loan terms covered 85 percent of the
price of the planes, at an interest rate of 8 percent and with repayments
spread over twelve years. He produced a telex from the Europeans confirming their offer.

Having been to Boeing at Seattle, he was now considering a purchase not
of five, but of up to twenty-five, planes. The package would consist of twelve
Boeing 767s, which were roughly comparable to the Airbus A-300, though
not ready for delivery till 1983; four Boeing 727s and nine Boeing 737s. The
727s and 737s were smaller, and Murdoch thought they would enable ATI
to compete with TAA in the years before ATI's big planes were delivered. If
Eximbank could provide comparable finance, the whole package might go
through. The full scope had not been decided, but on finance there had to be
quick agreement: Eximbank had to cover 85 percent at 8 percent interest.
He talked big and tough. The meeting broke up on a promise by Moore that
Eximbank would 'promptly develop a position' on terms matching Airbus
Industrie's financial offer.

To develop a position on so huge a loan, Eximbank normally took three
weeks. It was no simple matter to match the diversified offer made to ATI in
Europe, 40 percent was to be lent in French francs at 8.75 percent, 40 percent in Deutschmarks at 6.5 percent, and 20 percent in $US at 9.25 percent.
The differing interest rates were below the market rates in those three countries, whose levels were influenced by expectations of how each currency
would perform in coming years. Thus the German rate was lower because
the mark was expected to go up and the American rate higher because the
dollar was expected to go down. When an Australian borrower made repayments, he expected to repay the Germans more in terms of Australian
domestic currency than the Americans and he was compensated by the
lower interest rate. Of course, nobody was certain which way currencies
would move over a dozen years, and the risk was therefore spread over three
denominations. The diversification of the loan into several currencies was an
insurance policy.

In laying down his terms to Eximbank, Murdoch showed no concern for
spreading the risk. He wanted the money all in American dollars. He told
Eximbank that he expected the Australian dollar to remain strong; in other
words, he expected to spend fewer Australian dollars in repayment in due
course. Yet he also demanded a low interest rate on the loan; he wanted to
have his cake and eat it too. The day after the meeting on Vermont Street,

Boeing transmitted the gist of another conversation with Murdoch to Eximbank: 'Our deal is dead unless it's 8 percent or less'.[3]

The Eximbank was pushed hard and within a week the Board had a staff submission for its guidance. Three directors, including Moore, met on 26 February. Eight percent? The bank had not lent at so low a rate for months, the current borrowing cost was much higher, and in March it would be paying 13 percent to borrow. But the strongest objection at the meeting was to the size of the loan, calculated at $US656,854,000: 'Something in that just doesn't make sense to me,' said Thibaut de Saint Phalle, one of the directors. In his view, ATI would buy the Boeing 727s and 737s anyway; only the 767s needed to be covered so as to match the Airbus Industrie offer, and the smaller planes should be dealt with on separate terms. George Heidrich, a bank executive who had been to Melbourne in mid-February, had been told that the Boeing 737s would replace the existing fleet of DC-9 planes. Two of the three directors present were wary; only Moore supported the loan. But as nobody was sure just how many 767s Murdoch wanted, the decision was put off until Eximbank found out. Saint Phalle recalled saying after the meeting: 'Of all the cases I have participated [in] since I have been at the Bank, this is the one of which I feel least proud.'[4]

A greatly modified submission came before the Board two days later. ATI wanted only five 767s on a firm basis and Eximbank was prepared to lend around $US200 million at 8 percent to cover 85 percent of the purchase price. It would offer lower coverage and higher interest rates for the rest: on the 727s, half the purchase price at 8.375 percent, and on the 737s, 40 per cent of the price at 8.4 percent, plus a guarantee on a further 20 percent of the price, to be borrowed privately. The total loan now stood at around $US290 million. This proposal continued to have its critics inside Eximbank, and at the US Treasury, to whom all loans had to be referred, Murdoch's demands had caused unprecedented divisions, rumours circulated, leaks sprang, reporters made enquiries.

To Murdoch, the matter seemed settled. On 17 March he called a news conference in Melbourne and announced that ATI would buy a fleet of five Boeing 767s, four 727s and twelve 737s.

III

Judith Miller of the *New York Times* had been calling at Eximbank and else-where in early March. The day after Murdoch's Melbourne announcement, her paper carried an article she filed from Washington. It mentioned the $US290 million loan and its unusually low interest rate, Murdoch's lunch at the White House on the same day as his visit to Moore, the *Post's* endorse-ment of Carter, and sketched Moore's political career. She added that Ambassador Philip Alston had contacted Moore from Australia to check whether Moore knew of the 'prospective sale' of the Boeing planes.[5] The *Washington Post* and the *Wall Street Journal* joined the trail. On 21 March Senator William Proxmire, the chairman of the Senate Committee on Bank-ing Housing and Urban Affairs, and Senator Adlai E. Stevenson, the chair-man of its Sub-Committee on International Finance, wrote to Moore and to the Treasury, expressing their concern at the reports, and asked for delivery of all documents covering the loan. What they then saw led them to set two days for hearings in May.

A storm had broken over Murdoch. The case against him was put sharply by William Safire, a conservative columnist writing in the *New York Times* on 10 April. Safire recapitulated the coincidences and asked:

Lavishing on everyone concerned the benefit of every doubt and imputing to all the highest motives, doesn't this deal reek of at least the appearance of conflict of interest?

The press cannot defend the First Amendment with its hand out. Journalism cannot shut its eyes to the danger of conglomeration, where one division scratches a government back that in turn scratches the back of another division. 'There is a case that newspapers should have no interests outside publishing,' says Mr Murdoch who obviously does not think much of that case. 'What does the *Times* do before the FCC [the Federal Communications Commission which renews television licences]?

Publisher Murdoch should stop treating this as an insult to his integrity and start recognising the principle at issue: When journalism and government get too close, both suffer. His voluntary rejection of the financing would prove him a fast learner with a renewed appreciation for the fundamental American values.[6]

Senator Proxmire's Committee did not have a brief to police American values or rule on the proper relations between government and the press; its task was to oversee Eximbank. On the first day of the hearings it was overwhelmingly sceptical of the bank's action in offering the loan, but it also touched on the wider issues. Proxmire, a Wisconsin Democrat, who habitually criticised a wide range of subsidies paid to privileged groups and individuals, was thus suspicious of Eximbank. The ranking minority member, Senator John Heinz, a Pennsylvania Republican and a scion of the '57 Varieties' family, had often supported the bank's lending policy; on this occasion he was antagonistic. Senator Adlai Stevenson, an Illinois Democrat and a supporter of the bank, now raised his eyebrows in sympathy with Proxmire's. Proxmire began with the premise that government subsidies would depress the quality of American goods in the long run, and if other governments subsidised aircraft sales, the United States should at worst equal, not outbid, them. He drew attention to negotiations in Paris intended to get agreement on official subsidy levels and thought that the loan to ATI would undermine those. Stevenson agreed with Proxmire's opening statement.

Moore appeared with four of the bank's directors and two of its staff. He did not make an impressive showing: he insisted that the issue was competition, not political influence; the Airbuses were the first European planes to challenge the aircraft industry of the United States and this competition had to be met. Heinz put it to Moore that by stressing the urgency of a decision, Murdoch was using a well-established negotiating ploy, with which the bank should be familiar, and Moore admitted that Murdoch had obtained a fortnight's extension from Airbus Industrie, beyond the date first mentioned by him to Eximbank. The bank had not checked on Murdoch's statement to it. Moore agreed that he had received a note from Boeing mentioning Murdoch's appointment at the White House; when he saw Murdoch, he had completely forgotten about it. He knew that Murdoch controlled the *New York Post*, but was not aware of the Carter endorsement till a reporter for the *New York Times* suggested a connection. And Alston? Moore had heard from the Ambassador before the first Board meeting and let him know the decision of the second. The examination of Moore was resumed on 13 May, and after discussing the general issue of aircraft finance and the bank's close relation with Boeing, Moore had to answer questions about his relations with Carter and even his past travelling expenses. The Committee's guns pointed at Eximbank, not at Carter or Murdoch.

On the afternoon of the second day, Carter's associates took the stand. The first was Robert Strauss, the chairman of the Carter Re-election Committee. Proxmire was deferential, with a hint of irony in his remark that Strauss dealt only with people at the top. Did Strauss know Howard Squadron? He did, tolerably well; he had met Squadron eight or ten times, always to discuss the Middle East. He had met Murdoch once, at the '21', when Murdoch was in the company of Charles Allen, whom Strauss knew well. When the *Post* endorsed Carter, Strauss spoke to Murdoch to express his appreciation; he knew nothing of the White House lunch. McCleary followed Strauss to outline his contacts with Murdoch, and Tim Kraft, the man in Washington who fixed the meeting for 19 February, followed McCleary. Finally Philip Alston described his own role: he had first called Moore at the request of the Boeing representative in Sydney; he considered helping Boeing as part of the ambassadorial duties. He had once been a guest at Murdoch's property in Australia and on 15 March Murdoch was his guest at the Canberra residence, where they discussed the Boeing transaction.

In giving evidence, Murdoch benefited from the sympathetic atmosphere that had sprung up between the senators and the non-elected politicians, such as Robert Strauss, that afternoon. Taking his cue from Moore, who so carefully segregated his roles, Murdoch said, 'We have always been extremely careful to keep our duties as publishers quite separate from any other business interests, although we have also behaved in the most responsible ways as businessmen and all behaviour involves a public duty.'[7] He regretted the coincidence of the dates of the Vermont Avenue and White House meetings. The lunch with the President was unconnected with the aircraft purchase and he now thought he should have sent someone else to Eximbank. The *Post* frequently expressed early preferences on political races. In reply to a passage from William Safire's article which was read out to him, he commented that people were looking for conspiracies and that Safire worked for some who had 'other barrows to roll'. Murdoch did not find it unusual that President Carter should give more time to him than to the Prime Minister of Australia: 'Publishers tend to be asked to these things, particularly in election years.'[8] Somehow nobody asked why Boeing thought it relevant to tell Eximbank that Murdoch was seeing Carter on the same day.

Proxmire was charmed by Murdoch: 'Well, I want to say that you are a remarkable man, Mr Murdoch. You seem to know a whole lot about an industry which you've just gotten into. You are very refreshing, intelligent, and an effective witness, and responsive.'[9]

The senators ended the hearings and reached their conclusions. On 22 May, Moore received a letter telling him what the Committee thought: the ATI application had been handled sloppily; the loan offer showed a lack of regard for conserving the public's money; the provision of credit supporting aircraft sales was wasteful in some cases; the provision of half the bank's money to the aircraft industry, and much of that to Boeing, diminished its capacity to support other exports; and lending at rates several points below cost constituted an extraordinary subsidy.

The loan to ATI had been committed, subsidy or not. Murdoch looked as if he had joined the smartest of the international loan raisers, though not for very long. His main consideration in buying from Boeing was that ATI would repay in US dollars while the planes would earn their keep in Australian dollars, which were on the way up in relation to US dollars. Exactly the opposite happened in the following three years. In the first ten months of 1982, Australia's currency declined sharply in value, and early in March 1983 it was officially devalued by another 6 percent. Thereafter it briefly crept up again, but far short of Murdoch's expectations.

IV

Though New York was the newspaper gamble on which he had so far wagered the biggest stake, Murdoch could afford to sit back in the second half of 1979 and the first half of 1980. The controllers of the *Daily News* were losing direction faster than circulation.

The first move by the Tribune Company in Chicago, which owned the *News*, was to change the top echelon in New York. Robert M. Hunt, the Tribune Company's President, replaced Tex James as publisher and Mike O'Neill, the editor responsible for the journalistic improvements of the past decade, was given vice-presidential status. The day Hunt arrived in the *Daily News* building on 42nd Street, he was taken to lunch by O'Neill, who brought a management consultant with him. Neither Hunt nor O'Neill thought such an outside adviser out of place. Both had spent close on twenty-five years in an organisation run by executives; if you have grown up behind protective corporate walls and don't know what to do next, you consult.

Captain Joseph Medill Patterson, who had founded the *Daily News* in 1919, died in 1946; his cousin, Colonel Robert McCormick, who inherited the *Chicago Tribune*, followed him in 1955. In the two decades after McCormick's death, the trustees for the heirs, who spoke for over half the Tribune Company's stock, controlled the Board and made policy. The watchword was prudence, and for a long time prudence paid. At the beginning of the 1970s the Tribune Company published more newspapers each week than any other American group, and three-fifths of them came out of New York. In 1975 the Tribune Company trust lapsed, but at least 18 percent of the votes remained in the hands of the former trustees. The corporate articles were changed so that an 80 percent acceptance was needed for a merger and, in

any case, the stock was not traded. Stanton Cook, the chairman, had started
as a production engineer; Bob Hunt began as a salesman of classified advertising. They had seen the *Tribune*'s politics shift from the dead Colonel's far
right position towards the centre and they had successfully moved into television. The Tribune Company controlled two newsprint mills in Canada
which cushioned it against cost pressures. The world was on the Tribune
Company's side.

But not in New York. The core readership of the *News* was blue collar and,
during the 1970s, 600,000 blue-collar jobs vanished in New York, a figure
roughly equal to the loss in the *News'* circulation. The lesson came home
after the 1978 strike, when the paper was squeezed between declining
revenues and rising costs. The strike settlement locked the *News* into staffing
levels close to those of 1970, while lower sales, and advertising rates that
could not be raised, brought less real income. On an industry comparison,
the Tribune Company was overgenerous in its staff payments: in 1976 it
spent 48 percent on 'compensation' (salaries, wages, pensions etc.), whereas
Dow Jones, the publishers of the *Wall Street Journal*, got away with 30 percent.[10] In 1979 the *News* came close to making a loss: on a revenue of $US300
million the pre-tax profits were $US5 million.

Early in 1980 the upper ranks had a presentation from Steven Starr, a
whiz-kid consultant from Boston. He drove home the fact of the decline in
sales and then graciously accepted that decline. The problem was not a lack
of readers, Starr explained, but a lack of the kind needed to sell advertisements. The paper should acquire some of the readers of the *New York Times*
in the upper middle class, and the way to get them was through an afternoon
paper sold in Manhattan, which would catch *Times* buyers on the way home.
Starr thought a circulation of 125,000 a good beginning; when the *Post*
closed, the new afternoon paper might reach 400,000.[11]

Murdoch's nerves were steady, though his loss figures were settling into
levels far greater than Dorothy Schiff's. In the year to 30 June 1979, the loss
on the *Post* was $US6.3 million; in the six months that followed, $US3.5
million.[12] To cut them back, he raised the retail price to thirty cents in
February 1980, while the *News* and the *Times* stayed at twenty-five. This
move suggested a closure of the *Post* and a great deal of wishful thinking was
done at the *News*, while Hunt, O'Neill and the sales director Henry Wurzer
spent months considering Starr's plan without seeing its flaw. The flaw was
that, whatever the intended targets of their new paper, it threw down a
challenge to Murdoch. He was already competing with the *News* by putting
the first edition of his 'evening' paper on the Manhattan stands at nine
o'clock in the morning, and his last edition started printing at 2.30 in the

afternoon. The *News* thought it could sidestep a confrontation by printing an hour later and calling the paper *Daily News Tonight*. Murdoch did not see that there was room for two.

In late spring the *News* began to hire journalists and on 19 June it approached the Allied Printing Trades Council, whose officials were delighted at the prospect of employment for 200 to 400 of their members. Two days later, Hunt announced an evening paper, to appear in several editions, some of which would include the late stock market prices. He fore-shadowed four lifestyle inserts, for both the morning and the evening papers, on four separate days of the week. The first reaction at the *Post* was that high costs would preclude retaliation with a morning paper, but having talked to the Allied, Murdoch made an announcement that amounted to competing with the *News* even in the morning. Just as the *News* pretended that it was not starting a separate evening paper so Murdoch adopted the formula that he was not bringing out a new morning paper, but merely starting his presses at one instead of seven o'clock in the morning. This fiction circumvented long union negotiations, which Murdoch knew were liable to get bogged.

Freed from the constraints that had bound him in 1978, Murdoch moved fast. The first early *Post* came out three weeks before the *Daily News Tonight* and in September he dropped its price back to twenty-five cents, making it fully competitive with the two morning papers.

The *News* stuck to the idea of chasing the *Times*' readers with its evening paper. O'Neill hired Clay Felker to edit *Tonight* and Felker took on a bevy of feature writers and columnists. He could not reproduce the splash of *New York* a decade earlier, for the *Times* had incorporated the magazine's consumer attractions and *New York* itself was still coming out. Yet *Tonight*'s ties with the morning paper were not cut; some reporters and columnists appeared in both papers. Murdoch, on the other hand, upgraded the *Post*. He gave it a Washington bureau and imported Maxwell Newton from Melbourne to write on economics. Newton had become a humbler man: his attempts to establish a newspaper group of his own had failed, he had gone into personal bankruptcy in 1977 and he did not feel strongly about leaving his creditors behind.

Felker left *Tonight* in June 1981, two months before it closed with a terminal circulation of 70,000. Neither he nor *Tonight*'s special writers fitted in with the hard-bitten reporters of the parent paper. He seldom had the last word on *Tonight*'s front pages, whose pitch was in too many directions. Bob Hunt had originally promised to spend $US15 million on the evening paper, expecting to draw on the profits made in the morning; at the time of closure, it was estimated that the two papers had jointly lost $US11 million over twelve months.

The *News* was still the largest daily paper in the United States, but Murdoch was chiselling away at it, chip by chip. While *Tonight* was being published, the *News* lost 40,000 sales a weekday and 200,000 on Sunday, while the *Post* improved by 125,000 and passed the 800,000 mark. Was Murdoch diabolically clever, outmanoeuvring the experienced New Yorkers, as Clay Felker suggested during the strike? Murdoch knew how to do one thing they didn't at the *News*: lose money without losing his nerve; he had had long practice, while they were easily panicked by this new experience.

V

A week before Christmas 1981 the Tribune Company put the *Daily News* on sale. Hunt's announcement of a $US11 million loss had been unwelcome in Chicago, where $US20 million had been laid out earlier in the year, on the purchase of the Chicago Cubs, a professional baseball team and $US190 million were committed on additional newsprint operations in Canada. Hunt's figure was announced in anticipation of talks with the unions, which did not take place; paradoxically sales had begun to pick up in past months, after the *News* started to promote 'Zingo' to meet the *Post*'s 'Wingo' – both versions of bingo, whose name had been registered by a third party. The figure that really worried Chicago, however, was announced much later: it was a projected loss of $US50 million for 1982, and this was truly disproportionate.

Salomon Brothers, who handled the intended sale, soon had applicants for information at their door, to whom they talked until March. Through a combination of two problems, however, the prospects dropped out one after the other. The purchase could only be viable if the buyer got the unions to agree to lower staff levels and perhaps a pay freeze; such agreements could only come about if the Tribune Company threatened to close the paper, in the absence of the unions agreeing, declaring one of the applicants to be 'the buyer of the last resort'. The second problem was that the Tribune Company had built up a liability of at least $US85 million in severance pay and pensions and that this liability would have to be met if the paper closed. The company was therefore reluctant to involve itself in an undertaking to close and pay out; it wanted the buyer to take over the liabilities and meet them in the event of later closure. On one view, it was selling an enormous deferred liability.

Murdoch showed no interest when the sale was announced. The *Post* was once more flexing its political muscle. Mario Cuomo, Ed Koch's rival in 1977 and now the Lieutenant-Governor of New York State, proposed to run for Governor late in 1981. On 25 January the *Post* had a front-page editorial saying 'ED KOCH FOR GOVERNOR', and on page three it carried a coupon asking those who agreed to this view to mail it in. Koch had not yet declared his intentions but, in the two weeks that followed, the coupon continued to be printed, together with headlines such as 'ODDS IMPROVING ON KOCH FOR GOVERNOR'. Late in February Koch entered the race. Cuomo took a jaundiced view of Murdoch journalism: 'The *Post* became what amounted to a political pamphlet for thirty days . . . The small political community that controls the early stages of every campaign is disproportionately influenced by something like the *Post* campaign: they read everything.'[13]

With other buyers dropping off, the Tribune Company arranged for Joe L. Allbritton to have thirty days from 1 April to negotiate with the unions and sign the sale. Allbritton, a Texan financier, had once owned the *Washington Star* and had recently bought the ailing *Trenton Times* from the Washington Post Company. The terms were generous to him: he would get the *Daily News* title and two printing plants without cash payment, but the Tribune Company would keep the building on 42nd Street and lease a part to him. As his opening move, Allbritton proposed staff cuts of 32 percent and a pay freeze. Stanton Cook made a public statement designating Allbritton as the 'buyer of the last resort', but the unions were wary and asked to see the letter of intent between the Tribune Company and the purchaser.

Americans think they know all the possible paths to buying newspaper companies. The straight and narrow is to offer a multiple of current profits; Murdoch had taken it at San Antonio, with the extra benefit of tax deductions from other losses he was about to incur. Path two is via an elderly owner who wants to retire; Murdoch followed it to the *New York Post*. Path three is through brawling shareholders, taking the side of one faction; Murdoch, a graduate of the News of the World Organisation contest, emerged victor from the *New York* melee. Path four: heavy losses, owner must sell – and this was the plight of the *Daily News*. The anti-trust laws, however, permitted a merger with a competitor only when this was the one alternative to closure and until Allbritton withdrew Murdoch could not bid. The fifth path had not hitherto been cut in the United States: Murdoch now sought to get into bed with the printing unions who would make the running for him.

Ted Kheel provided the entry cue. Still an adviser to the Allied, Kheel realised that one way out of the huge losses made by both the *News* and the *Post* might be a joint new printing plant producing both papers. He had no response to his proposal at first, but when Allbritton set stiff terms for staff cuts, some of the union leaders contacted Murdoch to sound him out about Kheel's suggestion. Murdoch came back with a modified counter-proposal: he himself would produce and print both papers in a single plant and under common ownership; he would guarantee employment and offer employees stock in the corporation owning both papers. Murdoch made his offer public and alleged that Allbritton was trying to bring about the *Post*'s demise, which was certain unless the unions extended the same concession to the *Post* as to the new owner of the *News*.

The warning was not altogether plausible. The *Post* operated on a much lower ratio of staff employed to copies printed than the *News*; it did not need heavy cuts to survive; it might in fact find it difficult to make proportionate cuts. Murdoch's private reasoning at that point is even harder to reconstruct. Without undue modesty, he could see himself as a more experienced newspaper man than Allbritton and could predict that the *News* would decline further under this newcomer to New York. He may, of course, have expected that his intervention would make agreement at the *News* more difficult, that a withdrawal would follow and that the *News* would then close. The expectation overlooked the huge pension liability haunting Chicago; he caught up with that fact before the end of the month, when the *Post* speculated in an article that the costs of closing the *News* might be much bigger than the $US85 million announced. Whatever his calculations, Murdoch was unable to stand back and let things take their course.

The deadline for an agreement between Allbritton and the unions was 25 April. The Tribune Company gave him another five days, but on 28 April, the curtain came down on the scene. Stanton Cook announced he was breaking off all negotiations because he considered Allbritton could not come to terms with the unions.

Late that afternoon, Murdoch dictated an offer to Cook's secretary in Chicago over the long-distance phone:

Since there are apparently no other qualified buyers of the *News*, I am advised there should be no legal barrier to purchase by News America Publishing Incorporated. Under these circumstances, I hereby offer to sign a letter of intent with Tribune Co containing the same terms as set forth in your letter of intent with Allbritton Communications Co. of 31 March 1982.[14]

Vintage South Australian red from the 1959 cask, it was served without grace. Murdoch failed to make out Chicago as it had failed to assess him in starting *Tonight*. A resilient Stanton Cook rejected the offer in a brusque answer:

The suggestion in your letter that you will obtain greater concessions from our unions than we or anyone else is not credible to us; if we were to conclude other-wise, the legal implications are both obvious and grave . . . We view your claim that you are presently a qualified buyer of the *News* as an anti-competitive and predatory act, and you should govern yourself accordingly.[15]

A headline in the *News* put it more succinctly: 'Trib to Rupert: Drop dead'.

Cook announced that the paper would stay in business, would consider spending $US50 million on a new plant and would start talks with the unions forthwith; in September, he achieved staff reductions of about 20 percent. But the four and a half months of uncertainty had done the *News* much damage; journalists left, advertisers booked space with the *Post* and, operat-ing round the day, the *Post* pushed past 900,000. By August, Murdoch once again felt confident enough to raise the retail price to thirty cents. The con-test returned to the guerrilla level of 1979. This suited him, for he now had a much bigger loser on his hands and was dividing his time between New York and London.

BOOKS

...e Leigh talks to some condemned

OVE...

CADILLACS

...oks at the
...es Bond and Maigret
...he books are better

in prisons a...

THE... ...PERS

Tomorrow

Death watch
The women who are

Tha...
Fa...

THE SUNDAY TIMES magazine

SPECTRUM

...sual television cele...
...'s son Tom Priestley: interview by Peter Lewis

...e life and work of

from one time to another

...om boy stens fo...

THE ART...

that we were close. We were
...onate but without showing it. He
...to push me into any career.
...so seriously he took my

...sing a bit of a s...
superb!
car...

...om A...

DAY TIMES

eview

Pre Glo...

...nnecessary and dangerous
arrogance.

Heart matters

From H. J. Tudgay Broomden

Popular femi...

'ebration of th...

a line to ...

"I'm a great pragmatist. When
opportunities present them-

...rm: Marshal Ogarkov (left), his successor Marshal...
...d President Chernenko, whose fading grip helped spark...

...rkov victim of h...
emlin power struggle

...SUNDAY ...
...es

FRIDAY PAGE

Chapter Thirteen

/// *Quality Street* ///

Of all big British newspapers, the *Observer* was best insulated against political pressures and least able to absorb economic shocks. It saw itself as the heir to a liberal tradition of fairness in argument and of scrutiny of the long-term effects of public policy; their observance secured the loyalty of the staff and the affection of many readers. Apart from a small stake in television, its owner, Observer Holdings, had not accumulated investments; and using more newsprint in each Sunday copy than the dailies did, the paper was more quickly shaken by the sharp rise in costs. It put up its cover price and lost around 150,000 average sales between 1974 and 1976, ending up below 670,000. But it was resilient; it cut its staff by a quarter, a relatively painless operation since many were part time; and it embarked on using the esteem it enjoyed as its survival kit.

Arnold Goodman went to see two successive Prime Ministers before the *Observer* was put on sale. The paper's shade of liberalism did not preclude a closer involvement with government: David Astor, the editor, had broken early with his mother Nancy's pro-appeasement Conservatism, was a champion of the welfare state and sometimes defended Labour budgets. The *Observer*'s independence was vested in two trusts: the Publishing Trust owned the building and most of the stock in Observer Holdings, the operating company; and the Editorial Trust, chaired by Goodman, chose the editor and had the task of maintaining the paper's character. When Goodman saw Harold Wilson, the Labour Prime Minister suggested an approach to IPC, but this group expressed reluctance to add a third Sunday to its list. A case for finance to buy new plant and retrench staff was then mounted to the current Royal Commission on the Press. By the time the Commission made

221

supporting recommendations, Wilson had left Downing Street. Goodman then talked to a sympathetic Jim Callaghan, without landing funds. As a staff writer put it later, by September 1976 'a feeling of despair was settling on the *Observer*'s trustees, and out of that mood, Goodman, as their chairman, approached Murdoch.'[1]

Had it been successful, the approach to Murdoch would have raised a major commercial problem. The *Observer* owed much of its viability in post-war Britain to its position on the quality side of the quality/popular distinction, which reflects the supposed spending power of a paper's readers, not merely their number. The distinction is entrenched in JICNARS, an annual readership survey jointly financed by newspaper proprietors and advertising agencies. JICNARS classifies readers into six categories – called A, B, C1, C2, D and E. A and B account for 13.5 percent of adults, but they are deemed to have much greater spending power per head; a substantial proportion of As and Bs in the readership makes a paper 'quality', and advertisers are willing to pay much higher rates, relative to sales, in quality than in popular papers. Until 1960 the *Observer* competed for these readers on Sunday only with the *Sunday Times* and, since then, with the *Sunday Telegraph*. As far as advertising was concerned, none of the three needed to worry about the much higher circulations of the *News of the World* and its runners-up; on the contrary, too demotic a readership could have imperilled the sale of advertising space – the readership, in short, Murdoch was so vigorously pursuing.

In September 1976, however, the *Observer* needed cash, and soon. In the past David Astor's family, which owned most of the stock, had been able to help with moderate sums. But David Astor retired in 1975, the assets were vested with yet another trust and the trustees could not be readily convinced that substantial advances were in the best interests of their beneficiaries. The sums were required to buy newsprint and mount a defence against the *Sunday Telegraph* which proposed to follow the *Observer* and the *Sunday Times* into colour supplements. Roger Harrison, the *Observer*'s managing director, thought Murdoch would understand these problems and Arnold Goodman therefore rang him in New York. Though deep into finalising matters with Dorothy Schiff, Murdoch flew in and was ready to buy. The immediate object, according to Harrison and Goodman, was to preserve 450 full-time and 400 part-time jobs; David Astor, still a director and trustee, more ambivalently remarked that 'an efficient Visigoth' was better than no buyer at all.[2]

Astor brought Donald Trelford, the thirty-eight-year-old editor, into the picture. The year before Trelford had been chosen by an unprecedented process. He had been deputy editor to Astor and was his predecessor's personal preference. After a short-list of six applicants had been drawn up, it was given to the journalistic staff for a veto, and Trelford passed the test. Astor now told Trelford, who had been involved in the previous moves, that Murdoch wanted Bruce Rothwell, the editor of the buried *Sunday Australian,* to become editor-in-chief. Such an appointment would affect Trelford, and at Goodman's suggestion Trelford went to New York to see Murdoch. Murdoch politely listened to a case for slow change acceptable to the staff. The impression left with Trelford, however, was that in Murdoch's view purchases were matters for proprietors, not editors and staff, and that his visit was regarded as an intrusion.

Back in London Trelford lunched with Rothwell, who did not seem to rejoice in Trelford's intervention. Some days later, as Trelford was driving through the congestion of Covent Garden, a pedestrian stepped into his slow-moving car and touched the bonnet as if to stop the vehicle. The pedestrian was Rothwell, who thereafter seemed to Trelford to bear an air of suspicion. On meeting Murdoch again, this time in London, Trelford learnt that Tony Shrimsley, a political writer for the *Sun*, would become editor under Rothwell; Trelford himself would hold the position of 'editorial director', loosely defined and without authority over the paper's contents. Shrimsley was a right-wing Tory; the choice foreshadowed a turn in the *Observer*'s policy. Murdoch confirmed that the paper would move downmarket, a move whose commercial implications Trelford did not raise. Having been close to the negotiations since 4 October, Trelford was not in a position to halt moves he did not wholly welcome; he was bound to silence.

The *Daily Mail* broke it on 21 October with a report that talks with Murdoch were in progress. The source of its information, immediately the subject of wild guesses, was probably one or other of the *Mail* journalists in New York with friends in the News group office: a call had gone out from there for Tony Shrimsley to return to Britain and see Murdoch. Once the *Mail* had published its report, Trelford called the *Observer* journalists together and outlined the talks. They did not like the prospect: Clive James, the Australian-born television critic, protested vociferously that he had not come to London to have Murdoch catch up with him. A delegation sought an appointment with the *Observer* trustees for that evening; questions were already being asked in the House of Commons. Murdoch, annoyed, issued a statement from across the Atlantic: 'In view of the breach of confidence that has taken place, together with the deliberate and orchestrated attempt to build this into a controversy, News International is no longer interested.'[3]

The day after this withdrawal, the *Observer* staff met again and voted that negotiations should continue with interested parties, not excluding News International. The publicity brought the directors new contacts and they took further initiatives. Sally Aw Sian, the Hong Kong proprietor whom one of the Astors flew out to see, did not find the figures financially attractive, and Associated Newspapers, who wanted a Sunday companion for the *Daily Mail*, said they would make the paper much more 'popular'. These contacts, in a sense, made purchase easier for Murdoch; he faced the possibility that the Government would issue a reference to the Monopolies Commission for its approval, and the failure of other buyers to show up could either avert the reference or favour him in the examination. The trustees had kept in touch with Murdoch; Trelford felt that he was in the middle of 'Macbeth'; Fleet Street mentioned Murdoch as the hot favourite.

Just as the trustees decided to finalise with Murdoch, Kenneth Harris, a senior *Observer* journalist, dined with Douglass Cater, the former editor of an American weekly and now associated with the Aspen Institute for the Humanities in Boulder, Colorado. The Aspen Institute was funded by Robert Orville Anderson, the head of Atlantic Richfield and, hearing of the *Observer*'s plight, Cater proposed to interest his patron, the wealthy head of the eighth-largest oil company in the United States. Six days later, having talked to two trustees, Anderson bought 90 percent of the Observer Holdings stock on behalf of Atlantic Richfield. Murdoch was irate when Goodman told him that the paper was no longer available, although he was later to tell the *Sunday Times*: 'My first reaction was one of tremendous relief; second, of personal grievance and annoyance, partly at myself for being sucked into the thing; and lastly, I've got to admit, that it's all for the best.'[4] The journalists of the *Observer* were also relieved. Trelford stayed in the editorial chair; in the first issue under the new proprietor, Atlantic Richfield was reported to have agreed to maintain 'editorial traditions and journalistic standards'.

The interlude gave rise to one of those many false impressions about Murdoch: he wanted, it was widely said, to buy prestige for himself with a quality paper. His proposals for future directions did not bear out that opinion; the *Observer* was another case of a 'fire sale', an ailing business whose editorial and financial ways he could overhaul. His failure to buy it freed him for a bigger attempt in the same line.

II

While Trelford fought for the *Observer*'s survival and independence, Harry Evans, the editor of the *Sunday Times*, battled to publish extracts from the late Richard Crossman's Cabinet diaries. Evans was a crusader for the right to publish. He established a reputation for fearlessness quite early in his editorship, when he launched an investigation into the Philby affair, against multiple pressures from high quarters and the threat of prosecution under the Official Secrets Act. The *Sunday Times* had a circulation big enough to worry any government in 1967, when it conducted its research on Philby; in the 1970s its resolution was backed by the resources of the Thomson Organisation, to whom a large income was now flowing from North Sea oil.

Since Thomson had bought the *Sunday Times* in 1959, its commercial record was unassailable; its sales rose from 900,000 to 1.5 million in 1967, and stayed near there in the 1970s. It made losses in 1975 and 1976; they could be put to one side as temporary. Yet all was not well at Times Newspapers Ltd. Roy Thomson, who became the first Lord Thomson of Fleet, had bought the weekday *Times* in 1966; he then promised the Monopolies Commission to meet the losses of the mendicant daily from the profits of the Sunday paper, and when those did not suffice, from Thomson Scottish Associates. This was done for the first half of the 1970s, until the liability was transferred to British Thomson Holdings, another entity in the Thomson group, in September 1975. In August 1976 Roy Thomson died; would his son Kenneth and the trustees of the family continue to pay the keep of the *Times*? In an interview on the BBC in June 1977, the second Lord Thomson (Ken) guardedly spoke of putting the Times papers on solid economic feet by getting the staff to agree to the introduction of new technology. Unless that could be done, there was 'plenty to worry'.[5]

Roy Thomson had picked a system for Times Newspapers after he had seen it at work in California: it had been developed by an American company, Systems Development Corporation. It was an obvious escape from the high printing costs of quality papers, which devoured an enormous amount of copy in each issue. To popular dailies, such as the *Sun* or the *Express*, typesetting costs were not a major consideration, and thus the quality papers could not count on a common approach with them to the unions about the introduction of the new technology. At any rate, the industrial structure in Fleet Street was highly decentralised; the chapels – the sub-branches of the unions at each workplace – had the last word, and each proprietor had to make a separate deal with them. These circumstances, with which Ken Thomson was thoroughly familiar, accounted for his initial caution.

With a similar caution 'Duke' Hussey, the chief executive of Times Newspapers, began to talk to national print union officials in April 1978; he had to put to them arguments which they in turn could convey to the chapels; and they had twice the usual job on their hands, for the *Times* and *Sunday Times*, housed in two separate but connected buildings in Gray's Inn Road, had separate sets of chapels. To make Hussey's pleas more persuasive, the full financial burden of the loss-making daily *Times* was shifted back to Times Newspapers in mid-1978: the losses would now stare people in the face, and Hussey could argue that the choice lay between the new technology and closure.

The negotiations came to grief over a small but consequential feature of the American system. It provided for a direct input from an electronic keyboard via the computer to a photosetting unit. As part of this system, employees in the advertising department, who had hitherto used typewriters and were not members of a printing union, were to take down classified advertisements by putting them directly into the system through electronic keyboards which would replace their typewriters. In other words, they would be setting part of the paper, hitherto a prerogative of skilled, unionised tradesmen. The typesetters of the two papers, who belonged to the National Graphical Association (NGA) resisted this proposal and raised a demand for what they called 'double key-stroking'. It meant that all copy for the papers was to go through the hands of NGA members, whether it had already been put into the system by someone else or not.

The NGA saw itself as particularly hard-pressed by the new system. It covered compositors as well as typesetters, and as a result of the new technology, it was already to lose 40 percent of the compositors. In the attempt to keep up NGA numbers at Gray's Inn Road, it made double key-stroking a central issue. The management could see no merit in this and all proposed compromises failed. Having set 30 November as the deadline for new contracts and accomplishing nothing, Times Newspapers ceased all operations on that day. The closure lasted for the best part of a year; it cost the Thomson group several times the subsidy paid out to cover the losses of the previous six years.[6]

The management had, perhaps, not fully realised what was involved in the closure. Having initiated the suspension, it issued dismissal notices to the printing staff and hence had to pay out severance dues. It issued the first batch of notices on 15 December and continued to do so in weekly batches of a hundred a week. In addition to severance, it therefore paid current

wages for nearly three months. The journalists had signed an interim agreement before the closure, the management honoured it and paid salaries
throughout the shut-down. This exercise was not only costly; it made the
printers more stubborn, for they doubted whether there was any intention
of shutting the papers for ever. As it waited for the Times management to
come to heel, the NGA established the double key-stroking principle at three
other work places; and when Times Newspapers re-opened in November
1979, it had to concede on this issue. The balance sheet showed a loss of
£stg39 million, though £stg20 million were written back as 'group tax relief'.
It was the biggest financial disaster Fleet Street had yet seen.

The closure also damaged circulations. The *Sunday Times* bounced back to
average sales better than those of 1978, but the position of the *Times* became
even more precarious. Before the closure, it had led the *Guardian* by 17,000;
in 1980, averaging 279,000, it was 100,000 behind.

When the *Times* was not there, correspondents from London told their
readers abroad that the paper was being missed: the British did not feel the
same without a letters page announcing the first call of the cuckoo in the
country's forests. The *Times* letters page was indeed superior to any in the
country; the 'leaders', a creation of the nineteenth century, were fluent, firm
and sometimes outrageous; the parliamentary reports and obituaries were
definitive; the auction-room coverage was unique; and until 1977, the
opinions of Peter Jay, its economics editor, had wide resonance. But the
Times was not the best paper for news: it missed stories, important enough
for other London papers to give them prominence, day after day. It relied on
a narrow range of contacts that led it, for instance, to forecast a victory for
William Whitelaw over Margaret Thatcher in the contest for the Tory leadership, or to impugn a dead Cambridge don as an accomplice of Kim Philby,
without being able to offer proof when challenged. Its exposé of corruption
among the London police in 1969 was the last occasion it set the cat among
the pigeons. It barely covered the Civil Service – in apparent deference to a
succession of governments – though it drew many readers from it. It chose
professional politicians, rather than coherent thinkers, as outside contributors. Summarising the paper's virtues after fourteen years as editor, William
Rees-Mogg produced a catalogue of what the *Times*, in contrast to lesser
papers, would not do, rather than what it had done.[7]

The computer took its time. In 1980 the pre-tax loss of Times Newspapers
ran to £stg13.9 million and relations between management and unions continued to be rugged. In August 1980 there was a journalists' strike on the
Times; Ken Thomson happened to run into Rupert Murdoch in a New York
airport lounge the next month and unbuttoned about British unions. In

October the *Sunday Times* was in dispute with one printing union and suffered large production losses; that month, Denis Hamilton, then chairman and editor-in-chief of Times Newspapers, was on a plane with Murdoch, bound for a Reuters meeting at Bahrein. Though he knew what was coming, Hamilton dropped only the vaguest of hints. Ken Thomson had by then decided that his organisation could not get co-operation from the unions and, on 22 October, announced that he would sell. The sale would be handled through S. G. Warburg, who went on to draw up a prospectus and fixed 31 December as the final date for bids. If there were no sale, the papers would close between 8 and 14 March; this was Ken Thomson's last message to the unions.

Murdoch held his move; he wanted to buy cheaply and waiting cost nothing. He also knew that legal requirements had changed since he bought the *Sun*. An owner of a paper with a circulation above 500,000 who sought to buy another paper had to be examined by the Monopolies Commission, unless the Secretary of State for Trade was satisfied that the paper to be acquired would not otherwise continue to exist. This requirement was enacted in 1973 and Murdoch was familiar with it, having negotiated with the *Observer* in 1976. At Times Newspapers, the situation was more complex: only the daily *Times* was in peril of extinction; the *Sunday Times* might survive. What was the position for a buyer of both papers, such as Murdoch, who already controlled vast circulations? Would he have to face the Monopolies Commission?

III

It was not the printers, but the editors and journalists at Gray's Inn Road who first stood in Murdoch's way. On the very day that the proposed sale was reported, William Rees-Mogg announced his intention to form a syndicate including journalistic and other staff members to buy the daily, and the daily alone; in future, the *Times* would be run more cheaply. The association with Thomson and with the *Sunday Times*, Rees-Mogg implied, had made the paper a target for unrealistic union demands.

Rees-Mogg was greatly liked by journalists in the building and beyond. Having started as an economics writer on the *Financial Times*, he knew his way around the City and could get backing. He had twice tried to get into Parliament as a Conservative, so there was no socialistic flavour to the staff involvement he proposed. It was a serious initiative; it was followed by a staff group, who incorporated Journalists of The Times Ltd (JOTT) with a parallel aim. The two efforts were merged under a committee headed by Sir Michael Swann, a former chairman of the BBC; Rees-Mogg was deputy chairman, with three business figures and two employees of Times Newspapers as the other directors. The committee put in a bid to S. G. Warburg on the last day of the year.

At the *Sunday Times*, Harry Evans agreed that the association of the two papers was undesirable. With the help of Donald Cruikshank, the general manager of the paper, and Bernard Donoughue, a journalist/academic who had been Harold Wilson's and Jim Callaghan's principal private secretary, he mounted a bid for the Sunday paper alone. The group privately considered a three-months closure, a reopening elsewhere, and printing on presses in three or four separate, cheaper locations. Low production costs were the key.

The Thomson group rejected these two bids, along with at least one other made for the *Times* alone. But the bids created an atmosphere in which editorial independence and journalistic integrity began to be important considerations.

Murdoch came to London on 8 December and told Gordon Brunton, the chief executive of the Thomson Organisation, the corporate umbrella in Britain, that News International could be a buyer. S. G. Warburg supplied him with a set of confidential figures on whose basis he elicited more. On 30 December he put in a bid: a million pounds, with the Sunday Times building thrown in and the redundant managers paid off by the sellers. This was bluff and so was Brunton's rejection, for S. G. Warburg had ten requests for figures and, along with Murdoch's, only those from Associated Newspapers, Atlantic Richfield, Robert Maxwell and the mining group Lonrho were deemed serious. Murdoch was told he had till 12 February to iron out difficulties, including terms with unions – an open invitation to continue negotiations.[8]

In his customary way, Murdoch put himself at the centre of attention by giving an interview to the BBC radio programme 'The World This Weekend' on 11 January. 'We might be making a bid, yes,' he confessed. No serious negotiations had taken place: the *Sun* and the *Times* did not and would not compete.[9] He brought the matter into the open and provoked counter-moves. The chapel of *Sunday Times* journalists issued a statement saying that Evans' syndicate alone appeared to offer adequate safeguards; the *Times* chapel deplored the secrecy surrounding the selection of appropriate bidders and thought that the record of 'proprietorial interference' raised doubts about some of them. Michael Foot, the Leader of the Opposition, asked the Prime Minister for an assurance that a bid by Murdoch would be referred to the Monopolies Commission; he did not get it. A motion calling for a reference was drawn up, to which Harold Wilson subscribed.

Though the Thomson Organisation would have nothing to do with journalists' bids, it set up a 'vetting committee' to scrutinize bidders' attitudes to the conduct of the papers. Denis Hamilton, who thought highly of Murdoch's bid, decided to make editorial independence an issue. He presided over the vetting procedure, assisted by Rees-Mogg, Evans and four 'national directors' who had been appointed in Roy Thomson's day to Times Newspapers Holdings Ltd, the controlling structure of the papers and related investments. The committee stiffened the conditions already in the Articles of Association of Times Newspaper Holdings: the number of national directors would be increased to six; editorial appointments and dismissals would be subject to the approval of a majority of these directors, who would also need to approve any future sale of the titles; editors would appoint and control staff, and separately decide on news and opinions printed – matters on which they would not be subjected to instructions from the proprietor or management.

Murdoch met the vetting committee, talked about his father and the *Australian*, and came through ninety minutes with flying colours. He was in good training, having recently faced tougher questions before the US Congress and the Australian Broadcasting Tribunal. Hamilton announced Thomson Organisation's approval of Murdoch and the journalistic conditions under which the papers would be run.[10]

Some of the print union officials were more than anxious to do business with Murdoch. After Michael Foot, the Opposition Leader, had sought an assurance that the sale of the Times papers would be referred to the Monopolies Commission, three general secretaries wrote to Foot asking him not to insist on a reference to the Commission. The industrial future of Gray's Inn Road was settled as expeditiously as in Bouverie Street. Staff were cut by 563, shifts reduced by 100 and the *Times Supplements* were to be printed outside London. Murdoch confirmed that the NGA would have control of keystroking when the switch to the electronic system took place. The overall staff cuts were slight and the papers remained the most heavily manned in London.

Simultaneously, Murdoch and the Thomson Organisation had to agree on final terms. Merv Rich, Murdoch's finance director, and Richard Searby, who was presented to Thomson negotiators as a future Chief Justice of

Australia, arrived in London. A reference to the Monopolies Commission remained a possibility, for after the proposed acquisition News International would control 30 percent of the national dailies and 36 percent of the national Sundays. To overcome the threat of a reference, S.G. Warburg supplied figures to the Government showing that the *Sunday Times* had lost £stg600,000 in the first eleven months of 1980. The matter was discussed at Cabinet level, and relying on the Warburg figures, John Biffen, the Secretary of State for Trade, waived a reference.

In rebuttal of these figures, the *Sunday Times* chapel of journalists said that a profit had been made at least in the past three months and that profits would be made in the future; it proposed legal action to force a reference. It was certainly puzzling that the Government refused to have this ambiguous situation resolved by a non-political body. When Roy Thomson bought the *Times*, before the legal requirements were sharply defined, he had to pass through the Monopolies Commission; and later that same year, when Lonrho, as owners of some Scottish papers, sought control of the *Observer*, they also had to submit to a close examination.

To mollify the journalists, Murdoch agreed to a further circumscription of his formal powers; two journalists would join the Board of Times Newspapers Holdings Ltd, and this Board would consider candidates for editorships before the national directors approved. Nothing like this limit existed elsewhere in Murdoch's group; there he marched in as Emperor. An array of Hildebrands, wielding spiritual authority, seemed to have brought him to his knees; yet they also absolved him as their papal predecessor had done.

The price tag was £stg12 million and included the Sunday Times building valued at £stg8 million. 'Mr Murdoch becomes the most powerful figure in the national press since Lord Northcliffe,' said the headline of a background article in the *Times*. Kept out of Sir Keith's former Melbourne office fifteen months earlier, he now stepped into the shoes of his father's friend, the 'Chief'.

IV

With the Archbishop of Canterbury and the Warden of All Souls, the editor of the *Times* is deemed to be part of 'the Establishment.' The historian Hugh Thomas, who gave currency to the concept in the 1950s, did not specify the power exercised by those who comprise it: the last time they had gone into effective action was during the abdication crisis of 1936. For those who believe that money isn't everything, the Establishment is a consoling thought; and indeed some millionaires lack clout in British political life, though Rupert Murdoch is not one of them. Rees-Mogg announced his resignation the day the sale was reported; his successor was chosen by the new owner.

Harry Evans, who had met Murdoch in 1969, was courted by him while the sale was still proceeding; his success at the *Sunday Times* weighed heavily in his favour. He could not resist the real opportunity of improving the daily nor the residual mystique surrounding it. When Murdoch asked him, he crossed the overhead bridge joining the two buildings and started to edit the *Times*. Design was one of his skills; he called in a professional to work out the details and within weeks, the paper had a new look. New typefaces appeared as the computer edged in; the back page began to carry important news and, a little later, a vigorous Tory columnist. Murdoch was pleased and displayed some of the April issues at the AAT hearings in Australia to show that changes under his ownership were for the better.

Evans had some less enviable tasks. He traced the source of the missing news to the division into day and night staff and then remained behind each evening to bridge the gap. Some of the senior staff resisted his suggestions; redundancies cost money and many were kept on. But the journalistic staff was too large: around 280 journalists were on the full-time payroll and some twenty special writers drew large retainers; at the same time, new talent had to be engaged to fill glaring gaps. In the other building, Evans had freely hired staff and pampered the best; they regarded him as a hero and, often, as a father confessor. The new recruits to the *Times* were a minority; they regarded the old-timers with suspicion. The appointment of a deputy editor, a strong aspirant to the succession at the end of Evans' promised seven years, showed how difficult it was to get things done. Louis Heren, at sixty-two the incumbent deputy editor, refused to move and ultimately accepted an associate editorship. Evans wanted Hugo Young of the *Sunday Times* and could not get him transferred. Murdoch and Hamilton suggested Charles Douglas-Home, the foreign editor, as a gesture to the 'old guard'.

Douglas-Home was an enthusiastic journalist and had been on the *Times* for seventeen years. He knew the staff and was a good administrator. He seemed to complement Evans: he had gone to Eton, served in the Royal Scots Guards and broadened his education as aide-de-camp to a Governor of Kenya. He was a nephew of Lord Home of the Hirsel, a former Prime Minister, and his political colour was true-blue. Evans was the son of an engine driver, had served in the Royal Air Force and read economics at Durham. He

put issues ahead of political allegiance, opposed capital punishment, supported abortion law reform and had a strong streak of compassion. Douglas-
Home asked to have access to all policy matters and Evans opened his in-
and-out correspondence to him.

Where would the new readers of the *Times* come from? The many readers
of the *Daily Telegraph*, the obvious target, were singularly satisfied with that
paper: 61 percent of them read no other daily and only 7 percent also read
the *Times*. The *Times* readers themselves were far less happy; only 31 percent
saw no other daily. Evans' most concerted effort was to cover Whitehall in
an informative way; no other national paper followed the developments in
the upper bureaucracy. In 1965 the *Sunday Times* had appointed Tony
Howard to a civil service round, and Harold Wilson, as Prime Minister, at
once ordered that all doors be closed to him. Choosing a soft approach,
Evans appointed Bernard Donoughue as assistant editor and put a group of
reporters under him. They carried out three major investigations and gave
running coverage of Whitehall.

The state of the economy, overshadowed by the paper's own crisis,
suggested other neglected issues. Margaret Thatcher had been in office for
two years; growing unemployment accompanied her attempts to apply
monetarist precepts. Her premises were beginning to be questioned: a
round robin signed by 364 economists was an early expression of malaise
and, from this, the *Times* took its cue to open a discussion. It commissioned
Frank Hahn, a Cambridge professor known for his opposition to monetar-
ism, to write a first article. Hahn characterised monetarist theory as ' in-
coherent and flawed' and challenged its advocates to explain why Britain
had enjoyed its greatest prosperity in the quarter century when Keynesian
policies were followed. From April to July, a debate went on in the business
pages: some articles defended the monetarist approach; others, with titles
like 'Crowding Out – is it an illusion?' and 'Why the monetarists are wrong
on unemployment' carried the challenge further into the Government's
camp. The discussion was part of a wider controversy within the Conservative Party, many of whose members refused to be born again into the
monetarist faith.

If the *Times* had any historic allegiance to the Tories, it felt a strain after
the formation of the Social Democratic Party (SDP) as did a surprising number of previous Tory voters. The SDP looked back to the days of prosperity
and consensus and allied itself with the Liberal Party for electoral purposes.
As the 'Alliance', the two organisations contested three by-elections in 1981.
At two of the three, the *Times* came out in support of the Alliance candidate.

The first was fought by Roy Jenkins, a former senior Labour minister and one of the 'Gang of Four' who left Michael Foot's party. The day before the ballot, the *Times* headed its first leader 'Roy Jenkins for Warrington'; it argued that the SDP avoided extremes, put forward a credible policy on unemployment relief and called the contest 'the by-election of the century.' Jenkins did not win, but cut the Labour majority, and heavily reduced the previous Tory vote. The *Times* called the result 'The Jenkins Effect'; though it was too early to say whether the SDP could become the principal Opposition party or whether a multi-party system might emerge, it hoped that the SDP would maintain its momentum. It went on to favour Shirley Williams, another of the 'Gang of Four', as the Alliance candidate for Croydon West, but it did not support the Liberal who actually ran and won this Conservative seat.

The SDP's wins were seen by some Conservatives as an internal lever to change Margaret Thatcher's more intransigent policies. The support of the *Times* ran on a parallel line. In November Shirley Williams was chosen by the Alliance to stand for Crosby in the Liverpool area, whose voters had given the Conservative candidate a majority of 19,000 in 1979. She received a tumultuous local welcome, and support in the *Times*. The day before the poll, a low-key leader said that readers should ask themselves what an individual candidate could contribute and found the case of a vote for Williams strong. The swing to the Alliance was nearly 25 percent; a first leader commented that Williams now represented 'quintessential Tory territory', a grim message to Thatcher in *Times* cypher.

Murdoch had taken a dislike to the 'Gang of Four' after he met them at lunch, but he did not take specific exception to the *Times* leaders. In the first half of 1981, he was kept busy by two collisions with Robert Maxwell. Maxwell had bought control of British Printing Corporation, the contractors for the *Sunday Times* colour supplement. Murdoch considered that Eric Bemrose, a subsidiary of News International short of work, could print the colour supplement and prepared to move the work there. The dispute heated up and Maxwell was willing to go to court. While this dispute developed, Maxwell, who had been buying into the book publishers William Collins Ltd, brought his holding up to 8 percent. The Collins family, who controlled the company, was divided. On behalf of one faction, Arnold Goodman contacted Murdoch, who agreed to buy the stock controlled by Jan Collins and his mother. As a result, News International held over 30 percent and had to make a public bid for the whole company, which was estimated to cost £stg20 million, more than Times Newspaper Holdings and the Sunday Times building together.

Maxwell and Murdoch settled their differences over the supplement a week before they were to face each other in court. They also did a good deal of other tidying up insisting these were quite separate matters. British Printing Corporation kept the contract: News International proposed to sell Eric Bemrose to Maxwell on ten-year terms. Murdoch bought Maxwell's holding in William Collins and News Ltd made a second public bid for the book publisher. The Collins board rejected this bid and Murdoch announced that he was satisfied with the 42.5 percent equity he now held. At the end of 1981 he bought an apartment in St James' Place, which chanced to be a stone's throw from the London headquarters of William Collins Ltd.

By then the circulation of the *Times* was approaching 300,000 but, with little reduction in the printing staff, heavy losses continued. On 8 February 1982 Murdoch provoked an atmosphere of crisis by sending a letter to all employees of Times Newspapers, warning them that the daily and Sunday would close 'within days rather than weeks', unless 600 jobs were shed. Times Newspapers expected to lose £stg15 million, a figure that would swallow the profits of the *Sun* and the *News of the World*. For a start, he wanted a reduction in the 671 clerical employees; 250 similar employees did the same task for the *Guardian* and the *Observer* combined.[11]

A week later it became known that the titles of the two papers had been transferred from Times Newspapers to News International. The move had been made the previous year to keep the industrial relations of the two papers separate. It now had more far-reaching consequences. If after a closure the liquidator moved in, the titles would not be part of the realisable assets; there might not be enough funds to pay outstanding wages and salaries; News International could reopen elsewhere without being bound by the conditions of the 1981 sale. The national directors had not been consulted about the transfer and one of them, Lord Dacre (Hugh Trevor-Roper), pronounced the failure a prima facie violation of the terms and a gross incivility. Rees-Mogg wrote to the Secretary of State for Trade and, on the BBC, called for the cancellation of the transfer.

According to Murdoch, the transfer was made on legal advice; after officials of the Board of Trade examined the matter, the titles were switched back. The closure did not eventuate. Announcing in March that 430 full-time posts and 400 shifts would disappear, Murdoch promised that the papers were now secure.[12]

V

The papers survived because their joint deficit was met by News International. Yoked together and tied to the old chapels, they had missed the
chance of economic independence a year earlier. What of their editors'
powers? Early in January, Murdoch reshaped the second echelon of the
Sunday Times with the acquiescence of Frank Giles, who had succeeded Evans
there. When the *New Statesman* alleged a violation of the agreement, Giles
informed it that only he could have taken the decisions.

In February, suggestions appeared in Fleet Street, first by word of mouth
and then in print, that Evans would not last at the daily. On 11 February the
front page of the *Times* carried a denial attributed to Murdoch in New
York:

Reports in competitive newspapers that Harold Evans is about to be replaced as
editor of the *Times* are malicious, self-serving and wrong. Mr Evans' outstanding
qualities and journalistic skills are recognised throughout the world, as are his
improvements to the *Times* over the past twelve months.[13]

Five days later, Evans was named Editor of the Year by Granada Television.

Evans' father was in a coma throughout February and died at the beginning of March. Murdoch encouraged him to take time off. On 9 March, the
day after his return, Evans was summoned to Murdoch's office and asked to
resign. Murdoch had already picked a successor: Charles Douglas-Home,
who had proposed his own resignation to Murdoch three weeks before.
Evans refused to resign; Murdoch flew to New York where Anna was preparing a party for his fifty-first birthday and the carriage of the 'resignation' was
left to Richard Searby as chairman of News Corporation and to Gerald Long,
as managing director at Gray's Inn Road.

Evans last saw Murdoch that day – a Tuesday and budget day, for which
the *Times* had mounted a special effort. By Thursday several versions of their
encounter were current in Fleet Street. On Friday the *Times* printed a 'no-
comment' from Evans and said that he was on duty as usual. The *Guardian*
reported at greater length that Murdoch had tried to sack Evans, that
Douglas-Home had told staff he had been appointed editor and that a senior
journalist described the scene as a 'lunatic asylum'. It drew attention to the
supposed role of the national directors in dismissals and appointments.[14] In
fact, the national directors had been told of Murdoch's intentions, but had
not authorised a dismissal.

Though Evans had said 'no comment', he wrote a leader under the title 'The Deeper Issues'. On the surface it considered the budget and the forth-coming by-election at Hillhead, where Roy Jenkins was once more standing for the SDP. It called the prevailing unemployment a social scandal and explained that, in backing Jenkins, it was not embracing the SDP. It thus traversed the issues on which the *Times* had taken a stand over the past year. More deeply, it was a coded resumé of the differences between Evans and Murdoch.[15]

Evans continued to be under pressure all Friday. For the greater part of the past twelve months, Murdoch had been elusive about the paper's own budget, but more recently Gerald Long had asked for drastic expenditure cuts. Richard Searby had been proposing terms of settlement to Evans' soli-citors: should he accept? The journalists were breaking into factions; should he sign? He had helped to write the guarantees for editorial independence; should he allow them to be nullified? He refused to settle and went home.

The next morning even the printed *Times* was in a state of confusion. One item had Murdoch announcing that Evans' departure had been agreed on; another had Anthony Holden, the features editor, alleging that Murdoch wanted an extreme right wing line and had complained about articles on British Rail, Poland and the SDP.[16] The *Guardian* was more pungent; it quoted Holden saying 'Mr Murdoch wants a poodle as editor and I'm not going to work for a poodle'; it canvassed possible disagreements among the national directors.[17] On Sunday a writer in the *Observer* put his finger on one source of Murdoch's strength: 'The staff and the directors were so divided – and so punch-drunk from the closure threats – that Murdoch went through them all like a knife through butter.'[18]

Time was working for Murdoch who stayed in New York. On the week-end, Lord Robens, one of the national directors, told BBC listeners that though it was the function of his group to approve appointments and dis-missals, it could act only if approached by Evans. Evans did speak to some of them; they could not meet before Wednesday. On Monday morning Evans was back in his office in a bouncy mood, but it wore off and late in the day he decided that the situation could not be prolonged. He contacted Independ-ent Television News, signed the lawyers' papers and announced his resigna-tion to the cameras. Two of the assistant editors resigned in his wake; a third was twice summoned before Douglas-Home, asked to account for his actions, and was then dismissed.

Evans received hundreds of letters from present and past colleagues; some spoke of the golden era of journalism that ended with his departure from the *Sunday Times*. He had believed in the safeguards he helped to set up;

he was a journalist, not an office politician. The idyll was at an end and he was shattered. A year and a half later, he published a detailed account of his experiences in a book. Under another proprietor, they would have made a fine serial and lifted the sales of the *Sunday Times*.

THE TIMES

SATURDAY JUNE 12 1982

Reagan fails to allay Berlin fear

resident Reagan, visiting erlin, proposed an extended ut line" between the Krem and the White House. But speech did nothing to allay fears of those Berliners cerned at his hard-line confrontation with Russia. As spoke, police fought street les with more than 2,000 ng people opposing his cies.
Page 5

365m limit r BSC

s of further job losses plant closures at the h Steel Corporation with the announcement external financing had limited to L365m. In the d States, a ruling that ean steel exports were threatened to deprive of one of its traditional ts
Page 17

ding on 'free ge eggs'

ter Peake was fined at Shrewsbury Magis Court for describing from hens housed in at his Shropshire farm e range" The case ught by the country's standards depart

ective killed RA bomb

Ulster Constabulary was killed when a mb exploded in a hed in Londonderry

Galtieri says Argentina will fight on regardless

By Our Foreign Staff

General Galtieri, the Argentine President, has no regrets over the deaths of hundreds of his young troops in the Falklands conflict. In an interview with the Italian journalist, Oriana Fallaci, published in *The Times* today, on page 4, he claims that Argentina will fight on, whatever the outcome of the battle for Port Stanley.

He invokes the Dunkirk spirit and says that Argentina will never accept a return to the position before the occupation of the islands. He calls Mrs Thatcher "politically inadequate" for the historical moment"

The United States is accused of "betrayal" for taking the British side after the breakdown of Mr Alexander Haig's mediation attempt. President Galtieri expresses his ultimate readiness to accept weapons from the Soviet Union. He claims that the Falklands crisis has paved the way for political life in Argentina.

But questioned about the thousands of former opponents of the military regime who have disappeared

FALKLANDS ROUNDUP

How warships died ... 5
Patrols near Stanley ... 5
Enoch Powell ... 12
Leading article, letters 13

place at Puerto Argentino (the name the occupiers have given to Port Stanley) is not so grave as you expect"

Even if the capital were to fall, he would not wonder if he had made a mistake. "Remember when, in the Second World War, the British were defeated at Dunkirk? Well, in 1945, they were in Berlin"

He denied that he had acted as he did because Latin machismo had convinced him that a British woman Prime Minister would not go to war.

Questioned about "the driving necessity" that made him invade, General Galtieri described the British threat to expel the group of Argentine scrap merchants from South Georgia in March as "the straw that broke the camel's back"

From Tony Samstag Southampton

The Queen Eliza

among them were 21 wounded, but only one who still Yacht Britannia with Queen

QE2 sails home to welcome fit for a que

FINAL
SPORTS EXTRA

NEW YORK POST

25 cents   AMERICA'S FASTEST-GROWING NEWSPAPER

40 warships steam to Falklands

BRITISH LAUNCH INVASION FORCE

... But in Argentina they're dancin' in the streets

New Red weapon

the loss of hu the long-term quences of the conflict.

The Pope arr at 3 pm to gre members of Catholic hierar boarded the kissed the gro Galtieri promptly knee and kissed ring

The Pope's livered in Spanish delicate offered the junta

THE Sun

8-PAGE WORLD CUP PULLOUT
—Begins on Page 13

£50,000 Birthday Bingo Bonanza
—Page 5
Lucky numbers
—Page 20

14p   THE PAPER THAT SUPPORTS OUR BOYS

King Arthur slams Lord Joe

LOVELY TO SEE YOU!

Oh, what a welcome   A PRETTY

Chapter Fourteen

/// *The Empire Strikes Back* ///

By purchasing the London *Times* without having won in New York, Murdoch committed his personal energies and a significant slice of corporate profits to two simultaneous, drawn-out fights. His failure to knock down the *Daily News*, followed by a poor balance sheet in June 1982, made him jumpy. He began a course of forward moves and backtracks; on occasion, his journalistic judgement was clouded and his business calculations were aberrant. Then he struck it lucky again and his horizon was wider than ever.

He had barely shed Harry Evans at the *Times* when he became Margaret Thatcher's brother in arms. They had grown together ever since the 1979 election, when his papers, like the majority of Fleet Street, supported the Tories. She was unsympathetic to those who had been snooty to him in the early 1970s; he expected economic recovery under her rule. 'It's going to take a lot to break down the snobbery and shibboleths to reverse the gentrification of Britain,' he told a gathering of advertising people in April 1981. Thatcher did not despise commerce, and in Murdoch's view she differed from the last six prime ministers, who liked to be photographed 'as either men of the countryside or men of the sea'.[1] In the Falklands conflict he gave her full endorsement; his key papers in three continents became her shrillest advocates.

On the first weekend of April 1982, Fleet Street was in chaos over the Falklands. The officials assigned to deal with the media were unprepared for action in so distant a place. The Ministry of Defence allocated five berths on the ships heading for the South Atlantic to newspaper reporters; their names were to be picked from a hat by the Newspaper Publishers Association. None of the five drawn worked for Murdoch's papers. Help came from

241

Bernard Ingham, the Principal Private Secretary at 10 Downing Street, who all that weekend talked to editors about policy, practicalities and finally more berths. When the first ships sailed, the *Sun* and the *Times* each had a reporter aboard the aircraft carrier *HMS Invincible* (then on sale to Australia); four days later, the *Sunday Times* had a reporter on the south-bound converted troop carrier *Canberra*.

In theory at least, the future of the Falklands was a matter for international mediation for some weeks. Thatcher's first task was to get acceptance for her Government's somersault from appeasement into the possible use of force. The Foreign Office and Argentina had been conducting talks for years; a mere eighty British marines were stationed at Port Stanley, the Falklands capital, when Argentinian forces overwhelmed them. The media had not prepared for the somersault. On 1 April the *Times*, with a long tradition of loyalty to the Foreign Office, ran a non-news item captioned: 'Impenetrable silence on Falklands crisis'. The next morning the British marines surrendered: the *Times* had led its front page with a report that the United Nations would meet. The Government would not confirm the surrender till eight that night and meanwhile summoned the House of Commons to the emergency meeting the next morning, a Saturday. The *Times* now faced a choice between its friends at the Foreign Office and the Prime Minister's imminent change of line.

On 3 April confusion reigned even in the paper's late edition. Simon Winchester, a correspondent for the *Sunday Times*, was on the spot and filed a cable with the daily, but was relegated to the third page. On the front page, a headline proclaimed that Lord Carrington, the Foreign Secretary, had expelled Argentina's diplomats, another that the Fleet was ready to sail, a third that the invaders' flag flew over Port Stanley. Only the first leader was clear-cut. The Argentinian action was 'Naked Aggression', it said, without example since the days of Adolf Hitler.

In the House of Commons, Thatcher had no choice but to announce retaliation. To her right were seventy Tory backbenchers addicted to Empire, to her left was Michael Foot, the Labour leader, who complained of 'betrayal'. Charles Douglas-Home had the weekend to write an approving mega-leader which he spread over half the editorial page on Monday. 'We Are All Falklanders Now', it proclaimed in fat letters. The British were an island race, one of their islands had been attacked, and with John Donne, it concluded that the bell had tolled for Britain. Hidden in the text was one of those messages the *Times* often carried from one small group of its readers to another. Douglas-Home questioned the capacity of John Nott, the Minister for Defence, to inspire confidence and he cast doubt on the standing of Lord

Carrington. The *Daily Mail* voiced the same uncertainties. That afternoon Carrington resigned and Nott offered to turn in his portfolio but was asked to stay. For the moment, one scapegoat was enough to keep everyone happy with Thatcher.

Striking a first shrill note the next day, the *Sun* proclaimed that the Foreign Office had been a haven for appeasers since Munich. The *Times*, perhaps conscious of its role in pre-war days, disentangled itself more graciously. Carrington, though having got it wrong, had provided a bridge for a Prime Minister coming into office without familiarity with foreign affairs; the Foreign Office, however, was responsible for intelligence and deterrence. This let the Prime Minister off all too lightly. Early in 1982 she had appointed Sir Anthony Duff as Deputy Secretary to her department as a channel for intelligence. With similar oblivion Lord Home, the editor's uncle (who had accompanied Neville Chamberlain to Munich), chimed in with an article saying that politicians not officials should be blamed for what had happened, without naming any politicians.

Despite this confusion, the *Times* had managed to move over into the Prime Minister's circle. As Rupert Murdoch put it in the next Annual Report of News Corporation, it was 'once again speaking with the authority which gave it its traditional place in Great Britain'.[2]

For most of April no shots were fired, the correspondents were immured on the ships and, even after the landings, their despatches were at the mercy of the Ministry of Defence, which controlled transmissions and preferred to release information in London. Murdoch's editors made up in fervour what they lacked in news.

Free from official restraints and with a lead time of five hours on British clocks, the *New York Post* reported events before they took place, and even when they didn't. On 2 April it said that a British Fleet had 'reportedly' been sent to mount a counter-invasion; on 3 April it had 40 warships steaming to the South Atlantic; on 5 April, a British 'armada' was on the way. To bring the war home to New Yorkers, James Brady wrote on 'Page Six': 'Like many of our diplomats, I worry about the domino theory. The Falkland Islands this week, the Sandwich Islands [ie., Hawaii] next, then maybe Coney Island. Who knows where the Argentinians, flushed with victory, will be stopped.'[3]

In Sydney, the *Australian*'s coverage was less frenzied. Australia's media were immune to the Falklands fever, and though the Prime Minister issued a statement in support of the United Kingdom, the Deputy Prime Minister, who had been working out a common approach to the EEC with Argentina, was miffed. The *Australian* did not catch up fully with its proprietor's enthusiasm until the middle of the month, and then began to set aside a whole section under the running lines: 'The Falklands Crisis' (14 April – 2 May), 'The Falklands War' (3 May – 31 May) and 'The Falklands Aftermath'.

Over those two months the *Times* worked hard at keeping the Falklands at the top of its first page; only the visit of Pope John Paul II pushed the islands off the prime place on its newsmap. For the *Sun*, the Falklands were equally serious business: for one historic day, the photographic models migrated from page three to page nine.

When nothing of note appeared on the telex machines, the *Sun* turned itself into the centre of attention. Kelvin MacKenzie, the thirty-six-year-old editor, was cut out for this act. On 20 April he launched a boycott on Argentinian corned beef with the slogan 'STICK IT UP YOUR JUNTA'. The *Sun*'s promotions department was so pleased with these five finely crafted words that it offered 'Sunsational' tee-shirts at two pounds each, carrying the slogan in big letters. Towards the end of April the journalists on the *Sun* went on strike, but the added load of bringing out the paper did not quench MacKenzie's fire. On 1 May he varied the slogan and its application: 'STICK THIS UP YOUR JUNTA'. 'THIS' was a Sidewinder missile, sponsored by the *Sun* and inscribed 'UP YOURS GALTIERI' by Tony Snow, the paper's correspondent aboard *HMS Invincible*. As Snow duly reported, it hit an enemy plane.

The war grew hotter when a British submarine sank the Argentine cruiser *General Belgrano* outside the exclusion zone declared by the British, and several hundred Argentinians drowned. The *Sun* summed up the event in one word 'GOTCHA!'. The Government had tried to present the conflict as a professional exercise: on the British side, the orders came from civilians, in contrast to the military junta on the other side. The televised face releasing the news was Ian McDonald, a career civil servant in the Ministry of Defence with a classics degree and a mother in Scotland. 'GOTCHA!' was a *faux pas*; Robert Harris later chose the headline as the title of his study of the unhappy relations between the media and the Government.[4]

It was a mere preliminary to the *Sun*'s next effort. The Argentinians retaliated by sinking the HMS *Sheffield*, and the dovish *Guardian* and *Daily Mirror* wondered aloud whether too high a price was being paid for the islands. The *Sun* now found the true enemy at home. It took its cue from Margaret Thatcher. In covering the conflict the BBC had pursued its long-term credibility with domestic and foreign audiences by sometimes quoting Argentinian sources along with British. On 6 May a Conservative backbencher asked the Prime Minister whether she could find time to watch radio and television and whether the British view was being presented in a way likely to give 'support and encouragement to our servicemen and their families'.

Her reply was that she understood the Argentinians were being treated almost as equals.

'Dare call it treason', the *Sun* headed its editorial the next day. It underlined the first sentence: 'There are traitors in our midst.' The *Sun* would not hesitate to use a word the Prime Minister had not used. As 'traitors' it named Peter Snow, the BBC's defence correspondent who had doubted a government version of the sea battles, the *Guardian* which had printed a cartoon with the line 'The price of sovereignty has been increased – official', and the *Daily Mirror* which had pleaded for the appeasement of the Argentinian dictators. Having hoisted the flag, the *Sun* pitched for sales: it declared itself sorry for those who read the *Daily Mirror*, a paper that had no faith in the country.

The *Sun* enjoyed more attention than popularity in the days that followed. A Labour member urged the Attorney-General to prosecute for criminal libel; the National Union of Journalists called the editorial 'odious and hysterical'; and the *Daily Mirror*, seldom drawn into controversy with other papers, ran a full-page reply. It called the *Sun* 'the Harlot of Fleet Street', but rejected public prosecution, because the verdict would run 'criminal but insane'. What would the *Times* have said under Rees-Mogg as editor and Thomson as proprietor? Under Douglas-Home and Murdoch, it failed to editorialise and printed an article by Simon Jenkins of the *Economist*, who found that the *Sun*'s editorial would have made Senator McCarthy blush.[5] The *Sun* dismissed its critics and adopted the slogan 'The paper that supports our boys'.

Murdoch was in New York for much of this time, preoccupied with the potential conquest of Manhattan Island, but he found time to make a personal plea for the war. The occasion was a dinner given by the American Jewish Congress to honour the first recipient of its 'Communications Man of the Year' award, who had been nominated by Howard Squadron, at once president of the donor and attorney to the recipient. Accepting, Murdoch told the 300 guests at the Hilton that the confrontation between Britain and Argentina was a useful reminder of what might happen in the Middle East: in both conflicts democracies were opposing dictators, and the case for supporting Britain was exactly the same as for supporting Israel. The applauding guests included Roy Cohn, a former aide to Senator Joe McCarthy, George Steinbrenner, the owner of the Yankees, and a bevy of elected officials. The American press was represented by two sons of the late Samuel Newhouse who had sold the delivery list of the *Long Island Press* to Rupert Murdoch.[6]

In 1982 the opinion polls showed Margaret Thatcher suddenly restored to popularity and the Alliance of Social Democrats and Liberals relegated to insignificance. Political commentators began to speak of 'the Falklands factor'. It did not work for Rupert Murdoch in the same way as for Margaret Thatcher. From average sales of 14.9 million in March 1982, the Fleet Street dailies rose to 15.2 million in May. The *Sun* lost 40,000 average sales while the *Daily Mirror*, its close rival, gained 95,000. Because the *Mirror* had started a promotion campaign before the conflict broke out, it is impossible to attribute the circulation trends of these two popular papers to the discrimination of British readers.[7]

All was normal again in June when the *Queen Elizabeth II* brought the first contingent back from the Falklands. The *Sun* celebrated the arrival of the men with a front-page photograph of a young woman baring her breasts in a waiting boat, ostensibly for the benefit of the passengers and crew of the liner.[8] At the end of that month, when other papers responded to the rise in newsprint costs that followed the decline of the pound sterling, the *Sun* briefly stayed at 14p to recapture readers.

II

On the morning before the 1982 annual general meeting of News Corporation in Adelaide, Murdoch recorded an interview with the ABC radio programme 'City Extra'. He talked soberly of the future of his newspapers; he would not buy any more, though having started negotiations for the Boston *Herald-American*, he entered a caveat excepting 'certain American cities'. The interviewer then put a more personal question: 'Is there anything of which you are frightened?' He paused and replied with a generality: 'A lot of people are very fearful of what is happening in the economy.'[9]

He expressed a mood spread widely among Australian businessmen. For the past eighteen months the global recession had been kept offshore by an anticipation of high demand for energy resources, but now it was settling over the continent. The decline was particularly unwelcome to News Corporation, whose Australian base was the only overall source of black figures in the report put before shareholders that day. The pre-tax profits made within the group had fallen from $A62.4 million in 1981 to $A12.8 million in 1982; the associated companies, contributing $A38 million, against $A28.6 million in 1981, had partly redeemed the result and to that redeeming sum, Ansett Transport Industries had made the largest contribution. The airline, however, was particularly prone to the shrinkage in demand during recession. As for the United States, there was still an overall loss; and in Britain, Times Newspapers and a new colour supplement to the *News of the World* were devouring most of the other surpluses.

The greatest immediate pressure came from high interest rates. The servicing of loans taken in since 1979 was swallowing large sums. These problems had been acknowledged by new appointments: Stanley Shuman of Allen and Co. Inc. had joined the Board; Richard Sarazen had returned to the organisation as full-time finance director, replacing Merv Rich who became vice-chairman. But there was no going back on some of the expansion and expenses already planned. A morning tabloid using the plant of the Brisbane Sunday paper had gone ahead. Larry Lamb came to Sydney via Western Australia, where he had worked for Robert Holmes a'Court, to edit the *Australian*. He shrunk the headline types, cut the staff, watched the circulation drop further and went back to London where he surfaced at the *Daily Express* some months later. Most of all, Rupert Murdoch himself was incurring new liabilities.

The least helpful was a deal with Robert Holmes a'Court. In characteristic fashion, Holmes a'Court had built up, over three years, a holding in Thomas Nationwide Transport, the partner of News Corporation in ATI. With a parcel of just under 10 percent, Holmes a'Court assured the TNT directors in 1981 that he was merely a passive investor. A year later the TNT directors decided to bring the stock holdings into line with the operational interlock between TNT and ATI freight operations they had created, and on 24 September 1982 they announced that they and their associates were in control of 23 percent of TNT stock. The major part of this holding was through ATI and an affiliated shipping company. Signalling an intention to stay in TNT, Holmes a'Court bought further small parcels.

Murdoch thereupon rang Holmes a'Court from New York proposing to buy the TNT holding, an offer that was promptly accepted. A first announcement put the amount at 20 million stock units, but it was superseded by a lower figure of 16.4 million. In the rush of events, the requirements of the new National Companies Act were overlooked: bidders for more than 20 percent in listed corporations had to follow procedures laid down in detailed schedules, which News Corporation had not done. At issue was the question whether the parcel bought by News Corporation should be counted with ATI's and perhaps others controlled by TNT. A long legal tangle followed; late in 1983 News Corporation's holding was down to 6.2 percent.

The terms which Murdoch arranged with Holmes a'Court indicated the constraints under which he was now working. The principal sum of $A32 million would not be paid for a year; until then, monthly interest would be incurred at the prevailing rate for commercial bills plus a small premium – a costly exercise. When he next bought the *Herald-American* in Boston (week-day circulation 228,000, Sunday 227,000, against the rival *Boston Globe*'s 517,000 and 750,000), he put down $US1 million and agreed to another $US7 million if and when profits were made. In February 1983 Murdoch went into even slower motion over the purchase of ATI's subsidiary Austa-rama, which held the Channel 10 licence for Melbourne and owned a small FM radio station. The Austarama operation was making a loss, the agreed transfer price was $A13.2 million, and payment was to be as late as June 1984.

The half-yearly profit figures, released in March, were the first encourag-ing sign in nine months; at the end of the month, an even better prospect showed on the horizon. Murdoch had been saying for two years that if the *Sunday Times* could do a million and a half copies on weekends (it sold some-what fewer), then the *Times* should be able to reach the half million mark on weekdays. Charles Douglas-Home now heard of an opportunity for a quantum jump: Gerd Heidemann, a staff reporter on the Hamburg weekly *Stern*, claimed he had unearthed Hitler's secret diaries and *Stern* was willing to sell their first English-language release. Murdoch was alerted.

The *Daily Mail* and *Newsweek*, who had also been approached by *Stern*, showed initial interest. Murdoch decided on a joint bid with *Newsweek* who would take the American rights while he would publish in Britain and Aus-tralia. Confident of the value of the material, *Stern* wanted $US4 million and insisted on spreading publication over eighteen months to get the maximum benefit in Germany. As a bargaining move, Murdoch held off and *Newsweek* dropped out.

From the beginning, the copyright to any of Hitler's writings presented complications; copyright ownership was quite a different matter from pos-session of the manuscripts. Who *did* own the copyright? A Bavarian court had decided that all of Hitler's property would pass into the possession of the State of Bavaria. A federal court had upheld the validity of Hitler's will, as a result of which his property passed to the Federal Republic. To resolve the situation, the Federal Archive was given the task of administering the copy-right and of securing more of Hitler's writings as they turned up. Accord-ingly, *Stern* submitted nine documents to the Archive: eight of them bore no relation to any diaries; the ninth was part of the section relating to Rudolf Hess, who had absconded to Britain during the war, though it was not pre-sented as a part of any diaries. With the object of acquiring further original documents, the Archive agreed that *Stern* could utilise its discoveries and that the Archive would then get possession of the documents.[10]

At *Stern* and among those with whom it negotiated, the publishing project was shrouded in secrecy; the documents themselves were kept in a Zurich bank vault. On the Murdoch side, less than half a dozen people were involved in the negotiations and none of them was expert in Hitleriana, where fakes were constantly being put on the market. Accordingly, Lord Dacre, one of the national directors, was sent to Zurich to give an opinion. Under the name Hugh Trevor-Roper he was an authority on Stuart England, the author of a post-war bestseller on Hitler's last days and the editor of some translated Nazi documents. Dacre judged the documents in Zurich to be authentic on the external and internal evidence and later set out his reasons in an article for the *Times*.

After mid-April, *Stern* moved its own publication date forward to early May and lowered its price for British and Australian rights to $US400,000. Murdoch bought and began to look for a way of having tasty extracts appear in London before *Stern*'s first instalment appeared. As a result, the *Sunday Times*, not the *Times*, would serve up the appetiser. A leak sprung, and on Friday 22 April 1983 Douglas-Home went on television vouching for the authenticity of the manuscripts. The next morning the *Times* published Dacre's assessment and made the impending publication front-page news.[11]

The secrecy surrounding the preparations was the mainspring of the humiliation that promptly followed. *Stern* had not carried out proper tests on the material; Murdoch had not done so either. Had he been more open within his organisation, he might not have been deceived so easily. The British Hitler biographer David Irving who had been shown some of the material in the previous year, decided that it was forged. He had good friends on the *Sunday Times*. The paper's staff remembered vividly the purchase of Mussolini letters in 1967, which turned out to be forgeries and were not published. The 'Hitler Diaries' were turned over to it late, but, remembering the Mussolini slip, the staff rechecked with Dacre, who continued to issue assurances. Once his article was published in the *Times* Dacre got cold feet; Murdoch pressed for publication.

The forgery was expertly baited for newshounds. Brian MacArthur, the deputy editor of the *Sunday Times* who had been appointed at Murdoch's personal behest, introduced the snippets with the observation that Hitler 'had made acid comments about other world leaders and demonstrated the tenderness of his love for Eva Braun'.[12] The manuscripts whitewashed Hitler. On existing accounts, for instance, the extermination of European Jewry had been decided at a notorious conference early in 1942; the 'Diaries' presented this decision as a resettlement plan, thus absolving Hitler from the worst of his crimes. This alone assured that the documents would be closely scrutinised by historians and challenged by Hitler's victims.

The challenges began at once. *Stern* held a pre-publication press conference on Monday; Dacre went to Hamburg, questioned Heidemann, the purveyor of the hoard, and his doubts increased. He now said so in public; so did David Irving who had been flown in by a rival German publisher and questioned the ink used in the manuscripts. *Stern*, with an increased print run, released the first instalment and followed with a second a week later. The *Sunday Times* held off the next Sunday, promising to publish after further authentication. As the number of highly qualified sceptics grew, *Stern* agreed to chemical tests on the originals and submitted the text to the Federal Archive. Within two days, the Archive's verdict of forgery came down. With hurriedly acquired samples, the *Sunday Times* commissioned a parallel laboratory examination and asked Norman Stone, a Cambridge historian who had recently worked on Hitler, to look at the German originals. The British examiners concurred in the German verdict.

At *Stern*, a part of the large Bertelsmann publishing group, journalistic, editorial and managerial heads rolled. At Times Newspapers, they merely bowed. 'Serious journalism is a high-risk enterprise,' the *Sunday Times* said in an apology to its readers.[13] Rupert Murdoch kept out of sight. It was just over twelve months since he had been appointed 'Communications Man of the Year' by the American Jewish Congress.

III

There had been no single moment when Rupert Murdoch established himself on the political right. His enmity to Whitlam Labor in 1975–6 had been followed by a campaign against his old South Australian friends in 1978. He had supported Margaret Thatcher in 1979 and Ronald Reagan in 1980 and had not deserted them thereafter. But his most lasting alliance was with Ed Koch, the changeable New York Mayor, whose constituents he was prudent enough not to affront with the spurious 'Hitler Diaries'. It was Koch's style of accommodation that Murdoch brought to bear on a tricky situation in Australia.

Towards the end of 1982 and again in February 1983, Murdoch spent several weeks in Australia, attending to the base, giving a reception at the Kirribilli Yacht Club and, at the request of Neville Wran, the Premier of New

South Wales, raising funds for the State Gallery. Wran was currently his closest senior contact in the Labor camp; he had cultivated the Premier when he took office in 1976 and the ties firmed after the partnership with Sir Peter Abeles, whose TNT did a good deal of business with the State Rail Authority of New South Wales and who had become a personal friend of the Premier.

It was an uneasy southern summer. Malcolm Fraser, Murdoch's childhood playmate, had twice been on the point of calling an election before the vacation, but put off a decision. The campaign broke out on 3 February 1983, a turbulent day in the course of which Bob Hawke replaced Bill Hayden as Opposition Leader and Fraser went to the Governor-General with a request for a double dissolution as the preliminary to the campaign. Leslie Hollings, once more editing the *Australian*, relished a fight in defence of the Government. 'FRASER versus HAWKE' ran the front page on 4 February; the day's editorial argued for 'strong, stable government', meaning under Fraser. Its editorial support was most pronounced after Hawke presented his economic policy, which the paper called 'a threat to freedom'. The news columns also favoured Fraser, whom photographs showed smiling and friendly, while Hawke invariably pulled a face.

For the duration of the campaign, the *Australian* sponsored public opinion polls, which showed Labor comfortably in the lead; the reports might have ranked as 'favourable to Labor' in a bias study, but the *Australian* had its own way of presenting them. Three days before the ballot, a poll showed 39 percent for the Coalition, 48 per cent for Labor. On polling day, the figures were 40 percent for the Coalition, 50 percent for Labor. The *Australian* reported the last result under the headline 'Latest poll shows Fraser gaining'; by orthodox arithmetic, Labor had made a net gain of 1 percent.

On his return to Sydney in the second half of February, Murdoch was more deeply impressed by the polls than the editorials. He had made earlier attempts to live down his unrewarding reputation as Labor's Publishing Enemy Number One. In 1980 a common friend had talked to Ken Cowley, the chairman of Mirror Newspapers, and to Bill Hayden, the Labor leader, in an effort to arrange a meeting between Murdoch and Hayden; Hayden rejected the feeler. Hawke was now standing on a platform of 'national reconciliation'. His strategists did not want vehemence from Murdoch's papers nor retaliatory vitriol from their own ranks. Murdoch was prepared to make contact with Paul Keating, the shadow Treasurer and John Button, the shadow Minister for Communications. By the end of the campaign, Labor headquarters were aware that Murdoch was anxious to see the issue of a third television licence in the Perth area as an outlet for the product of

his eastern channels. Since News Corporation was disqualified from controlling yet another channel, the proposed issue of a licence to a third party
would be no great embarrassment; it was awkward only because Robert
Holmes a'Court, who supported Labor on the state and federal levels,
owned one of the existing two stations in Perth.

The gregarious Hawke himself was easy to deal with. Murdoch had
lunched with him back in January 1976, when Hawke was federal president
of the Labor Party and Murdoch its *bête noire*. As the newly chosen Opposition Leader, Hawke's first major move was to avert a national strike in the oil
refineries, which would have given Fraser the opportunity to focus on the
issue of union power. Hawke's success particularly pleased his old friend
Abeles, whose ATI planes and TNT trucks would have been stalled by a fuel
shortage, a prospect that had worried Abeles for weeks.

How could Murdoch show fairmindedness without putting his papers'
political drive into reverse? A way out was to hand. Hawke had challenged
Fraser to a face-to-face debate; Murdoch offered a time slot on his channels
and sought Fraser's participation, without complete success. On the night of
2 March the two leaders made separate appearances on Melbourne's Channel 10. After the show Murdoch escorted Hawke through the back door,
where they were snapped by a press photographer.

Hawke won the election. By November 1983 Murdoch had nothing but
contempt for the loser Fraser: 'The poor chap is miserable . . . he is running
round the world with other ex-heads of government telling present ones
how to do their job.' He might have been talking about a former editor and
his replacement as he added: 'Bob Hawke has obviously had a brilliant
start.'[14]

Murdoch's commercial position had then improved. Though ATI's operations in the air declined and the arrival of the large Boeings, purchased in
1980, proved untimely, Abeles had made another successful investment.
Having been in and out of metals and mining on his personal account for a
quarter of a century, Abeles had put ATI into a 14.9 percent stake in Santos
Ltd, a central Australian gas producer, in 1980. In July 1983 further large
reserves of gas were confirmed, Santos stock doubled in price and ATI sold
its holding for $A188 million, a net profit of $A110 million after three years.
A special dividend distributed the profit to the two partners. Apart from
giving News Corporation cash, the distribution opened up another possibility. Murdoch had on occasion talked about selling News Corporation's
half of ATI, should the need for money arise. TNT would be the obvious
buyer, but it had not been flush with funds in the past. Having received a
parallel special dividend, it was in a better position. The annual results of

News Corporation to June 1983 were equally encouraging; pre-tax profits within the group recovered spectacularly, the North American operations were in the black, the *Times'* losses were down and the two British popular papers netted $A51 million, a figure equal to 51 percent of the group's post-tax profits of $A87 million.

Murdoch also hoped for a second infusion through Times Newspapers, which held a valuable parcel of stock in Reuters Ltd, the wire service. Reuters proposed to go public in the next twelve months and the parcel held by Murdoch might then be worth well over $A100 million and would be realisable. Since May he had also been watching Chicago, where the two Field brothers, who owned Field Enterprises, found themselves in disagreement about the future of the corporation's daily, the *Sun-Times*. Outstripping other bidders, Murdoch offered $US90 million in October, was accepted as the conditional buyer and settled for $US100 million in January 1984, when he took over. The profits of Field Enterprises were reputed to run between $US3 and $US5 million a year; he therefore purchased at about twenty times the profit, but the tax liability could once again be set off against the losses he was making in Boston, on the paper renamed *Boston-Herald*.

The Chicago purchase brought him into confrontation with the Tribune Company on its home territory. The *Sun-Times*, with a circulation of 639,000, was running second to the *Tribune* with 751,000. As Murdoch moved in, Mike Royko, the *Sun-Times'* popular columnist, moved to the *Tribune*. James Hoge, the *Sun-Times'* publisher, had already left, and in March showed up in New York, in charge of the *Daily News*. In its first six weeks under a Murdoch executive, the *Sun-Times'* average sales fell by 30,000. The Tribune Company learnt that Murdoch was not invincible; or was it just because he could not give Chicago much personal attention?

IV

Unlike Britain, the United States cannot easily be painted Murdoch-yellow with a single daily emanating from one city, such as the London *Sun*. If Murdoch were to extend his American operation with large steps, he had to take to the airwaves. Unfortunately for him, American communication laws prohibit foreigners from getting control of any one television channel; and the regulators of television look askance at cross-holdings between newspapers and television channels in any given area. Murdoch therefore began to explore newer forms of communication. In an interview in 1981, he ruled out cable television as too costly, but described satellite broadcasting as a cheaper way of getting into American homes. At the time he confessed that he had only 'spasms of interest' in these systems.[15]

The spasms became more regular after he engaged an Australian from the Institute for Future Studies at the University of Southern California to form a small research group. In the first half of 1983 News Corporation bought a majority holding in the ailing Satellite Television PLC, which provided a service from Britain to north European cable franchisers; and more ambitiously, it acquired control of the California-based Inter-American Satellite Television Network, whose name was changed to Skyband Inc. with headquarters on Third Avenue, under Murdoch's watchful eye. Skyband leased transponders on the SBS-3 satellite, scheduled transmissions over five channels for 1984 and budgeted a good deal of money to set up earth stations in outlying parts of the United States to receive the satellite signals. Murdoch was willing to debit these outlays against the next two years' profits of News Corporation, but early in November 1983 he blew a firm retreat. His planners had initially counted on a market of seventeen million rural households; the figure was revised down to two million to allow for the households that competitors could snatch. The beginning of the Skyband operation was put off for another eighteen months.[16]

The satellite broadcasting project made Murdoch look around for programmes to transmit. The demand could be enormous in two years: in the industry there were highly optimistic forecasts of eight broadcasting satellites with up to 200 channels. The needed programmes would be sought in existing studios and in libraries holding past feature films. On 23 August 1983 Stanley Shuman took Murdoch to the vacation house of Steven J. Ross, the chairman and chief executive of Warner Communications Inc. (WCI). Ross was in the course of buying a part of 'Showtime', the second-largest pay-TV channel in the United States and Murdoch thought he might like to participate in the purchase. But this was not all he had in mind. WCI had a large film-making studio and a library of movies highly successful in the past; and significantly, WCI stock was selling at a bargain price of about $US20 a unit, compared to over $US60 the previous year.

Ross showed no enthusiasm for Murdoch joining him in 'Showtime', but when Murdoch expressed a wish to buy WCI stock, Ross did not object. The next day Allen and Co. Inc. started to take in units at $US20.75 and at the end of September News Corporation announced that it held 1.7 percent of WCI, a proportion not without significance for a corporation whose holdings were widely dispersed.

The decline in WCI market prices, which was enticing Murdoch, had begun in December 1982 after Ross warned his stockholders that earnings for the last quarter of 1982 would be down and that he expected further difficulties in the first half of 1983. According to Ross the problem lay largely with Atari Inc., the subsidiary that manufactured computer goods based on silicon chips and, within Atari, from a drastic drop in profits from video cartridges, the software for Atari game machines, for which there had been a craze in the previous two years. Within ten days of Ross's warning, WCI stock tumbled from $US54 to below $US31.

As market analysts looked more closely at their recent darling, they came up with devastating dissections. They found that in 1981 and for part of 1982, Atari had command of nearly 80 percent of the video cartridge market. A cartridge costs a few dollars to make and retailed for $US20. With the cartridge craze Atari's revenue had grown from $US238 million in 1979 to $US1.2 billion in 1981, and the trading results from a loss of $US2.7 million in 1979 to a profit of $US286 million in 1981. The other Atari products did not count: the home computers, expensively promoted, were in the red and the coin-operated machines performed indifferently for their makers. The gloss was now off Atari cartridges, for there were as many as twenty rival manufacturers, providing competition and forcing down prices.

WCI held a large, though mixed, bag of tricks for the leisure market: crowd-pulling movies like 'The Extra-Terrestrial'; recorded music, with stars like Linda Ronstadt on contract; a diversified book publishing house; a national magazine distributor; and the monthly *Mad*. It also owned half of the money-loser Warner Amex Cable, which needed further funds for wiring its television franchise areas, and all of a smaller loss-maker, Knickerbocker Toys, which it was selling. Whatever other faults disillusioned analysts could now find, they agreed that just as Atari had made WCI a glamour corporation, so Atari's decline would sink its parent like lead. In the first half of 1983 WCI showed heavy losses.

As Murdoch continued to buy, the price of WCI stock was likely to recover somewhat. To get it all might cost him $US2.1 billion; to get half of it, over a billion.

The most fashionable way of financing a purchase of this size was the 'leveraged loan' with a high gearing of borrowed money to funds provided by the purchaser himself. To effect this, a purchaser might pledge to his lenders some of the assets inside the corporation he was buying and, on getting control, would sell off those assets and repay his loans. But the uncertainty over what was and what was not valuable inside WCI made a leverage deal difficult. Murdoch would therefore have to borrow on News Corporation's credit, backed by his personal reputation as an entrepreneur who knew what he was about. A section of Wall Street regarded him with considerable favour, a good opinion that spread to News Corporation whose stock was to reach $A11.50 on the Australian market, after a low point of $A1.60 in 1982. Murdoch could easily borrow a billion dollars, according to several commentators who were not called to produce that sum for him.

The first cloud appeared on the horizon when Herbert J. Siegel, a friend of Steven Ross and the head of Chris-Craft Industries, an investor in television stations, met Murdoch at a party in October 1983. In a brief conversation Siegel told Murdoch that 'Steve' had a lot of friends; not on Wall Street, Murdoch replied dismissively.[17] On 1 December, News Corporation announced that it had bought 6.7 percent of WCI. Siegel thereupon went to see Ross and proposed a plan to block an acquisition by Murdoch by making Chris-Craft the biggest stockholder in WCI. On 29 December the details of the plan were announced; WCI would acquire 42.5 percent in Chris-Craft's television stations and in exchange would issue WCI stock amounting to 19 percent to Chris-Craft. If Murdoch persisted with his plans to control WCI, he would have to top this holding; he might also meet with legal obstacles that debarred him from control of television stations, as he might do when he bought more WCI stock.

Murdoch, furious over the arrangement made by Siegel and Ross, began to file legal actions; Siegel and Ross counterfiled; Murdoch went to Switzerland to borrow money to buy more stock. Throughout January, the media obtained inexpensive though unrevealing communiqués on the public side of the contest. Siegel, Ross and Murdoch were meanwhile negotiating in private. In a first attempt to soothe Murdoch, Siegel offered to buy News Corporation's holding in WCI. The three men then met and Murdoch was offered a slice of 'Showtime', in which he had shown an interest the previous August. Murdoch replied with a public announcement foreshadowing a fight for stockholders' proxy votes, in an attempt to unseat the WCI Board; and Siegel renewed his offer to buy Murdoch out of WCI, to which Murdoch responded with an offer to buy Chris-Craft's holdings.

This first bout of negotiations stopped late in January; talks began again late in February, when Drew Lewis, the head of Warner Amex Cable, went to see Murdoch. Murdoch admitted that his plan to get control of WCI could be defeated by another large stock issue, and in a further talk with Lewis, mentioned $US35 as a price at which he might either buy or sell WCI stock. With a price in the air, negotiations got rolling. Murdoch agreed to sell his holding to WCI itself at $US31 a unit, totalling over $US172 million. News Corporation had bought 5.57 million units and made a profit of $US41.5

million on its dealings. WCI also agreed to pay $US5 million for the legal costs incurred and $US3 million for interest charges. This was not what Murdoch preferred. 'You can say I should have known better in the first place,' he told the *Wall Street Journal*, in a mood reminiscent of his disappointment over the London *Observer* in 1976.[18]

In his usual way he did not cling to the cash. With the help of additional credit from Great Britain and Australia, he bought a 5.6 percent stake in St Regis Corporation for $US65 million before the end of June 1984. A huge paper manufacturer, St Regis Corporation had been supplying Murdoch's companies with newsprint since 1976. The vertical tie into raw material is quite common among North American publishers; in this respect Rupert Murdoch was not breaking new ground. The open question was how far he would go in trying to get control of the paper manufacturer.

V

Picture a man in his early fifties: the forehead is furrowed over a pair of darting eyes; the suit fits closely over a slim body; he is facing a gathering, and as people's looks pass over him and away, he shifts from one foot to another. What does the posture mean? A burden of responsibility, a wish to get away from the quizzical curiosity he has invited, or just that Rupert Murdoch does not know the best foot to put forward?

He had relished his fame as keenly as any film star and had cashed in on it more shrewdly than anyone in Hollywood. By the middle of 1983 he presided over the printing of three billion newspapers a year, a hundred times as many as three decades before when he started in Adelaide. He was still most comfortable declaring himself in newsprint. His editors had learnt to tread a careful path between the public's expectations of what a newspaper should be and their boss's view of the world. He himself was not above making large concessions to special markets. On a small number of his publications, he abstained from putting his personal stamp: the radical *Village Voice* in New York, the donnish *Times Literary Supplement* in London, the housewifely *New Idea* in Melbourne might be owned by anyone else. Was he being mellowed by his success or honed down by necessity?

The profits of his group were now two thousand times larger than at the time of his Adelaide beginnings and a substantial part of them came from sources other than the media. He still gambled, but his borrowings ran into hundreds of millions, and the margin for error was proportionately smaller. For the greater part of his life, the rise of Rupert Murdoch to prominence and the expansion of the News group had run in tandem. The editorial and business, political and financial threads finally met in his hands; he would speak alternately of 'I' and 'we' without discrimination.

But in 1981 the corporate structure came under tight financial constraints, and in 1983-4 it took him an unprecedented seven months to get into and out of Warner Communications Inc. 'Is America a leap too far?' the *Economist* asked from London in an article touching on the most vulnerable point, the limits to the borrowing capacity of News Corporation.[19] These limits, though obscure, are the most severe of those constraints. They could only be shaken off if Rupert Murdoch were willing to loosen his proprietorial control and became just another large stockholder in a group whose ownership was spread widely. He shows no signs of doing so: all his efforts are bent on passing on dynastic control to his son, to succeed where his own father had failed with the Herald and Weekly Times. The furrows that mark his face declare his dilemma more openly than his balance sheets.

For the confident young Rupert Murdoch, financial discipline had been self-imposed. News Ltd, as the group was then called, paid low dividends in proportion to its earnings and financed its expansion from retained funds. Under Australian tax law, corporate profits are first liable to a company tax and, as dividends distributed to stockholders, are taxed again as part of the recipients' income. By keeping dividends low, the Murdoch family minimised its tax payments. But low market prices for stock tend to follow modest dividends and thus encourage corporate raiders in search of bargains. To forestall raids, Cruden Investments Pty Ltd, owned by the Murdoch family, seldom allowed its equity in News Ltd / News Corporation to fall below 40 percent; in the same vein of self-protection, Murdoch avoided raising funds by stock issues, which were intermittent and went to existing stockholders. When he finally needed extra funds, he got them from banks and the money markets.

News Ltd raised its first substantial bank loans to buy into the News of the World Organisation in London, but the subsequent prosperity of the daily *Sun* provided a huge cash flow, and a low dividend policy imposed on the British affiliate once again kept ample funds within the corporate structure. It was only in 1979 that large sums began to be raised outside. The growth in interest charges provides a first reading of this outside reliance. In 1979, just before Murdoch's expansionary burst in Australia, interest charges took $A6.4 million; the next three annual figures were $A15.4 million (1980), $A34.8 million (1981), $A51.8 million (1982) and $A57.1 million (1983). The sharp jump from 1980 to 1981 stemmed partly from the incorporation of the

British figures into those of the Australian-based group.

These interest payments were not only large; they seemingly carried high and rising rates. Calculated on the basis of the principal sums outstanding at the end of the financial year – $A120 million (1980), $A241 million (1981) and $A328 million (1982) – the rates work out at 12.8, 13.9 and 15.8 percent. If the calculation were made on the basis of the average of the sums borrowed at the beginning and end of each year, and not simply on the figures outstanding at the year's end, the interest rates would be even higher. Either way, they seem to have been above the prevailing market rates for reputable corporate borrowers, and News Ltd/News Corporation was certainly a better credit risk than Mexico or Argentina.

These rates are a puzzle in the absence of more information on the actual weighted average of the fluctuating principal sums over each year. A possible solution is that interest was incurred on credit obtained other than the sums the accountants were itemising as 'non-current' and 'current' liabilities. A balance sheet detective would soon notice another fast-growing item, the entry called 'trade creditors'. This figure stood at $A49.5 million in 1980; it then took off at high speed to $A191.9 million (1981), $A219.4 million (1982) and $A240.4 million (1983). If interest was incurred on part of these trade credits, the real borrowings would be much higher, and the average interest rates would come closer to prevailing market levels. In publishing it is quite common to finance newsprint purchases by short-term commercial bills, with the actual newsprint in store providing security. Nonetheless, why use this source of finance at all, at a time when short-term finance costs fluctuated wildy and were particularly high?

One possible answer lies with those obscure borrowing limits. Between late 1979 and early 1982 the News group raised Eurocurrency loans through Hambros to an announced total of $A185 million. The loan documents are not on public record. It is common practice in that market for the lenders to limit the total indebtedness of borrowers, expressing the limit as a ratio of borrowings to shareholders' funds as shown in the balance sheet. For non-mining companies, the ratio fluctuates around one dollar borrowed to one dollar of shareholders' funds. In February 1984, Murdoch told the *Economist* that a one-to-one ratio of *long-term* borrowings to shareholders' funds had been his ceiling.[20]

Counting only the liabilities entries in the balance sheets, the News group kept within this ratio. Its shareholders' funds were $A202 million (1980), $A302 million (1981), $A342 million (1982) and $A405.9 million (1983); its liabilities, 'non-current' and 'current' combined, were $A120 million, $A251 million, $A328 million and $A349 million for the corresponding years. No

slouches at balance-sheet reading, his bankers presumably allowed any borrowing short that may have been done through 'trade credits' beyond the
limiting ratio. But borrowing short to invest long in Warner Communications Inc was quite another proposition. At that point the weight of the
empire's commitments struck back at his personal ambitions.

Where could Murdoch go after he was shut out of Warner? There was
always Australia. His operations down under were still expanding: in
November 1983 the Townsville *Daily Bulletin* had been bought for $A19
million against a competitive bid, to secure a printing base in north Queensland. And now even Australia was to be girt by satellites. There would be no
direct broadcasting to television sets in the homes; in the old, comfortable
Australian way, the new technology would be used to link existing channels
to each other across the continent and a public agency would bear the costs
of putting the satellites into the sky. The market was ready to be divided up
into secure holdings and a submission from the News group to the Australian Broadcasting Tribunal argued for three networks to cover the
country, with Murdoch controlling one of them. He was not needed to put
the case in person; his name was enough. He was now one of the big fish in
the aquarium and had to be fed regularly. On Australia Day, late in January
1984, he accepted the A.O. (Order of Australia), a federal honour that comes
without such titles as 'Sir Rupert' or 'Baron Murdoch of Bouverie', which
North Americans never get right. When he came to Sydney in April to
attend a party for Peter Abeles' sixtieth birthday, he broke an absence from
his country longer than any since his student days.

He had seldom been remiss in spotting opportunities and in putting
together the means to seize them. In his hands, everything, everyone could
be an instrument. He was the most versatile player in Australia and among
the readiest in Britain and the United States, but what would he play? In his
earlier days, he would pick up the tunes his Australian contemporaries were
humming and amplify them. Those tunes were too provincial for him now.
He would sing public paeans for incumbent national leaders for consump-
tion in their respective countires, but cover himself with sceptical remarks in
private. He replenished his vocabulary with phrases from small-town
America – the family, strong principles, the red threat – even while he was
playing the most complex, cosmopolitan financial games.

He was on a random walk; and despite the ever greater accumulation of
means in his hands, he contributed more and more to the spreading confusion about ends.

THE TIMES

7, 200 Gray's Inn Road 'WC1X 8EZ, Telephone: 01-837

REAGAN IS TELLING LIES, SAYS 'TRUTHFUL' FERRARO

£1,000,0

Mossie explosion threat | Man acto

ONE of four me

TANKS A MILLION

When the FBI Is the Crimin

Appendix

NEWS LTD/NEWS CORPORATION LTD: GROWTH AND PROFITS

The bare statistics that follow can be interpreted with the help of a chronicle of the acquisitions made by the group. Though the details of these acquisitions, and some unsuccessful attempts, are given in the preceding text, they are briefly recapitulated here.

1923   News Ltd founded in Adelaide.

1930   Control passes to Herald and Weekly Times Ltd (Melbourne).

1951   Control passes to Cruden Investments Pty Ltd, a Murdoch family company.

1953   Rupert Murdoch takes charge of News Ltd, following death of his father, Sir Keith Murdoch (in 1952).

1954–6   Acquisition of minor interests in Western Australia and Victoria.

1958   Southern Television Corporation Ltd (60 percent News Ltd) is granted one of two commercial TV licences in Adelaide; starts transmission 1960.

1960   Purchase of Cumberland Newspapers Ltd (Sydney) and Mirror Newspapers Ltd (Sydney) – *Daily Mirror* (Sydney), *Sunday Mirror* (Sydney) *Truth* (Melbourne, Adelaide, Brisbane, Tasmania).

1963   Fails to get commercial TV licence in Sydney; takes up interest in Wollongong (NSW) TV licensee; acquires 25 percent equity in Television Corporation Ltd (Packer-controlled).

1964   Acquires 25 percent of Wellington Publishing Co., publishers of *Dominion* (Wellington, New Zealand) but agrees not to exercise control. Starts *Australian*, national daily based in Canberra.

263

1967   Sells stake in Television Corporation Ltd; acquires 100 percent of Southern Television Corporation Ltd.

1968–9 Acquires control of News of the World Organisation Ltd (London), publishers of *News of the World* (later renamed News International), but leaves equity below 50 percent; buys title of daily *Sun*.

1970–71 News of the World Organisation becomes largest stockholder in London Weekend Television Ltd.

1972   Buys titles of *Daily Telegraph* and *Sunday Telegraph* (Sydney).

1973   Buys Express Publishing Co. (San Antonio, Texas), publishers of *Express* and *News*.

1974   Starts *National Star* (later *Star*), national weekly (New York).

1976   Buys *New York Post* (New York); fails in negotiations for *Observer* (London).

1977   Buys New York Magazine Company (*New York*, *Village Voice*, *New West*).

1979   Buys United Telecasters Sydney Ltd (Sydney commercial TV licensee). Fails in bid for Herald and Weekly Times Ltd (Melbourne).
        Sells Southern Television Corporation Ltd.
        Buys 50 percent of Ansett Transport Industries Ltd, airline and road transport operator, and Melbourne television licensee.

1980   News Corporation formed as holding company for News Ltd; News International (Britain) becomes subsidiary of News Corporation.
        Sells out of London Weekend Television.
        Buys Times Newspaper Holdings Ltd (*The Times*, *Sunday Times*, *Times* Supplements).

1981   Buys 42.5 percent of William Collins Ltd, British book publishers;
        Buys Angus & Robertson, Australian book publishers.

1982   Starts *Daily Sun* (Brisbane).
        Buys *Herald-American* (later *Boston-Herald*), Boston, Massachusetts.

1983   Enters satellite television operations in Britain and US; US operation postponed.
        Secures purchase of Field Enterprises, publishers of *Sun-Times* (Chicago).

1983–4 Buys stock in Warner Communications Inc.; announces battle for control; withdraws from contest.

In the eleven annual periods from 1958 to 1968, when News Ltd operated chiefly within Australia, the rate of inflation was negligible. As Table I below shows, both shareholders' funds and post-tax profits expanded roughly ten-fold. (Australian pounds have been converted to Australian dollars.)

Table 1   NEWS LTD

	Shareholders' funds	Consolidated net profits
	$A '000	$A '000
1958	2416	246
1959	2545	432
1960	7223	762
1961	10080	454
1962	12026	823
1963	13406	1528
1964	20349	1619
1965	21049	1493
1966	21725	1566
1967	22245	2534
1968	24723	2512

Source: News Ltd, Annual Reports* (Accounting years end in June)

*The profit figures of News Ltd in those years sometimes included and sometimes excluded extraordinary items. Since the amounts involved in the items were not substantial, the differences created have been ignored.

From 1969 onwards News Ltd had major investments in Britain, but initially they affected group results only to the extent that a dividend was actually received. From 1971 onwards the group results include an 'equity' contribution, that is pro rata shares in the profits of 'associated' corporations, (corporations in which News Ltd held between 20 and 50 percent). Though not separately disclosed, the British contribution was by far the largest. Between 1971 and 1979 the total equity contributions accounted for about 48 percent of profits.

Table 2   NEWS LTD

	Shareholders' funds	Net profits	Equity contributions
	$A '000	$A '000	$A '000
1969	44,669	3476	n.a.
1970	48,850	4208	n.a.
1971	53,740	4554	2040
1972	59,525	6140	4556
1973	72,609	8040	4950
1974	80,347	6386	2140
1975	89,433	5607	2060
1976	96,119	11,398	4830
1977	106,675	13,994	6639
1978	118,506	13,419	5034
1979	144,309	21,546	11,196

Source: Sydney Stock Exchange Service (Accounting years end in June)*

*The figures produced by the Sydney Stock Exchange Service are more rigorous than those in the Annual Reports, excluding inter alia extraordinary items. They are generally a little lower than those in the Annual Reports.

The results of News International PLC (earlier called News of the World Organisation Ltd) are shown in Table 3. As a result of the scheme under which News Ltd obtained control of the British corporation, these figures included profits from some Australian operations. The British entity also took a half share in American investments and bore their losses. As profits were made from the *Sun*, News International followed News Ltd's Australian policies in keeping dividends low and accumulating funds: in 1976, for instance, net profits were nearly £stg 7.5 million, of which dividends took less than £stg 1.7 million. Until the end of 1979 News International's balance sheets ran to the end of December; in 1980 it became a subsidiary of News Corporation and adjusted its balancing date to June; in 1980 it filed results only for the six months January to June. Figures for this period are therefore not given in any of the tables in this appendix.

Table 3   NEWS INTERNATIONAL

	Shareholders' funds	Profits after tax
	£stg '000	£stg '000
1969	23,998	1890
1970	23,897	2154
1971	24,856	3005
1972	28,442	5615
1973	33,382	5351
1974	41,404	2524
1975	46,280	6224
1976	51,608	7496
1977	60,009	8976
1978	71,812	11,370
1979	81,899	12,155

Source: News International, Annual Reports.

In the latter 1970s, the exchange rate of the pound rose strongly against the Australian dollar (from being worth $A1.44 in late June 1976 to $A2.03 four years later). The group's rising British profits therefore gave a twofold boost to the results of News Ltd, expressed in Australian currency. By 1978 the profits of News International were higher than those of News Ltd, even after the equity share of the British profits was counted into the group results. By 1981, the results from Times Newspapers Holdings affected both entities. If Times Newspapers Holdings had not been purchased, the consolidation of the British profits into the group figures would have produced a huge rise. As it was, the overall profit started to fall. The next table shows the immediate impact of consolidation.

Table 4

	News Corporation Profits	News International Profits	North America Profit/(Loss)
	$A '000	£stg '000	$A '000 (computed)
1981	57,681	17,653	(8735)
1982	37,262	3,313	(1740)
1983	86,918	n.a.	15349

It should be noted that loan funds for North America are frequently obtained through the group and may not be charged in full to the North American operations. North American results are not filed in the United States, have been computed from News Corporation's Annual Reports and are therefore given in Australian dollars.

Notes

Notes to Chapter 1: Paper Chains

1.   Australia, Senate, *Debates* 1976, vol. S.67, p.359. For the context of that remark, see the final section of Chapter 6.

2.   Harold Evans, *Good Times, Bad Times*, Weidenfeld & Nicolson, 1983, p.369.

Notes to Chapter 2: Southcliffe and Son

1.   The chief archival source for Sir Keith Murdoch's life is the Murdoch Papers, National Library of Australia, MS. 2823. The Papers include an unpublished biography, C. E. Sayers, K.M., 'A Life of Keith Murdoch, Newspaper Reporter', which was commissioned by the family. Desmond Zwar, *In Search of Keith Murdoch*, draws substantially on Sayers. The files of *Newspaper News* report appointments, journeys and illnesses. I have also used the Fisher, Lyons and Hughes Papers in the same deposit.

2.   Supreme Court of Victoria, Probate Jurisdiction no. 455344.

3.   C. B. Bednall, 'A Temporarily Undesirable Person', unpublished manuscript, La Trobe Library, MS.5546.

4.   For information on Hugh Denison, and the *Sun*, see R. B. Walker, *The Newspaper Press in New South Wales 1803-1920*, Sydney University Press, Sydney, 1976, esp. pp.108-13.

5.   E. Ashmead-Bartlett, *The Uncensored Dardanelles*, Hutchinson, 1928, pp.239-49; Evidence by Mr Keith Murdoch, 5 February 1917, The Dardanelles Commission (copy held at the Australian War Memorial, Canberra).

6.   H.C.J. [Herbert Campbell Jones], 'Secret History/Anzacs at Gallipoli', *Sun*, Sydney, 23 May 1920.

7.   Churchill's remark was recalled by Keith Murdoch in his Evidence, The Dardanelles Commission, p.841; Hankey's Diary is cited in S. W. Roskill, *Hankey: Man of Secrets*, vol. 1, Collins, 1970, p.220.

8. 'The Murdoch Letter' (Keith Murdoch to Andrew Fisher, 23 September 1915), first published in *Herald*, Melbourne, 19–21 November 1968.

9. 'The Murdoch Letter'.

10. Keith Murdoch's Evidence, The Dardanelles Commission.

11. Keith A. Murdoch, 'The New Australians', *Sun*, Sydney, 9 November 1915; Keith A. Murdoch, 'Sweat and Labour: Anzac's Agony of Soul', *Sun*, Sydney, 10 November 1915.

12. From Our Special Representative, 'Dardanelles Mistakes/Ashmead-Bartlett Scathing', *Sun*, 28 October 1915.

13. From Our Special Representative, 'Diary of the War/Behind the Scenes', *Sun*, 17 November 1915.

14. From Our Special Representative, 'Diary of The War/Churchill's Eclipse', *Sun*, 1 January 1916.

15. For aspects of the relation between Hughes and Murdoch, I am indebted to L. F. Fitzhardinge, *The Little Digger 1914–1952*, Angus & Robertson, Sydney, 1979; and to the Hughes Papers, National Library of Australia, MS.1538.

16. Hughes to Murdoch, 4 November 1916, quoted in Fitzhardinge, *The Little Digger*, p.214.

17. Fitzhardinge, *The Little Digger*, pp.253–5.

18. The cables between Hughes and Murdoch are held in the Australian War Memorial, Canberra; they were not used by Fitzhardinge. George Steward was the Secretary to the Governor-General and held the official cyphers.

19. Murdoch to Hughes, 2 April 1918, Australian War Memorial Library.

20. Murdoch to Hughes, 4 April 1918, Australian War Memorial Library.

21. Murdoch to Hughes, 7 April 1918, Australian War Memorial Library.

22. From a Special Representative, ' The Byng Boys', 'Anzac Successes', 'Both Sides Bleed/Who Will Die First', *Sun*, Sydney, 1 April, 4 April, 7 April 1918.

23. F. W. Eggleston, quoted in W. J. Hudson, *Billy Hughes in Paris*, Nelson, Melbourne, 1977, p.117; G. E. Morrison Diaries, 1919–20, entries for 23 March, 10 April, 11 April, 13 April 1919, G. E. Morrison Papers, Mitchell Library, MS.312/26.

24. The Murdoch–Northcliffe correspondence between September 1915 and May 1922 forms part of the Northcliffe Papers, British Library, Add. MS.62179.

25. The importance of newsprint and its falling prices has been stressed by the economic historian H. D. Innis. The price series and circulation figures appear in Edwin Emery, *The Press and America*, Prentice-Hall, third edition, New York, 1972, pp.285 and 342. The international development of the mass circulation press between 1870 and 1914 is summarised in P. Albert & F. Terrou, *Histoire de la Presse*, PUF, Paris, 1974, pp.56–76. For Northcliffe's adaptations, see R. Pound & G. Harmsworth, *Northcliffe*, Cassell, London, 1959, p.205, and Robert N. Pierce, 'Lord Northcliffe: Transatlantic Influences', *Studies In Journalism*, 1975.

26. W. A. Swanberg, *Pulitzer*, Charles Scribner's Sons, New York, 1967; George Juergens, *Joseph Pulitzer and the New York World*, Princeton University Press, Princeton, 1966.

27. *Times*, 8 May 1920.

28. Valentine Williams, *The World of Action*, Hamish Hamilton, London, 1938, p.160.

29. Murdoch to Northcliffe, 12 March 1922, Northcliffe Papers.

30. Murdoch to Northcliffe, 7 December 1921, Northcliffe Papers.

31. See also [Cecil Edwards], 'Keith Murdoch, Spearhead of Expansion', *House News*, March–April–May 1961.

32. Quoted in Michael Cannon, 'Shaping the *Herald*', *Nation*, 29 June 1963.

33. Dame Enid Lyons, *So We Take Comfort*, Heinemann, London, 1965, p.168. For Lyons in transition, see P. R. Hart, 'Lyons: Labor Minister – Leader of the UAP', *Labour History* 17, 1970.

34. W. R. Rolph to Murdoch, 27 August 1935, Murdoch Papers.

35. Australia, House of Representatives, *Debates* 1935, vol.148, pp.2365–7.

36. Murdoch to Lyons, 25 November 1935; Lyons to Murdoch, 29 November 1935, Murdoch Papers.

37. Murdoch to D. L. McNamara, 6 February 1935, Murdoch Papers.

38. *Smith's Weekly*, 14 December 1935.

39. 'Germany's Bid for World Power', *Herald*, 8 October 1936.

40. Murdoch to C. L. Baillieu, 5 March 1937; 25 May 1937; 4 January 1939, Murdoch Papers.

41. Dame Enid Lyons, *Among the Carrion Crows*, Rigby, Adelaide, 1972, p.61.

42. For the appointment of the Director-General of Information, see Australian Archives, Canberra, SP195/1, item 3/1/1A, part 1. The Department of Information is discussed at length in John Hilvert, 'Expression and Suppression: The Department of Information 1939–45', unpublished MA thesis, Macquarie University, 1980.

43. John Curtin, 'The Task Ahead', *Herald*, 27 December 1941.

44. 'Australia's Part'; Keith Murdoch, 'An Australian View' (letter to the editor); *Times*, 28 December 1941.

45. MacArthur's phrase is quoted in D. M. Horner, *High Command: Australia and Allied Strategy 1939–45*, Australian War Memorial/George Allen & Unwin, Sydney, 1982, p.222.

46. Keith Murdoch, 'Unjust: Unreal: Unrighteous', *Herald*, 4 February 1943 and 'Mr Curtin in 1916', *Herald*, 5 February 1916.

47. Gavin Souter, *Company of Heralds*, Melbourne University Press, Melbourne, 1981, pp.271–2. For Menzies on Henderson, Menzies to Lionel Lindsay, 11 March 1942; on Packer, Menzies to Lionel Lindsay, 29 October 1947, Lindsay Papers, La Trobe Library MS. 1671–8.

48. From the reports on 'The Areopagus', *Corian*, December 1947 and May 1948.
49. *Corian*, August and December 1948.
50. Hugh Cudlipp, *Walking on the Water*, Bodley Head, London, 1976, p.203.

Notes to Chapter 3: Under the Grid

1. Murray Goot, *Newspaper Circulations in Australia 1932-1978*, Media Centre Paper no. 11, La Trobe University, 1978. Letter to the author from Alan E. Moore, Advertiser Newspapers Ltd, 1 April 1982.
2. Don Dunstan, *Felicia: The Political Memoirs of Don Dunstan*, Macmillan, Melbourne, 1981, pp.42, 61, 82.
3. Australian Broadcasting Control Board, *Report on the Hearings into Applications for Television Licences for Brisbane and Adelaide Areas*, appendix l, Canberra, 1959.
4. Australian Broadcasting Control Board, Public Hearing into Applications for Television Licences/Brisbane Area/Transcripts of Evidence, pp.79-93.
5. Australian Broadcasting Control Board, Public hearing into Applications for Television Licences/Adelaide Area/Transcripts of Evidence, pp.79-93.
6. For the account of the proceedings of the Stuart Royal Commission and the case against News Ltd and Rivett, I am indebted above all to K. S. Inglis, *The Stuart Case*, Melbourne University Press, Melbourne, 1961. Professor Inglis also permitted me to see the papers he deposited in the State Library of South Australia. The quotations are taken from his book.
7. Inglis, *The Stuart Case*, p.94.
8. Inglis, *The Stuart Case*, p.105.
9. 'Rejection of Takeover Bid for The Advertiser', *Advertiser*, 24 October 1959.

Notes to Chapter 4: Mirror Images

1. Souter, *Company of Heralds*, pp.342-4.
2. 'The Earldom of Giveaways', *Nation*, 12 March 1960.
3. Souter, *Company of Heralds*, pp.322-45.
4. From a letter of E. G. Waters, Secretary of News Ltd, to Secretary of the Stock Exchange of Sydney, 14 July 1961, from the files of the Stock Exchange, Sydney.
5. C. A. Pearl, 'The World of News', *Nation Review*, 14-20 May 1976.
6. 'Here is Reality', *Daily Mirror*, 29 July 1960.
7. Rupert Murdoch, 'Cuba Holds Key to Red Control over Latin America', *Daily Mirror*, 14 September 1960.
8. Presidential Papers, National Security Files, Box 8, J. F. Kennedy Library, Boston MA.
9. Australian Broadcasting Control Board, Public Hearing of Applications for a Television Licence/Sydney Area/Transcript of Evidence, 14 August - 30 October 1962, pp.46, 63, 67, 72.

10. Australian Broadcasting Control Board, Public Hearing of Applications for a Television Licence/ Sydney, p.5074.

11. John Query [Jack Paton], 'Wollongong's £1-million bait to lure Sydney's 2 million viewers', *TV Times*, 19 June 1963.

12. *Daily Mirror*, 22 March 1963.

13. Australia, House of Representatives, *Debates* 1963, vol. 38, pp.697–703.

Notes to Chapter 5: Wizards of the Oz

1. 'Shakespeare Editions', *Nation*, 11 August 1976.

2. Souter, *Company of Heralds*, p.356.

3. Souter, *Company of Heralds*, p.356.

4. K. S. Inglis, 'Enter the *Australian*', *Nation*, 25 July 1964.

5. 'State Aid and the privileged', *Australian*, 21 October 1964.

6. 'Editor attacks control of Press', *Canberra Times*, 9 March 1965.

7. Souter, *Company of Heralds*, pp.421–4.

8. 'On and off the beam', *Nation*, 18 November 1967; 'The Conpress Changes', *Nation*, 2 December 1967.

9. 'ASIO's Lawless Years', *Nation Review*, 2–8 December 1976.

10. Adrian Deamer, 'Being both Australian and national', Arthur Norman Smith Memorial Lecture, *Review*, 13–19 November 1971.

Notes to Chapter 6: Friends Like These

1. John Gorton, 'I Did It My Way', *Sunday Australian*, 18 and 25 August 1971; 1 September 1971.

2. G. J. Munster, 'After the Packer–Murdoch Deal', *Nation*, 10 June 1972.

3. 'Bias in newspapers denied by Murdoch', *Australian*, 6 December 1975.

4. Dennis Minogue, 'On the threshold', *Australian*, 6 December 1975.

5. 'Publisher explains payment to Labor campaigns', *Australian*, 7 August 1975.

6. K. R. Murdoch, 'Newspapers in the 70s', *Australian*, 16 November 1972.

7. 'Mirror Election Viewpoint', *Daily Mirror*, 23 November 1972

8. Australian Administrative Appeals Tribunal, Transcripts of Hearings, 16 June 1981, p.2538; Brian Toohey, 'Whitlam tells: Murdoch's diplomatic post bid', *Australian Financial Review*, 24 December 1975.

9. Piers Brendon, *Eminent Edwardians*, Penguin Books, Harmondsworth, 1981, p.45.

10. 'Future of Alwest Project Uncertain', *Australian*, 1 February 1975.

11. Gough Whitlam, *The Truth of the Matter*, Penguin Books, Ringwood, 1979, p.73. I have enlarged on this version.

12. Russell Schneider, *War Without Blood*, Angus & Robertson, Sydney, 1980, p.16.

13. John Kerr, *Matters for Judgment*, Macmillan, Melbourne, 1978, esp.pp.246–9; Whitlam, *The Truth of the Matter*, pp.90–91.

14. A number of documents on the dispute between Murdoch and the AJA can be found in Kym Bergmann, *The Press as King-maker: The Australian and the Federal election of 1975*, roneo, n.d.

15. Patricia Edgar, *The Politics of the Press*, Sun Books, Melbourne, 1979, pp.117–31.

16. 'Bias in newspapers denied by Murdoch', *Australian*, 6 December 1975.

17. Richard Hall, *The Secret State: Australia's Spy Industry*, Cassell, Sydney, 1978, pp.133–8.

18. Peter Michelmore, 'Rupert Murdoch talks about the facts in the Iraki affair', *Australian*, 5 March 1976.

Notes to Chapter 7: The Invader

1. A chronicle of the NOTW battle was kept by British and Australian newspapers at the time. Additional information is found in 'Mr Murdoch in London', *Nation*, 9 November 1968; and S. W. Somerfield, *Banner Headlines*, Scan Books, UK, 1979.

2. Somerfield, *Banner Headlines*, p.154.

3. Harwick Brophy & Philip Jacobson, 'How the Quiet Australian mixed up Maxwell's sums', *Times*, 25 October 1968. 'News of Mr Murdoch's World', *Economist*, 26 October 1968.

4. Somerfield, *Banner Headlines*, p.181.

5. Australian Broadcasting Commission, 'What Makes Rupert Run', 'Four Corners', 27 February 1971, transcript.

6. The circulation figures here and below have been taken from the *Reports* of the Royal Commissions on the Press 1947–49 and 1961–63, and the annual editions of *British Rates and Data*.

7. *The Press and its Readers* (a report prepared by Mass-Observation for the Advertising Service Guild), Art and Technics Ltd, London, 1949.

8. I owe some of these points to James Curran, 'The Impact of Television on the Audience of National Newspapers 1945–68', in Jeremy Tunstall (ed.), *Media Sociology*, Constable, London, 1970; and to a discussion with Mr Curran.

9. Somerfield, *Banner Headlines*, especially pp.187–90.

10. Ian Hamilton, 'Rupert and Robert', *Listener*, 9 October 1969.

11. Somerfield, *Banner Headlines*, p.141.

12. Nigel West [Rupert Alanson], *A Matter of Trust: MI5 1945–72*, Weidenfeld & Nicolson, London, 1982.

Notes to Chapter 8: At Sunrise

1. *Economist*, 19 October 1968.

2. 'Our Business Staff', 'Independent *Sun* Pledge by Murdoch', *Times*, 4 September 1969.

3.   Tom Baistow, 'Jumbo and the Mouse', *New Statesman*, 19 December 1969.

4.   *The Cecil King Diary, 1965–70*, Jonathan Cape, 1972, pp.293, 314.

5.   *The Cecil King Diary*, p.314.

6.   William Cooper, *Shall We Ever Know? The trial of the Hosein Brothers for the murder of Mrs McKay*, Hutchinson, London, 1971, p.196.

7.   William Cooper, *Shall We Ever Know?*, p.217.

8.   United Kingdom, House of Commons, *Official Report of Debates*, 5th series, vol. 811, p.202.

9.   For some of the details, I have drawn on the 'Insight' column, 'The Lost Weekend', *Sunday Times*, 28 February 1971.

10.   Stewart Harris, 'Murdoch says ITA statement "sensible"', *Times*, 27 February 1971.

11.   'A Staff Reporter', 'Mr John Freeman to head LWT', *Times*, 10 March 1971.

12.   Clive Borell, 'Police seek men who tried to sell Lambton pictures', *Times*, 24 May 1973.

13.   *News of the World*, 27 May 1973.

14.   'A staff reporter writes', *Times*, 28 May 1973.

15.   *News of the World*, 3 June 1973.

16.   *Press Conduct in the Lambton Affair: A report by the Press Council*, London, 1974, pp.17–18.

17.   *Press Conduct in the Lambton Affair*, pp.21–3.

18.   'Investigative Journalism?', *New Statesman*, 1 June 1973.

19.   More detailed figures can be found in Tony Bassett-Powell, 'You buy – we sell', in Harry Henry (ed.), *Behind the headlines – the business of the British Press*, Associated Business Press, London, 1978; 'Statistical Supplement', *Advertising Magazine*, no. 68, summer 1981; and *The National Newspaper Industry*, London, Interim Report of the Royal Commission on the Press, pp.35–7, for newsprint.

20.   *News of the World*, 6 January 1974.

21.   *News of the World*, 13 January 1974.

22.   *News of the World*, 10 February 1974.

23.   *News of the World*, 17 February 1974.

24.   *News of the World*, 24 February 1974.

25.   *Sun*, 27 February 1974.

26.   *Sun*, 8 October 1974.

Notes to Chapter 9: Give Me Your Poor

1.   'Sharp Circulation Increase', *New York Times*, 21 November 1976.

2.   James P. Sperba, 'Guts and Gore in San Antonio', *New York Times*, 26 December 1976.

3.   Philip H. Dougherty, 'Advertising: The *National Star*', *New York Times*, 4 February 1974.

4.   Philip H. Dougherty, 'The *Star* – a Publishing Meteor', *New York Times*, 24 October 1977.

5.   Stephen Birmingham, *Our Crowd: The Great Jewish Families of New York*, Harper & Row, New York, 1967, sets out the history of the Schiff family; Jeffrey Potter, *Men, Money and Magic: the story of Dorothy Schiff*, Coward, McCann & Geoghahan, New York, 1976, traces Dorothy Schiff's life. Further illuminating sidelights appear in Geoffrey T. Hellman, 'Publisher', *New Yorker*, 10 August 1968; Jack Newfield, 'Goodbye Dolly! A reminiscence of the New York Post', *Harper's Magazine*, September 1969; and Ken Auletta, 'Dorothy Schiff: "Maybe I am a Silly Person"', in *Hard Feelings*, Random House, New York, 1980.

6.   Newfield, 'Goodbye Dolly!'

7.   James Arthur Wechsler, *The Age of Suspicion*, Andre Deutsch, London, 1954.

8.   *New York Post*, 20 November 1976.

9.   John Consoli, '*National Star* owner to buy *New York Post*', *Editor and Publisher*, 27 November 1976; Robert Haupt: 'Murdoch: A disarming pirate', *Australian Financial Review*, 3 November 1976; Alexander Cockburn, 'Murdoch Tells All', *Village Voice*, 29 November 1976.

10.   Vartanig G. Vartan, 'How Murdoch Mobilised His Money', *New York Times*, 7 January 1977.

11.   The fullest of several contemporary accounts of the battle for *New York* was Gail Sheehy, 'A Fistful of Dollars', *Rolling Stone*, 14 July 1977.

Notes to Chapter 10: Post Mortems

1.   Alexander Cockburn, 'Murdoch Tells All', *Village Voice*, 29 November 1976.

2.   Rupert Murdoch, 'Ordinary reader, not elite, is key to successful newspapers: Murdoch' (text of an address), *Advertising Age*, 13 June 1977.

3.   *Editor and Publisher*, 30 July 1977.

4.   Rinker Buck, 'Can the *Post* Survive Rupert Murdoch?', *More*, November 1977.

5.   [Richard Harris], 'The Talk of the Town: Notes and Comment', *New Yorker*, 15 August 1977.

6.   Carey Winfrew, '"Son of Sam" Case Poses Thorny Issues for the Press', *New York Times*, 22 August 1977.

7.   Buck, 'Can the *Post* Survive Rupert Murdoch?'

8.   Buck, 'Can the *Post* Survive Rupert Murdoch?'

9.   Ken Bode, 'Punch's Near Miss', *New Republic*, 1 October 1977.

10.   Joshua E. Mills & Mitchell Stephens, 'The Election According to Murdoch', *More*, November 1977.

11.   Carey Winfrew, '50 of 60 Reporters on *Post* Protest "Slanted" Coverage of Mayor's Race', *New York Times*, 5 October 1977.

12.   Stephen Steinberg, *The Ethnic Myth*, Atheneum, New York, 1981, p.258.

13.   'Sunday *N.Y. Post* on drawing board', *Editor and Publisher*, 22 October 1977.

14.   A. H. Raskin, 'The Negotiation, I: Changes in the Balance of Power', *New Yorker*, 22 January 1979; 'The Negotiation, II: Intrigue at the Summit', *New Yorker*, 29 January 1979. I am indebted for a number of details to these articles. The strike, as seen from the *New York Times*, is outlined in two articles by Jonathan Friendly, 'The Story of the Newspaper Walkout: Some Successes, Some Miscalculations', *New York Times*, 6 November 1978; and 'Newspaper Strike: Murdoch Split Cleared Way for Pact', *New York Times*, 7 November 1978.

15.   Valerie Lawson, 'Murdoch's Aust. flying squad of journalists', *Australian Financial Review*, 31 July 1978; 'Murdoch's Dummy Trouble', *New Journalist*, September 1979.

16.   Raskin, 'The Negotiation, I: Changes in the Balance of Power'.

17.   'A separate peace at the *Post*', *Business Week*, 16 October 1978.

18.   Richard Reeves, 'The Last Big News Strike', *Esquire*, 5 December 1978.

Notes to Chapter 11: An Australian Base

1.   In this chapter I have drawn on arguments put and evidence presented to the Australian Broadcasting Tribunal and the Australian Administrative Tribunal at various times. This material can be found in the following documents:

(A)   Before the Australian Broadcasting Tribunal: an inquiry into the application by News Ltd and its nominees to purchase 5,788,633 stock units comprising 48.2 percent of the paid capital in United Telecasters Sydney Ltd; transcripts of proceedings ('Transcripts A').

Australian Broadcasting Tribunal: Commercial Station TEN-10 Sydney; inquiry into proposed acquisition of stock units by News Ltd; a report, Sydney, August 1979 ('*Report A*').

(B)   Before the Australian Broadcasting Tribunal: an inquiry into an application by Control Investments Pty Ltd, a wholly-owned subsidiary of the News Corporation Limited, to purchase up to 50 percent of the paid capital of Ansett Transport Industries Limited, which wholly owns Austarama Television Pty Ltd; transcripts of proceedings ('Transcripts B').

(C)   Administrative Appeals Tribunal: Nos N 80/109, N 80/111, N 80/112, N 80/113, N 80/114; transcripts of proceedings ('Transcripts C').

Administrative Appeals Tribunal (General Administrative Division): Nos N 80/109, N 80/111, N 80/112, N 80/113, N 80/114; decision, reasons for decision, 17 December 1981 ('Decision C').

2.   Transcripts A, pp.12–22.

3. Transcripts A, pp.60, 80, 72.
4. Transcripts A, p.222.
5. Transcripts A, p.222.
6. Transcripts A, p.223.
7. Transcripts A, p.235.
8. Transcripts A, pp.247-9, 250, 251, 266-7.
9. *Report A*
10. Mark Armstrong, 'Issues in the Court's TV Judgment', *Sydney Morning Herald*, 21 May 1980.
11. *Australian*, 21 November 1979.
12. 'Chanticleer', 'Murdoch goes for the quick kill', *Australian Financial Review*, 21 November 1979.
13. Re Australian Broadcasting Tribunal – *ex parte* Hardiman 1980 (High Court Decision), 54 *Australian Law Journal Reports* 314.
14. Transcripts B, pp.810-34.
15. Transcripts B, pp.911-19.
16. *Report B*.
17. Rupert Murdoch, 'Decade of opportunity', edited text of an address, *Australian*, 15 April 1980.
18. Transcripts C, pp.1001, 853, 867, 1008, 890, 997, 965.
19. Transcripts C, pp.2495, 2471-2, 2381.
20. *Decision C*, p.195.
21. Transcripts C, pp.2636-43.
22. *Australian*, 18 July 1981.

Notes to Chapter 12: Up in the Air

1. *Hearings before the Committee on Banking, Housing and Urban Affairs, United States Senate, 12 and 13 May 1980*, p.182.
2. Judith Miller, 'Eximbank Favors Loan for Murdoch's Airline', *New York Times*, 18 March 1980.
3. *Hearings*, p.340.
4. *Hearings*, p.25.
5. Miller, 'Eximbank Favors Loan for Murdoch's Airline'.
6. William Safire, 'Is That The Right Name?', *New York Times*, 10 April 1980.
7. *Hearings*, p.177.
8. *Hearings*, p.178.
9. *Hearings*, p.183.
10. Paul W. Sturm, 'Is There an Exorcist in the House', *Forbes*, 1 September 1977.
11. William A. Henry III, 'The Decline and Fall of the New York *Daily News*', *Washington Journalism Review*, March 1982.

12.   N. R. Kleinfield, 'New York Post's Deficit May Be Widening', New York Times, 12 February 1980. The figures were supplied by the Post in arbitration proceedings.

13.   Mitchell Stephens, 'Clout: Murdoch's Political Post', Columbia Review of Journalism, July–August 1982.

14.   Daily News, 1 May 1982.

15.   Daily News, 1 May 1982.

Notes to Chapter 13: Quality Street

1.   Laurence Marks, 'How a Newspaper made the News', Observer, 28 November 1976.

2.   Marks, 'How a Newspaper made the News'.

3.   Peter Strafford, 'Mr Murdoch ends Observer talks because of "controversy attempt"', Times, 22 October 1976.

4.   Stephen Aris & Peter Pringle, 'Observer: How Rupert reacted', Sunday Times, 28 November 1978.

5.   A staff reporter, 'Lord Thomson puts faith in technology', Times, 9 June 1977.

6.   Eric Jacobs, Stop Press: The Inside Story of the Times Dispute, Andre Deutsch, London, 1980. I am indebted to Jacobs' narrative, though my interpretation differs from his.

7.   William Rees-Mogg, 'Now the Times must fight for herself', Times, 23 October 1980.

8.   Stephen Aris & Eric Jacobs, 'How Murdoch Won', Sunday Times, 15 February 1981; Harold Evans, Good Times, Bad Times, Weidenfeld & Nicolson, London, 1983; other material was obtained by the author.

9.   Dan van der Vat, 'Mr Murdoch gives bid for Times group serious consideration', Times, 12 January 1981.

10.   Stephen Aris, 'Round one to Murdoch but two hurdles remain in bid for Times titles', Sunday Times, 25 January 1981.

11.   Donald Macintyre, 'Times to close unless 600 jobs go', Times 9 February 1982.

12.   Staff reporters, 'Murdoch: Times is secure', Times, 12 March 1982.

13.   'The Times', Times, 11 February 1982.

14.   Stephen Cook & staff reporters, 'Murdoch tries to sack Times editor', Guardian, 12 March 1982.

15.   'The Deeper Issues', Times, 12 March 1982.

16.   David Felton & Donald Macintyre, 'The Times and its editorship', Times, 13 March 1982.

17.   Stephen Cook & staff reporters, 'Warfare as Evans hangs on', Guardian, 13 March 1982.

18.   Laurence Marks, 'The Trouble with Harry', Observer, 14 March 1982.

Notes to Chapter 14: The Empire Strikes Back

1.   Rupert Murdoch, 'We must reverse the gentrification of Britain', *Advertising Magazine*, no. 68, summer 1981.

2.   News Corporation Ltd, *Annual Report 1982*.

3.   *New York Post*, 5 April 1982.

4.   Robert Harris, *Gotcha! The Media, the Government and the Falklands Crisis*, Faber & Faber, London, 1983.

5.   Simon Jenkins, 'When Soldiers Play Journalists and Journalists Play Soldiers', *Times*, 10 May 1982.

6.   Richard Johnson & Peter Fearon, 'AJC Names Murdoch its Communications Man of the Year', *New York Post*, 22 April 1982.

7.   Harris, *Gotcha!*, pp.54–5.

8.   *Sun*, London, 12 June 1982.

9.   Australian Broadcasting Commission, 'City Extra', 23 November 1982, tape, ABC Sound Archives, Sydney.

10.   Letter from Prof. H. Booms, President Bundesarchiv, to author, 19 July 1983.

11.   The early steps of this interlude are covered by: 'Hitlers Tagebuecher', *Spiegel*, 2 May 1983; and Nigel Hawkes et al, 'How a Scoop Turned Sour', *Observer*, 8 May 1983.

12.   Brian MacArthur, 'My Friends and Enemies', *Sunday Times*, 24 April 1983.

13.   'The *Sunday Times* and the Hitler Diaries', *Sunday Times*, 8 May 1983.

14.   Terry McCrann, 'Nobody is going to call this newspaper proprietor a dummy', *Sydney Morning Herald*, 19 November 1983.

15.   Peter Samuel, 'Interview: Rupert Murdoch', *Australian Business*, 9 April 1981.

16.   John Edwards, 'Murdoch: Taking News Corporation Into the Giant League', *Australian Business*, 30 November 1983.

17.   Bill Abrams & Laura Landro, 'Warner's Plan to Buy Back Shares From Murdoch Boosts Chris-Craft', *Wall Street Journal*, 19 March 1984.

18.   Bill Abrams & Laura Landro, *Wall Street Journal*, 19 March 1984.

19.   'Rupert Murdoch: Is America a leap too far?', *Economist*, 25 February 1984.

20.   *Economist*, 25 February 1984.

/// *Photograph sources* ///

page ii: Rupert Murdoch, 1980 (*Age*); **page xii:** Rupert Murdoch and Australian Prime Minister, Bob Hawke, 1983 (Herald & Weekly Times); **page 6:** *Smith's Weekly*, 14 December 1935; Keith Murdoch and son Rupert (Herald & Weekly Times); Adelaide *News*, 21 August 1953

page 38: Rupert and Patricia Murdoch, wedding day, 1956 (Adelaide *Advertiser*); Adelaide *News*, 21 August 1959

page 56: Sydney *Daily Mirror*, 8 June 1960; Sydney *Sunday Mirror*, 19 November 1961; Australian newspapermen, Kerry Packer, Warwick Fairfax, Ezra Norton (Herald & Weekly Times)

page 72: Rupert and Anna Murdoch, wedding day, 1967 (John Fairfax & Sons); first edition of the *Australian*, 15 July 1964

page 94: Rupert Murdoch and family, 1977 (Newsweek Inc., Bernard Gotfryd/Newsweek); Sydney *Daily Telegraph*, 25 February 1976; *Australian*, 26 February 1976; *Australian*, 27 February 1976.

page 116: Rupert Murdoch and Sir William Carr, chairman of News of the World organization, January 1969, after stockholders voted to link up with News Ltd (UPI); Rupert Murdoch, publisher of *News of the World*, talks with other press chiefs in September 1969 – (l. to r.) M. C. D. Hamilton, chairman of *Birmingham Post*, Rupert Murdoch, Lord Thomson and Sir Eric Clayson, editor-in-chief of Times newspapers (AAP-AP); *News of the World*: assorted headlines

page 132: As new owner of the London *Sun*, Rupert Murdoch looks at the first issue as it comes off the press in 1969 (Press Association, London); Rupert Murdoch with (l.) Albert Lamb, new editor of the *Sun* and (r.) Bernard Shrimsley, new assistant editor, 1969 (UPI); London *Sun*, 15 November 1969

page 150: Rupert Murdoch buys the *New York Post* from Dorothy Schiff, November 1976 (AAP-AP); *Time* magazine, 17 January 1977; *Newsweek* magazine, 17 January 1977

page 166: Rupert Murdoch and Lou Rudin, chairman of the Association for a Better New York, after an Association meeting, February 1977 (AAP-AP); *New York Post*, 15 August 1977; *New York Post*, 19 August 1977

page 184: Rupert Murdoch, proprietor of the television station Channel 10, and Richard Searby arrive at the Australian Broadcasting Tribunal inquiry, July 1979 (John Fairfax & Sons); *Australian*, 21 November 1979

page 204: Rupert Murdoch and Sir Peter Abeles (Herald & Weekly Times); *New York Post*, 1 April 1982

page 220: Rupert Murdoch announcing his bid to take over the London *Times* in January 1981, with (l.) Harold Evans, editor of the *Sunday Times* and William Rees-Mogg, editor of the *Times* (UPI); Rupert Murdoch and representatives of the print and press unions during the *Times* dispute, February 1982 (AAP-AP)

page 240: Rupert Murdoch meets US Defence Secretary Caspar Weinberger as San Antonio *Express-News* publisher Charles O. Kilpatrick (centre) looks on (AAP-AP); London *Times*, 12 June 1982; *New York Post*, 3 April 1982; London *Sun*, 12 June 1982

page 262: Rupert and Anna Murdoch arrive in London from New York during the Times newspaper crisis of 1982 (AAP-AP)

The index entry for Rupert Murdoch is meant to serve mainly as a list of contents; obviously the whole work is about Murdoch.

There are many references to News Ltd and News Corporation throughout the work. 'The rise of Rupert Murdoch to prominence and the expansion of the News Group had run in tandem.' (p. 258) The appendix on p. 263–8 covers all the details of this expansion and is the only reference listed in the index.

The form of names in the text, often somewhat informal, has been used generally in the index.

REVEL
22 TI
BY N

Iter
sir A

they a
derisio
by the
and t

pporters beaten up by police
d our leaders arrested.

Forty-one leaders of the
ansvaal Indian Congress, the
tal Indian Congress and the
ited Democratic Front
DF), to which they are both
liated, were arrested during
week of the elections. They
still being held under the
ventive detention provisions
the Internal Security Act. In
cases they have been served
h detention orders that run
l the end of next February.

The final turnout in the
dian election was 20.7 per
nt of registered voters, and
ly 16.6 per cent of all eligible
ers (see table). This was a
n lower percentage poll than
recorded in last week's
oured elections, where the

drags
ill in

boy
ruin
ma

Sir Joh Bjelke-Petersen

DEIDRE

o a problem, u'
essed envelope
unerie Street,
personally an

he would
ook after
er happy
of their

them and
re being
tely tried
she was
15 years
for a
tuated
couldn't
dn't last.

ger

ge to get
se to stay
ch other,
ext couple
was like a

t she was
s boy and
m a ring to

ICI
BA

when I
a father.

I had
my boyf
fool him
baby cou
this was
weeks af
Added
whereas
I did
before

iled
rg.

think that y
is going
to the mana
risk you tell
she and
ook advanta

risk your
k to work ar
word with yo

you hope yo
put it down t
e and star
h a clean slate.
continue to feel
tabls start look
d for another
don't hand in
until you
d one.

Hitler forgeries

The man who has confessed
to forging the 60 "Hitler
diaries" yesterday sorted them
out in a Hamburg court and put
them neatly in chronological
order for the benefit of the
udges.

It was "totally insulting...

a federal government to
pose unnecessary rules on the
States with a "holier-than-
thou attitude".

Senator Durack said the Bill
of Rights would open the way
for scrutiny of State electoral
laws.

Sir Joh described the proposed Bill of Rights as a re-
hash of the discredited Bill
proposed by former Labor
prime minister, Mr Whitlam,
and his justice minister, Mr
Murphy, in 1973.

He said: 'The Bill of Rights
takes away more rights that it
gives,' Sir Joh said in a minis-
terial statement to Parliament.

"My government and legal

Herr Konrad Kujau, aged 46,
a souvenirs dealer from
gart, then said he was told
them neatly in chronological

r Stern magazine reporter,
is also accused of
fraud, that the books
to be sent to Martin
n, Hitler's former depu-
outh America.

demann said the diaries
help to rehabilitate
n". But I begun to doubt
, Herr Kujau said.

Kujau is charged from the
£421,000 from the

From Our

forgeries,
aged 53, is
at least £44
which Stern
the diaries.

Continuing
which began
Kujau said h
books "tailor
which no his
"Heidemann
1982, that
seriously ill
my work", he

"But then i
March Heide
might be inter
the diaries. I
volumes to him
of money, which
their content,
Heidemann's mo

THUGS at a party stabbed
because he trod on someone's
dance.

By GEORGE HOLLI

Record producer Winston "Sc
childhood friend of reggae star
after being brutally attacked w
broken bottles and a machete.

Women among the 200 reveller
the illegal drugs party to mark
Notting Hill Carnival fled screaming
old victim collapsed,
pouring blood.

Tabinum was bundled
into a car by friends at
the party in Stoke New
London,
books driven to hospital, but
died from multiple wounds

The dead man had
worked closely with Mar-
ley and other reggae

Dancing

His heartbroken girl
Emma, 24,
at the couple's Nott-
Hill home yesterday:
nson was dancing
and when he stepped
mistake on someone's

This bloke pulled out
nife and stuck it in
and then two others
stabbed him while he
son the ground.'

HAT A SHOWER

Snooping neighbours re-
ted 200 people who
ed hosepipes during
ought restrictions in
rbyshire.

Field' tricks say

anyone from the National
Party who has asked Liberal
Members to stand," he said.

Asked if he was up to any
tricks over the appointment,
Sir Joh said he didn't need
any.

The reference was to a move
by him in 1975 when he appointed Mr Pat Field to fill a
vacancy caused by the death
of Labor's Senator Milliner.

Mr Field, an ALP member,
but not the party's endorsed
candidate, was automatically
expelled from the party.

The resulting alteration of
the state of the parties in the
Senate gave the then Liberal-
National Party Opposition the
numbers to block the Whitlam
Government's 1975 Budget.

This in turn precipitated Mr
Whitlam's dismissal by the
then Governor General, Sir
John Kerr, and the 1975 double dissolution.

Since the 1977
the Constitution provides that

fr
an
The
beer
tem
from
wo
th
sw

But
he w
list of
ral Pa

Howe
an ass
choose
first ch
move
lieved
taining
from th
the fir

them.

M IS BEST
STORIES!

HORROR

plunged from the top
deck during an office out-
ing for A and M record
company staff near Berk-
hamsted, Herts.

Last night Mike, of
Lambeth, South London,
was "stable" in hospital
with head injuries.

"I must apologise for Edna—sh
the day clearing out her h

Retirements
of Victorian

By JOHN LYONS

THE Victorian Opposi-
tion leader, Mr Kennett,
yesterday announced a
reshuffle of his shadow
cabinet following the
proposed departure of
three front benchers
from State politics at
the election expected in
March.

The major change in
the new inner shadow
Cabinet, intended to be
the composition of the
Liberal Party front
bench to face the elec-
torate, is the addition of
Opposition minerals and
energy spokesman, Mr
igby Crozier, to the 13-
ember inner shadow

Mr Kennett yesterday
d and star
fitted he made a mis

take excluding M
ler from the inne
net when it was
in June.

The shadow mi
has been reduced
26 to 23, with a
cabinet of 14. M
nett was forced to
the reshuffle follow
the announcement
the retirements at th
next election of the par
ty's education spokes
man, Mr Walter Jona
the employment and
training spokesman, Mr
Peter Block and the
community welfare ser-
vices spokesman, Mr
Don Baltmarsh.

Under the changes an-
nounced yesterday, the
attorney-general in the

Felicity

Felic
a pro
turn

A NEW
series
blaste
yeste
it w
S
Felic
shoo
Bath
ang
exc
on
bl

de
t
to

Arafat: "all parties concern

al conventio

The Isra
win the wa
their calcul
fighting oth
happened?
tance, and t
be the longe
history.

The Israel
sualties in
attrition bei
tinian-Leba
forces. As yo
resign becau
in Lebanon t
Shamir gove
early electio

Followie
we faced the
cy against wa
attacks c Tr
Tripoli it was
ried out son
dent mo an
attacked Am
but they skill
the Liby It's

st two years since Israel
hand the PLO withdrew
n that time, the Pales-
has suffered further
t two years Israel has
ents in the occupied
ed more Arab land
Palestinians. The
rocked by revolt and
Yet there are those
is stronger today
its history. Chair-
view, where is the
h are its problems?

st two years have
call that in 1982
Israeli decision to
lan was designed
wed by General
a light from the

te Israeli army in
time, the Israelis
half divisions, as
vy and air force.
n was to annihi-
y its infrastruc-